THE CHINA CHALLENGE

ALSO BY THOMAS J. CHRISTENSEN

Useful Adversaries: Grand Strategy, Domestic Mobilization, and Sino-American Conflict, 1947–1958

Worse Than a Monolith: Alliance Politics and Problems of Coercive Diplomacy in Asia

THE CHINA CHALLENGE

Shaping the Choices of a Rising Power

THOMAS J. CHRISTENSEN

W. W. NORTON & COMPANY

New York • London

For information about permission to reproduce selections from this book,
write to Permissions, W. W. Norton & Company, Inc.,
500 Fifth Avenue, New York, NY 10110

For information about special discounts for bulk purchases, please contact
W. W. Norton Special Sales at specialsales@wwnorton.com or 800-233-4830

Manufacturing by Courier Westford
Book design by Ellen Cipriano
Production manager: Louise Mattarelliano

ISBN 978-0-393-08113-8

W. W. Norton & Company, Inc.
500 Fifth Avenue, New York, NY 10110
www.wwnorton.com

W. W. Norton & Company Ltd.
Castle House, 75/76 Wells Street, London W1T 3QT

*For Clifford A. Hart, John J. Norris,
and Douglas G. Spelman*

*Loyal deputies, esteemed colleagues,
and valued mentors*

CONTENTS

ACKNOWLEDGMENTS

I am grateful to many people for assistance with this project. Several people assisted with research, including Idir Aitsahalia, Yan Bennett, Jia Zifang, Patricia Kim, Shaun Kim, Adam Liff, and Eugene Yi. Deserving special mention is Dr. Dawn Murphy, who provided expert research assistance, constructive comments on argumentation, and editing advice throughout the writing phases. For very helpful commentary on the draft manuscript, I am grateful to Victor Cha, Alexis Dudden, Alastair Iain Johnston, and Johna Ohtagaki. I am particularly grateful to Ms. Ohtagaki not only for providing expert comments but also for vetting the manuscript for security purposes at the U.S. Department of State. Denise Mauzerall, a climate scientist, very generously reviewed and commented on the coverage of climate change in the manuscript. I have benefited from copyediting and general advice about publishing from Jennifer Camille Smith. W. W. Norton's terrific publishing team, especially editors Tom Mayer and Ryan Harrington, expertly shepherded this project from proposal to publication.

From 2006 to 2008 I had the privilege and honor to serve as Deputy Assistant Secretary of State for East Asia and Pacific Affairs with responsibility for policy toward China, Taiwan, Hong Kong, and Mongolia. Since 2008 I have been a part-time consultant, a foreign policy expert, for the Secretary of State's Policy Planning Staff. I have learned a great deal doing that work and I hope that knowledge is reflected in this book, but the views and opinions expressed here are my own and do not represent the views of the United States government or the U.S. Department of State.

I am grateful to my wife, Barbara Edwards, and two children, Theresa and William, for their constant support. The book is dedicated to Ford Hart, John Norris, and Doug Spelman, who were the three office directors at the State Department's China and Mongolia Office and Taiwan Coordination Office during the time I served as Deputy Assistant Secretary. They were colleagues and mentors as much as they were my deputies. I am grateful to them for accepting a newcomer to the U.S. government as a boss and for doing everything they could to make our team as successful as it could be. They represent with extraordinary dignity, dedication, and skill one of America's greatest and most underappreciated assets, the United States Foreign Service.

PROLOGUE

IN DECEMBER 2006 IN BEIJING, I had the privilege of joining the U.S. government entourage for a historic event in the U.S.–China relationship: the launching of the inaugural Strategic Economic Dialogue (SED), a series of semiannual meetings created by President George W. Bush and President Hu Jintao. The U.S. team, headed by then–Secretary of the Treasury Henry Paulson, included nearly a dozen cabinet-ranked officials who were greeted in a capacious and well-appointed room in the Great Hall of the People by some fourteen Chinese counterparts at the ministerial rank, led by Madame Wu Yi, the impressive, highly energetic, and sometime acidly tough Chinese Vice Premier. For a scholar of U.S.–China relations, this seemed like something akin to the Versailles Conference of 1919.

As a Deputy Assistant Secretary of State responsible for policy toward China, Taiwan, and Mongolia, I had participated actively in the time-consuming preparation for the meetings, but given the lofty ranks and large numbers of U.S. principals present I was, of course, a backbencher at the meetings themselves. This provided something rare in my experience as a senior government official—time to reflect on the meaning of events as they were occurring. From the perspective of international history and U.S. domestic politics, the U.S. message struck me as most unusual. At the most basic level, Washington was saying: "We wish China well and want to help extend your fantastic run of double-digit growth rates. Chinese growth is good for everyone. Our biggest concern is that you are not doing everything necessary to maintain it."

By training I am a scholar, not a policymaker or politician. So I was amused at how far this message diverged from the expectations of some realist international relations theorists or the prescriptions of neoconservatives, who often view the U.S.–PRC relationship in zero-sum terms. In their view, a leading power and a democratic power like the United States should regard the rise of any rival, particularly an authoritarian one, with fear and suspicion and should take actions to hamper and delay its further growth. Instead, the United States government was clearly hoping that China's economy would continue to grow even faster than its own. Beyond just hoping, it seemed so concerned with helping that it sent most of its cabinet to China for consultations. Of course, the primary goal of U.S. economic officials was to provide a better environment in China for U.S. businesses and workers, but that hardly alters the basic point. The best way to pursue those goals, they believed, was to help, rather than hinder, China's economic development, the most important factor underpinning the fantastic rise in China's national power since 1978.

At the State Department, I worked more intensively on security and political issues than economic ones. But I saw great benefits for U.S. national security policy in the dialogue that Secretary Paulson and Vice Premier Wu had launched in the names of their respective presidents. Even though the dialogue did not produce as much as many hoped on the economic front, its constructive spirit—indeed its very existence—helped mightily. One of the most common postcolonial nationalist arguments in Chinese strategic circles and the Chinese media is that the United States' China policy is fundamentally designed to keep China down. In my experience, almost all aspects of U.S. China policy—from support for human rights, religious freedom, and democracy to Taiwan arms sales, controls on exports from the United States, limits on foreign investment in the United States, and the strengthening of U.S. regional alliances after the terrorist attacks of September 11—have been routinely portrayed in China as one of two negative things: either an external U.S. containment or encirclement policy or an effort to "split" or westernize (read: weaken) the Chinese nation. These propagandistic tropes are designed in large part to justify the CCP's continuing illiberal rule after Deng Xiaoping jettisoned traditional Communism in the late 1970s. Such accusations also aim to channel the Chinese public's considerable frustrations outward, instead of at the state. Unfortunately, the idea that U.S. policy is designed to thwart China's success has found an eager audience in China. Chinese of all ideological stripes date the beginning of the nation's modern history to the Opium War with Great Britain, in which China was defeated and forced to sign peace terms that constituted the first chapter in a "century of humiliation." China is extremely sensitive to the idea that it might again be bullied as it was in the nineteenth and twentieth centuries.

The American entourage at the SED could have been accused of a lot of things—preachiness, condescension, ignorance of China's local conditions—for telling a group of Chinese elites how best to manage their own economy. But it could not reasonably be accused of trying to harm China. Such accusations against the United States, at least since the 1970s, are absurd. With a few rare exceptions, such as restrictions on arms sales and military-relevant technologies, U.S. China policy in the past few decades has been nearly the opposite of our containment policy toward the Soviets throughout the Cold War and toward China itself in the 1950s and 1960s. In this period, the United States made an active effort to isolate and harm the target economies through tight restrictions on trade, investment, and technology transfer. Since the Chinese reform era began in 1978, no global actor has done more to assist China's rise than the United States. I have raised this point many times with Chinese interlocutors who are critical of the alleged containment strategy of the United States, and while I sometimes have seen anger and frustration in response, I have never heard an intellectually sound refutation of the point.

The second and perhaps most stunning aspect of the U.S. presentations at the SED was the pragmatism and flexibility the Bush administration officials brought to the table. Much of the U.S. message to Beijing ran almost entirely counter to what most domestic observers might expect from a large group of Republican political appointees. Of course, some of the prescriptions were in line with the ideological leanings of some of those officials. Several had extensive experience in the financial sector of the U.S. economy. More than eighteen months before the financial debacle of 2008, it was only natural for these self-confident financiers to call for opening up the Chinese financial sector to greater foreign competition and even majority foreign ownership, so as to spread the "cutting-edge innovations" and "best practices" of Wall Street to the Chinese economy. Also consistent with free market principles, China was asked to allow more flexibility in its exchange rate, with the ultimate goal of floating its currency on international monetary markets. But on the majority of issues, Bush administration officials were wisely and laudably recommending something quite different. Rather than calling for a smaller role of government in the economy, the U.S. representatives were stating that China needed to increase central state capacity by improving state regulatory and oversight institutions. Imagine a group of responsible Republicans calling for bigger government, and doing so in a country already ruled by Communists!

One of the concrete achievements of the dialogue during the Bush administration, for example, was the Chinese government's agreement to allow several U.S. Food and Drug administration regulators to be stationed in China to help foster the growth of the ineffectual Chinese inspection and safety bureaucracies. In the 2000s, the underregulated and undersupervised Chinese market produced contaminated baby formula for Chinese consumers, poison toothpaste for Latin America, tainted dumplings for Japan, and dangerous baby toys and pet food for North America. No country has the institutional infrastructure to inspect thoroughly the vast number of containers flowing into their ports from China, so even the biggest advocate of small government would have to recognize that a much more efficient way to tackle this problem would be to increase China's own governmental capacity to inspect factories and enforce safety standards before products leave the shop floor.

Similarly, a persistent theme of the dialogue was the need for better enforcement of intellectual property rights laws and regulations to protect not only U.S. patent holders but current and future Chinese innovators. Even in the financial sector, U.S. officials advised their Chinese counterparts to improve government regulation and oversight in corporate accounting to build a more secure, transparent, and stable environment for the development of Chinese stock markets, which, under their currently underdeveloped conditions, still supply a relatively paltry percentage of the overall capital fueling economic growth. The existing financial arrangements are not favorable to innovative companies that might produce cutting-edge technologies as China's economy develops beyond manufacturing.

I found most astonishing these Republican cabinet officials' advice on social welfare in China. These U.S. leaders were calling on Chinese officials to create a much better social safety net for China's unemployed, sick, and elderly. They recognized that Chinese citizens nervous about retirement or health emergencies were saving too much, thereby forgoing healthy levels of consumption. What a farmer in Jiangsu could have spent on an imported piece of electronics or an upgraded major appliance might instead be socked away for future medical bills. An improved social welfare system and greater currency flexibility and revaluation were seen as the best ways to address China's ballooning current account surplus with the United States and the rest of the world.

As an academic political scientist, it was clear to me that this group of conservative, free-market advocates at least tacitly understood and accepted what the more left-leaning social scientist Karl Polanyi argued long ago. The ideal of laissez-faire economics is, like most ideals, at best half myth; free markets are always embedded in an institutional and political context, without which they could not exist in the first place, let alone function well. The failure of U.S. regulatory controls to prevent the excesses of American lenders and investors would demonstrate this in spades in mid-2008. In China, the vast majority of domestic investment went from state-owned banks to relatively large state-owned enterprises, a trend that only accelerated with the stimulus package Beijing quickly implemented after the financial crisis struck the United States and Europe. If private equity firms, hedge funds, and insurers were too big to fail in the United States, they were too small to succeed in China, with its relatively anemic stock market.

Because of the legacies of Mao and of Communism around the globe, when many people envision the People's Republic of China, they see a Communist behemoth dictating economic activity at every level throughout the country. But despite the history of central planning from 1949 to 1978, the Chinese Communist Party (CCP) regime during the reform period has been very weak on everything from social security and health care provision to enforcement of environmental and safety regulations and protection of intellectual property rights. It is institutionally ill suited to move its market economy into the next phase of development. Beyond the high savings and low consumption that result from a poor safety net, the costs of both the degradation of China's physical environment and the suspicion in overseas markets of "Made in China" harm the economy as a whole. Without intellectual property rights, it is difficult for market forces alone to reward and thereby spur innovation because the interests of the innovators are undercut by pirates and copycats. The good news is that many of China's own officials readily recognized these problems during the SED meetings. They have been wrestling with many of them since the 1990s. So the Chinese spent more time discussing what was already being done and why they preferred gradual change than they did debating the basic premise.

While domestic observers might find the Bush administration's message ironic, the officials' advice exemplified the pragmatism with which the government has successfully engaged its Chinese counterpart in recent decades. This period of pragmatism dates back to the historic secret mission of National Security Advisor Henry Kissinger to China in July 1971. There is a reason for this approach, and it forms the core of this book. U.S.–China relations are far from a zero-sum game. Clear mutual suspicions and competitive aspects aside, China is not currently an enemy of the United States. It does not need to be contained like the Soviet Union. Nor should China become the kind of regional or global adversary that we have faced in the past, although that outcome, unfortunately, is still a distinct possibility.

China is indeed rising in regional and global importance. But a net assessment of China's overall economic, military, and political clout would reveal that it is nowhere near a peer competitor of the United States. Despite ominous predictions of U.S. decline and impending Chinese dominance, the traditional realpolitik view—that the U.S. should work to contain any rising competitor—limits our understanding of the challenges and opportunities that a rising China presents for the United States. While hardly a Soviet-style superpower, China is already powerful enough in economic and military terms, and, in international political affairs, in institutions like the UN Security Council, to disrupt a wide array of U.S. plans. That potentially gives China coercive leverage even though the U.S. military is superior to the Chinese People's Liberation Army, the U.S. technological base is incomparably more advanced than its Chinese counterpart (hence the concerted effort by Chinese entities to steal as much of that technology as possible), and U.S. per capita income remains several times that of China. While it will likely lack the power to dominate East Asia, let alone the world, for decades to come, the Chinese state still has a growing coercive capacity that poses serious potential challenges for Washington and its allies.

But even as we recognize and accept growing Chinese power, Chinese elites should have few incentives to use Beijing's growing international leverage to harm U.S. national interests so long as Washington and its many allies and security partners avoid counterproductive diplomatic stances. The two Pacific giants are already highly linked into a regional and global system in which each benefits from the other's growth and stability. One of the worst possible Chinese futures from a U.S. perspective would be not China's continued rise but its stagnation or even internal collapse. The latter development would carry grave economic and security implications, to which the United States and its allies are signally ill prepared to respond. The same can be said for China. While it is not too difficult to spin out scenarios in which tensions across the Taiwan Strait or over Sino-Japanese maritime disputes lead to a Sino-American conflagration, it is much easier to imagine scenarios in which the very real differences between the powers in the Asia Pacific are managed and peace continues to prevail over conflict. After all, China needs good relations with the United States and its regional allies, such as Japan and South Korea, to maintain economic growth. Moreover, Chinese leaders need such growth to maintain social stability at home, the real security challenge that keeps them up at night.

Despite falling far short of being a global superpower, China still has international heft. As the world's second largest economy, by some measures, the world's number one trading state, and the leading target of foreign direct investment, China is a critical component of the world economy. Like insurers such as AIG or investment banks like Goldman Sachs in the 2008 U.S. economy, China is too big to fail. Should the country fall apart, it would take the international economy down with it. But, as I will argue in this book, China is too big to fail in another sense, too. In a deeply globalized world in which security, economic, and environmental challenges require cooperative and multilateral solutions, China could make it much more difficult for the international community to tackle global problems such as international terrorism, proliferation of weapons of mass destruction, global financial instability, and global climate change.

If China willfully and spitefully obstructs the efforts of the other great powers, such endeavors will surely fail. But if China simply rides free on others and offers neither deliberate obstruction nor constructive support, it might still undercut those efforts. For example, by maintaining normal friendly and economically lucrative relations with pariah states like Iran and North Korea while others sanction them; by protecting its undervalued currency to preserve jobs in its export sector; or by spewing greenhouse gases with abandon, China can undercut multilateral efforts to halt nuclear proliferation, manage global financial stability, and limit climate change. This will be true even if China's national goals on these issues align with those of developed countries like the United States, European nations, and Japan. China has simply become too big in the international community to fail to pull its weight. And getting China to pull that weight will likely prove significantly more difficult for U.S. diplomats and policy leaders than preventing Chinese obstructionism or military aggression.

Never before has the world been so tightly integrated and interdependent. It is now more vulnerable than ever to transnational threats and contagions, sometimes emanating from relatively weak actors. But never before has a country as relatively poor as China on a per capita basis held such an important and powerful position in the international system. The combination of these two factors means that the post-Maoist version of the People's Republic of China—an inwardly focused developing country that since 1978 has generally kept a low profile in international politics—is, by necessity, going to be asked to contribute more to international stability than any developing country in history. China's well-cultivated sense of postcolonial victimhood renders requests for Chinese cooperation even more controversial at home, especially on issues that run against its recent diplomatic traditions. Given the CCP's near obsession with maintaining domestic stability and avoiding the kind of nationalist protests that helped destabilize the previous two Chinese regimes (the Qing dynasty and the Nationalist government), CCP elites might be very reluctant indeed to appear to their colleagues and to the Chinese public to be making sacrifices to satisfy the demands of other powers. This is true even if one can make a sincere and compelling argument that what is being asked of China is in China's own long-term national interest.

For all of these reasons, the United States and its allies will have a big challenge ahead. They need to maintain sufficient power and resolve in East Asia to deter Beijing from choosing a path of coercion or aggression with its impressively expanding material power. And they will need to simultaneously reassure China that the purpose of U.S. forces and alliances in the region is not to keep China down. Initiatives like the SED and its successor (the Strategic and Economic Dialogue) can help serve just such a purpose. More difficult still, the United States and other leading states will need to persuade China that it is in everyone's interest, including China's own, for Beijing to accept the challenge laid down by then–Deputy Secretary of State Robert Zoellick in an important speech in September 2005: China needs to become a "responsible stakeholder" in the international system, contributing more actively than in the past to help shore up the stability of the international system from which it has benefited so greatly. Recognizing that Chinese postcolonial nationalism is unlikely to soften, the diplomatic mission will be to maintain a strong U.S. security presence in East Asia and to persuade China that bullying its neighbors will backfire, while proactive cooperation with those neighbors and the world's other great powers will accelerate China's return to great power status.

As the leading State Department official focusing on China, I often testified before congressional committees and congressionally mandated commissions about China's rise and the U.S. response. My message was consistent and reflected a broad consensus in the interagency process: the goal of the United States, its allies, and all like-minded states should not be to contain China but to shape Beijing's choices so as to channel China's nationalist ambitions into cooperation rather than coercion. If we can demonstrate that Chinese nationalist greatness can best be achieved in the new century through participation in global projects, we will have accomplished this strategic goal. Such an effort will require us to better understand the meaning of China's rise and the domestic challenges Chinese leaders face. I am hopeful that this book can contribute to that effort.

THE CHINA
CHALLENGE

Introduction

TWO CENTURIES AGO, Napoleon Bonaparte is purported to have warned: "Let China sleep, for when China wakes, she will shake the world." For millennia China was arguably the greatest civilization on the planet, and for many previous centuries its most powerful empire. Its general malaise in Napoleon's time would only deepen due to internal decay, foreign invasion, and catastrophic domestic rebellions from the mid-nineteenth to the mid-twentieth centuries. Following the defeat of imperial Japan in the Pacific War and the completion of China's bloody revolutionary war on the mainland, Mao Zedong, founder of the People's Republic of China, would famously claim on October 1, 1949, that China had "stood up." But this was more a statement of aspiration than of fact. China was still poor, backward, and vulnerable, and Mao's peculiar ideological predilections would keep it that way for decades to come. It was really the peaceful economic transformation launched under CCP leader Deng Xiaoping in 1978 and the collapse of the superpower Soviet Union thirteen years later that made China appear to stand tall again among the great powers.

China's return to great power status is perhaps the most important challenge in twenty-first-century American diplomacy. By focusing excessively on China's material power relative to the United States, many analysts fall into one of two opposite traps. I call these camps optimists and pessimists. Pessimists exaggerate China's national power and the actual or potential threat of Chinese hegemony in Asia and beyond. They see China's emergence as a great destabilizing force, akin to the rise of the United States, Germany, and Japan in the nineteenth and twentieth centuries, and one that could easily lead to a new round of large-scale military conflict. Optimists, for their part, note that Chinese power will not catch up to that of the United States anytime soon. They believe that the United States should maintain economic and military superiority over China and are not overly concerned with every advance by the still vastly inferior Chinese military. They point out that China's per capita income is only one fifth that of the United States. Though a true trade superpower, many of its exporters are controlled at least in part by foreign investors. And while there is talk of the Chinese RMB (renminbi) becoming a future reserve currency, the U.S. dollar remains the global reserve currency and the safe haven of choice for global actors, including the Chinese government itself—even after the financial crisis of 2008.

Neither the optimists nor the pessimists are wholly correct. While the optimist is right that China is nowhere close to being a peer competitor, it is important to realize that security challenges do not come from peer competitors alone. One wise commentator at a U.S. government conference that I attended in the mid-1990s pointed out that we can talk all day about U.S. military superiority over China, but even during the Clinton administration China was already strong enough that Washington would hardly have been eager to challenge it militarily. What was true then is more than doubly true today given China's fast-paced military buildup since the late 1990s and the dispersal of U.S. forces around the world following the terrorist attacks of September 11, 2001.

Still, the pessimists do not give enough credit to the sustainability of U.S. leadership in Asia. For example, they often underestimate the value of America's unparalleled network of allies and security partners. Moreover, they often fail to appreciate how globalized economics, changes in military technologies, and the disincentives for territorial expansion have altered international politics since the early decades of the twentieth century, when a zero-sum view of politics still held sway.

Then again, one does not have to accept the pessimists' policy analysis to recognize China's recent accomplishments. China's economic clout is real and growing rapidly, especially since the 2008 financial crisis. China has been the main engine of growth for the world's economy since that time and, by some measures, has become the world's number one trading state.[1] In addition, China has provided an economic lifeline to exporters of all types: developed nations selling sophisticated equipment and developing nations selling commodities. One only needs to see the negative reactions in equity markets in the United States and Europe when China's economy falters to realize that China need not be economically dominant to be important; an economic collapse would arguably pose much greater risk to the United States than Chinese economic dominance. While an optimist might simply say that China's intrinsic global importance means we are all in the same boat, a pessimist might consider this one more sign of China's power over the United States.

As I learned from my interlocutors on several trips to China during an academic sabbatical in 2010–2011, the debate in the U.S. about China's status parallels a lively internal discussion about China's place in the world, or China's *dingwei*. Is China a developing country that should primarily focus on solving domestic problems or an ascendant great power that should assume a more assertive place on the international stage? The internal debate is, if anything, more intense than the debate outside of China, especially since, to many Chinese, the financial crisis seemed to raise China's power ranking quickly. Beijing weathered the storm better than perhaps any other major economy, quickly instituting a large-scale stimulus package and growing at nearly 9 percent in 2009. Meanwhile, the United States seemed to decline much more quickly than expected. Wall Street excesses, U.S. fiscal irresponsibility, and two lengthy wars all called American leadership into question. The wars in particular symbolized to declinists the type of U.S. imperial overstretch predicted in the scholarly writings of authors such as political economist Robert Gilpin and historian Paul Kennedy. They impacted both material power and the perceived superiority of U.S. economic and political institutions, what Harvard's global thinker Joseph Nye calls America's "soft power."

The debate within China is not only more intense than it is abroad, it is more consequential. The outcome will affect everything from China's ability to reassure its neighbors as its economic heft and military firepower grow to the Chinese Communist Party's willingness and incentive to experiment with domestic political reform at home and cooperative diplomacy abroad.

In a high-profile essay published in December 2010, the leading official in the foreign affairs system of China, State Councilor Dai Bingguo, offered an extraordinary analysis. He proclaimed that neither Chinese citizens nor foreigners should exaggerate China's rise or ignore the enormous domestic challenges that the Chinese nation still faces.[2] It is hard to imagine an American politician in a position of such authority making a speech that, in effect, stated that the current leadership had not yet accomplished as much as many foreigners and many of its own citizens believed.

Dai's message articulated a more humble and introverted Chinese *dingwei* than desired by those who believe China has already been restored as a leading great power. His essay was almost certainly aimed at two audiences. Most immediately, there were foreigners, who had become concerned, if not alarmed, about Chinese foreign policy posture in the two years following the financial crisis, when China responded brashly to unanticipated incidents on its periphery. As a result, the diplomatic trust that China had built since the late 1990s seemed to decline sharply. Since 1997 China had used multilateralism and economic integration to assure neighbors and the United States that its rise would not threaten their interests. This strategy worked extremely well until 2009–2010, when China managed to alienate the United States, Japan, South Korea, ASEAN (the Association of Southeast Asian Nations), and India through acerbic reactions to regional events and to the Obama administration's reiteration of long-standing U.S. policies. These reactions, described at length in Chapter 8, left very few countries in the region with a positive view of a rising China. Dai wanted to show that China had not intended to rock the boat and that Beijing's overall grand strategy had not changed in the past two years.

A second and perhaps even more important target of Dai's message was China's own hypernationalists, who had become more critical of Beijing's relatively passive foreign policy posture dating back to the era of Deng Xiaoping. They wanted China to push back against the United States and China's neighbors. As is almost always the case in Chinese politics, the domestic audience is more important than the foreign audience, and Dai was trying to lower the expectations of the public.

If Chinese history in the nineteenth and twentieth centuries was any guide, Beijing's failure to meet popular expectations of Chinese nationalist ambition could lead not simply to popular and elite disappointment but also to domestic instability, the security concern that has worried Chinese leaders for centuries. The Qing dynasty suffered and eventually fell from a combination of international humiliations at the hands of the British and the Japanese, among other great powers, and huge domestic uprisings like the Nien and Taiping rebellions in the nineteenth century, which left tens of millions dead and the central government anemic. The Nationalist (KMT) government of Chiang Kai-shek ultimately lost the Chinese Civil War in large part because the Japanese invasion undercut the legitimacy of the regime and provided an opportunity for the upstart Communists to tap nationalist frustrations. So in the lead-up to President Hu Jintao's January 2011 state visit to Washington, Dai Bingguo sought to set an official standard by which China's leadership should be judged by its own citizens. China was not, he argued, trying to supplant the United States as the supreme power in East Asia but rather to defend its sovereignty when challenged and to guarantee a stable international environment necessary to address China's domestic problems.

Dai's essay should have been soothing to pessimists outside of China, because it suggested China was not as powerful as they might expect. Some pessimistic observers, however, would read this as a "peace offensive." They believe that China had temporarily overreached in 2010, but in the process revealed its true intentions. Dai's essay also should have reassured the optimists: it is of course better for the United States and its allies for China to maintain the status quo and forgo righting perceived historical wrongs. It is also arguably better for China not to challenge U.S. regional leadership or its own neighbors, since conflict in the region would harm China as much as anyone.

But Dai's speech did not augur well for those who would want China to be more proactively cooperative on the world stage. Dai was telling his own people not to expect too much from the Chinese government, but he was also sending the same message to the world. This is a relatively safe position to take domestically, since there is almost no domestic constituency at present for collaborative efforts with the great powers of the world. Think of how unpopular foreign aid is in the powerful and successful United States. Now imagine lobbying for more such assistance in a much poorer country, especially one that has been kicked around in the past by the wealthier powers who are requesting greater participation. If anything, the nationalists who are frustrated by China's humility in foreign affairs and seem eager for China to take a more confrontational stance would be incensed if the Chinese leadership instead increased Chinese contributions to multilateral cooperation with former enemies and current rivals. Unfortunately for the United States, the domestic moderates find refuge not in Deputy Secretary Robert Zoellick's 2005 call for China to become a responsible stakeholder. Instead they cite more passive formulas, like Deng Xiaoping's famous expression (*tifa*) that China should "bide its time, and hide its capabilities" (*taoguang yanghui*), or Jiang Zemin's notion that the two decades before 2020 provide China a "strategic opportunity" (*zhanlüe jiyu qi*) to focus on domestic development.

My most farsighted Chinese interlocutors tell me that an addendum to Deng's original formula provides a small ray of hope. The addendum states that China should also try to "accomplish something" or "do some things" (*you suo zuo wei*), which President Hu Jintao purportedly embraced by adding the adverb "actively" or "assertively" (*jiji*). However, my more moderate interlocutors in China in 2010, many of them extremely critical of China's abrasive turn in foreign policy, warned me that under current conditions, if foreigners were successful in convincing China to be more assertive, it would likely not be as a responsible stakeholder, but rather something much more confrontational. The things China might try to accomplish, for example, could be coercing the PRC's neighbors—Taiwan, Vietnam, Japan, the Philippines—into accepting Beijing's interpretations of sovereignty. Facing the prospect of such aggressiveness, Chinese moderates generally support a more passive approach to Chinese foreign policy under the rubric of Deng's and Jiang's main dictums. They don't see passivity as a final direction for

China as a great power, but as a much more attractive current posture than the one their hypernationalist compatriots demand.

American pessimists will always spin the phrases *taoguang yanghui* and *zhanlüe jiyu qi* in the most negative sense. They worry that China might be biding its time for now, but once it is strong, it will no longer need to hide its capabilities and will use them to overturn the status quo. Similarly, one might argue that when the twenty years of strategic opportunity end, China will have successfully built up its domestic foundation and go on the strategic offensive. Those who are less pessimistic interpret *taoguang yanghui* and *zhanlüe jiyu qi* to mean that Chinese leaders are lying low and tending to their many problems at home. While much less alarming than the pessimists' spin, the optimists' interpretation should not be overly comforting either for those, like this author, who believe that we can no longer afford an introverted Beijing.

While Napoleon worried about China waking in the early nineteenth century, we need to worry about China napping in the early twenty-first century. A passive China is more likely to concentrate on stability on the Korean peninsula than to worry about North Korean nuclear weapons. A China worried about energy supply for its voracious industries and profits for its state-owned energy companies is much less likely to worry about Iran's nuclear developments and its support for international terrorism. A China that worries most about near-term job creation and its vibrant export sector along the coast will likely want to continue to suppress the value of its currency, turn a blind eye to Chinese theft of foreign intellectual property and trademarks, and avoid engaging in the potentially costly fight against global warming.

The new Chinese president, Xi Jinping, has two *tifas* of his own. One is "the China Dream" (*Zhongguo meng*). The second is his call for the United States and China to pursue a "new type of great power relationship" (*xin xing daguo guanxi*) based on trust and cooperation, rather than suspicion and conflict. We still do not know the character of Xi's Chinese national dream. Does the dream envision China settling historical scores on the international stage by recovering "lost" territories and putting former victimizers like Japan in their place? Or does it mirror the American Dream with increased prosperity and personal security for the average Chinese citizen? If it is the former, then we can expect a traditional great power rivalry between a rising China and the United States. If Xi's China Dream proves to be the latter, largely domestic in nature, the potential indeed exists for China to enjoy a new type of great power relationship with the United States, but it will need to join the United States and other great powers as a responsible stakeholder in the international system to see the true fulfillment of that ideal.

WITH THESE AMERICAN and Chinese debates in mind, part I of the book will investigate China's power from a number of different angles. Chapter 1 describes the breadth and depth of China's dramatic rise since 1978 in all dimensions of national power—economic, political, and military. Chapter 2 discusses why international politics in the twenty-first century are significantly different than in the nineteenth and twentieth centuries, and why this reduces the likelihood that China will be both willing and able to drive the United States out of the Asian region. Chapter 3 counters excessive pessimism from a different angle, discussing the many continuing sources of long-term U.S. superiority over China, including economic, military, and political factors.

We should not, however, push our criticism of excessive pessimism too far in the opposite direction. Chapter 4 explores the real challenges posed for the United States and its allies by China's newfound capabilities, and chapter 5 discusses how the security, economic, and environmental challenges that the United States and others face require unprecedented cooperation among the great powers. On this score, China's rise has created not so much a threat of domination as one of obstructionism and free-riding on the efforts of others.

Part II will discuss how well the United States has addressed the challenges of coercive diplomacy and global governance presented by a rising China in the decades since the end of the Cold War. Chapters 6 through 8 roughly track the diplomatic successes and missteps of the Clinton, George W. Bush, and Obama administrations. The book will conclude with some thoughts about the future based on the lessons learned since the end of the Cold War. With Xi Jinping as PRC president for the next several years, China will likely continue to rise in regional and global importance. By avoiding self-fulfilling prophecies of conflict or blithe optimism about the stabilizing effect of continued U.S. leadership, the United States and its allies and partners can better tackle the real challenges posed by China's rise—both managing regional security relations in East Asia and encouraging China to contribute to global governance alongside the other great powers.

PART I

UNDERSTANDING CHINA'S RISE

CHAPTER 1

China's Rise: Why It Is Real

CHINA'S RISE IN WEALTH, diplomatic influence, and military power since 1978 is real and it's stunning. For all the scars on his personal political history—from support for the disastrous Great Leap Forward in the late 1950s to the Tiananmen massacre in 1989—Deng Xiaoping will be remembered most by historians for launching the program of Reform and Opening. That program pulled hundreds of millions of people out of grinding poverty and allowed China to become a potent international actor for the first time since the first half of the Qing Dynasty, which spanned the mid-seventeenth to the early nineteenth centuries.

Deng's market reforms unleashed the pent-up economic energy of the Chinese people, who had suffered for more than two decades under Mao's postmodern version of Communism. Under Mao, market laws of supply and demand and basic economic concepts such as diminishing returns on investment were dismissed as bourgeois, imperialist myths. Expertise and management skills were valued much less than blind loyalty to Mao and devotion to the bizarre economic model he created in the late 1950s. Mao communized agriculture, localized industry, and commanded unrealistic production targets. He mobilized the population around utopian Communist economics and radical political activism. His goal was to have China catch up with the Soviet Union and the United States in a short time frame and position the People's

Republic of China as the leader of the international Communist movement. But his Great Leap of the 1950s and the Great Proletarian Cultural Revolution of the 1960s led instead to domestic economic disaster,
international isolation, and the premature deaths of some forty million Chinese citizens. In the late 1970s Deng Xiaoping would restore
market incentives and place an emphasis on skill and practicality rather
than ideological purity in professional promotion. Practical control of
agricultural land, if not ownership, was taken away from communes
and given to farmers. The reform program also injected market-based
pricing and incentives into the Chinese economy and opened China up
to foreign trade and investment. Officials, engineers, and scientists were
chosen for being expert, not "red." The resulting growth brought some
three hundred million people—about the size of the U.S. population
today—above the threshold of poverty as measured by international
organizations: an income of less than one dollar per day.

These results are unprecedented in world history. For the past
thirty-six years, China's economy has grown on an average of about
10 percent per annum in real terms (meaning adjusted for inflation).
Accordingly, the gross domestic product (GDP) of China has almost
doubled every seven years since 1979. And with a Chinese population
of 1.3 billion, the economy has moved from one that was poor but still
large to one that is now much less poor and truly gargantuan. China's
per capita income is still very modest compared to the wealthiest countries of the world, but the change is nonetheless astonishing. Official
per capita income rose from $220 USD in 1978 to $4,940 in 2011,[1] and
according to some measures using "purchase power parity," China's per
capita income was $9,300 in 2012 (an impressive figure, though it is
notable that the per capita income of the United States, by comparison,
was $50,700).[2] While still a developing country, China surpassed Japan
in 2010 to become the world's second largest economy, a feat simply
unimaginable in the early years of the reform era. At that time Americans were fretting about the economic recession of the early 1980s and
Japan was seen as the great power likely to surpass the United States in
the next cycle in the "rise and fall of the great powers," to use Yale professor Paul Kennedy's famous phrase.

The economic reforms have had more than just economic results.

The individual citizen's life is incomparably more energetic and free in China today than in the pre-reform period. My first trip to China was in the summer of 1987, the eighth year of the reform era. The anesthetic grip of socialism was still very strong on Chinese society. At midday, cities like Beijing and Shanghai, moving at a slow pace already, ground to a halt as the population rested and often slept for two hours, wherever they might be. This was the *xiuxi* period, a designated siesta for urban Chinese citizens, many of whom still worked in inefficient state-owned work units. By contrast, the energy on the contemporary streets of Beijing and Shanghai is palpable and sometimes overwhelming. Cranes rotate at construction sites in every direction, and one is more likely to find oneself stuck in stultifying traffic at midday than stepping around a slumbering deliveryman sleeping on his bicycle's flatbed. The slowly rolling bicycles of the 1980s urban landscape have been replaced by the twenty-first-century traffic of young professionals in new and relatively sturdy automobiles. In fact, China has become the largest market for new cars in the world and the lifeline of companies like GM facing declining domestic sales.

The government's often impressive efforts to build an infrastructure capable of handling this new burden has kept world-famous equipment companies like Caterpillar in the black despite diminishing demand in wealthier countries. Still, the growth in the new Chinese middle class has outstripped the growth of new roads; epic traffic jams in Chinese cities are a regular occurrence. Beijing now ranks alongside Mexico City as the worst in the world for traffic. In less thoughtful moments, the experienced traveler almost yearns for the slower but more predictable pace of Beijing's bicycle lanes, where coal couriers and relatively unstressed citizens spat out the sand and industrial dust blown downwind from the manufacturing centers and the Gobi desert.

Marketization has had a big impact on personal freedoms in China as well and thus constitutes what the political scientist Harry Harding aptly described as the People's Republic's Second Revolution.[3] In Mao's China, the Party secretaries in charge of state-owned enterprises had a degree of power over the workers that Americans simply cannot imagine. Local Party chiefs had near total control over the lives of their charges from cradle to cremation. They had authority over not only salary and career promotion but also education, health care, housing, retirement, and even permission to marry. Marketization changed this to a large degree by creating both a vibrant private sector outside of the state-owned enterprise system, to which disgruntled workers could escape from meddling Party chiefs, and a new standard of success— market competitiveness—for the state-owned enterprises themselves. The combination meant that Party chiefs in those enterprises needed to focus on something other than micromanaging the personal lives of their workers and could ill afford to alienate their most able staff lest they jump ship to the private sector. The personal individual space created by this process, even space to privately express disappointment with the state itself, moved China very quickly from what Ambassador Jeane Kirkpatrick had categorized in the Cold War as a totalitarian state to what she described as a typical authoritarian one. Nations living under the latter suffer from lack of democracy, free press, freedom of assembly, and often rule of law, but the life of the individual on a day-to-day basis is still much freer than under the ever-present thumb of totalitarianism. Along the same lines, the hope for positive future economic and political change in China is also much greater now than it was in the totalitarian Mao era, and hope for a better future may be one of the most underappreciated human rights of all.

China in the International Economy

IT IS HARD to use the words "equally dramatic" to compare almost anything to China's domestic transformation since 1978, but it seems almost fair to apply the phrase to China's foreign economic and diplomatic relations. China's whirlwind economic transformation was fueled by a fast-paced integration of the economy into global trade and financial markets. Deng did not just marketize the Chinese economy at home, he opened it up to foreign trade, investment, and competition in a way unimaginable in Mao's China. That process was accelerated further in the 1990s under Jiang Zemin and his market-oriented and highly urbane premier, Zhu Rongji. After many years of Maoist revolutionary diplomacy and self-imposed isolation, China's overall trade was less than $21 billion USD in 1978, a mere fraction not only of world trade but of China's own GDP. In the past decade, China became the largest trading nation in the world (if we exclude services),[4] the largest trading partner of almost all its neighbors, and the second largest trading partner of the United States (after Canada and before Mexico).[5] According to World Bank statistics, in the last year before the global financial crisis, trade was an astonishing 67.6 percent of Chinese GDP (compared to 29 percent for the U.S.).[6] In 2011, China's trade as a percentage of GDP had fallen to 58.3 percent (compared to 31.8 percent for the U.S.). In finance, China rose from almost no incoming foreign investment in 1978 to surpass the United States to become the world's top destination for foreign direct investment in 2012.[7] For many years, China has consistently outstripped all other developing countries as a target of foreign investment. In the last ten years, China has also begun investing abroad and has, famously or infamously, become the largest foreign purchaser of U.S. sovereign debt.

In the 1990s, politicians and diplomats in the United States and other countries belonging to the OECD (Organisation for Economic Co-operation and Development) began talking about integrating China into the international economy. While constructive and laudable, their policy pronouncements were really trailing, not leading, the existing trends in China's foreign economic relations. The policies of Deng and the reformers who followed him, along with the market forces those policies unleashed, did more to link China to the global economy than the conscious strategies of foreign capitals.

Deng also curtailed Mao's revolutionary evangelism abroad. Ending the hectoring about the evils of capitalism, feudalism, and revisionism in Communist states dispelled fear of China among its non-Communist neighbors and provided Beijing the opportunity to forge cooperative relationships with an enormous number of actors, most notably recent former enemies such as Japan and the United States. Perhaps most dramatically, in 1992 Beijing formally recognized a democratizing and capitalist South Korea (ROK), a former enemy. And Beijing did so despite the expressed dismay of longtime Stalinist ally North Korea. Normalization of the PRC–ROK relationship planted the seeds of a robust economic relationship in which China today is South Korea's largest trade partner and favorite destination for Korean foreign direct investment. Hyundais assembled in China from Korean parts populate the new fleet of taxis in Beijing. Having ridden in their tinny and fragile predecessors, I can say that these solid sedans are a great improvement not only for comfort but for safety.

On a similar note, despite a bitter wartime history and opposite positions in the Cold War, China and Japan had long had trade relations, even during the Cultural Revolution. But these trade relations deepened significantly in the reform era. Especially since the mid-1990s, Japanese direct investment in China has increased rapidly. This means that when Chinese nationalist protesters call for boycotts of Japanese products, as they did in Shanghai in March 2005 and around the country in fall 2012, Chinese leaders themselves become extremely nervous, in part because so many of the Japanese products marketed in China—from cars to electronics—are made by Chinese workers.

Chinese economic integration with Southeast Asian countries, though somewhat less dramatic, has also been impressive. China's free-trade agreement with the Association of Southeast Asian Nations (ASEAN), which had been negotiated several years earlier, was fully implemented in 2010. Not only is China a major economic partner of these countries, but because it is the last assembly point in a transnational production chain that exports to the rest of the world, Southeast Asian states routinely run trade surpluses with China because they export both raw materials and manufactured parts into the Chinese assembly behemoth. This provides strong incentives in the ten ASEAN capitals and Beijing to maintain positive diplomatic relations despite maritime sovereignty disputes in the South China Sea and a history of Chinese Cold War belligerence and meddling in places such as Vietnam and Cambodia.

Turning to China's west, in recent years China has overtaken Russia as the main economic partner of the former Soviet republics in Central Asia, an understandable source of pride for Chinese diplomats and a predictable source of jealousy in Moscow. By financing long-term energy deals, building pipelines for the importation of crude oil and natural gas into China, and providing a steady supply of cheap and relatively high-quality consumer products, China has become indispensable to these states. In the past several years, even China's economic relationship with India has blossomed. Sino-Indian trade grew from $2 billion in 2000 to $73.9 billion in 2011.[8] China became India's largest trading partner in 2008. This dramatic growth in trade has overcome several major political hurdles. China and India have ongoing border disputes (all of China's other sovereignty disputes on land have been settled). Indians advocating expansion of India's nuclear program and navy have expressed concern about China's rising power and frustration with Beijing's special relationship with India's longtime rival, Pakistan. China has equally felt frustration over India's sheltering the Dalai Lama's government in exile and Delhi's general sympathy for Tibetan nationalist causes.

China's deepening economic relations with Africa, Latin America, and the Middle East are no less dramatic. In 2009, China overtook the United States as Africa's number one trading partner.[9] It is difficult to obtain credible reporting on China's overall investment in Africa, in part because Chinese aid and investment are famously nontransparent. Moreover, the mix of investment, infrastructure loans, and export-import bank financing makes for murky accounting. But some numbers are available and give the sense of the pace of change.[10] In 1980 China's trade with sub-Saharan Africa was less than $1 billion. In 2012 it was $123 billion.[11] Chinese state-owned enterprises (SOE) and government agencies have combined corporate investments and infrastructure loans and investments to increase the flow of oil and other natural resources from Africa to China. For example, China offered infrastructure financing in Ghana as that West African nation's new oil field came online. China made a similar $6 billion loan to the Democratic Republic of the Congo, apparently to support the export of minerals to China.[12] Although China imports a great deal of oil and other natural resources, its trade with the continent is relatively balanced as it sells manufactured goods of nearly the same value each year to the continent. China has also made large-scale investments in telecommunications (the Chinese firm Huawei, for example, has established a major foothold) and in the financial sector (note the Chinese state bank ICBC's acquisition of 20 percent of South Africa's Standard Bank). Many small and medium-sized Chinese enterprises now operate in Africa and, for better or worse, constitute the main interface between China and local populations.

China's trade with Latin America skyrocketed in the first decade of the century. In 2000 trade was a mere $10 billion. By 2012 it had grown to $258 billion, an increase of 2,480 percent![13] As with Africa and the Middle East, the vast majority of the exports to China from Latin America are natural resources, and 90 percent come from four resource-rich countries: Brazil, Chile, Peru, and Argentina. China is the largest export destination for the first three on that list. Chinese consumer and industrial products find good demand in the region, as well. In particular, the first internationally marketed Chinese car—the Chery—is very popular in Latin America (as it is in the Middle East and sub-Saharan Africa), and a joint venture was created to assemble the vehicles in Brazil, with a plant opening in Jacarei, Sao Paolo, in September 2014. China's investment in Latin America is still in its nascent stages and does not constitute a large percentage either of Chinese investment abroad or of incoming investment in the region. Chinese statistics on such investment are cloudy, but from the best publicly available reports it seems that, as of 2010, only about 13 percent of China's overall investment was dedicated to the region, the vast majority of which is heading to tax havens in the Cayman and Virgin Islands.[14]

Although it hardly seems possible, China's economic footprint in the Middle East grew faster still in the past fifteen years, the period in which China transitioned from a net exporter of energy to the world's leading importer. In 2011, China overtook the United States as the Middle East's largest trading partner. As the political scientist Dawn Murphy outlined in compelling testimony on Capitol Hill in June 2013, China's imports from the Middle East (primarily composed of petroleum and gas) grew from $3.8 billion in 1999 to $160 billion in 2012. The Middle East accounted for 55 percent of China's crude oil imports. China's top crude oil suppliers in the region are Saudi Arabia (22 percent), Iran (12 percent), Oman (8 percent), Iraq (6 percent), Kuwait (4 percent), and the United Arab Emirates (3 percent). But, as with Latin America, the trade is hardly a one-way street. China's product exports to the Middle East have dramatically increased over the last twenty years. They ballooned from $6.5 billion in 1999 to $121 billion in 2012. China's primary exports to the Middle East are light industrial products (including consumer electronics and appliances), textiles, clothing, machinery, and economy cars. In addition to product exports, the Middle East is a huge service export market for China's construction, telecommunications, and finance industries. Contract services by construction firms are a particularly important segment of those services. In 2011, China's construction services in the Middle East amounted to $21 billion.[15]

China in Multilateral Diplomacy

IN 1968, at the height of the Cultural Revolution, China maintained only one ambassador abroad. In the last years of Mao's reign (1971–1976) and then in the Deng era, the Chinese converted from radicalism and self-isolation to a more familiar realpolitik foreign policy based on national sovereignty, national interest, national power, and national wealth. As is often the case with recent converts, however, China in the 1980s and early 1990s employed realpolitik with a fervor and purity long abandoned by its previous practitioners in Europe and the Americas. By the early 1990s China had become, as I wrote in a 1996 *Foreign Affairs* article, "the high church of realpolitik" and as such treated multilateral organizations, even many of the ones it had joined in previous decades, either with indifference or suspicion.[16] Groups like ASEAN and the ASEAN Regional Forum on security matters were viewed by some nervous Chinese security analysts as opportunities for the Southeast Asian Lilliputians to tie down the Chinese Gulliver, with the United States and its allies providing the stakes and the rope. Humanitarian interventions in places like Somalia and Bosnia were viewed with concern and even fear as Chinese "realists" worried that they were veiled efforts to increase the power of the United States and NATO.

For all the potential downsides of a hard realpolitik view of the world, such an approach to international relations was, from the point of view of the United States and its East Asian partners, still preferable to Mao's revolutionary evangelism of the 1950s and 1960s. Mao had actively supported armed revolution in several neighboring states and, in the late 1960s, even criticized the Soviet Union for being too moderate and for seeking peace deals to settle regional conflicts. As I have argued elsewhere, without that evangelism the Korean War may never have happened and the Vietnam War would likely have been much less costly.[17] But given its built-in suspicions of other powers and obsessions regarding the protection of sovereignty, China's realpolitik view of the world carried its own problems for the United States and China's neighbors. In the mid-1990s, for example, China adopted coercive policies toward Vietnam and the Philippines regarding long-standing island disputes. While the weak Filipino navy and coast guard was pinned down by bad weather, the Chinese military occupied and built structures on a previously uninhabited coral reef aptly named Mischief Reef.

Beijing claimed that the structures were built as innocent havens for Chinese fishermen legitimately working the waters around the reef. Of course, the Chinese behavior sparked angry accusations in Manila against the Chinese government. The Filipinos argued that any building on their reef was an invasion. They also doubted that the structures were built primarily for the safety of fishermen, claiming instead that this was part of an expansion of Chinese military activities in the South China Sea.

But even as early as 1996 there were hints of a new, more positive change in China's diplomacy, as China signaled that it might for the first time embrace multilateralism, particularly through ASEAN, Southeast Asia's premier multilateral organization. Designed in the 1960s to build economic cooperation and reduce political and military mistrust among the region's non-Communist countries, ASEAN expanded after the Cold War to include all ten Southeast Asian nations, including the organization's former nemesis, the Democratic Republic of Vietnam. By 2000 China had become much more active in institutions in which it had previously been a relatively passive member, such as the ASEAN Regional Forum, a group of regional and global actors under ASEAN leadership that discuss security problems and promote confidence-building in the region. More impressive still, in 1996 and 1997 China actually helped build two important regional organizations from the ground up. China founded and offered headquarters to the Shanghai Five, a multilateral group consisting initially of Russia, China, and three Central Asian republics of the former Soviet Union that would eventually expand and morph into the current Shanghai

Cooperation Organisation (SCO). The purpose of this organization is to fight terrorism and "splittism" (a derogatory term given to ethnic or regional independence movements), to reduce mistrust and build confidence among the members, and to foster economic cooperation. China also helped found ASEAN Plus Three, a group of the ASEAN states, China, Japan, and South Korea. Significantly, neither organization includes the United States, while the latter includes four U.S. treaty allies—Japan, Korea, Thailand, and the Philippines. China had long complained about the inordinate influence of U.S. bilateral alliances in the region and it now had a venue to engage several of those allies without U.S. officials present.

In the past decade, China's regional multilateralism has expanded to include the China–ASEAN Free Trade Area (CAFTA),[18] signed in 2002 and enacted in 2010; a 2002 China–ASEAN Declaration on the Conduct of Parties in the South China Sea, designed to build confidence and reduce tensions over China's maritime territorial disputes with Vietnam, Brunei, Malaysia, and the Philippines; the Six Party Talks on Korean denuclearization, which China helped found and has hosted since 2003; and the East Asia Summit, a large organization founded in 2005 and initially comprising the ASEAN Plus Three together with India, Australia, and New Zealand.

As with the SCO and the ASEAN Plus Three, the United States was not initially a member of the East Asia Summit, since President George W. Bush refused to take the necessary step of signing ASEAN's 1976 Treaty of Amity and Cooperation (the TAC). That treaty calls for noninterference in the internal affairs of signatory states. But during the George W. Bush administration, the United States was trying to increase pressure on the Burmese junta to improve its human rights record, release political prisoners, and reform politically. As part of President Obama's announced "pivot," in which the United States allegedly would return to Asia, his administration made it a priority to sign the TAC and join the East Asia Summit. President Obama attended the summit for the first time in November 2011.

Somewhat ironically, China had initially embraced multilateralism in the second half of the 1990s in part as a tactical response to the United States bolstering its own bilateral military relationships. Moreover, Beijing began viewing such organizations as a way to reassure China's neighbors that China's "peaceful rise" would benefit them. Adopting a zero-sum view of these trends, many influential observers in the United States and the East Asia region worried that Chinese diplomatic power was growing at American expense. During the Bush administration, some prominent Democrats who would later join President Obama's policy team complained that the proliferation of organizations that included China but not the United States and the insufficient attention to those that did, such as the ASEAN Regional Forum, meant that China was "eating our diplomatic lunch" in Asia while the United States was distracted with wars in Iraq and Afghanistan.[19]

China's embrace of multilateralism went beyond Asian regional forums. In 2000 China was the engine behind the creation of the Forum on China-Africa Cooperation (FOCAC). In 2006 China hosted a giant conference in Beijing on China-Africa cooperation, inviting the heads of all African states and receiving positive RSVPs from almost all. Among those absent was Libya's Qaddafi, a man gifted at alienating even the most sympathetic regimes. At the meetings, President Hu Jintao promised some $5 billion in concessionary loans.[20] President Hu's frequent visits to the region (he made six trips to the continent after assuming the presidency in 2003) also bolstered China's multilateral diplomacy with Africa, as did extensive peacekeeping activities on the continent and high-profile assistance programs such as underwriting the new headquarters and conference center for the African Union in Addis Ababa, Ethiopia. In 2003 China established the Forum for Economic and Trade Cooperation between China and Portuguese-speaking Countries, which includes Portugal and several former Portuguese colonies in Africa, Latin America, and East Asia.[21] The China–Arab States Cooperation Forum was established in 2004.[22] In the following year, China and several Caribbean countries established the China-Caribbean Economic and Trade Cooperation Forum.[23]

And then there is China's role in the world's most prominent multilateral organization: the United Nations. China's recent rise to prominence in the United Nations is more than a simple function of its permanent seat on the Security Council. After all, the PRC has held that seat since 1971, when it replaced Taiwan in the seat allotted to China in the original UN Charter. But Beijing kept a low profile in the United Nations in its first two decades of participation. In the past twenty years, however, China has become much more active in New York. For example, early in this century China became the largest contributor of peacekeeping forces of all the five permanent members of the UN Security Council (the United States, Great Britain, France, Russia, and China). China participated in crafting various UN resolutions and presidential statements on Iran, North Korea, and Libya, among other issues.

Americans have appreciated China's contributions to these UN efforts, but Beijing's persistent efforts to water down resolutions aimed at its economic and political partners in Pyongyang and Tehran have disappointed Washington and many other capitals.[24] Worse still, a more assertive China sometimes directly defies the wishes of the United States and like-minded nations by wielding a veto or threatening to do so to block unwelcome resolutions aimed at some of Beijing's more unsavory diplomatic partners. Whereas Beijing had previously reserved its veto to punish countries that maintained diplomatic relations with Taiwan instead of mainland China, in the past several years China has threatened vetoes or actually vetoed draft resolutions aimed at Sudan, Burma, Zimbabwe, and Syria.

Such vetoes are still relatively rare but they signify something important. While China has certainly warmed to multilateralism, it has not gone so far as to wholeheartedly embrace the newest multilateral efforts to create global governance by supporting active enforcement of new international concepts such as "the responsibility to protect," which requires states to prevent crimes against humanity within their national borders. Beijing elites view such doctrines as a free pass for great powers to intervene in the domestic affairs of weaker states and for democracies to destabilize authoritarian governments. And while many developing countries with postcolonial forms of nationalism share the PRC's skepticism and concern about the concept of responsibility to protect, the PRC is the only one with the institutional and material power to prevent effective implementation of the concept by the other great powers.

China's important role in the United Nations was driven home to me during my two years as a State Department official. In July 2006 I was sworn into office as the Deputy Assistant Secretary of State focused on the portfolio of policies toward mainland China, Hong Kong, Taiwan, and Mongolia. As a career China specialist I was surprised to find myself soon thereafter occupied with a crisis in Lebanon. Israel had launched air assaults in the southern part of the country. Among the casualties were two Chinese peacekeepers stationed there as part of the UN mission. The Chinese government was understandably upset about the casualties. But it soon became clear to me and my colleagues that we needed to do more than express condolences to the Chinese government for the tragic loss of life, which, of course, we did. We needed to maintain China's cooperation with the UN while preventing the organization from adopting language and actions unacceptable to Israel, the key U.S. partner in the region.

Following the invasion of Iraq, the Bush administration had a reputation as unilateralist, and its nomination to UN ambassador of the often acerbic John Bolton, who appeared skeptical about the basic value of the institution, served only to enhance that reputation. But I quickly learned that the administration of George W. Bush turned to the UN Security Council earlier and more often than any of its predecessors to address security and humanitarian problems. So when there was trouble in Lebanon I needed to be briefed on the situation so that I could advise the senior officials in charge of Middle East policy about what China might do at the UN Security Council. This pattern would repeat itself over the next two years in policy crises involving Sudan Darfur, Zimbabwe, Burma, Iran, and North Korea, just to name a few. In all of those cases, the Bush administration relied on the United Nations to coordinate the response of the international community to the destabilizing problems in these regions. In several instances, China, not the Bush administration, played the unilateralist role, arguing that the UN Security Council was not the appropriate venue to address humanitarian conditions inside strife-ridden Zimbabwe or a poor, authoritarian, and incompetently ruled Burma. On that "principled" basis, China would sometimes veto resolutions drafted by the allegedly unilateralist United States.

China's multilateral reach in global affairs also expands beyond its role as an increasingly active UN Security Council member. In 2001 China joined the World Trade Organization as arguably the most important member from the developing world. During George W. Bush's second term and continuing into the Obama administration, China was welcomed by the United States and other leading economies as a key member of multilateral discussions of international finance (the G20) and the global environment (the UN Convention on Climate Change). In this process, China reasserted itself in a role that Mao himself had tried to establish, albeit under a revolutionary flag: the People's Republic of China as a champion and leader of the developing world. Now as a major global market player, China also takes a leadership role among other emerging economies to ensure that their interests are taken into account by the rich OECD countries in global forums. The American investment firm Goldman Sachs named one such grouping the BRICS, an acronym for Brazil, Russia, India, China, and South Africa. Goldman Sachs arguably did China a big favor. One of the few deep commonalities in Chinese foreign policy from the most radical phases of Mao's rule to the most pragmatic phases of the post-1978 reform era is the PRC projecting itself as a natural leader of the developing world. Whether analysis imitates life or life imitates analysis, China seemed to revel in being seen as the leader in the new grouping.

China's Military Modernization

IN THE 1980s Deng emphasized economic growth, not military modernization. He did this for straightforward domestic reasons but also to further reassure China's diplomatic and economic partners that China's ongoing rise did not pose a severe security challenge. Deng, a former general with strong control over the People's Liberation Army (PLA), successfully placed military modernization as the fourth of four modernizations in China's long-term grand strategy (preceded by agriculture, industry, and science and technology). Following China's rather humiliating performance in the war it launched against Vietnam in 1979, purportedly to teach Hanoi a lesson, Deng cut the bloated and unskilled Chinese military of six million soldiers by millions of personnel in the 1980s, slashing the military budget both in real terms and even more dramatically as a percentage of China's gross national product. At the outset of the reform program, China's military budget had been between 8 and 10 percent of GNP, an enormous burden on

China's still modestly sized national economy. Under Deng, this percentage fell to less than 2 percent by the early 1990s.

But through Deng's reform process, China built the economic infrastructure and wherewithal to allow for impressive military modernization efforts. Such development began in the years immediately before his death in 1997 and has accelerated impressively since 1999. Even though China's economy has grown at the searing pace of 10 percent per year since the mid-1990s, the military's official budget has enjoyed still faster growth.

PRC MILITARY SPENDING
1995–2013

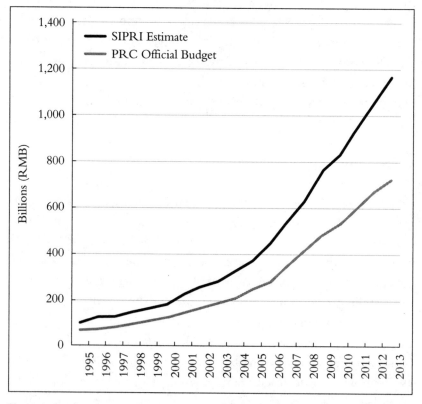

Figure 1. Graph compares China's officially declared defense budget for the years 1995 to 2013 with estimates of China's actual defense spending by the Stockholm International Peace Research Institute.

Sources: SIPRI Military Expenditure Database, 2014, http://milexdata.sipri.org; and Global Security.org, http://www.globalsecurity.org/military/world/china/budget-table.htm.

PRC OFFICIAL DEFENSE BUDGETS COMPARED TO U.S. GOVERNMENT ESTIMATES 1996–2009

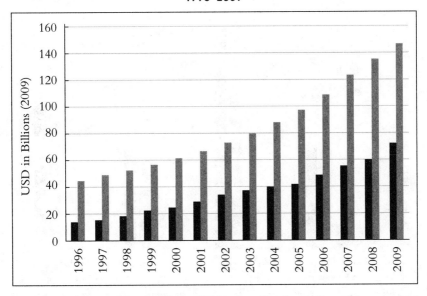

Figure 2. Black bars indicate the PRC's official budget. Gray bars indicate U.S. government estimates of China's actual military spending.
Source: *Military and Security Developments Involving the People's Republic of China 2010*, Annual Report to Congress, Office of the Secretary of Defense, p. 42.

In a process of reverse-engineering that Chinese civilian companies have practiced regularly with foreign firms' technologies, the PLA first imported and then learned to build an impressive set of weapons systems, including submarines, advanced fourth-generation aircraft, cruise missile systems, advanced air defenses, and satellite and radar systems. As will be discussed in chapter 3, many of these systems form the backbone of doctrines that China is designing to use against the United States, its allies, and its security partners. (See Appendix 1.1–1.8.)

China has developed a more modern military across the board but has focused special attention on certain technologies and doctrines. One of the areas to draw special attention has been China's development of a larger and more sophisticated arsenal of ballistic missiles. Many are conventionally tipped, short-range missiles arrayed in the Nanjing Military

CHINESE MILITARY FORCE MODERNIZATION TRENDS
2000–2010

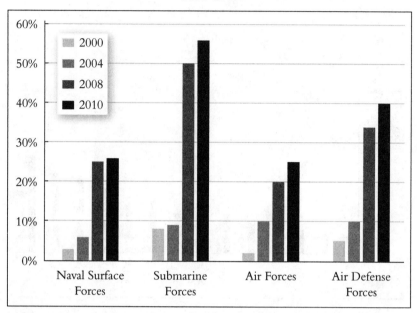

Figure 3. The bars represent the percentage of the force that is modern as defined by the U.S. Department of Defense. For surface combatants, "modern" is defined as multimission platforms with significant capabilities in at least two warfare areas. Modern for submarines is defined as those platforms capable of firing an antiship cruise missile. For air forces, modern is defined as fourth-generation platforms (Su-27, Su-30, F-10) and platforms with fourth-generation-like capabilities (FB-7). Modern surface-to-air missiles (SAMs) are defined as advanced long-range Russian systems (SA-10, SA-20), and their PRC indigenous equivalents (HQ-9).
Source: *Military and Security Developments Involving the People's Republic of China 2011*, Annual Report to Congress, Office of the Secretary of Defense, p. 43.

region, opposite Taiwan. What makes them impressive is their pinpoint accuracy and their reported ability to deliver sophisticated payloads, such as submunitions, that could damage runways and ports and slow the activities of personnel involved in repair and recovery operations on those sites. But China also has longer-range conventionally tipped missiles that can reach not only Taiwan but the territory of U.S. allies such as Japan, South Korea, and the Philippines. Since the United States has large and important bases in both Japan and South Korea, these systems could also pose direct challenges to the U.S. military.

A new source of concern for the U.S. Navy has been the Chinese development of a fundamentally new weapon system, an intermediate-range ballistic missile with a warhead that is reported to have a terminal guidance system for use after reentry into the atmosphere. Such a sophisticated system could potentially give China the ability to attack from Chinese soil large U.S. capital ships, such as aircraft carriers, far out at sea. This could compromise one of the United States' key advantages in a conflict in China's maritime periphery—the ability to operate U.S. naval aviation near Taiwan or other potential regional flash points.

In January 2007 China dramatically demonstrated antisatellite capability (ASAT, in DoD speak) by obliterating one of its own satellites in low-earth orbit with a ground-launch missile. The test was a success by kinetic standards but proved disastrous for China's diplomacy, as it was launched with no prior notification and executed in a fashion that significantly increased the overall amount of debris orbiting the earth. Many countries' diplomats, including myself, immediately called to express concerns to their Chinese counterparts. China was the first country to test such a system following the end of the Cold War. If ever fired in a crisis or conflict, Chinese antisatellite missiles could potentially destroy not only military satellite systems but civilian ones on which global communications have become so dependent. From a purely U.S. perspective, China seemed to be developing systems that might be used to compromise the clear U.S. advantage in space-based systems that allow for surveillance, reconnaissance, and over-the-horizon targeting for U.S. forces in war. International response to the Chinese test was immediate and forceful. My colleagues in the United States government and I did not exaggerate when we said in formal diplomatic complaints (démarches) to the Chinese that all space-faring nations around the globe were upset by the test. In January 2011, the PRC set off a smaller diplomatic firestorm with the publicized test flight of China's new stealth fighter-bomber, the J-20. The timing of the flight was unfortunate; it coincided with a trip to China by U.S. Secretary of Defense Robert Gates, who had planned the visit to smooth over tension following the Obama administration's notification to Congress that it intended to sell a large tranche of arms to Taiwan. Gates, reportedly upset that China had chosen this time for the test, raised the issue with

President Hu. Backbenchers at the meeting reported that President Hu seemed surprised to hear of the incident and checked with his military advisor regarding Gates's information. The public reports of the meeting led to some speculation outside of China, certainly overblown if not fully inaccurate, that the military had somehow wriggled free of civilian control in China.[25]

Beyond the realm of conventional weapons discussed above, China has also been modernizing its nuclear forces to make them more diverse, easier to deploy, and harder for the United States or other potential adversaries to destroy in a preemptive strike. Until very recently, according to public reports, China's strategic nuclear forces aimed at the United States were a relatively small number (about twenty) of liquid-fueled missiles in fixed positions. They would need to be fueled and mated with warheads in a crisis, a process that could take several hours, if not longer, and might make the systems vulnerable to a U.S. preemptive attack. Those ICBMs were first deployed in the 1980s. Traditionally, Chinese strategists and defense intellectuals envisioned the prospect of a nuclear first strike, a preemptive attack on Chinese nuclear facilities with U.S. nuclear weapons. In the past decade or two, Chinese experts also began to worry that U.S. missile defenses and conventional strike weapons could theoretically cripple China's nuclear arsenal without the United States using nuclear weapons itself. For all these reasons, China has been working persistently since the late 1980s to create a larger number of mobile solid-fueled systems that would be harder for enemies to target and easier to launch without time-consuming fueling and mating. China also has a program to develop submarine-launched, nuclear-tipped ballistic missiles in an effort to create a stealthier and more diversified deterrent. Even with this modernization, China will have far fewer nuclear weapons than the United States and will lack the capabilities to launch a crippling first strike against the U.S. nuclear deterrent. So it seems reasonable to argue that China seeks a credible second-strike capability, a deterrent force designed to eliminate U.S. first-strike options and thereby provide China a guarantee that it would be able to level unacceptable damage against the United States, even under the most severe instances of U.S. military attack.

The development of new hardware aside, there has been a more fundamental shift in China's defense posture. In the 1990s, in large part because of increasing tensions in relations between mainland China and Taiwan, the Chinese military began changing its doctrine. The earlier version emphasized defense of the borders of the PRC and domestic stability operations. Chinese security elites focused almost exclusively on maintenance and development of a land army. Since the 1990s, however, the Chinese leadership began giving more attention and resources to the Chinese PLA Navy and Air Force. Initially the new navy and air force investments—surface ships, submarines, advanced cruise missiles, and fourth-generation aircraft—seemed designed as coercive tools against Taiwan, if Taiwan moved toward formal legal independence, and against the United States, if the latter chose to defend Taiwan in any conflict across the Taiwan Strait.

Since the founding of the PRC in 1949, Beijing has claimed that Taiwan is China's sovereign territory, but it has not been under PRC control. From 1945 to 2000, the island was under the rule of the CCP's Civil War enemy, the Chinese Nationalist Party, or KMT, bearing the flag of the Republic of China (ROC). As the ruling party of the ROC, the KMT claimed that it was the legitimate ruler not only of Taiwan but of the mainland as well. In the middle 1990s, the KMT under its first Taiwan-born leader seemed to abandon the traditional KMT position that there is one China and Taiwan is part of it. Instead Taipei appeared to be moving in the direction of permanent, formal political separation of Taiwan and the mainland. The Clinton administration offered a visa to President Lee Teng-hui to visit his alma mater, Cornell University, in June 1996. In so doing, U.S. officials ignored Beijing's entreaties and reversed previous reassurances that Washington would not issue such a visa. A crisis erupted. PRC missile and surface exercises near Taiwan in July 1995 and March 1996 were followed by the deployment of two U.S. aircraft carrier battle groups to the waters near Taiwan by the Clinton administration. The Chinese government reportedly realized just how few military options it had to coerce Taiwan, let alone the United States, and thereafter accelerated its deployment of ballistic missiles opposite Taiwan and the development of naval and air assets for such contingencies.

This process would intensify dramatically in 1999 after President Lee Teng-hui stated to a German reporter that he viewed the cross-Strait political situation to be "special state to state relations," thus suggesting to worried mainland analysts that he was asserting independent state sovereignty for Taiwan. Chinese concerns would only grow in 2000 when Chen Shui-bian from the traditionally pro-independence Democratic Progressive Party was elected president to the first of two terms. The PRC defense budget would increase even more rapidly in the next several years following Lee's interview, at a rate of about 15 percent per annum at a time of little inflation in China. At this time, increases in defense spending outstripped economic growth, sometimes by considerable margins.

Even following the 2008 election of a more accommodating Taiwan president, the KMT's Ma Ying-jeou, the defense budget has continued to grow at an impressive rate. While avoiding provocative saber-rattling, Beijing continues to build potent capabilities that can threaten Taiwan. Ostensibly this buildup addresses the Chinese fear that Taiwan might again embrace pro-independence politics, but that is probably not the entire story. Chinese elites almost certainly regard a favorable military balance as a source of political leverage against Taiwan. Beijing's ultimate objective is unification of the two sides of the Taiwan Strait on Beijing's terms.

Not everything in the world of PRC power projection is about Taiwan, however. In 2004 Hu Jintao announced that the PLA would undertake "new historic missions." Although his use of the phrase remains relatively vague, the new missions seem to require new power projection capabilities for combat and noncombat operations, such as humanitarian assistance and disaster relief. After all, beyond Taiwan, China has maritime sovereignty disputes with several of its neighbors, including U.S. allies such as Japan and the Philippines. Its many claims in the South China Sea would require much more Chinese naval and air power than China currently possesses if they were to enforce all of those claims (see chapter 4 for a map of China's territorial disputes). Chinese security elites have also expressed concern about the protection of China's economic lifelines at sea—the Sea Lines of Communication—such as the Malacca Strait and the South China Sea, through which flow China's vital resources and trade.

There are other less traditional roles for the Chinese military. As China invests increasingly abroad under Beijing's "go out" strategy, millions of Chinese citizens find themselves living in locations far from home. Chinese state-owned enterprises often invest in locations that are politically unstable, and Chinese citizens in such places can find themselves real or potential victims of kidnapping or in the crossfire of civil conflicts, as more than thirty thousand PRC citizens did in Libya in 2011. In the past, the PLA has lacked the capability to get ships and planes so far from home to assist those citizens. Finally, the PLA would like to increase its involvement in more straightforward humanitarian and relief operations. Although Hu's introduction of the concept of new historic missions apparently predated the great Indian Ocean tsunami of 2004 by two days, the events of December 26, 2004, and their aftermath could only have helped convince Chinese elites of the need for better power projection and logistics capabilities in the region. Beijing reportedly was embarrassed by the way in which the United States and other armed forces were able to respond quickly and effectively, sending military assets to Indonesia while China lacked the planning, humanitarian assets, and strategic lift necessary to provide immediate disaster relief in its own backyard.

Some of the Chinese responses to the new historic missions should please China's neighbors more than others. The Chinese development of a hospital ship, for instance, should generally reassure foreigners about the positive aspects of China's rise. Chinese peacekeeping operations around the world, as previously mentioned, are also a generally welcome manifestation of increasing Chinese wherewithal. Similarly, by all accounts, Chinese naval assets have played a very active and constructive role in the UN-sponsored antipiracy operations in the Gulf of Aden, even though maintaining naval forces so far from China and coordinating with a multinational force have posed real challenges for China.[26] Politically, the Chinese effort underscores that, as a major trading state, China shares with other global powers an interest in preserving a peaceful and stable global commons. But other aspects of China's recent military behavior have troubled neighboring capitals. Beijing's purchase and refurbishing of a Ukrainian aircraft carrier, first launched for sea trials in 2012, and the apparent plan to build more carriers at home are, for obvious reasons, viewed differently in the region than the aforementioned hospital ship. The same can be said for the development of new cruise and ballistic missile systems, advanced fighters and bombers, some of them employing stealth technology, and the expansion and modernization of China's already impressive submarine force.

CHINA'S RISE IS REAL, and there is a reason that it has drawn the attention of so many observers and leaders around the world. But like most dramatic and new phenomena, China's economic, political, and military rise is often exaggerated and its meaning misunderstood. The next two chapters address these common mistakes.

CHAPTER 2

This Time Should Be Different:
China's Rise in a Globalized World

W HEN GREAT POWERS RISE, there is often real trouble. The examples are both numerous and horrific. Modern German history alone provides a series of demonstrations. The punctuated and violent rise of Bismarck's Prussia and the German successor states helped cause several great power wars in the late nineteenth and early twentieth centuries, including the two most brutal armed conflicts in world history. In Asia, the rise of Japan after the Meiji Restoration also led to several wars from the 1880s to 1945 involving Japan, China, Russia, Great Britain, and the United States.

There have been partial exceptions to what seems like a general rule of international relations. The rise of the United States and the decline of Great Britain as a global leader in the late nineteenth and early twentieth centuries did not lead to conflict between the two democracies. In fact, they would be allied together in two subsequent world wars against a rising Germany, in the Cold War that followed, and ever since. But even in that instance, structural transition was not truly peaceful. As I argued with Columbia professor Richard Betts in 2000, if China handles disputes with its neighbors as poorly as the United States did in the late nineteenth century, East Asia is in for a very rocky ride.[1] Racism under the thin academic patina of social Darwinism and the yellow journalism of a jingoistic press helped spark the Spanish-American war over Cuba, which in turn placed the U.S. military in a costly counterinsurgency war in the

Philippines. The ostensible reason for conflict was a nebulous naval incident in Havana Harbor with American casualties that became a national
rallying cry for war ("Remember the *Maine*, to hell with Spain!").

It does not take great imagination to see how similar factors could
contribute to Chinese belligerence as it pursues expansive maritime
claims against rivals like Japan, Vietnam, and the Philippines. Those
nations are often treated with derision, condescension, or both in Chinese nationalist circles. The prospect of U.S. intervention in such disputes and in relations across the Taiwan Strait could eventually lead
China to mimic another nineteenth-century American concept, the
Monroe Doctrine, which sought to prevent further European imperial incursions in the Western Hemisphere. In fact, some U.S. scholars
like Princeton's Aaron Friedberg already ascribe to China the goal of
"extruding," or expelling, the United States from its regional bases in
neighboring countries. Friedberg and others believe China plans to target the United States and its regional allies and security partners with a
combination of economic and military coercion and diplomatic persuasion to achieve this goal. In this scenario, either the United States would
leave of its own volition, fearing conflict with a rising China or, more
likely, would be deprived of regional partners because no Asian actor
would want to run the risk of alienating or provoking Beijing by maintaining traditional security ties with the United States.[2]

Friedberg lays out his argument with typical intelligence and care.
While I find scant evidence in Chinese strategic writings to support
this claim about Beijing's intentions at present, it is definitely a real and
dangerous possibility for the future. Avoiding such a turn in Chinese
doctrine and ensuring its failure if it were adopted, in that order, should
be priority goals for U.S. policy in the region. If such a doctrine were
actually adopted by China and proved successful, the decline of American power would be severe indeed. But even a failed attempt by China
to expel the United States from the region would likely be fraught with
crises and military conflicts. For this reason, University of Chicago professor John Mearsheimer has adopted an even more pessimistic stance
than Friedberg, declaring that China's rise cannot be peaceful because
it is inevitable that China will pursue what Friedberg calls extrusion,
whether such an effort proves successful or not.[3]

Despite these dreary historic precedents and prognostications, there are reasons to be more sanguine that the rise of China can be managed in a way that preserves both American power in East Asia and regional peace and stability. Two related arguments about the destabilizing effects of the rise and fall of great powers predict that China's rise will hurt regional and global stability. I hope to show that both are wrong. The first is a purely structural argument, based in the strategic history of past disasters associated with the rise of new challengers in the international system. The rise of new rivals destabilizes the international system by creating opportunities for territorial expansion and leads to intense spirals of tension among the great powers. The greed and fear created by these shifts in the distribution of great power capabilities result in crises among the great powers that lead to large-scale war and massive suffering.

The second argument is a corollary of the first and has less to do with material power and more to do with the international norms, institutions, and rules of the road. Scholars of institutions like the UN and the International Monetary Fund (IMF) often claim that the international rules and institutions in place at any time were previously set by the leading power at the apex of its hegemony over the system. The more cynical version of this theory suggests that such a hegemonic leader would only set up institutions that disproportionately benefit itself, not the system as a whole. When the leader's power declines in comparison to a rising rival, it is only natural, then, that the up-and-coming rival would want to revise or even overturn the existing rules and create new institutions that disproportionally benefit the rising state. So at the close of World War II, the United States sought the end of European colonial preferences in trade and finance and the creation of free trade regimes and a global financial system. According to the most cynical interpretation, Washington did not do so altruistically to create a more prosperous and stable world but rather because the United States was economically much more competitive than the remaining European great powers after World War II. In the current day, if China wanted to undercut existing international institutions in order to foster new ones that benefited itself more and the United States less, the process of change could damage near-term global cooperation on economics, security matters, humanitarian crises, and environmental problems and thus prove fundamentally destabilizing.

Fortunately, in the case of China's ongoing rise, there are several reasons to doubt these two arguments. The kinds of temptations that led to great power wars during previous power transitions are much less prominent in Asia today than they were in the Western Hemisphere and Asia in the past. Substantial changes in global economics and politics have made the current international system more robust than previous systems. Broader economic trends have made territorial conquest of colonies less tempting, and changes in both economics and weaponry have decreased the need for invasion and conquest of either peer competitors or their smaller allies. Furthermore, the institutions set up by the United States and its allies after World War II were beneficial not just to themselves but to all states willing to open up their economies to a rule-based global order. No country has benefited from that global order more than China, particularly since it joined the World Trade Organization (WTO) in 2001. Since domestic stability is paramount for the CCP and the maintenance of that stability depends in large part on economic growth, I can see few reasons why China would intentionally seek conflict with its trade and investment partners or undercut the institutional framework that has enabled its historic economic development.

Globalization and Forces for Peace in East Asia and Beyond

THE FIRST STRIKING DIFFERENCE between contemporary East Asia and the world of great power politics of the nineteenth and twentieth centuries is that for normative, economic, and strategic reasons, colonialism is dead and so are the temptations for the competitive territorial expansion that went along with it. The scramble for Africa that led to spiraling tensions among European great powers in the lead-up to World War I is unimaginable today. For dramatic effect, pundits often compare Chinese investment, aid, and trade policies in Africa and Latin America to those of the other great powers in an effort to portray a similar scramble. But investment and aid are hardly the same as those historical exercises in zero-sum competition. Not only are the economic incentives and business models of the great powers very different today than they were for European powers in the late nineteenth century, but China cannot project significant combat military power anywhere near Africa, even if it were to decide for some hypothetical reason to fight for physical control of places where it has significant investments, such as Sudan, Nigeria, or Libya. And if we look at contemporary Asia itself, where China increasingly *can* project military power, the conditions that drove imperial Japan to compete for colonial control of East Asia largely do not exist.

One of the key reasons is economics. Colonialism was never a particularly smart economic plan for the imperial great powers, as they generally spent more on imperial management and defense than they gained from economically dominating their subjects (as opposed to simply trading with them). But the information revolution that followed the industrial revolution, combined with the diversification of natural resources such as oil and gas, has made ownership of additional raw materials and land much less important to the overall wealth and national security of advanced economies. China does have preexisting disputes over energy resources with its immediate neighbors. But even with that important exception, it is difficult to imagine that China, Japan, the United States, and Russia will find themselves fighting over previously unclaimed areas of the world for the purpose of gaining monopoly control of the resources there.

Economic developments over the past 150 years provide major disincentives for great power conflict, even in times of structural shift. The ratio of the value of innovation and skill to raw inputs like natural resources and cheap, unskilled labor has never been greater and is likely only to grow. Scholars like Carl Kaysen had argued that advanced industrialization made war among the developed nations extremely less likely because it could not be profitable for the winner.[4] The wars that occurred in the first half of the twentieth century were an atavism of a preindustrial era in which aggression could pay because the victor could enjoy more easily exploited booty, namely land, resources, and a new source of cheap, menial labor. One scholar, Peter Liberman, countered this thesis convincingly by analyzing German conquests in industrialized parts of Europe, such as Czechoslovakia in the early phases of

World War II. In those instances, aggression provided Germany great added wealth and military wherewithal. While Liberman's point is convincing that some wars among industrial powers proved profitable and strategically valuable for the aggressor, it is highly doubtful that the same logic would apply to today's knowledge-based transnational production. In Liberman's work, aggressors like Hitler's Germany merely needed to gain the acquiescence of the conquered country's workforce.[5] In a world of transnational production, with logistics webs created by the need for on-time delivery, the aggressor state would also need to persuade a diverse set of foreign innovators, suppliers of key components, and logistics companies to continue doing business with the aggressor after the invasion.

Pessimists like to proclaim that economic interdependence cannot trump security concerns and thereby keep the peace. After all, by some measures such as trade as a percentage of GDP, there was nearly as much trade interdependence between the great powers in Europe before World War I as there is today. In particular, Great Britain and Germany developed very robust trade relations even as they prosecuted a major arms race in the first decade of the twentieth century. Some realist analysts gleefully cite Norman Angell's prediction just before World War I that the new economic patterns of the day meant that great power was unthinkable.

But such crude measures of trade do not capture the newer forces of globalization. The world is not just more interdependent now than ever before, it is interdependent in a way never seen before. Conflict among the great powers would do even more damage than in the past. Today, transnational production and the flows of capital in foreign direct investment (FDI) that fuel it are much different than before World War I. In the 1980s, Princeton University's Helen Milner wrote a trailblazing study describing how the development of transnational production by multinational corporations had changed the leading economies of the world. Final products are now assembled from parts made in multiple countries. Firms now buy and trade products with themselves across state lines. Large and politically influential producers, therefore, are now both importers and exporters and cannot safely lobby for protectionism in the face of foreign competition as they have in the past. For example, major U.S. firms like Apple and General Electric routinely manufacture products with inputs made in several countries. Raising tariffs in a country that assembles final products could raise the price of imported inputs, thereby raising the cost of their exported products. And those final products could easily face retaliatory tariffs in foreign markets. Milner points out that in 1929 only 2.5 percent of U.S. manufacturing was performed multinationally, while as early as 1977 20 percent was.[6]

Almost two decades later, Dartmouth's Stephen Brooks built on Milner's findings and argued that transnational production and FDI in manufacturing had expanded to such a degree that even arms manufacturers rely on complex supply chains and expanded intra-industry trade (trade across national borders by companies based in multiple countries). He argues that it might now be difficult for many countries to prosecute extended wars because they would not be able to guarantee weapons procurement from enemy countries or from noncombatant third countries.

Brooks points out that what distinguishes interdependence today from interdependence before World War I is that transnational production (or, as he puts it, "the globalization of production") barely existed in that earlier era. Manufacturing economies were investing in the developing world, particularly for the purpose of natural resource exploitation, more than in other advanced manufacturing countries. In 1914 three-quarters of global FDI was spent on things like oil and coal, and that capital flowed to destinations outside the United States and western Europe. In the 1990s, natural resource investment constituted only 11 percent of FDI. Moreover, investment largely stayed within the developed world as North America and western Europe absorbed well over half of global FDI.[7] Before World War I, arm's-length trade—the trade in final products and resources—was the rule of the day. Multinational production and intra-industry trade barely existed. By 1992, Brooks writes, the value of international production activities of multinational corporations outstripped global arm's-length trade by more than two to one.[8]

This trend has only accelerated since the 1990s, in large part because of the integration of East Asia into a multinational production base with China as the core. Brown University's Edward Steinfeld argues that in the early 1990s China created an unprecedented form of Asian manufacturing growth. By opening itself up to investment and linking itself to transnational production chains, China has become a regional production hub involving money, know-how, and components from many countries. The Chinese economy is not only highly dependent on exports, especially for a large economy, but China's exports are produced in China by foreign-invested firms at a rate never before seen in history.[9] In many instances, the lion's share of value, which lies in innovation and branding, is enjoyed by the foreign firms. So, countering Thomas Friedman's famous argument, Steinfeld cleverly argues that the world is not really flat, it is hierarchically integrated with technologically advanced economies like the United States, not China, at the top of the ladder.[10]

In 2008 more than half of Chinese exports were created by foreign-invested firms. China offers those firms a competitive mix of a cheap but relatively educated labor force, good infrastructure, and political stability. And while the technological sophistication of Chinese exports has increased, foreign firms create an even larger percentage of the more sophisticated products in the Chinese export portfolio than they do of the less sophisticated ones. Fully 90 percent of Chinese exports that are labeled high-tech are produced in China by foreign-invested firms. Moreover, they are for all intents and purposes "assembled in China," not made there; many of the high-value components are imported from China's Asian neighbors by foreign-invested firms, then assembled in China. Those products might more accurately be labeled "Made in Asia" or even "Made on Earth!"[11] Steinfeld offers the example of an iPod assembled in 2005 in a Taiwanese-owned plant on mainland China using American and Korean know-how and a hard drive made by a Japanese manufacturer, itself with a factory based in China that uses components imported into China from third countries.[12]

The degree of interdependence and transnational production within Asia alone is already very dramatic and appears to be deepening. In an important article on the early post–Cold War era, Aaron Friedberg called East Asia ripe for rivalry.[13] He cited several factors that made Asia less stable than Europe, but a key one was intraregional trade; that is, trade between China and other regional nations like Korea and Vietnam. Writing in 1993, Friedberg pointed out that even though many of the high-growth economies in East Asia were major exporters, most of the trade went toward the advanced economies of the United States, Europe, and Japan. But only a decade later, intraregional trade outstripped extraregional trade in large part because of the decisions made by President Jiang Zemin and Premier Zhu Rongji to open the Chinese economy. In 2005, at the Beijing Forum, Japanese scholar Takashi Inoguchi argued that Northeast Asia was quickly transforming itself into a region with the incentives for community-building found in western Europe.[14]

Since the 1990s, the People's Republic of China has replaced the United States as the largest trade partner of most Asian economies. That list notably includes U.S. allies South Korea and Japan and security partner Taiwan. Japan had long been China's largest trade partner (if one does not count the EU as a single economy), but the relationship only recently became reciprocal. In 2004 China replaced Japan as the number one target for neighboring states' exports as well. At the same time, the ten ASEAN countries' trade with China began to rival their trade with the United States and subsequently has surpassed it. The ASEAN countries routinely run surpluses with China since they, like Taiwan, supply many inputs for products that are assembled in China and then exported. In fact, more than half of Chinese imports are used in Chinese export industries. By one calculation, in 2006 foreign value added stood at 50 percent of the overall value of China's manufactured exports. And for higher-tech products, foreign value added stood at 80 percent.[15] Not only are over half of China's exports produced by foreign-invested firms, these foreign-owned companies are increasingly Asian-owned.[16] In the mid-2000s, year-on-year Japanese FDI in China outstripped U.S. investment, and South Korean investment in China has rivaled that of the United States since the latter part of the 2000s.[17]

While the economic incentives might now be there to support Professor Inoguchi's perhaps overly optimistic prognosis for an Asian economic community akin to Europe's, unfortunately many political, historical, and cultural hurdles remain. We will examine those problems in chapter 4. In a provocative 2012 article entitled "A Tale of Two Asias," scholars and former U.S. government officials Evan Feigenbaum

and Robert Manning ask an interesting question in a time of rising
security tensions. They place East Asian intraregional trade at 53 percent
of the total. But they ask whether the obvious incentives for cooperation will trump the hypernationalism, historical memories, and current
sovereignty disputes creating tensions among the nations of East Asia.[18]

As with most such questions, the proper answer to Feigenbaum and
Manning's is probably not a simple yes or no. While transnational production and interdependence is certainly no guarantee against war, it is
still a major force for peace. In addressing why, we should consider the
implications of the pessimists' scenarios in which China tries to bully
the United States and "extrude" it from the region. The number one
security issue for the leadership of the Chinese Communist Party is to
stay in power and maintain social stability. Job creation is critical to
that mission, so it is hard to imagine China wantonly harming or even
threatening to harm the economic relations that provide such a large
percentage not only of China's trade but also its annual GDP.

The table opposite uses the relatively conservative estimates for
China's trade as a percentage of GDP offered by the IMF (the World
Bank suggests that over 50 percent of China's 2011 GDP is in trade,
while the IMF's 2012 statistics result in a lower figure: 47 percent).[19]
Whichever figures one chooses, it appears that Beijing would be ill
advised to harm these economic links through coercive measures. If
one assumes that China upsetting the current order would also alienate
U.S. allies and like-minded states in both the European Union and East
Asia, a Chinese coercion campaign against the United States and other
advanced economies operating in East Asia might have potentially catastrophic consequences for Beijing's effort to produce jobs. In 2012, trade
with the United States and U.S. allies and security partners constituted
39 percent of China's overall trade, and that trade stood at 19 percent of
China's overall GDP. If one adds the EU as a set of like-minded states,
then the United States and its friends and allies occupy a majority position (54 percent) in Chinese trade; that trade constitutes a stunning 26
percent of China's GDP.

A study of Chinese foreign direct investment produces similar
results. Approximately one-third of official FDI entering China comes
from the United States and its formal allies and security partners in

CHINA'S TRADE WITH THE UNITED STATES, U.S. ALLIES AND SECURITY PARTNERS IN ASIA, AND THE EUROPEAN UNION 2012

		China's Exports	China's Imports	Total Trade	% of China's GDP	% of China's Total Trade
United States		353	129	482	6%	12%
Formal U.S. Allies in East Asia	Japan	152	178	330	4%	9%
	Republic of Korea	88	167	255	3%	7%
	Australia	38	79	117	1%	3%
	Philippines	17	20	37	0%	1%
	Thailand	31	38	69	1%	2%
Allies Total		326	482	808	10%	21%
Nonallied Security Partners in Asia	Singapore	40	28	68	1%	2%
	New Zealand	4	6	10	0%	0%
	Indonesia	34	32	66	1%	2%
	India	48	19	67	1%	2%
	Mongolia	3	4	7	0%	0%
Security Partners Total		129	89	218	3%	6%
EU-27		373	213	586	7%	15%
World		2052	1817	3869	47%	

Figure 4. Numbers represent billion USD.
Sources: Trade information from International Monetary Fund (IMF), Direction of Trade Statistics database, 2013, www.imfstatistics.org. Accessed via Global Insight database. GDP information from World Bank, http://www.worldbank.org/en/country/china.

Asia.[20] This figure, while large, actually grossly underestimates the role of the United States and its partners. Forty percent of China's overall official "FDI" flows from Hong Kong, a special administrative region of the PRC itself.[21] Moreover, a large percentage of that FDI comes from the mainland itself. It is being "round-tripped" to gain beneficial tax and other incentives given to foreign-invested firms on the mainland, or simply to launder ill-gotten profits.[22]

**NET FDI INTO CHINA FROM THE UNITED STATES AND U.S. ALLIES
AND SECURITY PARTNERS IN ASIA
1990–2012**

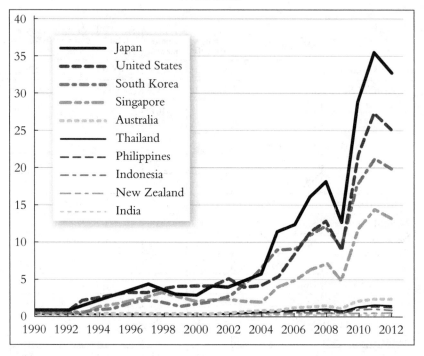

Figure 5. Numbers represent billion USD. Data from 2006 to 2012 are estimates prepared by the Economist Intelligence Unit (EIU) World Investment Service. Data for Mongolia is not available from this source. Organizations and scholars analyzing the Chinese economy employ a variety of methodologies to measure FDI inflows to China and thereby derive widely ranging figures for each year. The EIU estimates tend to be on the high end of that range. The rate of change and the relative ranking of countries in the overall portfolio of China's incoming FDI in the EIU database are, however, consistent with those created by databases using other methodologies, and it is those aspects of the graph above that are most important for the analysis here. Source: EIU World Investment Service (online), Economist Intelligence Unit, https://eiu.bvdep.com. Accessed September 16, 2014.

Why would China try to use economic leverage against these benefactors especially for the purpose of ending those alliances? Why would China not try to avoid security policies that triggered military conflict with these actors? For reasons offered in later chapters, the other leg of CCP legitimacy, nationalism, might trump rational economic calculations under certain circumstances, such as escalating tensions over mari-

**NET FDI INTO CHINA FROM THE UNITED STATES AND U.S. ALLIES
AND SECURITY PARTNERS IN ASIA
2012**

		FDI into China	% of China's Total Inward FDI
United States		25.13	8%
Formal U.S. Allies in East Asia	Japan	32.85	11%
	Republic of Korea	19.80	7%
	Australia	2.21	1%
	Philippines	1.31	0%
	Thailand	1.37	0%
Allies Total		**57.48**	**19%**
Nonallied Security Partners in Asia	Singapore	13.26	4%
	New Zealand	0.28	0%
	Indonesia	0.84	0%
Security Partners Total		**14.38**	**5%**
World		296	

Figure 6. Numbers represent billion USD. Data for India and Mongolia are not available from this data source for 2012. India and Mongolia both provide only small amounts of FDI to China. See the caption for figure 5 for discussion of the EIU database.
Source: EIU World Investment Service (online), Economist Intelligence Unit, https://eiu.bvdep.com. Accessed September 16, 2014.

time sovereignty disputes, but all things being equal, the contemporary economic realities should prove a major force for peace.

The U.S. Alliance System and the Lack of True Multipolarity

NOT ONLY ARE the straightforward economic incentives and relationships different now than during the late nineteenth and early twentieth centuries, so are the strategic concerns. That earlier world was one in which territorial conquest, even of other great powers, seemed desirable and plausible. Multipolarity and alliance politics played a significantly destabilizing role in European and Asian security before 1945. In Europe before the two world wars, the existence of several powerful states created opposite but equally deadly forces for instability. Before World War I, almost all European capitals held the misguided belief that offense provided the military advantage on the battlefield. That misperception led to the prediction that early victories in war would likely accumulate. Allies in these opposing camps tied themselves tightly together so as to maximize the momentum of their initial punch should war occur. As a result, escalation to World War I occurred quickly following what otherwise would be relatively small perturbations—tensions in the Balkans pitted the interests of Russia, tightly allied with France, against those of the Austro-Hungarian Empire, tightly allied with Germany. Before World War II, multipolarity created a nearly opposite dynamic. World War I had bogged down into a defensive war in which great powers wore each other down in the trenches. A misplaced belief among European powers in the hardiness of defenses allowed Hitler to pick off victims piecemeal and accumulate power before the future allies could coordinate their efforts. By the time the Allies rallied to counter Nazi Germany, the task of defeating Berlin required a massive conflagration.[23]

In pre–World War II Asia, a desire for territorial acquisition fueled Japan's imperial aggression against first a relatively weak China and then a relatively passive United States. According to Michael Barnhart, Japanese strategic leaders had learned the standard lessons of World War I regarding the attritional nature of great power war and the need for an autarky, an economy with a resource base and markets that are firmly under one's own control. Japan was concerned about the United States and Britain, both great powers present in East Asia, but its main long-term concern was the prospect of conflict with the resource-rich Soviet Union. Japan remained a resource-poor island nation with little strategic depth. The acquisition of Manchukuo in northeast China and the later invasion of China were, in part, designed to rectify that situation. Instead the campaign in China proved costly and violent and alienated the United States, on which Japan ironically had become more dependent for natural resources. When the United States started to pressure Japan through sanctions and embargoes over the occupation of China, the Japanese militarists decided to ally with Nazi Germany and attack U.S. and British bases in the Pacific.[24]

East Asia today is not divided between opposing alliance systems. In fact, almost all important actors in the region besides China and Russia are either formal U.S. allies or security partners. Despite the recent overtures to Moscow of China's new leader, Xi Jinping, soon after he took office, Russia and China themselves are not aligned and their relationship is a complex mix of cooperation and mistrust. Moreover, east of central Asia, Russia itself is no longer a significant Asian military actor, at least not in the conventional sphere. In the western Pacific, the United States enjoys alliances with many regional actors, like Japan, Australia, South Korea, Thailand, and the Philippines, and security partnerships with others, such as Singapore and Taiwan. But the alliances do not at all resemble the ones that helped launch World War I. The United States does not rely on, say, the Philippines for survival, as Germany did with Austria-Hungary or France with Russia prior to World War I. So a dispute over an uninhabited rock between China and the Philippines or even China and Japan seems much less likely to escalate into World War III in the way that the shooting of an archduke in Sarajevo sparked World War I.[25]

For its part, China itself lacks any strategically important allies. For all its destabilizing behavior, North Korea is hardly a "pole," yet it is the closest thing that China has to an ally in the western Pacific. Given the continuing U.S. alliance with South Korea, one can imagine destabilizing scenarios on the Korean peninsula that could greatly raise Sino-American tensions, or even conceivably lead to Sino-American conflict. For example, if North Korea were to collapse internally, both China and the United States might send in forces to secure nuclear materials and provide stability. Those forces could conceivably come into conflict, particularly if, as is all too likely, they had failed to plan and coordinate such activities in advance.

But the thought processes behind such clashes would almost certainly be quite different than those of leaders in Europe in 1914 or even of leaders in Washington and Beijing in 1950 at the outset of the Korean War. The Korean War escalated because the United States intervened to defend South Korea out of worry over the security of its future South

Korean and Japanese allies if it did not. Those allies were important because Washington was in a nascent global competition with the Soviet Union, itself allied with China and North Korea. When the increasingly successful UN force secured South Korea and prepared to cross the 38th parallel and defeat the North Korean military once and for all, Mao and his comrades worried about the fall of their North Korean ally and the prospect of a future invasion of China by the United States and Japan from the territory of a unified and anti-Communist Korea. Beijing decided to confront advancing U.S. and UN forces on Korean soil instead, with disastrous consequences for everyone but the North Korean regime. While China would hardly welcome a unified Korea under Seoul's leadership today, can anyone in China or anywhere else imagine the United States crossing the Yalu with ground troops to attack northeast China from a future unified Korea? Of course not. Even if common sense in Washington did not prevent the Americans from launching such an attack, we can be sure the leaders in Seoul would not permit the United States to use their territory for such a pointless and dangerous adventure. It is even harder to believe that China would take massive risks and pay astronomical costs to actively assist the North in a war with the United States and the ROK.

The Role of Nuclear Weapons

IN ADDITION TO the lack of true multipolarity, there is another difference between twenty-first-century Asia and the world before World War II: nuclear weapons. Unlike the United States, Germany, and Japan in the nineteenth and twentieth centuries, China is rising as a nuclear power into a world in which several other great powers have nuclear arsenals (including a few of China's immediate neighbors and the United States itself). The existence of these weapons does not preclude war, but it makes conquest much more difficult to imagine and thereby removes entirely one traditional incentive for great power war: an effort to invade, subdue, and occupy the territory of a great power or its ally. Even if China, the United States, Russia, and India somehow decided to abandon all of their nuclear weapons in the twenty-first century, a scenario in which these states tried to conquer each other entirely through blitzkrieg attacks or long attritional wars would still seem fantastic. With nuclear weapons, the scenarios seem simply ridiculous.

When the fear of domination and occupation by other great powers goes away, so do some of the ancillary reasons to become aggressive. China will almost certainly continue to fear the United States and other great powers, but it has little incentive to launch full-scale invasions of South Korea and Japan in an attempt to surround or occupy those U.S. allies in the way that Germany did to France and Belgium in the early stages of both world wars. Similarly, it is hard to imagine contemporary Japanese concerns about great power competition and dependence on mineral resources overseas leading Japan to launch colonial wars of occupation against Asian neighbors as it did in the 1930s. More likely scenarios include limited coercive struggles in Asia over disputed territories, shipping lanes, basing rights, and so on, and these could always escalate. But American and Chinese nuclear weapons should provide a major incentive for prudence and caution on all sides.

Will China Change the Rules Once Its Power Increases?

AS ITS POWER RISES, will China seek to undermine and ultimately replace existing global institutions? This is the source of debate among theorists who see institutions as by-products of national power and as tools for the powerful and what might be labeled "integrationists." The most prolific and influential of this latter group is Princeton professor G. John Ikenberry. He agrees with the pessimists about the decline of America in relative power terms, though he is less concerned about either the severity of that decline or its political meaning. Ikenberry argues optimistically that there is no reason to think that a rising China, as well as other emerging actors, cannot be integrated into what he calls a "liberal international order," a series of multilateral arrangements and norms originally set up by the United States and like-minded states after World War II.[26]

Critics think Ikenberry's vision is a pipe dream: integrating a rising authoritarian China into that liberal order under the umbrella of multilateral cooperation will prove difficult if not impossible. The order would only survive, they argue, if China were to transform itself radically at home, abandoning authoritarianism and becoming more like America, or if the United States managed to maintain clear international leadership. Scholars with diverse political leanings and varying levels of pessimism agree on this point. They believe that a rising China, especially an authoritarian one, will want to rewrite the rules of the current international order, not accommodate itself to those rules. Agreeing with Ikenberry that the existing international order is, at its core, "Western," Georgetown professor Charles Kupchan argues that such a liberal order was crafted in large part by the United States and its democratic allies after World War II in ways that served their selfish interests. Authoritarian postcolonial nationalists in Beijing and elsewhere have simply lacked the power to overturn it, his argument goes. But if China and other non-Western actors such as Brazil and India continue to rise, that will all change.[27] British academic Martin Jacques concurs, arguing: "Given that China promises to be so inordinately powerful and different, it is difficult to resist the idea that in time its rise will herald the birth of a new international order."[28] Coming from a neoconservative angle, historian Robert Kagan and Georgetown's Robert Lieber agree with this aspect of Jacques's argument regarding differences in Chinese and Western political culture but, along with Aaron Friedberg, believe that the United States and its allies can and should stave off such an outcome in part by maintaining the U.S. position of military preeminence in Asia.[29] For his part, Kupchan seems to think that, if sustained, a U.S. strategy of preeminence would lead to a spiral of tensions and otherwise avoidable conflict.

It is ironic that authors on both sides of this debate use terminology that underscores the differences between China and "the West." By doing so they lend ammunition to supporters of CCP authoritarianism, who portray concepts like "westernize" and "westernization" (*xihua* or *xifanghua*) as insidious tools of power politics designed to weaken and subjugate the Chinese nation. "Westernization" is often spoken of in the same vein as foreign advocacy for ethnic and regional separatism in China, or *fenhua*.[30] In a paper entitled "Western System versus Chinese System," Peking University professor Pan Wei rejects China's integration with the allegedly Western world order and defends China's domestic system and traditional foreign policy approach in zero-sum terms: "While the West tries to undermine the Chinese System and place China in the U.S.-led global regime of hierarchy, China strives for equality and independence in coexistence."[31] Cosmopolitan reformers in China seem to recognize this problem when they advocate borrowing political, economic, and social ideas from abroad to foster China's modernization. For example, in 2003 Peking University's Wang Jisi called for a fusion (*ronghe*) of the best ideas of East and West. He drew distinctions between this kind of healthy "globalization" and the much less palatable concept of westernization, which smacks of imperial superiority and bullying to the Chinese.[32]

Of course, it is the intention of neither the optimists nor the pessimists to give ammunition to conservatives in the PRC government or undercut cosmopolitan reformers, but that is exactly the effect of their rhetoric. The international institutions are not intrinsically Western, even though they have their roots in the post–World War II consensus. Are mathematics essentially Arabic or Asian because they originated there? Many great concepts have their origins in European cultures—physics, modern medicine, et cetera—but that does not make them all particularly European. On a more practical level, the greatest beneficiaries of that system have not always been the leaders who created it. Yes, as the political scientist Robert Keohane argued in the 1980s, the international system was created under U.S. leadership and it is difficult to imagine how it could have been otherwise. But from its outset the system—including aspects such as the General Agreement on Tariffs and Trade, the International Monetary Fund, the World Bank, and the United Nations—was designed to benefit all rule-abiding members. In conjunction with the Marshall Plan and with American tolerance for infant industry protection in western Europe and Japan, the institutional system was intended to allow poorer American allies to grow even faster than the United States. Yes, the United States benefited, but others benefited even more and that was no accident. Japan, for one, was an enormous beneficiary of this system, and any westerner who has spent any time in that country might find jarring its common inclusion in the Western world. Japan is economically successful and democratic, but it is not Western in any other discernible way. The same can be said of South Korea and Taiwan. Since presumably Asian, African, Latin American, and Middle Eastern countries should all want to be successful, perhaps they all then strive to be "Western." In this way I find Ikenberry's thesis about the potential expansion of the liberal international order persuasive, even if I find ironically counterproductive the one adjective, "Western," that he uses to describe it.

And this gets us to China. Since 1978, there arguably has been no greater beneficiary of the existing international order than China. By integrating into that order with a speed and intensity rarely seen in the developing world, China has built a vibrant economy that has pulled hundreds of millions out of poverty and, ironically perhaps, has legitimized the ruling Chinese Communist Party in a post-Communist world. We may grumble about Chinese investment restrictions and the favoring of state-owned enterprises, but as Edward Steinfeld has pointed out so well, China has opened itself up to international investment, international trade, and transnational production to such a degree that China is essentially playing by our rules. Now that it is so deeply entrenched, why would China want to change international trade and financial institutions fundamentally, particularly when it has been doing so well within that system? What would the changes look like (and here I am not including as a fundamental change a simple increase in China's voting rights within existing institutions)? What set of global institutions would China endorse to replace the existing ones? I have never seen any evidence that Chinese elites have a blueprint for a new international system to promote once China becomes sufficiently powerful to implement it. And even if they had such an abstract notion, I doubt it would be easy to gain a consensus in China about what a Chinese-centered international order should look like. China has helped form new regional organizations such as ASEAN Plus Three and the Chiang Mai Initiative, a regional currency-swapping institution. Globally, China has taken a leadership role in the BRICS, the aforementioned grouping of emerging markets, and on climate change and energy issues has aligned with a slightly different grouping of emerging economies, BASIC (Brazil, South Africa, India, and China). And, as discussed in chapter 1, China has formed several new multilateral dialogue forums with nations of the developing world. But none of these trends pose a fundamental challenge to the UN, the IMF, and other leading international institutions. In 2014, the BRICS economies formed a development bank of their own, but it remains to be seen if this bank will pose any significant challenge to existing institutions or even if its members will be able to sustain the internal consensus necessary to make the bank effective. The same can be said for the recent Chinese proposal for the Asian Infrastructure Investment Bank, which, unlike the preexisting Asian Development Bank, would not include the United States.[33] Even if these new organizations prove effective, and even if China plays a large role within them, as will surely be the case, they might simply supplement rather than undercut the existing institutions in which China and the United States both play a role.

One might argue that Chinese firms and the Chinese government do not play by the existing rules of the road in international commerce, whether they are gaining advantageous financing from Chinese state-owned banks for energy deals, stealing intellectual property, computer hacking, insisting on technology transfers as part of business deals between Chinese state-owned enterprises and companies from advanced economies, or dumping products to gain market share. There is no doubt that all of these problems occur and that they are serious issues for foreign businesses and, ultimately, for the long-term health of China's own economy. But they do not constitute the rewriting of international rules to somehow benefit China at the expense of others. They simply constitute cheating or free-riding on existing rules, an entirely different kettle of fish. While China would like to have more voice in the IMF (and the United States would not object), there is little sense that China wants the organization to change fundamentally in its form or function. Nor does it seem that China would like to change the rules at the WTO.

The issue of simple rules violations is akin to another major problem that will be discussed in later chapters: China's willingness to help maintain the international order from which it so benefits. China is not necessarily behaving worse than developing countries have behaved in the past, but China is so large and globally influential, more than any developing country in history, that even standard levels of rule-breaking might hamper the international system. The United States and the other leading economies applied this logic when China negotiated its accession to the WTO in 1999–2001. Because of China's overall size and the danger that Chinese protectionism and export of products with artificially low prices would undercut support for free trade agreements in the world's leading economies, China was asked by the United States and the member states of the European Union to follow a stricter liberalization protocol than other developing countries, making it harder for China to protect its agricultural and manufacturing sector through subsidies and tariffs, rendering it easier for others to retaliate against China for the dumping of underpriced prod-

CHINA'S TRADE WITH THE UNITED STATES AND U.S. ALLIES AND SECURITY PARTNERS IN ASIA
1990–2012

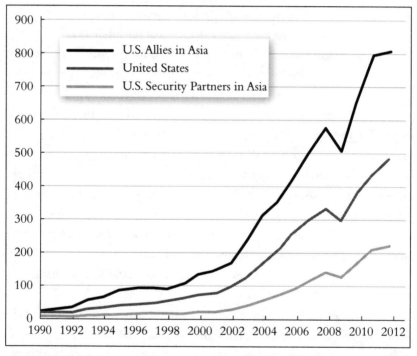

Figure 7. Numbers represent billion USD. U.S. allies include Japan, South Korea, Australia, the Philippines, and Thailand. U.S. security partners include Singapore, New Zealand, Indonesia, India, and Mongolia.
Source: International Monetary Fund, Direction of Trade Statistics database, 2013, www .imfstatistics.org. Accessed via Global Insight database.

ucts, and providing more protections for foreign firms operating in China than were found in other developing countries that were members of the WTO.[34] The results were startlingly successful in terms of both the growth of China's trade and the growth in foreign direct investment into China. Businesses no longer worried nearly as much about the prospect of trade wars with the Chinese state and invested accordingly. The table on page 60 gives a good sense of the growth of trade since China joined the WTO in 2001, especially with regional actors. The graph on investment on page 48 shows the sharp related rise in incoming FDI following China's WTO accession.[35]

We can go further still with this analysis and recognize that, on at least one score, China is a conservative force for protecting the *twentieth-century* rules of the international order. It is the United States, the Europeans, and Japan who are rewriting the traditional rules in the twenty-first century. The demise of the Soviet Union led to a sharp uptick in humanitarian military operations led by the United States and its allies, beginning with the intervention in Somalia in 1992 and followed by those in Bosnia and Kosovo. This apparent breakdown in the norm of noninterference worried Chinese elites, especially after being subjected to sanctions following the Tiananmen massacre of 1989. Many Chinese observers also feared that the more interventionist norms might provide pretexts for the United States and its allies to expand their power and create instability in regions where China had growing economic interests. In negotiations that were lubricated in part by the September 11, 2001, terrorist attacks launched from Al Qaeda bases in Taliban-governed Afghanistan, the United Nations in 2005 legitimized international humanitarian intervention against regimes that failed to protect their own or foreign populations from violence. China initially signed on to this new international Responsibility to Protect (R2P), albeit with a number of predictable caveats, reservations, and conditions. The gist of R2P is that states have more than a responsibility to respect the sovereignty and rights of other states: they also have a responsibility to prevent mass violence against citizens within their borders or beyond their borders whether that violence is perpetrated by state or by non-state actors. The clear implication for the United States and like-minded states is that violation of this norm should lead to international pressure

CHINA'S TRADE WITH THE UNITED STATES AND U.S. ALLIES AND SECURITY PARTNERS IN ASIA
1990–2012

	PRC Trade with U.S. Allies in Asia	% of PRC Total Trade	PRC Trade with the United States	% of PRC Total Trade	PRC Trade with U.S. Security Partners in Asia	% of PRC Total Trade	PRC Total World Trade
1990	21	18%	12	10%	5	4%	117
1991	27	20%	14	10%	6	4%	136
1992	34	21%	18	10%	6	4%	167
1993	52	27%	28	14%	8	4%	195
1994	66	28%	35	15%	9	4%	237
1995	83	30%	41	15%	12	4%	281
1996	90	31%	43	15%	13	5%	290
1997	95	29%	49	15%	16	5%	325
1998	90	28%	55	17%	15	5%	324
1999	104	29%	61	17%	16	5%	361
2000	136	29%	75	16%	23	5%	474
2001	144	28%	81	16%	23	4%	510
2002	170	27%	97	16%	29	5%	621
2003	232	27%	127	15%	39	5%	851
2004	309	27%	170	15%	57	5%	1155
2005	363	26%	212	15%	72	5%	1423
2006	426	24%	263	15%	90	5%	1761
2007	505	23%	303	14%	117	5%	2175
2008	581	23%	335	13%	143	6%	2561
2009	504	23%	299	14%	126	6%	2207
2010	671	23%	386	13%	172	6%	2974
2011	798	22%	444	12%	213	6%	3643
2012	806	21%	481	12%	218	6%	3869

Figure 8. Numbers represent billion USD. U.S. allies include Japan, South Korea, Australia, the Philippines, and Thailand. U.S. security partners include Singapore, New Zealand, Indonesia, India, and Mongolia.
Source: International Monetary Fund, Direction of Trade Statistics database, 2013, www.imf statistics.org. Accessed via Global Insight database.

and even, on occasion, military intervention, as was executed successfully in Libya in 2011 and attempted unsuccessfully in Syria through the United Nations Security Council in the following three years.

The Annan Plan for peace and political reconciliation in Syria failed in part because China and Russia vetoed multiple UN Security Council draft resolutions. The Chinese leadership did not do so because it is trying to revise the international system; it is trying to prevent revision of that order, which had been based on the inviolability of state sovereignty. China similarly vetoed draft resolutions on Zimbabwe and Burma while I served at the State Department. Chinese diplomats expressed the basic idea that humanitarian concerns within borders, no matter how severe, are not the purview of the UN Security Council. According to my Chinese interlocutors, China abstained on a resolution allowing the use of force in Libya in 2011 only because a veto risked alienation of the Arab League and the African Union. But when the scope of the initial UN-sanctioned operations expanded from protecting the citizens of Benghazi from massacre to the active overthrow of Qaddafi's regime, China became resolutely conservative on R2P proposals and has refused to budge on Syria despite heavy criticism from some states in the Middle East and beyond.

The real challenge facing the United States and like-minded states in the West and in Asia is not to prevent China from overturning the international order but rather to convince China that it would benefit from supporting concepts like the responsibility to protect. The initiatives are rooted in part in a recognition that domestic political instability and suffering can carry global implications. And, as I have argued above, few countries have more to lose from global instability than China. These are not easy tasks, but the hurdles to achieving them have less to do with increases in Chinese power than they do with China's self-absorption. China is a developing country with a potentially unstable domestic order and conservative views on sovereignty. We only feed into those tendencies by labeling institutions as "Western." Chinese patriots have every reason to reject a demand that they become "Western," but no reason to reject high standards of compliance with universal norms of free market economics, intellectual property rights protection, and nuclear nonproliferation, as well as basic standards of universal human rights and the spread of democracy itself. After all, those values are shared by three democracies immediately to the PRC's east—South Korea, Japan, and Taiwan—and many of them are shared by Hong Kong, an administrative region of the PRC itself.

WHILE THE RISE of new powers has historically led to bloody and sustained conflicts, this time should be different. A rising China has more reasons to avoid military and economic conflict with the United States and its allies than any previous rising power. In the next chapter, I will offer another significant reason for thinking that China will be unlikely to launch a destabilizing challenge to the United States in the foreseeable future: the likelihood that the United States will continue to be much more powerful than China for decades to come.

CHAPTER 3

Why Chinese Power Will Not Surpass U.S. Power Anytime Soon

C HINA'S RISE IS REAL, as discussed in chapter 1. And for reasons that will be discussed in the next chapter, China's increased military, economic, and political power poses challenges for U.S. national security and regional stability in Asia. But we need not panic. Not only does China have many disincentives for aggression, but it is not likely to catch up or surpass the United States in terms of comprehensive national power anytime soon.

There is a growing chorus that portrays China as being on a clear path to economic, military, and diplomatic supremacy. For example, Martin Jacques predicts China's impending hegemony in the title of his book *When China Rules the World*.[1] Economist Arvind Subramanian similarly argues that "China's dominance is a sure thing," going beyond Jacques and claiming that, by his measures, China has already caught up with the United States in overall economic power and will be fully dominant by 2030. He writes, "Chinese dominance is not looming. In some ways, it is already here."[2] Witnessing China's economic activities in Asia, Africa, Latin America, and the Middle East, others have prematurely extolled China's growth in diplomatic "soft power."[3] A more balanced approach is offered by the scholar David Shambaugh in his book *China Goes Global,* which recognizes China's increasing economic activity around the world but also the limitations in the increased political power that flows from that activity. Shambaugh cleverly labels China "the partial power."[4]

Pessimistic commentators like Jacques and Subramanian ignore too many sources of Chinese weakness and American strength. In addition to viewing trade and investment in the developing world as a realpolitik competition between great powers, a highly questionable proposition, these studies often exaggerate the political leverage enjoyed by countries that are purchasing raw materials. Moreover, there are several negative factors for China's reputation in these areas. China's extractive business practices have led to resentment of Chinese companies, including some high-profile instances of violence in Africa. Democratization in Latin America and Africa has led to a political backlash against China's support for states like Zimbabwe. The Arab Spring in the Middle East has also complicated Beijing's relations with some members of the Arab League as Beijing joins Russia in blocking the international community from pressuring Assad's regime in Syria.

In military matters, China's defense modernization does pose real problems for the United States, but the scope of that newfound military power is often exaggerated by scholars and public officials. Too often these observers approach military net assessments as if they are tallying a sports score, with each country getting a certain number of points for each counted asset. But even though the United States still does well in such a competition with China, numbers are not everything. A more sophisticated analysis would take into account the quality of systems, the quality of personnel, and the wartime experience of the two militaries. Such a study reveals that China is unlikely to have the military wherewithal to become a global peer competitor of the United States for decades to come. Chinese strategic writings, even those not meant for foreign consumption, seem to recognize China's shortcomings. They often refer to the need to develop strategies that overcome China's relative military weakness in comparison to a potential great power foe. While they discuss closing the gap in overall military power, there is almost no sense that such a goal will be achieved anytime soon. It seems then that Americans often give the Chinese higher grades and aspirations than Chinese military officers themselves are willing to accept.

For similar reasons, China is also unlikely to have the wherewithal to deny the United States access to the western Pacific, a goal that the Pentagon believes China is pursuing under the distinctly

American concept of "anti-access/area denial" (or A2AD in DoD-speak). As with Friedberg's concept of extrusion, I have seen in my research no Chinese-language equivalent to these terms in authoritative strategic writings. The closest Chinese term is "counterintervention," but this concept has more to do with raising the costs to intervening foreign forces than to physically preventing their entry in the first place. This does not mean that China will not adopt such a strategy of exclusion, only that it currently seems to lack the capability and intention to do so.

Another central problem with the pessimist school, also known as "declinists," is that they underrate U.S. power in the region in part because they do not fully appreciate the Asian alliance network that the United States created after World War II. Moreover, pessimists often worry excessively about China's diplomatic inroads in East Asia and Central Asia and around the world. Since these have grown exponentially since the mid-1990s, it must then be the case that China is closing the diplomatic power gap with the United States. But this approach to diplomacy misunderstands the function and importance of multilateral international groupings and underestimates the difficulties that any one country has in using those organizations as tools for selfish power projection. Pessimists reveal a jealous zero-sum mind-set in the language they use when referring to organizations in which the United States does not actively participate. Instead of mentioning who is included in such organizations, pessimists and declinists emphasize that the United States is excluded. By doing so, they portray otherwise healthy regional organizations designed to build confidence and increase cooperation among their members as daggers pointed at America's heart.

Taking them in turn, we shall see that there are many reasons to doubt China is taking over the world economically, militarily, or diplomatically.

Economics

JUDGING FROM PUBLIC opinion polls in the United States and Europe, the era of U.S. economic leadership is over and China is already the strongest economy in the world. Following the 2008 financial crisis, a majority of Americans seem to believe that China is the world's leading economy and a majority of Europeans seem to think that China has or will surpass the United States as a global superpower.[5] Perhaps these respondents have been affected by breathless media coverage and zero-sum political spin by politicians on the outsourcing of American and European jobs. Some respondents might have been influenced by more scholarly arguments like those of Martin Jacques, Arvind Subramanian, and Christopher Layne.[6] These authors have declared the period of U.S. leadership over and, with varying degrees of hyperbole, China a current challenger and/or a future leader on the world stage.

If we study the issue carefully, we find that the rumors of the death of U.S. economic leadership have been greatly exaggerated. In emphasizing China's remaining challenges and persistent U.S. advantages in the twenty-first century, a diverse set of authors—Joseph Nye, Dan Drezner, Michael Beckley, Robert Lieber, and Joseph Joffe—all subscribe to a thesis regarding U.S.–China relations pioneered by Harvard's Alastair Iain Johnston and Sheena Chestnut Greitens. In 2009 the Harvard scholars asked by what measures China was rising as a potential peer competitor with the United States.[7] Even three years later, by the most generous estimates of Chinese GDP (the purchase power parity, or PPP, formula favored by the World Bank), the United States economy was still 26 percent larger than China's.[8]

And even if the OECD is correct that continued growth in China and continued malaise in the United States will allow China's GDP (measured by PPP) to surpass that of the United States by 2016, this alone would not make China an economic peer competitor with the United States.[9] China's population is between four and five times larger than the United States's, and in 2012, even with the most generous PPP measures, its per capita income was less than one-fifth that of the United States (by one measure, U.S. per capita income was $50,700 and China's $9,300).[10] At least until the 2008 financial crisis, the gap in per capita GDP between the United States and China had actually grown in absolute terms since the end of the Cold War. This is true because, as in military affairs, China was growing from such a low starting point. In order to turn domestic economic wherewithal into political clout on the international stage, states need to mobilize wealth for national policy purposes, usually through taxation. Per capita GDP is a good measure of how easy or difficult it will be for any state to extract any amount of money from individual citizens for arms, foreign aid, and so on. It is also a good measure of the relative cost to citizens of income sacrificed when economic sanctions that harm trade and investment are leveled for reasons of power politics. Anyone who is familiar with progressive tax systems will understand this basic concept. A $100 tax on a Chinese person earning $3,000 per year carries a much larger marginal cost than a similar tax on someone earning many times that much. The same holds true for the hundred dollars that a Chinese citizen might lose if trade and investment relations were to break down with Japan or Korea over a political difference.

As an illustrative exercise to demonstrate the limits of China's economic power, it is useful to deconstruct the most dramatic of the theses about U.S. economic decline and the rise of Chinese economic supremacy. In 2011 Arvind Subramanian argued for impending Chinese domination of the world economy in the pages of *Foreign Affairs*. But a look at his measures of manifested dominance shows the underlying weakness of his thesis. First he argues that China "convinced the African countries in which it invests heavily to close down the Taiwanese embassies they were hosting." But is dominance really measured by the ability to get relatively weak countries to recognize a huge country of 1.3 billion rather than an island state of 23 million, especially when the vast majority of the world's nations already recognize the PRC rather than the Republic of China on Taiwan? If so, then the currency of dominance has been greatly devalued. The United Kingdom closed its embassy in Taiwan in 1950; Japan in 1972; the United States in 1979. Did they do so because of Chinese dominance? What might be seen as more remarkable is that Taiwan has been able to maintain as many diplomatic allies as it has by using its own combination of economic incentives and a more attractive political system than mainland China.

Pessimists like Arvind Subramanian also like to cite any moves in the economic sphere that undermine the dollar. For example, Subramanian pointed to the recent phenomenon in which trade transactions among several Asian and Latin American countries can now be settled in yuan (Chinese renminbi). While certainly a sign of growing Chinese economic importance, it hardly poses a challenge to the indispensability of the U.S. dollar as a global reserve currency. The fact that settlement in yuan (RMB), still a currency that does not float on international markets, is even notable only underscores the true importance of the U.S. dollar in the international marketplace. That importance actually might have grown with the financial crisis, as the dollar has fared much better than its only possible convertible competitor, the euro. I do not find the concept of economic dominance very useful in reference to either China or the United States because economics is far from a zero-sum competition. But if I had to cast such a concept in concrete terms, I might find no better example than the U.S. role in the international financial system *after* the financial debacle of 2008. Despite the revelation that terrible policies and habits in the world's leading economy levied tremendous economic losses not only on the United States but on the rest of the world, public and private economic entities around the globe, including the Chinese government, still came to the United States to buy Treasury bills and stocks on Wall Street. Why? Because one has to put one's money somewhere, and the strongest economy with the best and most stable institutions will be the preferred safe haven in a storm, even in a storm created by that economy's own faults. If there is such a thing as economic dominance, it must be the ability for a country to remain the clear economic system leader even when its own economy has taken such a terrible blow.

Pessimists often underestimate the major problems brewing in the Chinese economy as well. To his credit, Subramanian recognizes early on in his article that China's economy faces many structural problems that will be difficult to solve. They include an aging population and inefficient and environmentally damaging energy usage fostered in part by government subsidies. He also cites an overreliance on exports that was created in part by a systematically undervalued currency. If we were to update his list, we might mention the credit crunch that was created when the new Chinese leadership tried to rein in excessive and ill-advised loans at the local level by what are referred to as "shadow banks."[11] Subramanian therefore projects lower levels of growth from now until 2030 (7 percent per annum) than China has witnessed from 1978 to present (11 percent per annum). This is all fine. But a logic problem arises when he then lists as a major indicator of Chinese economic dominance the fact that China continues limiting the value of its currency despite the objections of the United States and others. China's stubborn "beggar-thy-neighbor" approach on currency actually causes long-term domestic instability in China by artificially reducing the sales price of exports and increasing the purchase price of imports, a trend that perpetuates the overreliance on exports for growth and reduces domestic consumption as a percentage of GDP. So what is actually a source of economic weakness becomes an alleged source of dominance.

This contradiction relates to China's much-vaunted surplus in foreign currency reserves—Beijing has become the largest foreign holder of U.S. Treasury bills in the world. Whatever leverage this relationship might provide China, and it is almost certainly quite limited because China would never have an economic incentive to sell off the bills precipitously, the stockpile of Treasury bills is also arguably as much a sign of economic weakness for China as it is economic strength. China's continued disproportionate dependence on exports as a job creator, its fear of domestic inflation, and its subsequent need to "sterilize" its current account surplus with the world compels China to purchase bonds in the United States and elsewhere. In this instance, "sterilization" simply means shipping overseas the foreign reserves accumulated through exporting more than is imported. The only other ways the state could manage that problem would be to allow inflation or to allow its own currency to revalue. Inflation could harm the economy and cause social instability among the many urban citizens and government workers on fixed incomes. Revaluation could cost China manufacturing jobs because it would hurt the competitiveness of exports and increase the competitiveness of imports. But China need not buy U.S. Treasury bills with this excess capital. It could purchase physical assets with the money, invest in stock markets in other countries, or shift from U.S. dollars to a wider basket of currencies. All of this has happened to some degree, but there is little sign that China has significantly slowed down its purchases of U.S. Treasury bills. The main reason, to return to my earlier point, is that despite the financial crisis, and to some degree because of it, the attractiveness of the U.S. bills as a *relatively* secure and highly liquid safe haven (in comparison to other investments) has only increased. To understand this, one has only to look at interest rates. Compared to, say, Spain, the United States has to pay a very low amount to borrow money because it is seen as a low-risk borrower.

The danger that China might sell off bonds precipitously to coerce the United States appeals to many commentators, including Chinese ones. In 2010 nationalist commentators prescribed such a strategy following the announcement of a new tranche of U.S. arms sales to Taiwan. But the government was wise not to take such advice. Indeed, the scenario makes little sense. For example, Subramanian posits that China in the future might hold $4 trillion in U.S. debt. If we grant him that, then we would also have to assume that China will have remained overly dependent on exports for continued growth and will not have broken its addiction to sterilization as a means of keeping exchange rates and inflation low. But even if this proves to be the case, why would China want to sell off a large initial portion of its bonds for the intended purpose of hurting the U.S. economy, one of its largest markets for exports? China would likely lose a huge amount of money in the first round, when its remaining bonds dropped precipitously in value. But more important, by damaging the U.S. economy and basically threatening economic warfare, China would almost certainly have done severe damage to a major export market and a source of foreign direct investment. Reducing the overall purchasing power of the United States and upsetting it politically would also risk reciprocal economic punishment.

Some worry that China might be able to use this economic leverage over the United States as a nonviolent way to undercut U.S. alliances in Asia. This would be the equivalent of Friedberg's extrusion through the use of economic statecraft rather than military coercion. It is not unheard of for states to use financial or trade power to influence the security policies of other states. As Cornell's Jonathan Kirshner argued in his excellent book *Currency and Coercion*, Washington was able to leverage its position as the holder of the global reserve currency in 1956 to dissuade London from escalating militarily against Nasser's

Egypt. That crisis was sparked by Cairo's claim of control over the Suez Canal. The United States believed that the British, French, and Israeli military and diplomatic response to the Egyptian move threatened to alienate Arab nationalists and drive them permanently into the Soviet camp. Moreover, there was some concern that the crisis could escalate to World War III if the Soviets were to intervene directly against U.S. allies in defense of Egypt. Washington's threat was to undercut the value of the British pound sterling on international markets to punish its ally if London refused to back down. London reluctantly complied with Washington's demand and settled the Suez crisis largely on Egypt's terms.[12]

Subramanian raises this example himself in discussing how China might use its alleged financial power to drive the U.S. military from East Asia. But the analogy does not hold. First, the dispute between Great Britain and the United States was among friends and allies, not potential adversaries. Washington, the holder of the leading reserve currency, was acting within an alliance hoping to avoid giving the Soviets unearned leverage in the Middle East and to prevent a local crisis from escalating into a global one. In Subramanian's scenario, China would be an adversary forcing the United States out of its alliances, not an ally counseling restraint, however muscularly, on an overly belligerent friend. Thus, the political goal that Subramanian ascribes to a future aggressive China would be much harder to achieve than the one Washington accomplished in 1956. Moreover, the economic weapons in Beijing's arsenal would be much less potent than those Washington could aim at London in the early Cold War, as today the United States, not China, remains the holder of the leading reserve currency.

The last measure of Chinese dominance employed by pessimists—trade power—reveals an outdated view of the political leverage that trade provides. Subramanian argues that China can exclude U.S. companies from its markets as a punitive measure in order to change U.S. foreign policy. Consistent with Subramanian's claim, Chinese partners have reportedly withheld market access to pressure foreign companies such as Ford Motor Company, General Motors, Kawasaki, Siemens, and BASF to transfer technology directly or, less directly, to build research and development centers adjacent to their factories and offices in China, thereby training Chinese engineers who can then depart to Chinese firms. The CEO of BASF, Jürgen Hambrecht, reportedly derided this practice as "forced disclosure of know-how" in a meeting with Premier Wen Jiabao and Chancellor Angela Merkel.[13] Individual American companies are reluctant to go public with their complaints on this score lest they spoil their relations with Beijing.[14] One particularly bold CEO, GE's Jeffrey Imelt, did publicly complain, albeit abstractly: "I really worry about China. I am not sure that in the end they want any of us to win, or any of us to be successful."[15] But such Chinese practices are very different from Subramanian's concern about China "offering or denying countries" access to markets for the purpose of altering their foreign policy. First of all, China still generally exports more than it imports (hence the current account surplus and resulting hoard of Treasury bills). Moreover, it depends on those exports to produce jobs and maintain social stability. If China tried to close off its economy to all imports from a major economy, especially a market as large as the United States, the inevitable retaliation against Chinese products would have enormous ramifications for China's own export industries. By grossly violating its WTO commitments, Beijing would also damage its attractiveness as a location for foreign direct investment. This would only exacerbate a growing problem for China, which is that other Asian countries are looking like increasingly attractive alternatives for foreign investment. With its impressive rise in wealth, China's laborers are demanding higher wages, making them less competitive in certain industries than workers in places like Vietnam and Bangladesh. Especially since China's own trade sector is heavily dependent on foreign-invested firms, as outlined in chapter 2, China would not only be shooting itself in the foot by sanctioning major countries like the United States, it would be shooting itself in the head.

Persistent U.S. Strengths and Chinese Challenges

BEYOND FINANCE, if one looks at more traditional measures of national economic power, such as global share of manufacturing output, the United States still seems very strong. Despite China's impressive rise, as Lieber reports, in 1978 the United States accounted for 22 percent of global manufacturing, and it still accounts for between 17 and 20 percent today.[16] While the fact that China has caught up to the United States in that period is a tremendous feather in the cap of the reform program launched in 1978, China has between four and five times the population of the United States, and a major part of its manufacturing sector is for exports that have been created for foreign markets with foreign know-how and management skills.

Even the most exuberant analyses of China's economic prospects recognize that China suffers from other institutional, legal, and normative hurdles to becoming a global leader. Innovation is one of those areas of weakness. Corruption, the lack of independent and private academic research institutions, and the lack of intellectual property rights protection all hinder China's development in a global marketplace that rewards innovation. Robert Lieber presents three separate rankings of the top twenty academic research institutions in the world, one list from the United States, another from China, and the third from the United Kingdom. The majority of the top twenty universities on all three lists are American; no Chinese university appears on any of them.[17] China has invested a tremendous amount in its educational institutions in the past few decades, and for the first time university professors can live solidly middle-class lives in China's largest cities. But Chinese academic culture emphasizes numerical measures of success, such as quantity of publications, rather than originality of thought. It has neither well-developed professional norms nor regulatory oversight to prevent fraud, plagiarism, or other forms of intellectual property theft. Without such institutions, China is unlikely to produce top universities soon. In the corporate sector, the United States is still the clear leader in innovation as well. One need only look at America's high percentage of global patents in fields like green technologies and nanotechnologies.[18] For related reasons, China also trails far behind the United States and the Europeans in international branding, which is essential to gaining and sustaining a loyal customer base for finished products.[19]

There are several other problems related to its economy that could stall China's fast-paced economic growth. They include demographics and the pernicious effects of China's one-child policy. As Michael Beckley points out, the ratio of workers to pensioners will drop faster in China than in any country in human history: from 8 to 1 today to 2 to 1 in 2040. Because of relatively liberal immigration policies and high birth rates, especially among recent immigrants, the United States is the only advanced economy in the world with a growing population and a growing work force.[20]

Similarly, while there is fairly widespread understanding in China that a major structural change must take place to reduce dependence on trade and foster more domestically driven growth, my interlocutors in 2010–2011 suggested that there is no consensus among top leaders about how to proceed and no leader who combines the personal power and imagination to drive through needed changes without a broad consensus. Along similar lines, China lacks institutions like developed stock markets to channel capital into the most dynamic sectors of its economy. The infusion of new capital into large infrastructure projects as part of the post-2008 stimulus package may have only exacerbated problems related to corruption, local debt, environmental degradation, and eminent domain controversies.[21] The new government under Xi Jinping launched reforms at the Party's third plenum in 2013 that addressed precisely those problems, but whether the PRC government can adequately tackle them remains to be seen.

China's Economic Inroads in the Developing World

DESPITE THE COMMON usage of terms like "a new scramble for Africa" in media circles, the idea that China and the United States are competing for influence there is extremely ill conceived. In my experience as a U.S. government official, neither the United States nor the Chinese government viewed the relations of the other with African countries as part of a zero-sum struggle for global influence. And even if one were to accept such nineteenth-century logic, China would hardly look like the dominant great power in either Africa or Latin America. Of course, it is notable that China has become Africa's largest trading partner since the financial crisis. But U.S. trade with the continent is still large despite a sharp decline in the past few years.

As recently as 2008, U.S. trade with sub-Saharan Africa outstripped China's by a considerable amount ($107 billion USD to $83 billion USD).[22] Few lauded U.S. "dominance" in the region at that time, nor would such a conclusion have been warranted. Since then, China's trade with sub-Saharan Africa grew by half and U.S. trade dropped by nearly one-third (in 2012 China's trade was $123 billion USD and U.S. trade was $73 billion USD).[23] One reason for the increase in Chinese trade is that China's economy is increasingly dependent on imports of foreign oil, of which sub-Saharan African nations are a major supplier. In 2013 China surpassed the United States as the world's largest net importer of oil.[24] Still, China's exports to sub-Saharan Africa have grown even more quickly than China's growing energy imports from the region, in part because Chinese energy supplies from Sudan were disrupted by the ongoing tensions between Khartoum ("Northern" Sudan) and newly independent South Sudan. Despite this disruption, imports still constituted nearly 20 percent of the increase in China's trade with the region since 2008,[25] and the vast majority of the value of Chinese imports from the region are in natural resources.

Another, more important reason that Americans should not panic about these trends in African trade is that the change in the U.S. trade portfolio can be explained largely by energy markets. U.S. energy production at home has increased sharply, and U.S. imports of oil have dropped sharply due to the shale gas revolution; thus, energy imports from Africa have dropped precipitously. Overall trade with Africa is not a problem. In fact in 2012, U.S. exports to sub-Saharan Africa actually increased by 7 percent, faster than U.S. export growth to the rest of the world (4.5 percent). But U.S. imports from Africa dropped 33 percent in the same year.[26] Much of that drop was in the oil sector (oil imports fell 38 percent), followed by precious stones and metals (imports of these commodities fell 25 percent).[27] Declines in these imports hardly represent U.S. economic weakness. Moreover, global U.S. firms like Exxon Mobil still produce a great deal of oil in Africa even when their downstream destinations are outside the United States. Most important, since U.S. oil imports from Africa dropped because of development of the domestic energy market in the United States, the decline should probably be viewed as a sign of U.S. economic strength.

The rhetoric about energy independence in the United States on both sides of the political aisle is fundamentally misguided and misinformed. Oil is a globalized commodity and no one can cut the United States off from supply because of the diversity of energy producers and the power of the U.S. Navy. And even if the United States produced all of its energy at home, regions like the Middle East would still be strategically important to Washington because the readily available energy resources there would still produce windfall profits for its owners on global markets. Especially since most of those owners are still states, it will still matter greatly to Washington whether the regimes there are friendly or antagonistic to the United States and its allies. Even now, the U.S. imports from the Middle East are limited, but the region is still of great strategic importance.

For this reason, the bipartisan call for energy independence on security grounds is a domestic political canard. But the opposite argument would, if possible, be even more absurd. A country certainly does not become more influential on the international stage by importing more energy and natural resources from any given country or region. No one would argue that we would improve our political power in places like the Middle East or Venezuela by buying more oil from those places. But when Chinese energy imports increase and U.S. imports drop, some analysts begin to worry about Chinese "dominance." Suddenly, Chinese energy dependence becomes a source of national power and U.S. energy independence a cause of national weakness. This makes no sense.

Of course, trade is only one aspect of economic relations in any case. It is difficult to measure China's financial relationship with Africa, given the challenges of drawing lines between aid, loans, and investments. China sometimes gives large discretionary infrastructure loans, for example, to countries in which Chinese state-owned enterprises have invested. These loans and projects are sometimes designed to help get products to port—building roads, rail, and port facilities, for instance—but they are also ways to grease the wheels for energy and resource investments Chinese firms may have made. In recent years, the gap between Chinese and U.S. aid to Africa has been closing, but in most standard categories, the U.S. position still compares very well with China. According to a leading scholar of China's relations with Africa, Deborah Brautigam, U.S. government aid to African countries in 2008 outstripped the closest Chinese equivalent of foreign direct assistance by a very wide margin of almost five to one.[28] This was the result of several years of increases under President George W. Bush, who placed very heavy emphasis on AIDS treatment and prevention under PEP-FAR (President's Emergency Plan for AIDS Relief) and on conditional aid under the norms of the Millennium Challenge initiative. Today, the United States is still the largest provider of overseas development assistance (ODA) to Africa. In contrast, in 2013 China placed about sixth on the list of overall OECD ODA donors, just above Sweden and below France.[29] Chinese aid to Africa is growing, but that increase must be considered in context. According to 2013 estimates, Chinese aid to Africa had risen to approximately $3 billion USD, much larger than before but still less than 40 percent of the U.S. total of approximately $7.75 billion.[30] (See Appendix 3.1.)

According to UN data, China's foreign direct investment in sub-Saharan Africa stood at $3.1 billion in 2011, while the United States invested $5 billion. Accumulated investment even more strongly favored the United States over China, with total stocks of $58 billion USD and $16 billion USD respectively.[31] That said, both U.S. and Chinese FDI are dwarfed by EU investment.[32] While recognizing the U.S. "lead" in such figures, we should still understand that the competitive metric itself is not very useful. Nobody calls the EU "dominant" in Africa. If the Chinese and American numbers were reversed, this would still have bigger implications for the people and corporations involved in trade and investment than for Chinese or American national power. In June 2008, Jim Swan, my counterpart in the Africa Bureau of the State Department, and I testified to the Senate Foreign Relations Committee. I can remember seeing looks of some surprise when I stated that China had in fact played a positive role in Africa: "On an abstract level, China's own domestic economic reforms and opening up to the outside world provide a good example for some of the more insulated economies on the continent. And on a more concrete level, we believe that China's investment in infrastructure and in building businesses in Africa provide positive results for the African people."[33] A few of the senators and their staffers seemed puzzled that we didn't want or believe there to be a zero-sum competition with the Chinese in Africa.

As my colleague, Mr. Swan, pointed out that day, if we consider commonly used instruments like Chinese government preferential financing for Chinese companies operating in countries like Angola or Nigeria or those in China exporting to Africa, the combined numbers for Chinese aid, investment, or both would be much higher. But even if we grant China much higher figures, it is not entirely clear that China would gain great political leverage because of it. Many of these countries have diverse outlets for their natural resources, for example, and the prices are still largely determined by international market forces, not by special deals with China or anyone else.

Even when the importing country enjoys something close to a monopoly position as a purchaser of globally available resources from any given supplier, the purchaser does not necessarily enjoy a privileged political position in the relationship. Witness the U.S. relationship with Venezuela. The United States has long been by far the largest purchaser of Venezuelan oil, and oil is by far Venezuela's most valuable economic asset. Moreover, much of the Venezuelan crude is refined in the United States before it returns to Venezuela or is sold elsewhere as combustible fuel. But Washington not only does not dominate the country, it held little sway over its obstreperous and outwardly anti-American leadership under Hugo Chavez, who famously referred to George W. Bush as the devil, praised Iran, and maintained close ties to Castro's Cuba. Realizing this when I was at the State Department, I often chuckled when I saw ominous news reports regarding the political implications of new energy deals that China was cutting with Venezuela. These seemed to be the same kind of credit-for-energy swaps that China had signed in Africa. The prediction was that Venezuela would be able to diversify its export markets and increase oil flows to China. The implication was that this would give China great political influence in America's backyard. Indeed, Venezuelan exports to China eventually did increase. In 2012 Venezuela reported that exports of oil to China increased 30 percent, to 600,000 barrels per day. U.S. official estimates put the figure at a much lower 260,000 barrels of crude per day (for

2013).[34] But even the higher Venezuelan figure is smaller than the flow of crude to the United States, which even at half of what it was in the late 1990s was still over 800,000 barrels per day in 2012 and 2013. Furthermore, Venezuela still depends on U.S. refineries. It has no parallel in its relationship with China.[35] The more important point is that, since Washington has had so little influence on Venezuelan policies at home or abroad even when it was an unrivaled leader in Venezuelan energy markets, it is hard to imagine that somehow the United States lost and China gained significant influence in the process of increased Venezuelan exports to China. If eclipsing the U.S. in oil purchases from Venezuela buys China as much influence in Venezuela as we enjoyed during the Bush administration, we can only wish Beijing the best of luck with that.

China has also run into political problems in Africa. Postcolonial nationalism and democratization in sub-Saharan Africa in particular has at times exposed China to criticism for its investments in resource extraction and special relationships with shady governments. China's investments in Zambia were so controversial that they became a major issue in a presidential campaign there in 2006, with the challenger blasting the incumbent for facilitating Chinese exploitation of Zambia's resources. Six years later, in August 2012, Zambian miners killed a Chinese mine manager during a conflict about wages.[36] In April 2008 South African dockworkers refused to offload Chinese weapons being sent to the odious government of Zimbabwe during civil violence in the lead-up to elections there. Other countries followed the lead of the South African labor union and refused docking rights to the Chinese ship. The ship eventually headed back to China fully laden. U.S. State Department officials, as is the wont of the U.S. government, attempted to take credit for dissuading the Chinese government from delivering the weapons. It is true that we had requested that Beijing recall the ship. I had participated in that process, as had officials in several other like-minded states. But the influence of angry Africans seems a much more important part of the story and a more meaningful message to Beijing than anything officials in Washington or Europe could ever muster. As China worries about the long-term stability of its relations in the developing world, it will have to weigh the trends of democratization and popular demand for justice against the benefits of cozy state-to-state relationships with unpopular tyrants.

China's overall economic relationship with Latin America has also deepened significantly since the 1990s. Again, in my experience the U.S. government tends not to view these relationships as a zero-sum struggle. But even if we adopt the zero-sum optic as an exercise, the U.S. position would still seem very secure. U.S. trade with Latin America outstrips Chinese trade by a very wide margin. In 2012 China's trade with Latin America was 30 percent of U.S. trade with the region (Chinese trade was $258 billion USD; the United States' was $856 billion USD).[37] Chinese investment numbers have been growing—FDI in 2010 totaled $10.5 billion USD. But those numbers are still dwarfed by U.S. investments, which according to the OECD amounted to over $44.5 billion in that year.[38] Moreover, by far the biggest target for Chinese "investment" in Latin America still seems to be the Cayman Islands, with the British Virgin Islands in second place. According to a U.S.– China Economic and Security Review Commission report, in 2009 73 percent of Chinese investment to Latin America went to the Caymans and 22 percent to the British Virgin Islands.[39] For 2010, if we subtract $3.5 billion USD investment to the Caymans and $6.1 billion USD to the British Virgin Islands, Chinese FDI to Latin America is only $0.9 billion for that year, or only 1.3 percent of China's global FDI.[40] This suggests that a big portion of the Chinese money is being reinvested back into China as faux foreign direct investment by Chinese entities that want the tax and other benefits enjoyed by foreign-invested firms. Some of the money flowing through the Caymans might also be a shelter for ill-gotten gains on the mainland. Of course, a large piece of the U.S. investment in the region is also to places like the Caymans and Suriname, most likely for tax haven purposes, but even accounting for this phenomenon, U.S. investment in the region for more productive purposes is still many times higher than the Chinese figures. For example, in 2012 U.S. net investment in two major South American economies, Brazil and Argentina, was over $12 billion USD.[41]

On the trade front, as is the case with the United States in Venezuela, the Chinese imports from the region are largely raw materials and agricultural products, commodities that have globally determined prices. (The productive parts of Chinese investment in the region are also heavily skewed toward extracting such raw materials.) As is demonstrated by the U.S.–Venezuela case, the purchase of such commodities does not give the buyer inordinate political power over the seller, which has many potential outlets for sale of its products in a global marketplace. It is difficult to see how China could use its newfound position in these markets to do serious damage to the American economic interests in the region, let alone to create leverage to harm U.S. national security interests in the Western Hemisphere.

The Military

IN VIRTUALLY EVERY ASPECT of military hardware, the United States military remains superior to the PLA in quality, quantity, or both. When we consider software and arguably its most important subcategory, the experience and training of military personnel, the United States holds an even more commanding lead. For reasons that will become clear in the next chapter, I personally do not put much weight in direct comparison of numerical indicators, free of context, to judge military advantage. But it is still a useful exercise to refute the arguments of American declinists on their own terms.

The defense budget of the two countries is as good a place to start as any other (see graphs and tables in chapter 1). Although China's defense budget has increased impressively since the late 1990s, so has the American one since 2001, more than offsetting in absolute terms any Chinese gains on this one measure. This is true even if we disregard the numbers in the official Chinese budget, which tend to be much smaller than foreign estimates of actual Chinese spending on the military. So, for example, by U.S. government estimates in 1996, the PLA budget was approximately $42 billion USD, while the U.S. defense budget for that year was $307 billion. The difference favored the United States by about $265 billion. In 2009, after many years of double-digit growth of the Chinese defense budget, the U.S. government estimated the Chinese budget to be a much larger $150 billion. But even the lowest estimate for U.S. defense spending in that year, excluding the costs of the wars in Iraq and Afghanistan, was $494 billion. The difference favored the United States by $344 billion USD, even more than in 1996.[42]

Any quantitative measures of national power, the kind many political scientists prefer, would conclude that the United States military lead is enormous and almost historically unprecedented. One of the most popular figures, used often by critics of Pentagon budgets, is that the United States spends considerably more on its military than the rest of the world combined. A member of the declinist school might counter that these budgets are not a source of strength but long-term weakness: imperial overstretch will sap American economic power and will be one of the causes of America's decline and China's eventual rise. Martin Jacques in particular focuses on imperial overstretch by the United States as a cause of both economic decline and military weakening. He writes, "In [the] future the American economy will find it increasingly difficult to support such a military commitment."[43]

But history does not support such a conclusion. It will be jarring to many readers to learn that the United States has maintained its high level of post–Cold War defense spending without a significant tax on its economy. Even when one factors in the wars in Afghanistan and Iraq for a budget of $739.8 billion in 2012, the financial burden of U.S. defense spending (5 percent of GNP) is smaller than it was in 1986, at the height of the Carter-Reagan buildup that contributed to the end of the Cold War (6–7 percent of GNP).[44] By that same measure, the current burden is much smaller than the defense burden on U.S. taxpayers during the 1950s, when as a result of the early Cold War and fighting in Korea, defense expenditures averaged more than 10 percent of GNP. Especially since the U.S. economy was much smaller even in the 1980s, let alone the 1950s, than it is now, the marginal value of the burden on the U.S. taxpayer has not been nearly as great in recent years as it was during the Cold War. What is equally notable is that the U.S. economy grew at a healthy clip in both the 1950s and the 1980s, calling into question the notion that high levels of defense spending necessarily sap national economic power.

The costs of America's recent wars in casualties and dislocated families are, of course, great indeed. And those costs may render the United States very cautious in the future about subsequent interventions. Also, legal and political obstacles in the United States make it easier to cut defense budgets than many other aspects of government spending in periods of ballooning federal budgets and fiscal challenges such as ours. Discretionary spending, which includes the defense budget, will always be cut under any austerity measures because entitlements like Medicare, Social Security, and government pensions are nondiscretionary and tend to be legally protected. This is one reason that the recent budget sequestration hit the Defense Department so hard. But this set of complex problems, while important to the future of U.S. defense spending, has little or nothing to do with the common complaint one hears in punditry and media circles that excessive defensive spending has harmed the U.S. economy. President Eisenhower famously warned about a military-industrial complex and perhaps he had a point, but the U.S. economy grew most quickly in the 1950s and 1960s, when defense budgets as a percentage of GNP were considerably higher than in subsequent decades. Many citizens may not like the policies behind the large defense budgets or how the defense dollars themselves are spent, but one cannot sustain the argument that somehow the defense budget is undercutting the overall economic foundations of U.S. power.

In terms of the quality of weapons, there is no category of military hardware, save perhaps the antiship ballistic missile under development in China, in which China has anything approximating an advantage over the United States. That one exception comes from the simple fact that the United States has not tried to develop conventionally tipped land-based ballistic missiles. Ballistic missiles are not a very efficient method to deliver conventional ordnance. Plus, the United States has many other options. Such a weapon is quite important for China and must be taken seriously, but its importance lies in its potential utility as a coercive tool, not as a game-changing hegemonic weapon that would allow China to dominate the region, let alone the world.

Because of the sheer size of the Chinese military, I am sure there are entire categories of weapons in which China's numbers outstrip our own, but raw numbers do not mean as much in measuring military power as technological sophistication. When one factors in quality, China looks much weaker than the United States. This is evidenced by China's own recent history. China's two-million-person army is much leaner and more efficient than its decrepit six-million-man army of 1978. China's submarine force is considered much more potent today than it was in 1995, but the number of diesel attack submarines is down from seventy-four to sixty-six. How can this be? The answer is simple: a larger percentage of those sixty-six submarines are considered modern weapons systems. They are harder to detect, can stay submerged longer, and carry much more advanced weapons packages than their forebears. The older and more numerous weapons had no such advantage.

This all shows that modernization matters. But while China's modernization from a backward force in 1978 to its current status is a true achievement for Beijing, a Chinese optimist can only say that the glass is now one-third full, while a pessimist can say that it is still two-thirds empty. The U.S. Department of Defense estimated that in 2010, despite more than a decade of surging investment, less than 30 percent of PLA naval surface forces and air forces and 40 percent of air defense forces could be considered "modern."[45] Even China's more modern systems have had real difficulties and tend to trail far behind the parallel systems of the U.S. military in terms of combat effectiveness. It is important for submarines to be able to stay submerged for a long period of time; this favors nuclear submarines over diesel-powered ones. China now has nuclear-powered subs and is building more. It is also developing a more sustainable submarine-based nuclear deterrent with ballistic missiles aboard nuclear-powered submarines (SSBNs). But from public reports, Chinese nuclear-powered submarines are still very loud.[46] And since the whole point of a submarine is to avoid detection, noise greatly reduces their effectiveness and greatly increases their vulnerability. According to the 2009 Office of Naval Intelligence (ONI) report, the Jin-class, China's newest and most advanced SSBN, is noisier than similar submarines built by the Soviet Union three decades ago.[47] Moreover, the United States has advanced experience and technologies for tracking enemy submarines that China lacks. Even China's most modern equipment, including indigenously built fourth-generation fighters, are widely considered to be one or two decades behind their counterparts in the U.S. arsenal.

Some of China's recent high-profile military developments provide good examples of the PRC's persistent overall military inferiority. In January 2007 China destroyed one of its own satellites in low earth orbit in an unannounced exercise of its ground-based antisatellite (ASAT) system. Besides the troubling debris belt left behind, this mission also concerned the United States and other countries because the Chinese military now seemed to pose a new threat to satellites on which civilian economies and militaries around the world rely. But this hardly represented a breakthrough technology. After all, the United States had tested a ground-based antisatellite weapon in the 1980s. And as part of its massive missile defense effort since then, the United States has developed an array of weapons capable of intercepting ballistic missiles both within the earth's atmosphere and in outer space (what is called "exo-atmospheric intercept"). Defense cognoscenti have long realized that any ballistic missile defense weapon with the latter capability, like the ship-borne SM-3 missile deployed on U.S. Navy destroyers in the Asia Pacific, can rather easily be used to hit satellites in low earth orbit if they are operating at altitudes similar to those of the ballistic missiles. In 2008 the U.S. Navy found occasion to destroy a tumbling U.S. satellite that threatened to crash into the earth's surface with a ship-borne missile. In what was dubbed Operation Burnt Frost, the target, which was much more difficult to acquire and hit than the target in the Chinese test, was fully destroyed by a system that is already widely deployed. And it was done in a highly professional and careful manner that prevented the creation of any significant debris field from forming and which, it should be said, created little diplomatic fallout.

Next we can look at the famous (or infamous) test flight of the new J-20 stealth fighter by the Chinese military during the visit of Defense Secretary Robert Gates in January 2011. That test flight was notable in part because stealth technology is difficult to develop and because of its timing, which many Americans believed was designed to send a signal to the visiting entourage. But if we are keeping a score card in comparing American and Chinese military developments, a rudimentary test flight of a stealth plane to simply show that it could fly underscores just how far China's military modernization program trails the United States. Public reports place the first U.S. stealth aircraft flight in 1981, and the U.S. military doctrine assumes the use of an array of stealth fighters and bombers deployed at home and abroad, the most advanced of which may be the F-22 Raptor, an air superiority fighter with ground-attack capability that rotates through USAF bases in Japan, among other locations. Test-flying a plane is the most preliminary step in the long march to making the equipment combat ready and, more important, integrating it into existing forces and doctrine to make it a useful tool for the rest of the military. A Pentagon spokesman said just after the publicized test that it was far too early to tell whether or not China had actually created a "fifth-generation aircraft" (referring to a truly stealthy warplane).[48] Even optimistic (from a Chinese perspective) estimates put such an integration process several years out, and some U.S.-based experts like Tai-ming Cheung doubt that China can achieve those results that quickly. He recently opined that U.S. government estimates that the J-20 might go into service by 2018 were "wildly optimistic."[49] Moreover, according to multiple public sources, China still lacks the capability for serial production of turbofan jet engines for its most advanced fourth-generation aircraft and thus remains dependent on Russia to procure these critical components.[50]

Finally, we have the much-publicized deployment of the Chinese aircraft carrier for sea trials in 2012. On the one hand, this is indeed a new capability for the Chinese military, which has traditionally emphasized defense of the homeland and the sea corridors near the Chinese coastline, where so much of China's wealth lies. While significant, particularly to China's weaker neighbors, a Chinese carrier can hardly be seen as a game changer that closes an overall gap with the United States. After all, the Chinese bought their vintage, Cold War–era carrier from Ukraine, hardly a leading military power. Both the United States and its former enemy and now regional ally Japan have had the ability to operate carriers since the 1920s! The United States currently has eleven nuclear-powered carriers, and the massive and sophisticated battle groups that accompany and protect them are fully trained and in operation.

Merely having a carrier in service does not mean it is inviolable. The United States has decades of experience from World War II through the Cold War in tracking and destroying enemy carriers. In one World War II battle, Midway, the United States sank four Japanese carriers, the *Akagi*, *Hiryu*, *Kaga*, and *Soryu*. Fortunately, during the Cold War, the superpowers avoided the kinds of direct military conflict that would entail attacks on carriers. But both sides trained extensively for such missions, and in many ways carriers today are much easier to track and hit than they were then. Given the massive expense of the carriers themselves and the even greater expense of the carrier battle groups that need to accompany and defend them, combined with the relative ease with which they could be sunk by the United States, a realpolitik, zero-sum analysis might lead one to hope that China would build many more carriers, not fewer. Already many sophisticated U.S. defense analyses worry more about the future vulnerability of U.S. ships to attack by Chinese missiles and torpedoes than they do about any offensive threat posed by Chinese carriers. One U.S. defense expert who generally frets greatly about trends in China's defense modernization once half-joked to me, "When I dream happy dreams, they are full of new carriers: Chinese carriers."

Another area that gets a great deal of press is cyberwar. There is little doubt that China has developed a large cadre of government-sponsored hackers and cyberwarriors, and it is difficult to make the distinction between the two, as the capabilities that allow one to penetrate any network and spy on it often track very closely with the capabilities to disable and destroy that network. James Mulvenon, a political scientist turned cyberanalyst in a U.S. think tank, has done much of the best publicly available work on how cyber attacks on U.S. forces could complicate U.S. military operations in the western Pacific. In 2012 he presented some of his findings at Princeton University, pointing out that while combat orders and other sensitive communication would be done on classified systems that are much harder to penetrate, U.S. military operations still rely on relatively vulnerable unclassified systems for logistics purposes. In chapter 4 we will discuss how such Chinese capabilities might prove very important in a coercive struggle with the United States. But one does not need to conclude that China somehow has a lead in cyber warfare capabilities or that the United States has a particularly large deficit in terms of cyber vulnerability. It is difficult to know from publicly available sources which Pacific country enjoys the advantage in cyber warfare. The U.S. government rarely discusses U.S. offensive capabilities, though public reports suggest that cyber attacks were used extensively in Iraq, for example. There has also been widespread public speculation about U.S. and Israeli cyber attacks on the Iranian nuclear program in programs called Stuxnet and Flame. In 2012 General Keith Alexander, the U.S. general in charge of Cyber Command, broke silence when various reports had suggested that somehow the United States was unilaterally vulnerable to foreign cyber attack. He said, "I can assure you that, in appropriate circumstances and on order from the National Command Authority, we can back up the department's assertion that any actor threatening a crippling cyber attack against the United States would be taking a grave risk."[51] In 2013 he went further, stating that the U.S. government believes U.S. cyberoffensive capabilities are the "best in the world."[52] Since the flight of National Security Agency contractor Edward Snowden, many in the United States and China seem to believe that the NSA has the ability to penetrate large swathes of China's cyberspace. Since penetration is the essential element to cyber attack, this would imply a serious U.S. cyber warfare capability against China. Still, U.S. superiority on this score, even if it exists as General Alexander suggests, does not necessarily provide great safety or comfort, as we will discuss in chapter 4.

In addition to having larger numbers of more advanced weapons systems than China, the United States has a massive advantage in training and war-fighting experience. Take the several hundred Chinese fighter aircraft, for example. They are not only outmatched by thousands of superior U.S. planes, but U.S. pilots receive much more training time on flying their aircraft than their Chinese counterparts. Moreover, since the bulk of the PLA is still not considered modern, the Chinese units that use weaponry deemed modern face a challenge not shared by their U.S. counterparts: they need to try to integrate with units of widely varying capabilities, a task that is not easy to accomplish. Finally, while they may find fixes to these problems, the fact will remain that China has not been in a major international conflict since 1979, when Deng Xiaoping ordered the ill-fated ground invasion of Vietnam. Chinese units performed rather poorly in that fight, but that is not as important as the fact that only the most senior Chinese officers have any war-fighting experience at all. The experience they do have from that fight is largely irrelevant to most contemporary military challenges China might face. This is particularly true at sea and in the air in the western Pacific. By contrast, the United States military has been in harm's way somewhere in the world in almost every year since the launch of Operation Desert Storm in January 1991.

Besides technology and experience, allies represent one of the biggest military advantages that the United States enjoys in comparison to China. Michael O'Hanlon points out that the United States alliance system comprises some sixty allies, which, if one includes the United States itself, constitutes some 80 percent of global military spending.[53] Similarly, in his book *Liberal Leviathan* John Ikenberry has presented data comparing U.S. alliances with China's security relations abroad to show the lopsided lead enjoyed by the United States on this score. The United States has formal defense commitments with sixty-two actors around the world.[54] China only has a formal alliance with North Korea and a very strong security partnership with one other Asian country, Pakistan. It has defense cooperation and an arms trade relationship with Russia, but mutual mistrust between the two makes it very hard to label it an alliance or security partnership in the same way that one could describe the U.S. relationship with South Korea and Australia (alliances) or Singapore and Taiwan (security partnerships). These alliances and security relationships give the United States more than just additive power in a conflict; they provide permanent basing rights in many cases and, in others, the right to use ports and airstrips for exercises and in certain emergencies. In addition, they provide intelligence sharing and local awareness regarding geography, weather, and the like that serve as a major force multiplier for American power. While, for reasons offered in chapter 4, this does not necessarily mean that the United States should cut its defense budget or become complacent about the security challenges posed by a rising China, it seriously undercuts arguments that China is quickly closing the gap with U.S. military power or on course to dominate the international system.

Diplomacy

MANY CRITICS OF U.S. foreign policy have pointed out that China gained at America's expense in the diplomatic sphere during the George W. Bush administration. Not only did the United States not always attend at the highest-level regional gatherings of which it was a full participant, such as the ASEAN Regional Forum, but it was not a participant, or more nefariously put, it was excluded from other regional organizations, such as the Shanghai Cooperation Organisation, ASEAN Plus Three, and the China–ASEAN Free Trade Area. Adopting a zero–sum approach to these issues were influential experts like Randall Schriver and Aaron Friedberg, both of whom served in the Bush administration, and Kurt Campbell, a former Clinton administration official and later President Obama's Assistant Secretary of State for East Asian and Pacific Affairs. A leading think-tank executive officer during the Bush administration, in June 2005 Campbell organized a seminar in which I participated, albeit as the loyal opposition, "With One Hand Tied: Dealing with China During a Period of Preoccupation." Later in the same year, he wrote, "Rarely in history has a rising power made such prominent gains in the international system largely as a consequence of the actions and inattentiveness of the dominant power. Indeed, Washington has been mostly unaware of China's gains within the past few years, many of which have come at the expense of the United States."[55]

Public intellectuals joined these scholars in bemoaning the potentially dangerous nature of Chinese diplomatic and economic inroads in the region and beyond. A common concern was that China might undercut U.S. relations with allies such as Japan, South Korea, the Philippines, Thailand, or even Australia, as the latter became dependent on exports of raw materials to China. In a *New Republic* article, Joshua Kurlantzick worried about China's engagement in bilateral and multilateral diplomacy and economic activities not only in Asia but in more distant regions like Africa and Latin America. His fear that Chinese soft power had become so great led him to conclude that "China may become the first nation since the fall of the Soviet Union that could seriously challenge the United States for control of the international system."[56] In a *Washington Post* column entitled "China's Moment," Charles Krauthammer even worried that the Chinese-led Six Party Talks on Korean denuclearization might prove successful. This, of course, did not come to pass. But from my perspective as a former member of the U.S. delegation, North Korea's scrapping of its nuclear program would have been most welcome in Washington. Nevertheless, Krauthammer worried that Chinese prestige and power would grow greatly at the expense of the United States if the talks were successful.[57]

There are still several shortcomings in such criticisms. At the most basic level, dating back to the early post–Cold War period and the writings of Aaron Friedberg and others at that time, it has been an explicit goal of the United States to encourage China and its neighbors to collaborate more in multilateral settings. The idea was to reduce historical mistrust and security dilemmas attendant to the collapse of the Soviet Union and the rise of China. As often happens in American policy circles, when one problem is replaced with a solution, the solution itself becomes the new problem. When China has poor diplomatic relations with its neighbors, we worry about spirals of tension and rivalry that could destabilize the region. But when China gets its house in order diplomatically, embraces multilateralism, and reassures its neighbors, we worry about lethargy among our allies and the potential that they might jump on the bandwagon with a rising China against U.S. interests. But if we adopt the fearful realpolitik attitude that China's diplomatic engagement and attendant prestige will harm our interests, then we have made fear of diplomatic success a reason for not trying to gain Chinese cooperation in the first place!

It is important, whenever possible, for U.S. officials to attend regional meetings at the same protocol level as the Asian hosts. So when Secretary Condoleezza Rice missed two of four annual meetings of the ASEAN Regional Forum from 2005 to 2008, it was predictable that Southeast Asian nations worried about the implications for U.S. dedication to the region. Similarly, the United States should join regional organizations where appropriate, and I applauded the Obama administration's willingness not only to join the East Asia Summit but to make its meetings meaningful. In November 2011, for example, the president and his advisors kept concerns about the South China Sea maritime disputes on the agenda despite China's resistance. But there is no need to join every organization. It is only natural for Asian states to have some groupings that do not include the United States, and it is not necessarily a signal of an anti-American conspiracy or a great boon for Chinese power when they do.[58] No one in either the United States or China talks about the huge power advantages over China that the United States enjoys because it is a member of the Organization of American States or the North American Free Trade Agreement, both of which include the United States but "exclude" China. Moreover, many of the Asian groupings of this type include U.S. friends and/or allies, so the United States is not in the dark about their activities. ASEAN Plus Three, for example, includes four U.S. treaty allies and a security partner in Singapore.

These organizations generally contain enough internal diversity that it is difficult for them to sustain a cohesive policy over time that runs against U.S. interests, even when some or most of its members might attempt occasionally to use them for that purpose. In the Shanghai Cooperation Organisation, for example, differences emerged between Russia and China and several other members about independence for Abkhazia and South Ossetia, formerly parts of Georgia. China's opposition scuttled Moscow's hopes to gain the organization's support for the 2008 invasion of Georgia, which had been cleverly launched while the world was distracted by the Beijing Olympics. In the 2005 SCO meeting in Astana, Kazakhstan, the SCO did make a vague statement about opposition to long-term basing in Central Asia by outside powers. Such language would seem to target the United States, which had basing rights in Uzbekistan and Kyrgyzstan at the time to prosecute the war in Afghanistan. But Washington swiftly dispatched démarches to member states ensuring that such an episode would not be repeated. In general, to the degree that the SCO fulfills its mission of reducing violent extremism in Central Asia and building cooperation and trust among its members, it hardly challenges U.S. interests. Arguably such organizations actually further U.S. interests. It is unclear what U.S. membership would add. There are real costs to membership in any such organization because they hold true summits. The president of the United States would need to make another lengthy journey abroad every year for that summit, with all the enormous opportunity costs for the national security establishment and domestic policy-making that come with any presidential travel abroad. Or the president would have to delegate a subordinate to represent him or her, which could carry real diplomatic costs. As mentioned above, during the George W. Bush administration the United States lost some diplomatic standing in Southeast Asia when the president sent the deputy secretary of state instead of the secretary to the ASEAN Regional Forum, Asia's premier security dialogue. The same general logic holds true for China's participation in multilateral forums in the Middle East, Africa, and Latin America, as discussed in chapter 1. The United States should simply maintain and enhance its own diplomatic portfolio in these regions without viewing with counterproductive envy every forum that includes China but not the United States.

As part of its otherwise poorly named "rebalancing," "return to Asia," or "pivot" to Asia, the Obama administration found a good balance in handling these problems. It upgraded U.S. representation at existing forums and signed ASEAN's Treaty of Amity and Cooperation, thus paving the way for U.S. participation in the East Asia Summit. Moreover, it helped mobilize the regional actors in such a way that the summit successfully addressed serious regional security issues for the first time in its existence. But the administration wisely neither tried to join nor tried to undercut the authority of the other organizations that do not include the United States.

Recent trends in the East Asia Summit and the ASEAN Regional Forum demonstrate that China's growing activity in regional multilateral organizations does not provide impressive power resources for China in relation to the United States. To the contrary, when Chinese diplomacy became much more acerbic toward its neighbors in 2010 over issues related to North Korean belligerence toward South Korea and sovereignty disputes in the South China Sea and East China Sea, the majority of members of both organizations took positions closer to that of the United States than of China. In 2012, the ASEAN summit did fail to reach a consensus criticizing China for bullying Vietnam and the Philippines over maritime disputes in the South China Sea, but it appears that China had to pressure the chair, Cambodia, to prevent such an outcome. Such experiences make PRC leaders see the organizations as at best neutral and at worst a partial check on Chinese ambitions, rather than as an easily manipulated tool of those ambitions. China's relationship with ASEAN and other East Asian multilateral organizations can hardly be seen as an unalloyed asset that China can use against the United States in a zero-sum struggle for power.

China's diplomatic influence in the region has, however, grown, as has its military and economic wherewithal. These factors, combined with geography, alliance politics, and sovereignty disputes, create true challenges for U.S. national security policy. China will not replace the United States anytime soon as the world's greatest economic, military, and political power, but international politics is more complicated than self-proclaimed "realist" balance-of-power theories allow. Materially stronger powers do not always prevail over weaker ones in international disputes and in limited wars, and they are even less often able to deter those weaker powers from challenging the stronger powers and their allies in the first place.

CHAPTER 4

Why China Still Poses Strategic Challenges

ENJOYING SUPERIOR POWER is preferable to the alternatives, but it is no guarantor of peace. Nor does superior economic and political power guarantee that a nation's political goals will be achieved. A China that lags behind the United States in terms of economics, soft power, military capabilities, and alliances can still pose major challenges to U.S. security interests, particularly in East Asia. Weaker powers have often challenged stronger ones. As John Arquilla has argued, the initiator of great power wars has more often than not proven to be the loser.[1] Arquilla's work challenges the realist notion that superior powers should deter aggression from weaker states. Leaders in weaker states often miscalculate the balance of power and overestimate their prospects for success—or they understand the distribution of overall capabilities but challenge stronger ones anyway. They might do so because they believe that they can achieve limited political aims: to coerce stronger powers into concessions on some specific set of issues. Often the calculus takes into account the political willpower of the two sides to pay costs over a contested issue and the perceived importance of the issue. Leaders' perceptions of those realities are more important than the physical and political realities in determining whether a nation will initiate a limited conflict.

Most of international security politics involves political battles over limited political and territorial aims. Brute force struggles such as the two world wars are important, but they are the exception, not the rule. The struggles for national survival in the late nineteenth and early twentieth centuries informed realist balance-of-power theories developed in the mid-twentieth century. But even in that dark period, there were many crises and limited wars involving coercive diplomacy. And during the Cold War, the United States often found itself in combat with weaker actors with high degrees of resolve, such as in Korea and Vietnam. More recently, we have witnessed a vastly superior U.S. military confront difficulties in the face of insurgencies in post-invasion Iraq and Afghanistan. With that historic backdrop, consider the strategic challenges posed by a modernizing Chinese military today. Although China is hardly a military peer competitor of the United States, the United States has fought no military since World War II that is anywhere near as impressive as Chinese forces are today. And even in World War II, the formidable axis powers—Germany, Japan, and Italy—did not have nuclear weapons that could strike the United States. Contemporary China does, and that fact could, in specific circumstances, limit the willingness of a U.S. president to exercise all aspects of U.S. conventional military superiority.

China's military modernization concerns American strategists because Beijing has intelligently focused its development on new capabilities that expose U.S. forces deployed far from the United States and close to China to various risks. By doing so, Chinese elites might gain confidence that they have increased coercive leverage against Washington or against its allies and security partners. The United States relies on bases in those places and cooperation provided by regional actors for power projection not just in Asia but around the world. In this sense, while the U.S. alliance system is a great source of U.S. power and has no equivalent in the Chinese security portfolio, it is also a source of vulnerability to Chinese punishment: China can try to dissuade those allies from cooperating with the United States or can strike directly at U.S. forces at bases relatively close to China to cause pain to the more distant United States. Chinese coercive strategies can thus raise the costs of U.S. intervention in the region even if China cannot prevail in a full-scale conflict. So, while responsible Chinese elites might view the Chinese military as weaker than the United States, and their strategic writings suggest that they almost universally do, they might still be emboldened by certain new coercive capabilities under development. This is particularly true if they believe that the issues at stake matter more to China than to the United States. Chinese leaders might believe they have greater resolve regarding sovereignty disputes, for example, even if their military is not as powerful as that of the United States. Observers around the world have noted U.S. withdrawal from Vietnam, Somalia, and Afghanistan when costs to the United States were raised by significantly weaker actors. By endangering American and allied military assets in the region, Beijing can raise the prospective costs of U.S. intervention. The strategic goals would be to deter U.S. intervention, delay effective deployment of U.S. forces until local actors have been subdued, or compel U.S. withdrawal if the United States decides to intervene in an extended conflict with China.

In such a campaign, military pressure might be brought to bear against not only the United States but also key U.S. allies and security partners such as Japan, South Korea, Taiwan, the Philippines, Thailand, Singapore, and Australia. Beijing has invested an impressive amount of resources, especially since the late 1990s, in military capabilities designed to project power offshore and strike the assets of the United States and its allies. Many hundreds of accurate, conventionally tipped ballistic missiles threaten Taiwan's fixed assets. A smaller number of these missiles can reach U.S. bases in Japan and the western Pacific as well. According to the Pentagon, one version of an intermediate-range ballistic missile, the DF-21, can hunt and kill large capital ships at sea by using terminal guidance, the ability to steer a warhead toward its target after it reenters the earth's atmosphere from space. If deployed and integrated into China's existing doctrine, the DF-21D or antiship ballistic missile (ASBM) could threaten American aircraft carriers, home to several thousand American service personnel and a tremendous amount of firepower and ammunition, making it both an attractive coercive target and an important military target.[2]

To challenge American sea power, the Chinese navy has developed a large number of submarines armed with advanced torpedoes, cruise missiles, and sea mines. These would be supplemented with a large fleet of smaller naval and civilian surface vessels, including the Houbei-class fast missile boat, that could be used to fire cruise missiles, lay mines, and help locate U.S. forces for targeting by other Chinese assets. China has also invested in a large fleet of fourth-generation fighter planes and advanced air defenses to try to offset the qualitative and quantitative advantages enjoyed by the United States. Chinese surface ships and aircraft can also launch cruise missiles at ships at sea and against fixed targets on land. In 2007 and 2009 China demonstrated the ability to strike satellites in low earth orbit. Along with electronic warfare and cyber attack capabilities, these assets could also serve to reduce America's clear advantage in the realm of what the Department of Defense calls Command, Control, Communications, Computers, Intelligence, Surveillance, and Reconnaissance (C4ISR). In combination with the other weapons systems listed above, these assets can be force multipliers that allow the Chinese military to threaten a greater number of American and allied soldiers, sailors, and airmen. Such perceived coercive capability might embolden the Chinese leadership in potential standoffs.[3]

It is important to remember that these capabilities do not give Chinese leaders confidence that they can prevail in an all-out struggle with technologically more sophisticated militaries like the United States. On the contrary, Chinese strategic writings assume that Chinese forces are likely to be weaker and less technologically sophisticated than those of unnamed, advanced great power enemies. Chinese strategists hold little hope of closing the gap of overall military power with the United States anytime soon, but this is hardly a cause for passivity among Chinese strategists. Instead they write about the "inferior defeating the superior under high-tech conditions" through a combination of skill, timely strikes on key targets, and superior political resolve.[4] The goals of the proposed attacks on a physically superior enemy are as much to affect the psychology of the enemy and the cohesion of its regional alliances as they are to denude the enemy's physical capacity to fight over the long run.

In Washington security circles, I often encounter melodramatic language about the threat to U.S. access to the western Pacific. Such talk might be good for securing budgets for the Pentagon and, in particular, for the U.S. Navy and Air Force. But the hyperbole is intellectually inaccurate and politically counterproductive in several ways. In recent years, the Department of Defense has coined a new term, anti-access/area denial, or A2AD, to describe Beijing's newfound capabilities and the doctrines that accompany them. The idea is that China is trying to deny the United States military access to the waters and airspace near China's coastline. But while DoD descriptors have changed, my research and conversations in China over several years suggest that the current Chinese strategy has been in place since the 1990s at the latest. I outlined that strategy in a 2001 article in the journal *International Security* entitled "Posing Problems without Catching Up."[5] China has long sought to affect the psychology of a militarily superior United States and its regional allies by posing potentially costly military challenges to forward-deployed U.S. forces. What has changed in the interim is not so much China's strategy but its capability to execute that strategy. Starting from a humble base, China has for the first time developed the ability to project naval and airpower offshore in a serious way. Defense budgets have grown even faster than China's rapidly expanding economy. But China could not physically deny military access to the western Pacific should the United States resolve to go there. The only area in which China might have a technological edge is with the antiship ballistic missile. The United States has eschewed production of such a weapons system not because it cannot build them but because to do so could violate certain Cold War–era arms control agreements and because Washington has other more effective methods than ballistic missiles to strike at distant moving targets.

Ironically, perhaps, the phrase A2AD and other buzzwords ascribe to China more coercive leverage than Beijing has earned during its impressive military modernization. If the Chinese military modernization campaign is aimed as much at affecting American psychology as it is at crippling American forces—and everything we know from Chinese doctrinal writings suggests that it is—then Beijing has already scored a direct hit. When the United States discusses publicly the notion that there are areas of the world its military cannot penetrate, it has the potential to undercut not only U.S. resolve but also allied resolve, since third parties would naturally wonder if China can actually physically prevent the United States from intervening on their behalf in a regional crisis. This perfectly serves China's doctrinal purposes.

A second problem is that, by using terms like A2AD, the likes of which I have never seen in the Chinese military literature, the United

States is suggesting that U.S. forces would have to fight hard and early simply to gain access to what would otherwise be a closed theater of operations. Since access is a prerequisite for any coercive diplomatic role, such an exaggerated view of China's capabilities could have devastating escalatory implications in a real crisis. In other words, rather than adopting a more measured approach, U.S. commanders may decide to launch large-scale electronic warfare and precision strike operations merely to get U.S. forces into the theater. Some U.S. strategists have even publicly discussed a nascent U.S. doctrinal concept, "air–sea battle," some versions of which call for large-scale kinetic and blinding operations against China's "kill chain"—missile sites, command and control nodes, submarines, submarine bases, et cetera—to be launched early in a conflict to protect forward-deployed U.S. forces.[6]

Even against a conventionally armed weaker power, such an early escalation of conflict would be frightening, particularly to U.S. allies within range of Chinese missiles and conventional forces. Moreover, the United States might appear the aggressor and China the victim, reducing U.S. political advantages with both allies and neutral states alike. But there is a more basic issue: the United States has never in its history launched such a robust conventional attack against the homeland of a nuclear-armed state. Since the 1980s China has had a small and backward force of liquid-fueled missiles capable of reaching the continental United States (according to public reports, China has about twenty such missiles). Since they are relatively small in number and the missiles would require a good deal of time to be fueled and mated to warheads during a crisis, many inside and outside of China have doubted whether or not Beijing possessed what in nuclear parlance is a "secure second strike": the ability to level unacceptable damage against an adversary even after absorbing the most concerted preemptive attack (or first strike). We are not sure how Chinese leaders themselves viewed the survivability of the traditional Chinese nuclear deterrent, particularly in a world in which the United States has developed much better conventional strike weapons, greater reconnaissance capability, and missile defenses as a partial insurance policy against missiles that might survive a U.S. preemptive strike. But China is developing a significantly larger set of solid-fueled mobile missiles, and each potentially could have multiple warheads. This would provide a much bigger challenge for U.S. targeting units and even bigger risks for a U.S. president if he or she wanted to contemplate a first strike on China's nuclear weapons.[7]

On the opposite side of this strategic equation, a more robust second-strike nuclear capability for China should foster greater confidence among China's leaders during a crisis than they have enjoyed in crises in the past. In coercive diplomacy—or military engagements short of full-scale wars of survival—psychology and perceptions are even more important than military reality. So even if U.S. leaders were already sufficiently wary about China's traditional nuclear deterrent to eschew first-strike options, and even if they view the modernization program in China as merely an upgrade of China's preexisting deterrent, we cannot be sure whether Chinese leaders sincerely believed that the older arsenal could have survived a first strike. Any added confidence Chinese leaders gain by the nuclear modernization might give them added resolve in a crisis.

One could posit that talk of nuclear escalation is simply Cold War science fiction. After all, both sides have nuclear arsenals. So even if China has for the first time established a secure nuclear retaliatory capability against the United States, it would never have any rational incentive to use it unless the United States were to attempt a massive nuclear first strike against China out of the blue, an extremely unlikely scenario. Such a scenario is rendered even less likely, so the logic goes, by U.S. conventional superiority and the options that such advantage provides U.S. leaders short of the nuclear threshold.

Assessing Chinese nuclear modernization recalls Cold War–era debates about the role of nuclear weapons in deterring superpower aggression. During the Cold War, hawkish theorists in the United States claimed that there was something called the "stability-instability paradox," meaning that since both the United States and the Soviet Union enjoyed secure nuclear arsenals that could obliterate each other, nuclear weapons, in effect, simply canceled one another out. By this logic, stability at the nuclear level—known as mutually assured destruction (MAD)—allegedly fostered a robust rivalry at the conventional level. The argument ran that a conventionally superior power would know that its conventionally inferior rival would never have a rational reason to escalate to the nuclear level because such escalation would lead to an unacceptably devastating nuclear retaliation. This was a hawkish analysis in Cold War America because it was widely believed that the Soviets and their allies enjoyed conventional superiority over NATO forces in central Europe. U.S. hawks believed that Soviet conventional superiority posed a danger that strategic nuclear weapons could not neutralize because of the stability-instability paradox. So the Soviets might be emboldened by allied weakness unless conventional NATO forces were beefed up and/or bolstered by tactical and theater nuclear weapons that could be used short of a full-scale nuclear war to offset those Soviet conventional advantages.[8]

Less hawkish Cold War critics of this viewpoint, such as Robert Jervis and Thomas Schelling, believed that nuclear deterrence cast a much larger shadow over the behavior of nuclear-armed states than the hawks allowed. They believed that attackers seeking to change the status quo would have to consider the threat of escalation from conventional war to nuclear war. Defenders of the status quo could manipulate what Schelling famously called the "threat that leaves something to chance": the dangerous prospect that limited, conventional warfare could escalate at "time t +1" in ways such that no one could accurately predict at "time t," and that escalation to the nuclear level could occur as the tensions spiraled. In other words, an actor could not easily exploit its conventional superiority for fear of unleashing an unintended escalatory process that would end in nuclear conflict. That both superpowers deployed tactical and theater nuclear weapons to the European theater bolstered this analysis. Those deployments provided a slippery slope between conventional and nuclear combat that the Soviets could hardly ignore when plotting a conventional attack.[9]

It is important to remember that the U.S. and NATO, while possessing inferior conventional forces, were defending the recognized status quo in western Europe. And one of the underappreciated stabilizing factors in the Cold War was that—with the notable exceptions of volatile areas like West Berlin—the geographic lines between the two ideological camps in Europe were fairly clear and mutually accepted. Schelling and Jervis theorized that this made for relatively stable superpower relations in the Cold War, an analysis consistent with psychological theories developed by Amos Tversky and Nobel laureate Daniel Kahneman. Tversky and Kahneman's work on prospect theory demonstrates that, in general, humans accept higher risks and pay greater costs to defend what they believe to be rightfully theirs than they will to acquire new possessions.[10] Applying these findings to Cold War Europe, Jervis asserted that, even if the United States and NATO could not prevail in a conventional physical struggle with the Soviets and the Warsaw Pact, they could successfully deter the Soviets from invading western Europe by raising the prospect that they would exact unacceptable costs on the Soviets to defend the status quo in this geostrategic game of chicken.[11]

Perhaps ironically, in the post–Cold War world, it is the more optimistic and more dovish Americans who subscribe to the stability-instability paradox. Since the United States has the upper hand conventionally and the potential adversary, China, is the weaker state with a nuclear deterrent, then the two states' nuclear deterrents cancel each other out and the United States should be able to contain Chinese aggression through conventional deterrence. Bolstering this argument is China's declared "No First Use" policy, or NFU, a doctrine that, if strictly defined and fully sincere, would mean that China would only use nuclear weapons in response to a nuclear attack on China. Rigid adherence to such a principle on China's part would preclude a slippery slope between conventional and nuclear war and would add to other clear disincentives for China to escalate to the nuclear level in a shooting war. By corollary, in peacetime and in crises short of war, a rigid adherence to NFU would also reduce the political leverage provided by China's modernized nuclear force. Strictly speaking, if China rigidly adheres to NFU, then only a proposed U.S. nuclear strike on China—an unlikely event—would make China's nuclear weapons relevant to U.S.–China coercive diplomacy.

Although I would hardly consider China trigger-happy with nuclear weapons, there are a series of factors that blur the line between conventional and nuclear conflict between the United States and China. Chinese doctrinal writings generally take China's No First Use pledge seriously. Unfortunately, the good news stops there. One problem is the vague definition of "No First Use." One authoritative military book declares Chinese "nuclear retaliation" to be "actions implemented under nuclear conditions (or conditions of nuclear threat)."[12] Unfortunately, any engagement with the United States military might be deemed as posing a "nuclear threat" to China, so the parenthetical is not entirely reassuring. Moreover, China has to worry not only that the United States might be able to take out its nuclear deterrent in a crippling nuclear first strike, but also that a combination of increasingly powerful, fast, and accurate conventional strike weapons, cyberwar and electronic warfare weapons, and missile defenses could make the United States capable of countering the Chinese nuclear force without using nuclear weapons. According to Chinese strategic writings, these new U.S. capabilities have provided an added incentive for China's nuclear modernization. There is little expectation among American experts that China would allow conventional strikes to destroy its nuclear arsenal simply because those enemy missions were carried out with conventional weapons. This makes China's No First Use doctrine seem even more elastic.[13]

Authoritative Chinese writings about nuclear weapons and doctrine reveal yet another problem. One key book written for officers in the PLA's Second Artillery discusses conditions under which China might "lower the threshold" of nuclear deterrence: It states:

> Lowering the nuclear deterrence threshold refers to a time in which a stronger military power with nuclear missiles relies on its absolute superiority in high-tech conventional weapons to conduct a series of medium-level or high-level air strikes and our side has no good methods to ward this off; the nuclear missile corps should, according to the orders of the supreme command, adjust our nuclear deterrence policy without delay, taking the initiative (*zhudong*) to implement a powerful nuclear threat, thereby blocking through coercion (*shezu*) the stronger enemy's sustained conventional air strikes against our side's important strategic targets (*yi fang zhongda zhanlüe mubiao*).[14]

Since the military is under the control of the civilian leaders of the Party, there is no speculation in the writings about when, if ever, China would feel compelled to carry through on such threats, but the entire discussion of "lowering the threshold" for deterrence relegates the concept of No First Use to the status of a guideline, not a rule.

That China's newly developed conventional weapons overlap significantly with its modernizing nuclear arsenal further complicates the issue of escalation. It is largely, though not exclusively, solid-fueled missiles and submarines that give China, for the first time, the ability to threaten U.S. forces and regional bases with conventional strikes. But solid-fueled missiles are also the backbone of China's modernizing nuclear force and the same service, the Second Artillery of the People's Liberation Army, controls the weapons and the command and control system for both conventional and nuclear systems. The second leg of China's nuclear dyad will be submarine-launched nuclear missiles capable of reaching the United States. Public reports suggest that these systems are in the advanced stage of development.

With this knowledge in mind, it is worrisome to consider conventional conflict scenarios involving Chinese threats to U.S. forces deployed in the western Pacific. To reduce casualties and to prevail, U.S. military commanders would have a strong incentive to try to attack, blind, and disable Chinese submarines, missiles, and their relevant command and control nodes on the mainland. But given the overlap of the conventional and nuclear systems, if the United States were to launch such attacks, it might prove difficult for Chinese leaders to know that these same strikes were not designed also to disable China's nuclear dyad as well. In U.S. strategic history, never has a president ordered a sustained conventional attack against the homeland of a nuclear power, and never before has there been so much overlap between the conventional and nuclear arsenals of a major nuclear power as we see in China. Of course, if the president were to choose not to exploit U.S. conventional advantages out of concern for potential escalation to the nuclear level, then China's nuclear modernization would have successfully reduced the practical utility of the U.S. conventional military advantage. This would be an intended effect. The aforementioned doctrinal book states that China's strategic rocket force is an "effective nuclear means by which to level the playing field with stronger enemies."[15]

Given the arguments laid out by Jervis and Schelling, one could take comfort in the notion that only a very aggressive China would want to unleash dangerous forces by challenging the status quo in the East Asian region. For reasons laid out in chapter 2, some new aspects of modern international politics and economics should dissuade Beijing from such brazen adventurism. But one must curb unalloyed optimism because in contemporary East Asia there are many sovereignty disputes, particularly in the maritime domain. Indeed, there is nothing close to a mutually accepted territorial status quo among potential belligerents. China itself has active disputes with many of its neighbors, including U.S. allies and security partners such as Japan, the Philippines, and Taiwan and important nonallied states such as Vietnam, Malaysia, and Brunei.[16] In addition, China has overlapping exclusive economic zones (EEZ) at sea under the UN Convention of the Law of the Sea (UNCLOS) with even more states, including South Korea, another U.S. ally, and Indonesia.

Such disputes are dangerous because all potential belligerents can believe that they are defending sovereign territory and the status quo. There does not need to be a clear aggressor for there to be trouble. Per Tversky and Kahneman's prospect theory, if both sides believe they own the disputed territories, then the game of chicken is much more likely to lead to a head-on collision than if one side is trying to change the status quo.

Such tendencies among individual humans can become even more pronounced for governments, which have to worry about the strategic and domestic political consequences of appearing not to defend the status quo. On strategic grounds, if a nation is willing to back down on an issue related to one's proclaimed sovereign territory, that nation will lose face, thus undermining its positions on other matters. So, in any given dispute, a country like China or Japan, with multiple island disputes, has to worry about the implications for future negotiations not only with the rival disputant but with third-party onlookers (Japan also has island disputes with South Korea and Russia; the PRC has disputes with Taiwan and four other countries in the South China Sea).

The situation only looks worse when one factors in the domestic political interests of governments, who are loath to look weak on issues that touch on nationalistic pride. If a state fails to defend its sovereign claims, then its own people can hold it to task. This is true everywhere but is particularly salient in East Asia, where the national ideology of states like Vietnam, the Philippines, Malaysia, and China itself are steeped in postcolonial resentment and the narrative of liberation from foreign bullying. When all the actors involved have such emotional and

SOUTH CHINA SEA TERRITORIAL CLAIMS

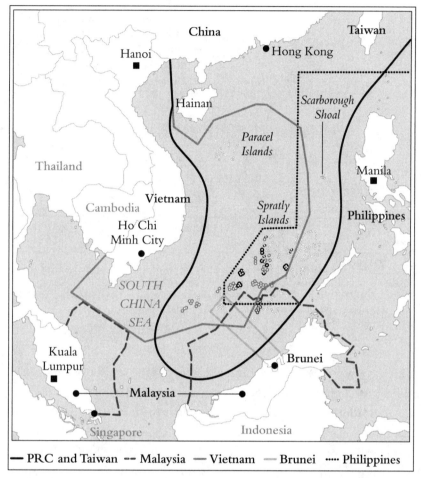

Figure 9. The map outlines the identical claim of the People's Republic of China and the Republic of China (Taiwan) and the claims of the four other nations in the dispute.
Source: http://www.southchinasea.org/files/2014/09/China-claims-a-big-backyard.png.
Editor: David Rosenberg

strategic incentives to stand firm, the mix becomes very volatile—perhaps volatile enough that fishing and energy disputes over uninhabited rocks in the East and South China Seas can escalate to shooting wars.

In China, continued Party rule is the top security goal. If there is any doubt about this, please note that the People's Liberation Army is dedicated not to China as a nation but to the Chinese Communist Party.

EAST CHINA SEA TERRITORIAL CLAIMS

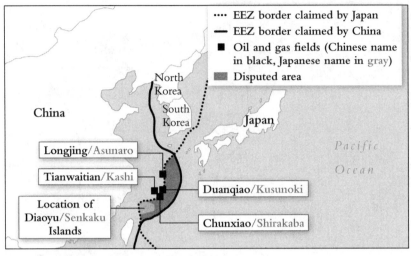

Figure 10. The map outlines the overlapping claims of China and Japan in the East China Sea, and the known oil and gas fields in and around those overlapping claims.
Source: "East China Sea," U.S. Energy Information Administration (EIA), September 25, 2012, http://www.eia.gov/countries/regions-topics.cfm?fips=ECS.

This has always been the case since the days of the revolution, and if the rhetoric of Xi Jinping and the recently selected leadership of the Party is any indication, it is not going to change anytime soon. One major problem for the Party in recent years has been the increase in "mass social incidents" (protests and riots) and the suggestion that Chinese society is increasingly unstable. Before the government stopped publicly discussing the number of such incidents in the middle of the past decade, it was already reporting as many as 87,000 per year.[17] Extrapolating from those trends, some analysts estimate that there are more than 100,000 of these every year in China today; one Chinese academic study in 2010 put the number as high as 180,000.[18] There is little doubt from my many recent trips to China that the public and the government alike are concerned about the long-term stability of China in a way that they have not been since the years immediately following the Tiananmen protests and massacre of 1989. Citizens seem frustrated by official corruption, eminent domain problems related to the fast-paced growth of cities and infrastructure, environmental degradation, and the unbalanced distribution of wealth. Adding to the unease of Chinese elites are uncertainties about the sources of future Chinese economic growth, particularly since the financial crisis called into question the reliability of markets abroad. There is, therefore, a growing consensus that China needs to restructure its economy to become less dependent on trade and investment and to increase the role of domestic consumption, but there is no consensus on how to achieve this transformation or at what pace.[19] All of these changes can create new controversies and dashed expectations, thus sparking new challenges to social and political stability.

Since jettisoning Maoist Communist ideology in the reform period, the nominally Communist CCP has legitimized itself through fast-paced economic growth and by nationalism. It portrays itself as an increasingly capable protector of Chinese interests and national honor. The ways that the CCP has managed domestic dissent in China renders nationalist issues such as Taiwan or other sovereignty disputes particularly delicate. The central government in China has successfully ridden the waves of popular discontent by keeping protests local and small and keeping the protestors out of the Party. The higher authorities have often been able to paint themselves as the solution to local problems by coming in to quell protests, making arrests when necessary, firing and replacing local officials, and paying off some of the aggrieved citizens. Still, the increasing frequency of the protests is alarming to Chinese officials.

One reason potential nationalist humiliation is so worrisome to the central government is that people angry at the state for other reasons can take the opportunity of such a humiliation to criticize government policies using politically correct slogans fostered for decades by the government's own "patriotic education" campaigns. Take, for example, the urban protests that arose across China over a nationalist issue: Japan's central government had purchased the disputed Senkaku Islands from a private Japanese family in 2012. One angry Chinese man held a placard that read: "Oppose Japan, Oppose America, Oppose Price Inflation!" (*Fan Ri, Fan Mei, Fan Zhangjia!*)[20] In so doing, he was linking a serious domestic concern with protests over international humiliation. Even when the topics of protests appear to remain international in nature, they can have dangerous domestic repercussions for the Chinese economy and political stability. So protestors targeting "Little Japan" (*Xiao*

Riben) often call on their Chinese compatriots to boycott Japanese products (*Dizhi Rihuo!*). But a boycott, if enacted, would severely harm China's own economy. Many products in China bearing Japanese brands
are made in-country by Chinese workers in Japanese-invested factories. Many other domestic and international firms operating in China
depend on Japanese parts in their transnational production chains. Chinese officials are well aware of the irony. Anti-Japanese protestors in
China often carry portraits of Chairman Mao, indirectly criticizing
contemporary leaders for their lack of fortitude on the international
stage in comparison to Mao.

Popular calls for national action have grown all the more dangerous for the central government as individuals and disgruntled groups
around the nation can increasingly communicate through social media.
Furthermore, as with most governments and militaries, there is plenty
of sincere nationalism within the CCP regime. Protestors in the future
then might find sympathetic ears inside the state security mechanism.
Moreover, military or civilian elites who are unhappy with their colleagues' lack of fortitude on international issues could stir up popular
protest through expanding media channels to pressure more moderate leaders to change policy or, at the extreme, to help drive them
from office. In fact, frustration with insufficiently robust resistance to
the United States, Japan, and Vietnam, for example, has already been
expressed in the mainstream press in China, sometimes by active duty
or recently retired military officers. (More broadly, that press, although
more open than in earlier decades, is still ultimately controlled by the
state.) For these reasons, nationalist humiliation, particularly as it per-
tains to issues such as Japan or Taiwan independence, is the third rail of
Chinese Communist politics.

Of course, China has no regional monopoly on nationalism or
domestic political concerns related to foreign policy. Strong strands of
postcolonial nationalism run through Filipino, Vietnamese, and Malay-
sian politics. And citizens in these countries are no less certain than
those Chinese protestors that their countries are the rightful owners
of disputed islands. Japanese prime ministers have sat atop extremely
shaky coalition governments for the past ten years while the Japanese
public believes that the Senkaku Islands are rightfully Japanese and that

China only became interested in the islands after natural resources were discovered in the seabed around them in the late 1960s. While only a few Japanese rightists seem eager for a fight over the islands, no Japanese leader wants to appear ineffective or weak in the face of Chinese pressure. If all sides are willing to run high risks to avoid humiliation and defend national honor, then coercive diplomatic crises become very dangerous games indeed.

The United States finds itself in the unenviable position of having alliances or security relationships with three of the actors with which China has territorial disputes (Japan, the Philippines, and Taiwan) but no position on any of the sovereignty disputes themselves. In the case of Taiwan, the U.S. legal position on its sovereignty has been "undetermined" since the U.S. decision to enter the Korean War on June 27, 1950. The consistent U.S. government demand since the 1970s has been that the two sides of the Strait should work out their differences peacefully and that each side of the Strait should avoid actions that unilaterally change the status quo in cross-Strait relations without the acquiescence of the other. In general this means that the United States opposes mainland China's use of force or the threat of force to compel Taiwan into unification against the will of the Taiwan people, and it opposes actions by Taiwan that move the island in the direction of permanent legal independence from the broader Chinese nation without the consent of Beijing. In the case of the largely uninhabited islands, rocks, and reefs in the South China Sea (Paracels and Spratlys) disputed by China, Taiwan, the Philippines, Vietnam, Malaysia, and Brunei as well as the case of the uninhabited rocks in the East China Sea disputed by Japan and China (Diaoyu in Chinese and Senkaku in Japanese), the United States takes no position on the sovereignty of the islands, even those claimed by U.S. allies. This is part of a global maritime legal policy in which the United States takes no position on disputed islands but simply insists that disputes be settled peacefully and in accordance with prevailing international law so as not to disturb freedom of navigation. The only partial exception is the Senkakus. In 1971, the United States transferred control of the islands to postwar Japan as part of the reversion of Okinawa. The Americans did this despite the protests of mainland China and Taiwan. The United States never recognized Japan's sovereignty over the Senkaku islands, however, just its administrative control. But it is notable that the United States claims that the islands fall under the purview of Article V of the U.S.–Japan Security Treaty in a way that the United States has never asserted for any of the Filipino claims in the South China Sea.

WHILE WASHINGTON ENJOYS military superiority over China, it is increasingly the case that China enjoys military superiority over most, if not all, of the United States' regional friends and allies. It may be this factor, above all others, that proves China's rise is real. So when, exactly, would the United States choose to intervene in support of its friends and allies? The question is complicated by Washington's status as a nonclaimant on the sovereignty issues. For its part, China has somewhat cleverly, if at times clumsily, deployed maritime security forces and civilian ships instead of PLA Navy assets to assert and protect China's claims. This puts the onus of escalation on the other disputant and places Washington in the extremely uncomfortable position of urging restraint on its ally while trying to dissuade China from continued provocations and manipulation of risk. The United States has its own reputational reasons not to appear indifferent or weak in the region, but it also has reputational and other strategic reasons not to allow its weaker allies to drag it into a conflict, especially a conflict over uninhabited rocks!

One can see how the real world of international security politics can diverge sharply from the predictions and concerns of the allegedly "realist" balance-of-power theories. One can also see why a China with inferior conventional and nuclear capabilities in comparison to the United States can still pose serious problems for the United States and its regional friends and allies. Unlike a brute-force struggle for regional or global supremacy, coercive diplomacy is a bargaining process. As Thomas Schelling argued during the Cold War, for coercive diplomacy to work, the target of one's efforts must not only understand the credibility of one's own threat of intervention and punishment but must also be credibly reassured that if it forgoes aggression or some other transgression it will not be punished anyway. Otherwise, it has no incentive to comply with the demands being leveled. So in the context of U.S.–China relations, the United States needs to credibly threaten to defend its own interests and the interests of its allies without at the same time suggesting to Beijing that Washington is preparing the means with which to harm China's security interests regardless of Beijing's behavior. This is no easy task, particularly given the ambiguous nature of the maritime sovereignty disputes. Any U.S. military units capable of intervening in the region could, from a Chinese perspective, also be used to promote revisionist goals at the expense of China. Along the same lines, it is a challenge for China to develop coercive capabilities designed to protect what it sees as legitimate interests without, in the process, appearing to those actors to be threatening, aggressive, and destabilizing.

The combination of ambiguous and contested political claims, geography, and military technology make managing East Asia while China rises a complex task, particularly since there are more than two actors involved. In the Taiwan context, for example, any combination of U.S., Taiwanese, or Japanese military power that could be used to deter China from forcing Taiwan into unification with the mainland against its will might also be used for the purpose of protecting Taiwan's moves toward permanent legal independence from mainland China. Similarly, any combination of PRC coercive capabilities designed to deter Taiwan's unilateral declaration of formal independence from the mainland could also be used to compel unification with the mainland against Taiwan's will. The fact that both Taiwan and the mainland can adopt political initiatives deemed provocative by the other side only makes the headaches in Washington all the greater. The same applies to Japan and the Philippines, formal U.S. allies with whom China has maritime disputes.

The United States needs to balance its deterrence of mainland aggression against the need to reassure China that Washington does not seek to promote provocative policies by its allies nor change its own neutrality policy. The challenges in this may become even more difficult as China's own rise exacerbates tensions with the United States and its neighbors and, along with the discovery of energy resources in the seabeds around the islands, accelerates other claimants' timetables for pursuing and consolidating their claims.

But the problems are not insurmountable. As we will see in chapters 6 through 8, the United States and China have ridden these often choppy waters successfully since the end of the Cold War. There is no reason to think that they cannot do so in the future, particularly if we all fully understand that recent history and draw the appropriate lessons from it.

CHAPTER 5

Global Governance:
The Biggest Challenge of All

Deterring Chinese aggression toward its neighbors and the United States will be increasingly challenging, but there are many reasons to be hopeful. China has major incentives to avoid unnecessary conflict, and after decades of a global Cold War, the United States government is highly experienced in the practice of coercive diplomacy. But no government has experience tackling the least appreciated challenge: persuading a uniquely large developing country with enormous domestic challenges and a historical chip on its national shoulder to cooperate actively with the international community. For the many reasons already offered, China has an interest in the stability of the current international system, but that does not easily translate into China helping to pay the costs to maintain that system.

Two stark facts underpin this challenge. First, China is by far the most influential developing country in world history. Second, globalization has made the world so interconnected that the behavior of every great power has become very consequential. As a result, China is being asked to do more at present than any developing country has in the past. Moreover, the intensity and diversity of those requests are only going to increase with the continuing rise of China and the deepening of globalization. If China actively tries to block efforts at improved global governance, many international problems will be extremely difficult to solve.

But even if China simply tries to lie low and ride free on the efforts of others, we will have great difficulty managing some of the globe's biggest security, economic, environmental and humanitarian problems.

There are a number of reasons why it will be so difficult to convince China to assert itself in the role of responsible stakeholder described by then–Deputy Secretary Robert Zoellick in his thoughtful and influential September 2005 speech. Zoellick correctly argued that China had benefited greatly from the security and prosperity created by a stable, rule-based international economic and political order.[1] But China had contributed a disproportionally small amount to maintain that order. Zoellick recognized that one of the great challenges facing diplomats in the United States, Europe, and Japan was to persuade China to do more to contribute to the global commons. So far the record of this effort is at best mixed, and there are real reasons to be concerned that the other great powers will continue to have a difficult time encouraging China to do more.

The goal here is analysis, not moral judgment. China's postcolonial nationalism often leads Chinese commentators to level over-the-top accusations against the United States and other great powers, suggesting that their entreaties to cooperation have some nefarious intent. But Chinese analysts and officials also make more thoughtful, logical, and compelling arguments for why China should be treated differently than advanced industrial nations. Compared to all other great powers and medium powers, China's per capita GDP is quite small and its social and political challenges incomparably larger than any other great power. China's per capita GDP in 2013 was the same as Ecuador's. Nobody is expecting Ecuadorians to contribute greatly to global governance—not so for the Chinese. While China has the largest holdings of foreign reserves in the world and has run a current account surplus with the developed world for decades, it also has a nascent and underdeveloped social security system at home and more than 100 million people still living in abject poverty. So when, for instance, it is asked to use its foreign exchange reserves on a large scale abroad to prop up economies in Europe, many in China wonder about the social justice in such a proposal. Why should a developing country with the frailest of safety nets bail out rich social democracies with per capita GDPs several times

China's simply because those states are now realizing the results of many years of profligate government spending?

China, the world's largest emitter of greenhouse gases, also needs to burn carbon to continue to grow. Developed countries dispersed massive amounts of CO_2 into the atmosphere as they industrialized and have only in the past two or three decades turned their attention to the negative results of that behavior. But the world's most advanced economies have also become much more service-oriented, so the realization comes at a relatively convenient time in their economic histories. Chinese leaders and scholars also correctly point out that those same advanced countries benefit from consuming the cheap products manufactured in China's coastal greenhouse gas belt, often by firms owned in the countries complaining most loudly about Beijing's emissions.

China is a major importer of natural resources and has energy firms that are entering the global marketplace relatively late in the game. Chinese officials and commentators argue that China cannot be so finicky as to turn down oil and gas partnerships with regimes considered unsavory in Washington, Tokyo, and European capitals simply because those partnerships might serve to undercut global humanitarian or nonproliferation efforts. So China does lots of business with perpetrators of mass killings in Sudan, supporters of terrorism and violators of the Nuclear Nonproliferation Treaty in Iran, and other questionable suppliers. Chinese leaders can also point to the long history of close relations between unsavory oil-producing regimes and the United States, Great Britain, and France. With its own authoritarian rule, its recent history of the use of military force against civilians, and its own recent experience with international sanctions and condemnation, Beijing is also predictably less comfortable than the capitals of the advanced liberal democracies with condemning, sanctioning, and intervening in authoritarian regimes in the developing world.

Fortunately, there are solid responses to these Chinese arguments, some of which are accepted by segments of China's elite. All are based in long-term thinking and a recognition that China has benefited and continues to benefit greatly from the economic stability and security of the current international system. Nuclear proliferation, terrorists finding safe haven in poorly governed states, financial instability in its export markets, and potentially catastrophic changes in the global climate would all affect China at least as much as they do any of the advanced democracies. But such a holistic, over-the-horizon approach to current issues is difficult to market in any country, democratic or authoritarian. It is a particularly hard sell in a country like China with very pressing near-term challenges. All countries, even authoritarian ones, have domestic politics. Chinese leaders worry increasingly about domestic stability and regime legitimacy as the distribution of income grows more stilted, more people lose their land in eminent domain cases, urban housing becomes unaffordable, and widespread corruption remains largely unchecked. Citizens have recently gained many new forms of electronic communication, with a resulting rise in the number of protests against local government officials. Moreover, the CCP has made postcolonial nationalism a major pillar of its legitimacy. In that context, arguments for expending resources and forgoing economic and diplomatic opportunities in order to coordinate China's policies with former enemies such as the United States, Japan, South Korea, and one-time European colonialists are a tough sell in China and could easily be exploited by nationalist critics in the increasingly robust print and electronic media. For this reason and others, the former State Department official and scholar Susan Shirk has called China the "fragile superpower."[2]

Diplomats from the United States and its allies have enjoyed limited success in convincing China to make near-term sacrifices. Such entreaties might appear to be a trap designed to undercut China's overall national power. For example, Professor Pan Wei at Peking University argues that deeper Chinese integration in what he sees to be a hierarchical U.S.-led international order would make China subordinate to the United States. He rejects "pressure [on] China to undertake more 'international responsibilities' and follow 'international standards' as defined by the existing regimes in the global hierarchy." He complains that China is often a "victim . . . of that hierarchy," citing China's non–market economy status in the WTO as one example.[3] In a somewhat more subtle fashion, another Chinese scholar warns against the danger of China being passively "pulled by the nose" by "the West and international society" into accepting excessive international responsibilities that are divorced from China's actual national capabilities. If China falls for this, he warns, it will become a "loser in the international competition" (*guoji jingzhengzhong chengwei shibaizhe*)."[4]

Like Pan, many Chinese commentators view Zoellick's challenge to China as a ruse to get China to foot the bill for something that will benefit the United States and other countries much more than China. Rather than accepting Zoellick's arguments that global governance is a shared mission of all the great powers, they wonder why China should "help" the United States with its problems. After all, Washington continues to sell weapons to Taiwan and support Japanese military enhancements. Since Chinese elites are worried about regime stability and personal promotion within the CCP, they are likely more concerned about the domestic political need for near-term job creation at home than the future effects of long-term global warming. They are also likely worried about nationalist domestic reactions to the appearance that they have thrown longtime diplomatic partners like North Korea under the bus at the request of the United States, the EU, and Japan. Professor Pan states succinctly, "China is not keen to help the West to oust their disliked regimes and create enemies for itself."[5] Leaders' concerns about such reactions at home might outweigh any perceived benefits of explaining the long-term connections between regional instability in poorly governed environments and the harm to China's own national interests. The connections are real and appear to be understood by at least some Chinese leaders, but they are not the stuff of bumper stickers. As one interlocutor put it in 2011, calls for intense cooperation on global projects evoke little emotion in comparison to attacks on the "hegemonic" United States or an "unrepentant" Japan. So when Americans and others ask China to be more assertive on the international stage, they should be careful what they wish for.

The reality, however, is that those countries have little choice but to foster Chinese activism. China's sheer size and its deep connections to the global economy as both a producer and an importer mean that the world cannot afford to give China a pass. China is the world's largest trader of manufactured goods, one of the world's largest importers of natural resources, the world's largest emitter of greenhouse gases, a close diplomatic and economic partner of several of the world's worst proliferators and failed states, and the holder of the largest reserves of foreign currency. When the other great powers seek cooperation from China on international security and humanitarian, economic, and environmental problems, China can undercut the efforts without even intentionally doing so. It is in this sense that China is too big to fail to pull its weight on global governance.

Nonproliferation

ONE OF THE MORE SERIOUS security challenges facing the international community is the growing number of actors who have developed or who are developing nuclear arsenals. The most dangerous situations are created when particularly aggressive and unreliable regimes seem to be producing fissile radioactive material and developing nuclear weapons technology and missile delivery systems. The poster children for this concern are North Korea (DPRK) and Iran. Previously one could include Saddam Hussein's Iraq and Muammar Qaddafi's regime in this category, but both dictators were forcibly removed from power. The latter had apparently given up his nuclear ambitions before he was overthrown by a coalition of international and domestic foes, a perceived betrayal that Chinese analysts note readily in discussions of Iran and North Korea. The former had suspended his nuclear pursuit after his previous efforts were discovered following the first Gulf War but hid this fact from the world and even from many of his own generals. According to the Duelfer Report, a postmortem of the WMD debacle of the second Iraq War, Saddam maintained his long-term nuclear aspirations, awaiting the breakdown of international sanctions against his country to restart his nuclear weapons program.[6] But the Second Gulf War removed him from power and there is no evidence that the successor regime in Iraq has such an aspiration.

In South Asia, India and Pakistan have recently developed nuclear weapons arsenals against the wishes of the international community. There seems to be significantly less concern that those two countries will either exploit their arsenals for aggressive purposes or intentionally transfer the weapons or nuclear material to third parties, whether those parties are states or nonstate actors. The main concern about Pakistan, deeply rooted in its modern history of proliferation, is that subnational actors with access to the weapons program will export weapons or relevant materials or technologies or that the state will lose control of its weapons program due to domestic instability (or, somewhat less likely, that the entire state will be taken over by radical Islamic forces and become more like Iran in its political orientation).

North Korea and Iran pose overlapping but somewhat different challenges. North Korea has a long history of aggression against the United States and its two Northeast Asian allies, South Korea and Japan. It also has a record of selling missiles and nuclear technology to Iran and Syria. Finally, North Korea has been estimated to produce one-third of its national GDP through state-sponsored criminal activity abroad.[7] Given the high value of nuclear weapons and fissile material, the temptation for North Korea to proliferate will be great, particularly if the nascent arsenal of weapons and stockpile of fissile material were to grow significantly. Iran has also reportedly cooperated with Pakistani entities and North Korea on the development of fissile material and delivery systems. Meanwhile, Iran has been a major supporter of terrorism in the Middle East and around the world and Iranian officials are outwardly hostile toward the existence of Israel and toward Sunni Muslim regimes in the Arab world. Those states, of course, worry about eventually being targeted by Iranian nuclear weapons, but more abstractly, and perhaps realistically, they also worry about how a perceived nuclear security blanket might embolden Iranian aggression at lower levels of violence, either directly by Iranian state agents or by proxies such as Hezbollah.

These fears have led many states and the International Atomic Energy Agency to actively oppose the development of a North Korean or Iranian nuclear weapons capability. In reference to both countries, the United States has deemed such a development "unacceptable." This word is, however, more easily uttered than acted upon, and short of extremely risky and potentially escalatory conventional military attacks on the two countries' facilities, the United States and its diplomatic partners can only pressure the two regimes to give up existing programs and then verifiably cease any future nuclear weapons development.

Without strong multilateral pressure, this diplomatic goal moves from the very difficult to the near impossible. If any major economy provides support and succor to the target of multilateral economic sanctions, then the rest of the international community will likely fail to pressure the target nation. By maintaining what it views as its traditional relations with North Korea and Iran, China has become the largest trader and investor in both countries. In the case of North Korea, China's ally dating back to the first half of the Cold War, China has arguably been the sole lifeline for the Kim family regime in Pyongyang, supplying almost all of its fuel, much of its food, and the vast majority of its trade and international financing.[8] In the case of Iran, China has maintained more normal relations, but as the Europeans and Japanese reduced or eliminated their positions in Iranian energy and trade sectors, China on several occasions moved in to fill many of those gaps, signing large upstream energy deals in the oil and gas sector and becoming Iran's largest trade partner.[9]

By all accounts and all indications, Beijing sincerely opposes the development of nuclear weapons in North Korea and Iran. It is also fair to say that China does not have the power or authority to micromanage the decisions of Pyongyang or Tehran, though the especially close economic relations that China enjoys with both countries likely gives Beijing much more influence there than Chinese diplomats are willing to concede. But the problems that the United States and like-minded states have in getting China to level effective pressure on these two countries are less rooted in China's limited influence than in China's own priorities and perceptions.

Regarding North Korea, Beijing could, quite simply, choose to strangle Pyongyang out of existence. The mutual recognition of this reality in Beijing and Pyongyang lends China significant leverage. But the PRC has a range of ideological, strategic, and economic reasons not to pursue such a course and is wary of the intentions of those calling for more sweeping sanctions that could lead to the DPRK's demise. However much China dislikes the prospect of a nuclear North Korea, Beijing has generally valued stability on the peninsula, including the stability of the regime in North Korea, over denuclearization.

As for Iran, a complex combination of postcolonial ideology, commercial interests, concerns about energy security, and the perceived need for a geostrategic counter to U.S. dominance of the Middle East all make China reluctant to alienate Tehran or to take actions that might destabilize the regime there. As we will see in chapter 8, China's behavior toward Iran seemed to improve from 2011 to 2013 from the perspective of the United States and its allies, but it is unclear exactly why China scaled back relations with Iran in those years. Unfortunately, the slight warming of relations between Tehran and Washington that allowed for the November 2013 interim agreement on Iranian nuclear activities (and the extension of that agreement a year later) became the occasion for China to sharply ramp up its economic interactions with Iran, especially in the energy sector. Iranian leaders have been rather frank in saying that they feel reduced pressure in their ongoing negotiations with the United States and Europe because they can rely on Beijing and, to a lesser degree, Moscow, even if the others continue to sanction their country harshly.[10]

North Korea

TWO REASONS ARE most commonly offered for China's reluctance to pressure Pyongyang. These arguments are not so much wrong as they are incomplete. The first is an issue of security, economics, and public health. North Korean collapse could open an unwelcome flow of millions of North Korean refugees into northeast China, a headache that China would rather do without.[11] North Korean refugees would likely be poverty-stricken, poorly educated, and, in many cases, exposed to virulent diseases, like drug-resistant strains of tuberculosis, that would tax the nascent social safety net in northeast China. The poor living conditions and exploitation of the tens of thousands of North Korean refugees already in Manchuria has also been a major source of international criticism for China, and multiplying that problem would hardly be a welcome outcome in Beijing.

The second reason why analysts believe that Beijing wants to avoid a North Korean collapse is China's often conservative, realpolitik view of international security challenges. Beijing's leaders, as with leaders in most places, like predictability. The situation on the peninsula following North Korean collapse would be highly unpredictable, but even the predictable outcomes would present problems. At a minimum, the collapse of North Korea would deprive China of a relatively friendly buffer state between it and the U.S. regional alliance system. South Korea, an American ally, would certainly move into the void left by Pyongyang's collapse and unify the peninsula under Seoul's leadership.[12] Since the U.S.–ROK alliance would likely survive Korean unification, the United States position in the region might be greatly strengthened by the collapse of the DPRK. U.S. forces might even return to North Korea for the first time since the early stages of the Korean War. Preventing the basing of U.S. forces just across the Yalu River border from China was one of the major reasons for China to enter that war in the first place. Why would China now help bring about the results it fought so hard to avoid and do so at the behest of its former Korean War enemy, the United States?

These two arguments help explain China's reluctance to level severe sanctions against North Korea. But, I believe, they only tell part of the story. In fact, the problems discussed above, while real, are relatively manageable. I am sure China would be concerned about refugees, but the entire North Korean population is only just over 20 million people, the size of one major Chinese metropolitan area like Chongqing or Shanghai. Moreover, Beijing could take actions to stem the flow of these refugees into China by setting up humanitarian base camps in the Yalu River valley on the Korean side of the border or limiting refugee transit deeper into China by deploying more security forces to the northeast if many were to try to cross the river into China. While it is true that China currently refuses to allow the UNHCR, the UN Refugee Agency, to set up offices in northeast China along the North Korean border to process refugees, it does so in part because it believes the organization will determine that the refugees deserve protected status as political refugees, and such a conclusion would severely harm Beijing's relations with Pyongyang. That concern would likely go away if North Korea collapsed because there would be no regime to upset. After a DPRK collapse, international agencies could operate in northeast China and assist China and Seoul in returning Korean refugees to a unified, democratic Korea without fear of persecution.

The legacy of the Korean War, I believe, is important, but not simply because China wants to avoid the stationing of U.S. troops near its border. American troops on the border would certainly be unwelcome in Beijing but would hardly pose the threat they were perceived to pose to the young Communist nation in the early Cold War. In 1950 when Washington dismissed Chinese threats and U.S. forces crossed the 38th parallel to unify the peninsula under UN control, China was concerned that U.S. forces in northernmost Korea would eventually be used for an invasion of China by the United States and, perhaps, Japan. Such a concern had no actual foundation in U.S. strategy at the time, despite General MacArthur's occasional bluster, but it was hardly a symptom of a fantastic imagination or paranoia. China had been invaded through Korea by Japan in recent decades, and at that time, the PRC was terribly poor, militarily weak, suffering from ongoing civil war, isolated from the regional economy, and allied with the Soviet Union, and thereby ideologically sworn to oppose the United States, South Korea, and Japan.

Today none of that is true. China is now a nuclear power with an increasingly impressive conventional military. It is a major economic hub for regional investment and trade, including for South Korea, Japan, and the United States. After the death of Mao and the adoption of a live-and-let-live pragmatism under Deng Xiaoping, the PRC abandoned the business of exporting its ideology abroad. In fact, realpolitik replaced revolutionary evangelism to such a degree that, for all intents and purposes, the PRC was aligned with the United States against the Soviet Union for the last decades of the Cold War. Ironically, perhaps, there has only been one possible exception to Beijing's abandonment of ideological evangelism in the post-1978 era: North Korea. Of course, now the content of that evangelism is very different than in the Maoist era. Beijing has consistently tried to convince Pyongyang to develop a domestic market economy and to open its hermetically sealed economy in the manner of Deng Xiaoping's reform program.[13] So in this military, economic, and ideological environment, can anyone really imagine a unified Korean peninsula under Seoul's leadership becoming a launch pad for invasion of the PRC, even if U.S. bases were created within spitting distance of China's northeast? (That is not to mention that such a military posture would be both unnecessary and unwise in the first place, even if Washington's South Korean allies were, for some bizarre reason, willing to allow it.) It should, therefore, be possible for Washington and Seoul to reassure China that a unified Korea would pose no direct security threat to the Chinese border.

But Korean unification under Seoul's leadership provides a deeper political challenge for Beijing than the viability of North Korea as a buffer state. A unified Korean peninsula would be democratic and, after a multiyear struggle to integrate the societies of North and South, it would also likely be prosperous, stable, and respected by its neighbors and the global community. These outcomes arguably would pose a much bigger challenge to the domestic legitimacy of the CCP than U.S. forces based in Korea could ever pose to China's national security.

The CCP's narrative about the Korean War also provides domestic legitimacy to the regime as the protector of the Chinese national interest. The war is a source of great honor and pride for the People's Liberation Army in particular. As mentioned above, the PLA has its primary loyalty to the Party, not the nation. But of course it wants to market itself as the defender of the Chinese people, not the Party's executioner of Chinese protestors, as it was in June 1989 at Tiananmen Square. Nothing serves that purpose better than the history of soldiers of a young PRC heroically protecting China by defending neighbor and ally North Korea against the advancing, militarily superior, and allegedly imperialist United States.

In terms of regime continuity back to "the founding of the nation" in 1949, Mao's legacy needs to be preserved in some fashion. The CCP's desire to remain linked to that earlier era is demonstrated every day by Mao's portrait over Tiananmen Square. One of the many reasons why CCP propaganda leaders believe the Soviet Union collapsed was that in 1956 Nikita Khrushchev opened up the Pandora's box of internal Party turmoil by his sweeping condemnation of the previous supreme leader, Josef Stalin. But there are only a few major events left from the Maoist era that can still be celebrated in the reform era to salvage the reputation of the self-absorbed leader. After all, his idiotic economic plans of the late 1950s and nihilistic political ideas of continuing revolution in the 1960s killed many more Chinese than the Japanese imperialists ever managed to do. For the CCP, there needs to be a story of Mao's patriotism and strategic genius on the international stage to offset the widely recognized and relatively freely discussed economic and social disasters that he unleashed at home. The main narrative is that Mao, for all of his faults, got China back on its feet again and defended the nation against the great powers. He united China and stood up to the outside world, playing a weak hand with great strategic acumen and creating a foundation on which Deng Xiaoping and his successors could build the more powerful and successful China of today. China's "victory" in the Korean War, along with the impressive nuclear and missile programs launched in the 1950s and 1960s, are at the center of CCP historians' effort to save Mao's reputation as a great leader.

China's current dysfunctional relationship with North Korea is sealed in a great deal of blood. I honor the courage and sacrifice of Chinese soldiers in Korea, as does every U.S. Korean War veteran whom I have ever met. And one should never discount the nobility and bravery of a soldier because of the mistakes of the leaders who sent him into combat. But I sadly view the Korean War's estimated one million Chinese casualties (including at least 200,000 dead and many more wounded) as additional victims of Mao's many mistakes. These people were killed and maimed protecting China against the phantom threat of future U.S. invasion shared by Mao and Stalin alike. Moreover, that threat only materialized in their minds because Mao and Stalin had preapproved the North Korean aggression that started an otherwise avoidable war. China's prize in this allegedly victorious war was to save a North Korean regime that started the unnecessary war in June 1950 and has, ever since, been among the most notorious and repressive in the world.

For obvious reasons, the CCP, and particularly the PLA, have a different story. They view the fallen among the "Chinese People's Volunteers" as martyrs who rallied behind the call of a great and farsighted national leader. Together Mao and the soldiers protected the Chinese nation against long-term external threats. Part of that story has to be the righteousness of the North Korean cause. For China now to cause the collapse of that regime and have its archives opened and history rewritten by the South Koreans could do great damage to the legacy of both Mao and the PLA. Recognizing this, one Chinese expert half-jokingly said to me that if North Korea were to collapse precipitously, it is possible that U.S. and ROK special forces might race into North Korea to secure weapons of mass destruction while PLA special forces might race to secure the North Korean archives!

The treatment of Korean War history in China to date demonstrates the sensitivity of the war for the CCP. The reality is that in 1950 North Korea invaded South Korea in violation of a UN-sanctioned agreement after World War II to temporarily divide the peninsula at the 38th parallel, pending eventual peaceful unification. The war was entirely avoidable. The founding leader of North Korea, Kim Il-sung, managed to manipulate a nervous Stalin and a relatively reticent Mao into supporting his preplanned invasion of the south. Kim's misguided theory of victory was that the south would crumble quickly and the United States would not intervene, at least not promptly enough to make a difference. He proved disastrously wrong. UN forces under MacArthur's command effectively intervened and, alongside South Korean forces, destroyed the North Korean forces in the south and then drove north to unify the peninsula. Mao and his colleagues went through a torturous process to decide whether or not to intervene to save North Korea. In mid-October, Chinese forces entered North Korea in large numbers, executed a brilliant deception strategy against MacArthur's overextended troops, and famously drove U.S. forces on the longest U.S. military retreat outside of the U.S. Civil War. Following an effective counteroffensive by U.S., ROK, and UN forces in early 1951, the Chinese and North Korean forces were driven back north of the 38th parallel. After another two and a half years of bitter fighting, a July 1953 armistice would reestablish roughly the same prewar division of the peninsula. Among the hundreds of thousands of Chinese casualties was Mao's only son.[14]

In retrospect, the lead-up to and execution of the war could have been portrayed in various different ways in China. A less revolutionary regime than Mao's CCP or a more self-confident one than the CCP has been since his death might have recognized the chairman's disastrous decision in May 1950 to approve Kim Il-sung's initial invasion. But Mao's decision and even the meetings in Beijing with Kim Il-sung that provided the occasion for it were kept secret from the Chinese people for decades. Several years after the Cold War ended, the meeting was eventually reported in Chinese secondary histories. Chinese censors must have realized that they could not keep the lid on these facts forever. The earlier official CCP accounts seemed particularly cartoonish and propagandistic in the light of Soviet and Eastern European archival materials that came to light after the collapse of the Soviet empire. Those archives document Mao's role before the war, his critically important meetings with Kim, and his communications with Moscow. The histories now published in the PRC acknowledging the Mao-Kim meetings generally portray Mao as aware of Kim's plan though skeptical about the wisdom of it on strategic grounds. Ultimately, however, he is portrayed as having little choice but to give Kim the green light because his main ally, Stalin, had put him in an untenable position by conditionally approving Kim's invasion if Mao also approved.[15] Mao could hardly say no, the story goes, without appearing like a weak Communist ally who, like Tito in Yugoslavia, was more of a nationalist than a truly internationalist ally. This was especially true as Mao would need Soviet help in defeating his civil war enemy on Taiwan and rebuilding the economy from decades of war. So Mao is not portrayed as the master of events but, as one Chinese scholar put it, rather as someone who had been presented with a fait accompli (*jicheng xianshi*) by Stalin.[16]

In this interpretation Mao avoids direct blame for helping to cause an unnecessary war that led to so many Chinese casualties, mobilized the United States for the global Cold War (the U.S. defense budget would triple in the first year of the Korean War), and rendered permanent the separation of Taiwan from the PRC (before the outbreak of the Korean War, the Truman administration seemed prepared to let Taiwan fall to the Communists if it were attacked). In my opinion, while Mao was indeed placed in a tough spot by Stalin, he was still responsible for giving Kim the green light. Mao had final veto power over the war itself and chose to support it.[17] But in the PRC, publishing such a conclusion would still be considered subversive because it would kick out the last leg of Mao's three-legged stool. He could then be viewed as a terrible economic, political, and national security leader of the PRC. How could one justify keeping his portrait over Tiananmen?

The particular sensitivity of the Korean War in Chinese history was driven home to me during my extended travel to China over a sabbatical year in 2010–2011. Fall 2010 was the sixtieth anniversary of the Chinese entrance into the war. In my time on the hotel gym's stationary bicycles, I saw television documentaries and news coverage of public events memorializing the heroic efforts of the Chinese soldiers in Korea. The documentaries underscored the tight links between the soldiers in the field and the patriotic citizens back home who volunteered money, clothes, and whatever they could muster for the front-line troops defending the young nation's security in the mountains of Korea. The intensity and language of this programming made it feel as if there might still be a cold war between the United States and China.

One speech in that year struck me as particularly anachronistic given the history of U.S.–China relations since Nixon's visit in 1972. The current Chinese president, then Vice President Xi Jinping, a worldly leader who is hardly a left-wing firebrand, remembered the struggle in words that seemed lifted from Chinese newspapers in the early Cold War. He stated:

> The war [was] imposed by the imperialist invaders on the Chinese people. After the Korean Civil War broke out, the U.S. Truman administration brazenly dispatched troops there for armed intervention, launching a comprehensive war against Korea. Ignoring warnings on several occasions by the Chinese government, [U.S. troops] crossed the 38th parallel and pressed forward close to the Yalu River and the Tumen River in the China-Korea border areas. . . . At this critical moment and at the request of the Korean party and government, the CCP Central Committee and Comrade Mao Zedong stood high and saw far, judged the hour and sized up the situation, and resolutely made the historical policy decision on resisting aggression and aiding Korea to protect our homes and defend the country . . . Our heroic soldiers and commanders of the Chinese People's Volunteer Army . . . crossed the Yalu River in high spirits, with no thought for their own safety fought side by side with the Korean people and armed forces in bloody battles for two years and nine months, and won a great victory in the War to Resist America and Aid Korea. . . .

[The Chinese People's Volunteer Army] set a brilliant example of utilizing the weak to defeat the strong (*yi ruo sheng qiang*). . . .

In the past sixty years, the Chinese people have never forgotten the great fighting friendship forged in the blood of the people and troops of China and Korea. To commemorate the victory in the War to Resist Aggression and Aid Korea is . . . to carry forward the spirit of resisting America and assisting Korea and to provide a powerful spiritual driving force for upholding and developing socialism with Chinese characteristics.[18]

One could hardly hope for a better summation than Xi's own words for why it would be domestically difficult for the CCP and the PLA to now be seen by an increasingly restive Chinese population to be suffocating North Korea at the behest of the United States. This version of the Korean War has multiple benefits for the CCP. It ties the revolutionary generation of the CCP tightly to the reform generation and bolsters Mao's image as a patriot and strategist; it even links Mao's military strategy to the current asymmetric doctrine of the weak defeating the strong to counter the United States, which is described in greater detail in chapter 4. It is also notable what is not in the speech. The war "broke out" as if it were a thunderstorm, not a premeditated act of North Korean aggression. And, of course, no mention is made of Mao's prior approval of that aggression.

Aside from the allegedly great victory over the "American imperialists" in the Korean War, the PLA has only fought two other large-scale international battles: a clear victory over India in 1962 in a border war and a clear military defeat at the hands of the Vietnamese in 1979 after China launched its "pedagogical" invasion of that country. The former is not highly trumpeted in China, perhaps because India is not granted sufficient respect in Chinese strategic affairs to warrant attention. The war with Vietnam is played down for more obvious reasons. The Korean War, in this sense, is unique and irreplaceable and, unfortunately for the rest of the world, it had the effect of saving North Korea and leaving the peninsula divided to this day.

None of this is to say that it is impossible for U.S. diplomats to encourage China to pressure North Korea and to urge Pyongyang to forgo new conventional military provocations on the peninsula or to limit or even abandon its nuclear activities. Like many other U.S. officials, I have spent countless hours myself trying to do just this. And there is reason to keep trying. There has been variation in China's behavior, and Beijing has at times toughened its stance toward North Korea—for example, signing on to and enforcing (with varying degrees of energy) several UN Security Council resolutions targeting Pyongyang or signaling Beijing's displeasure bilaterally through diplomatic and economic measures. The history of those changes will be outlined in chapters 6 through 8. I will just state here that it seems that China is often angered by the intransigence of its dependent ally. Beijing worries about the prospect of a second Korean War sparked by Pyongyang's belligerent behavior against the South or by U.S. preemption against WMD and missile programs. Even short of war, Beijing does not like the indirect effects for China of Pyongyang's provocative actions of recent years in the conventional realm (artillery attacks on South Korean islands) and in the realm of WMD (nuclear detonations and missile tests). These serve not only to embarrass Beijing as North Korea's protector, but to tighten U.S.-led regional alliances, as they did in 2010. In that year, North Korean attacks on South Korea stimulated those allies' military activities and cooperation in the region. When both Japan and South Korea improve coordination with Washington in areas like missile defense, antisubmarine warfare, and intelligence sharing, those developments could offset some of the hard-won gains of China's own military modernization. Also, Chinese experts understand that there is no guarantee that South Korea and Japan will permanently eschew nuclear weapons programs of their own if North Korea continues down its current path. In a nutshell, China has to constantly weigh the benefits of a stable North Korea against the costs and burdens that Pyongyang creates for China's regional security posture.

Iran

THE INTERNATIONAL COMMUNITY has been trying to monitor and curb Iran's nuclear activities for three decades. Despite Tehran's plea that its uranium-enrichment programs are for purely peaceful and scientific purposes, few intelligence analysts outside of countries friendly to Iran, like Russia and China, place much value in that claim. Iran has been accused by the United States, the European powers, and Japan of a clandestine nuclear and missile program designed to create a deliverable nuclear arsenal. And especially after the WMD debacle in Iraq, it is notable that the International Atomic Energy Agency has also flagged Iran for noncompliance with the inspection protocols of the Nuclear Nonproliferation Treaty, of which Iran is a signatory.

Since 2006 the UN Security Council has passed six sanctions resolutions that target Iran. The strictest of these resolutions was UNSCR 1929 on June 9, 2010, which banned certain weapons sales to Iran and placed on global blacklists various banking and industrial firms and individuals involved in Iran's nuclear and missile programs. Significantly, China voted for that resolution. But, as Erica Downs and Suzanne Maloney point out, the real squeeze on Iran's finances and economy have come not so much through the UN sanctions regime, but the series of unilateral policies, laws, and regulations adopted by like-minded states in North America and Europe to punish Iran for its intransigence. Those are stricter and more sweeping than the UN sanctions themselves. China has by all public measures complied with the UN sanctions but has not adopted separate unilateral measures against Tehran. In fact, in the process of drawing the six sanctions resolutions, Beijing has actively and rather infamously worked to water them down so as to ensure that Iran's biggest banks and energy sector were not included on the UN's Iranian target list. Chinese diplomats routinely argue that anything more would harm the citizenry of Iran and China's legitimate economic interests in the Iranian economy. As Downs and Maloney argue:

> Driven by economic interests, as well as sympathy for Iran's grievances, China is the only major player still active in the Iranian oil patch. Whereas firms from most other countries have retreated due to international pressure and Iran's unfavorable business climate, China and its companies adhere only to the letter of Resolution 1929, which contains no explicit restrictions on energy investment or trade. China has thus emerged as the linchpin of

the international sanctions regime against Iran and, by extension,
of the effort to forestall Iran from acquiring a nuclear capability.[19]

The Chinese economic interest in Iran is clear. China became a net
importer of energy in the early 1990s, and its biggest source of imports
is the Middle East and Persian Gulf region. Iran is the second biggest supplier of China's oil from the region and provides 12 percent
of China's overall oil imports (only the Saudis supply more).[20] In 2011
China imported 500,000 barrels a day from Iran. For reasons that will
be explored further in chapter 8, those numbers reportedly fell by about
25 percent in 2012 but are still quite substantial.[21]

Iran also provides fine opportunities for Chinese energy firms to
gain experience in developing upstream oil and gas fields and, in the
process, make profits in an area in which its international competitors
are at a severe disadvantage. Downs and Maloney wrote in 2011, "These
NOCs [national oil companies], which are powerful political actors,
may try to convince Beijing that gaining access to Iran's hydrocarbon
reserves is worth the risk of U.S. sanctions against Chinese companies.
The incentives of Chinese firms are both financial (Tehran reportedly
buys the gasoline at a 25 percent premium above the market rate) and
political (Beijing opposes U.S. sanctions as extraterritorial legislation
that harms the Iranian people)."[22] Finally, sanctions have left Iran cash-
strapped, allowing China to trade manufactured goods and service
contracts for energy in ways that profit Chinese industries, which have
become Iran's largest trade partners and major players in Iran's infrastructure and telecommunications projects.[23]

The political reasons for China's reluctance to sanction are worth
exploring further. In his magisterial review of China's historical relations with Iran, John Garver offers the many political and material reasons why China is reluctant to cooperate more actively with the United
States and others in pressuring Iran. At the deepest historical level,
China and Iran have a lot in common. This may seem jarring given
the fact that today Iran, despite the patina of democracy, is ruled by a
small group of revolutionary Islamic mullahs and China is ruled by an
avowedly atheist Marxist-Leninist state. But if we strip away the surface
ideology, we see a shared ideology of postcolonial nationalism. Prior

to the era of European imperialism, both China and Iran (Persia) were great empires with advanced cultures. They once ruled over almost all that they saw. They were centers of advanced learning and technology that lent them tremendous prestige. Both nations blame "the West," initially the Europeans, for stealing away that national greatness, interfering in domestic politics, and creating "semicolonies," to use Mao's phrase for pre-1949 China. Since 1989, both countries have been subjected to unilateral sanctions by the United States, Europe, and Japan, in part because of events in their domestic politics. Both object in principle to such sanctions, which they view as "extraterritorial."[24]

In part because of Mao's desire to portray himself as a leader of the developing world, he rejected great power arms control agreements that limited the number of nuclear powers. Even after the PRC became the first developing country to produce deliverable nuclear weapons in the 1960s, China remained wary of international agreements that would deprive others of the right to develop such weapons. This partially explains the history of China's past nuclear cooperation with countries like Pakistan and Iran.

China came late to the realization that increasing the number of nuclear powers did not serve its own interest. And as its growing economy needed more energy, Beijing wanted increased access to more foreign civilian energy technology. So Beijing signed on to the Nonproliferation Treaty only in 1992, twenty-four years after its initial adoption. Still under international sanctions itself following the Tiananmen massacre of June 1989, Beijing was not eager to alienate states on behalf of the United States. It took several more years for China to adjust to the norms of the regime and to take seriously the notion that for the treaty to have teeth, sanctions against nonnuclear signatories who violate its protocols are necessary. Nineteen ninety-two was also the first year of the post–Cold War era and the year after the U.S.-led coalition's decisive victory in the First Gulf War. As Garver points out, for geostrategic reasons, Beijing was concerned about U.S. and NATO domination of the Middle East and Persian Gulf as well as other areas of the world.[25] That concern grew after the United States invaded Iraq in 2003. As two Chinese scholars argued in 2010, for security and economic reasons, China needs more than ever to preserve good relations with Iran, which is a great power in an important region of the world. They warn that if the current regime were to fall and the United States and Europe held great sway over the successor state in Iran, it would have strongly negative repercussions for China's security and long-term economic development. So they counsel their government to ensure that only peaceful diplomatic means are used to address the Iranian nuclear issue and that nothing is adopted in that process to threaten the stability of Iran's current regime (*zhengquan*).[26]

Finally, as will be explored in the next chapter, in 1992, the same year that China signed the Nuclear Nonproliferation Treaty, President George H. W. Bush announced the sale of 150 F-16 aircraft to Taiwan, a move many inside and outside China deemed to be a violation of a 1982 communiqué between the United States and China on Taiwan arms sales. Significant arms sales would take place during all subsequent administrations as well. On a principled level, many Chinese ask why China should restrict its activities with Iran at the behest of the United States when Washington ignores its own commitments regarding China. On a more practical level, China's military and technical cooperation with Iran has provided Beijing leverage over countries like the United States and Israel, because Chinese diplomats could suggest a quid pro quo of limiting or eliminating that cooperation in exchange for more cooperative American and Israeli policies toward China. Although Chinese diplomats have become more subtle on such matters in recent conversations than they were in the 1990s, they still clearly link China's cooperation with the United States on global affairs like Iran and Washington's behavior on issues that touch on China's self-defined core interests, like Taiwan and Tibet.

This gets to the central intellectual problem that needs to be overcome to gain persistent Chinese cooperation on such matters: China will not cooperate to "help" the United States; Chinese leaders will need to understand that preventing Iranian nuclear development and belligerence is in China's own interest. In chapter 8 we will discuss the Obama administration's apparent success in getting China to at least limit its energy activities in Iran during the early part of its second term. But for our broader purposes beyond Iran, it will be important to understand whether China was acting in the spirit of the UN security resolutions that Beijing helped pass (less likely) or whether the reductions in purchases were purely the result of Chinese firms fearing U.S. unilateral sanctions if they did not limit their activities in Iran (more likely). The reasons matter because we know that China objects in principle to the unilateral U.S. sanctions, and one wonders for how long they will comply with them. Fortunately the prospect of business opportunities in the United States that flow from the shale oil and gas revolution may mean that China's NOCs have a long-term interest in avoiding U.S. sanctions to gain investment opportunities in the U.S. market. On the other hand, one worries that any U.S.–China dust-up over Taiwan or disputes between China and Japan in the East China Sea might lead China to "punish" the United States by increasing its activities in Iran.

As with North Korea, the degree of real or apparent coordination between China and the United States has varied over the past ten years. Some of this has more to do with Iran than the United States. China has its own problems with Iran. Iran has flouted international demands for transparency in its nuclear program and rejected proposals that would allow it peaceful scientific research on nuclear energy to such a degree that even China and Russia are not willing to stand in the way of some sanctions. And even in the best of political times, Tehran makes things famously difficult for its economic partners both in reaching deals and then, especially, in implementing them. As Downs and Maloney report, there has also been political resentment in Iran toward China because the PRC did in the end sign on to UN Security Council resolutions aimed at Tehran even after it worked to water them down. Some of the frustration toward China has taken the form of complaints about China's strong position in the import sector for consumer goods, with accusations that Chinese products are shoddy and below Iranian standards.[27] But as with North Korea, the posture of the United States also matters in affecting China's behavior toward Iran. As early as the 1990s, long before Chinese NOCs considered investing heavily in the United States, China did not want its relationship with Iran to seriously harm its relations with the United States. More directly, China does not want to see additional warfare in the Middle East and Persian Gulf region, already affected heavily by the wars in Afghanistan and Iraq, the civil war in Syria, and the unrest in Egypt. A U.S. or Israeli air strike on Iranian facilities could escalate into a regional war. Even if Beijing analysts deem the United States as too war-weary for such an adventure, they cannot rule out an Israeli strike, especially given Israel's strike on a Syrian nuclear facility in 2007 and Prime Minister Benjamin Netanyahu's impassioned speech about Israeli "red lines" on Iran at the September 2012 United Nations General Assembly meeting. Unlike the Korean peninsula, Iran does not border China, so the prospect of conflict there is not as pressing. But Beijing still has no interest in seeing further war in a region on which China, much more than the United States, is reliant for energy imports. The resulting energy price spike alone would likely have a major impact on China's energy-intensive export industries. Even if Beijing believes that diplomacy will not stop Iran's nuclear ambitions and continues to try to limit sanctions targeting that country for practical and ideological reasons, Beijing's leaders might still pressure Iran to some degree to preserve international negotiations and reduce the likelihood of a preemptive war.

Climate Change

OF ALL THE GLOBAL ISSUES on the U.S.–China agenda, achieving sustained coordination and cooperation on climate change might be the most challenging. A blizzard of factors makes it difficult to get both the United States and China to make the necessary compromises to limit future greenhouse gas emissions in a verifiable manner and thus encourage other major economies to travel down the same path. In late 2014, for the first time, there were some reasons for guarded optimism that cooperation might improve, and there have been some recent signs of progress in both countries. But to date, neither country has shrouded itself in glory on this issue. As one former U.S. government official quipped in a private conversation, "No one can say that the United States and China cannot cooperate. We cooperate every day in destroying the planet." He portrayed the United States and China as codependents, each blaming the other's behavior for its own lack of serious action on climate change. In 2008 William Chandler, the Carnegie Endowment's expert on climate, similarly labeled the dysfunctional U.S.–China relationship on climate change "a suicide pact."[28]

The United States is a democracy. Elected officials have to worry about near-term economic performance and job creation to stay in office, and the system has so many built-in checks and balances that the executive branch, no matter how green it might be in its orientation, cannot simply dictate national emissions reductions without significant Congressional support. There are regulatory measures that the executive branch can take to reduce greenhouse gas emissions by reinterpreting existing environmental laws, as the Obama administration did, increasing requirements for fuel-efficiency standards in automobiles and including carbon emissions as a pollutant under the Clean Air Act. But even these actions created a domestic backlash and, in the case of the Clean Air Act, a legal challenge. In the 2014 midterm elections, Republicans gained control of both houses of Congress, and the majority leadership promised to fight implementation of the new regulatory measures. Moreover, it is much more difficult for presidents to gain sufficient domestic support to secure congressional ratification of any international treaty negotiated with foreign countries. The Constitution requires a supermajority of the Senate to approve any treaty.

Forgetting this basic reality, many domestic critics have unfairly blamed the administration of George W. Bush for rejecting the Kyoto Protocol. The Bush administration performed poorly on global environmental issues (as did the first-term Obama administration). Most of these failures can be put in the category of sins of omission, but the failure to accede to binding international treaties was not one of those sins. The implication of some of the criticisms of the Bush administration seems to be that if Al Gore had been president in the first decade of this century, the United States would have signed on to international treaties like Kyoto that limited U.S. emissions. After all, Al Gore won the Nobel Peace Prize for his work on climate change (and, perhaps, like Barack Obama, for simply being an American leader who was not George W. Bush!). But this is naïve, to say the least. Kyoto had almost no backing on Capitol Hill from either party during the Clinton administration, in which Gore served as vice president, and the idea that a President Gore could have turned zero support for international climate treaties into a supermajority is simply fantastic.

One would think that China, as an authoritarian state, would find it easier to make sacrifices on greenhouse gas emissions than the democratic United States. But this too would be naïve. As stated above, all countries have domestic politics, and the CCP is concerned with something even more serious than elections: regime survival. Job creation and nationalism are the two main pillars of CCP legitimacy, and climate change negotiations touch directly upon both. There has been a clear correlation between China's economic growth and its burning of fossil fuels. To curb that growth in the near term for abstract long-term environmental reasons would be controversial enough. But it would be much more controversial still to do so at the behest of the United States and other wealthy economies that are still much bigger polluters than China on a per capita basis and historically have created the bulk of the accumulated greenhouse gases in the atmosphere today.

One of the best ways to think about climate change is to view it as an example of what social scientists call a collective goods problem. All nations on the planet would enjoy the benefits of reduced rates of greenhouse gas emissions (and all inhabitants will suffer if the predictions of environmental scientists prove accurate regarding global warming at current trajectories). But nations will benefit from the limiting of greenhouse gas emissions regardless of whether they limit their own emissions, and even the nations that have sacrificed the most to limit emissions will still suffer if others do not follow suit and the planet warms. This type of situation creates enormous incentives to "free-ride" on the efforts of others. Particularly in larger group settings, individual members of the group will have strong incentives to free-ride and the result will be a failure to provide the collective good.

There is at least some good news on climate change. A small number of actors produce a large amount of the greenhouse gases. In fact, as the largest per capita emitter among the world's leading economies and the largest national emitter, respectively, the United States and China account for fully 40 percent of the greenhouse gas emissions in the world.[29] If we consider the 25 countries of the European Union a unified actor for regulatory purposes, then four actors, the United States, China, the EU, and India emit a whopping 64 percent of global emissions. Since securing cooperation in a small group of actors is much easier than in a larger group, and since serious cooperation between Washington and

Beijing alone would have global impact, there is at least some hope that the two largest emitters or even the four largest emitters could cut a deal that might produce something significant. In theory, for better or worse (mostly worse), in coming decades China might emit such a large percentage of greenhouse gases on its own that it might have selfish incentives to limit global climate change by constraining emissions even if others can ride free from the benefits. The situation would be improved if one could demonstrate that the direct costs of climate change to the top emitters will actually be much higher than currently expected, for example by demonstrating that severe weather and national catastrophes hitting the United States and China are definitely linked to climate change. Many commentators unsurprisingly emphasize that link when calling for urgent action, but the scientific grounding for such arguments is not nearly as solid as arguments that emphasize temperature changes, droughts, and rising seas. Another possibility would be to demonstrate that creating better carbon-free or low-carbon energy sources and more efficient machines and buildings is not only good environmental stewardship but good economics. If that were proven to be true, a healthy and competitive race to be the lowest carbon economy would replace the temptation to ride free. But while politicians laudably state that they want to grow the green jobs of the next century, and China is certainly no exception on this score, there is still nothing on the horizon that rivals the burning of fossil fuels in terms of cheap energy output for large-scale economic use. Renewables like wind and solar are intriguing supplements, and nuclear energy is also an important source of electricity, but carbon is still king and the king, sadly, has a very stable reign. So the economic sacrifices involved in limiting carbon use are still real and the collective goods problem thrives.

In the case of China, the factor that is most likely to spur it to persistent constructive action is the domestic problem of fine-particulate, ground-level air pollution, which is choking cities up and down the coast and into the central parts of China as well. Many of the same processes that produce greenhouse gas (GHG) emissions also produce very unhealthy levels of air pollution for Chinese citizens. Air pollution is a major political problem for the CCP, especially in northern China, where experts believe poor air quality is lowering life expectancy by

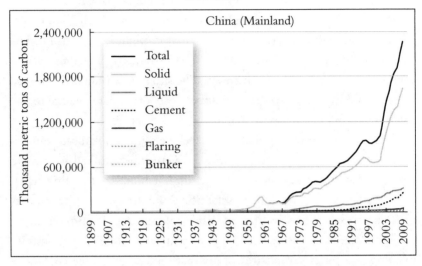

Figure 11. Graph traces the sharp increase in China's CO_2 emissions by source.
Source: T. A. Boden, G. Marland, and R. J. Andres, "Global, Regional, and National Fossil-Fuel CO_2 Emissions," 2013, Carbon Dioxide Information Analysis Center, Oak Ridge National Laboratory, U.S. Department of Energy, DOI:10.3334/CDIAC/00001_V2013, http://cdiac.ornl.gov/CO2_Emission/timeseries/national.

several years.[30] Unfortunately the two problems—climate change and fine-particulate air pollution—do not fully overlap. As will be discussed further below, while energy produced from noncarbon sources can reduce both forms of pollution, one leading carbon-based method of reducing ground-level pollution from burning coal, the use of coal-based synthetic natural gas as a substitute, creates significantly more greenhouse gases than burning coal itself. Moreover, reducing just the air pollution without reducing greenhouse gases actually exacerbates climate change by removing the cooling effects of ground-based pollution, which reflects solar energy away from the planet's surface.

As we drill deeper into the problem we see why the United States has been so unwilling to take significant actions unless the largest global emitter, China, agrees to do so in a verifiable manner. China is the world's largest consumer of fossil fuels and ranks low on energy efficiency. Moreover, nearly 70 percent of China's primary energy supply is produced by coal, the least green way to produce energy but by far the cheapest in China. And even though China imports coal for various economic reasons related to transport and chemical makeup, coal is still plentiful in China, which enjoys several decades worth of reserves. By contrast only about 25 percent of U.S. energy is produced by coal, and this will decline with new discoveries of oil and natural gas.[31] Figure 11 shows the staggering increase in China's CO_2 emissions just in the past several years (most of it from burning coal).

China itself has made advances in the use of natural gas, which is significantly cleaner than coal, and, as Thomas Friedman is quick to note in comparing China to the United States, Beijing has invested heavily in the production of solar panels, nuclear energy, wind farm technology, green buildings in major cities, and so on.[32] China has made a very large government commitment to investment in renewable energy (an impressive $473 billion in the five-year plan ending in 2015). But heavy reliance on the burning of fossil fuels is expected to continue.[33] Already, China is not only the world's largest greenhouse gas emitter, it is estimated to produce twice as much carbon dioxide as the United States.[34]

Nuclear energy provides a fine example of how China's overall growth and continued reliance on fossil fuels tends to subsume even the grandest plans to create alternative sources of energy. Despite the Fukushima disaster in Japan, China is going ahead with the largest program to increase nuclear power in human history. China currently has twenty-two nuclear power reactors in operation and twenty-six new ones under construction.[35] Compare this to the United States, which has not built a new nuclear plant since the Three Mile Island accident, or the EU, which is cutting back on nuclear power after Fukushima. Given the limited expertise in China and the lack of a solid regulatory infrastructure to govern the construction and operation of the plants, even the biggest fans of nuclear energy should be nervous about this initiative on safety grounds. But from the perspective of mitigating climate change there is something else that is sobering. After the massive buildup, the share of electricity output in China by nuclear energy will move from a tiny number (about 2 percent) to a significantly higher but still tiny number (5 percent) by 2020 (and, of course, electrical power itself is a subset of overall energy consumption).[36] China's overall demand for energy is growing so fast that even building twenty-six new nuclear power plants will only make a small dent in its overall mix of energy sources.

Without significant Chinese limits on greenhouse gas emissions, serious U.S. limits will be harder to sustain. Perhaps the most prominent complaint about the Kyoto Treaty was that it excluded from any responsibility some of the most prominent emitters in the developing world, such as China, India, and Brazil. Without countering the argument that those countries are free-riding on U.S. sacrifices, it would be very difficult for the Obama administration or any future administration to adopt and get Congress to pass new laws that limit U.S. emissions beyond the reductions caused by positive non-policy factors like the "shale gas revolution" created by fracking technologies. Coal is much dirtier than natural gas, so new access to cheap natural gas should, all things being equal, serve to reduce greenhouse gas emissions. One problem, of course, is that the same increase in U.S. natural gas frees up more American coal for export, and as far as climate change is concerned, it does not really matter where that coal is burned, even if the U.S. emissions figures might look better because of fracking. Further reductions might be caused by other market factors: any future increases in the price of gasoline and the efficiencies they would promote in the auto industry, and the further off-shoring of manufacturing jobs and their replacement with jobs in relatively clean service industries in the United States. And the executive branch has some regulatory room to maneuver along these lines without passing new laws, as the Obama administration demonstrated in its second term by raising fuel-efficiency standards for cars.

But just as the United States has serious reason to include the world's largest emitter in any agreement, China has a series of arguments to counter demands that it take more dramatic action to limit emissions that might risk damage to its future economic growth. Those arguments can be simplified into four categories: history, population, moral burden, and globalization of production. History was the theme raised by Chinese representatives at the international climate conference in December 2006 in Bali, Indonesia. The amount of CO_2 in the atmosphere is cumulative in nature, so it only makes sense to look not only at current emission levels but historical ones. China's historical emissions were estimated in 2002 to stand at 7.6 percent of the global total since 1850 in one study, while the United States stood at number one in the world at a staggering 29.3 percent (more than all twenty-five EU countries combined), or nearly four times China's total.[37] Of course China will close the gap over time. If it does not do so already, China will soon emit twice as much carbon as the United States on an annual basis. And by 2011 China's cumulative historical emissions were already almost 11 percent of the total while the United States had fallen to just over 26 percent.[38] Even when the historical gap disappears on a national level, Chinese representatives will be able to fall back on another compelling argument: China's population is between four and five times that of the United States, so it is only natural that it emits a lot of greenhouse gases. In 2012 each U.S. citizen was responsible for between two and three times the per capita carbon emissions of their PRC counterparts.[39] This is true even though U.S. energy generation is cleaner and much more efficient than Chinese energy. In fact, American citizens consume about seven times as much energy as their Chinese counterparts. "What if the Chinese used energy like the Americans?," asked William Chandler in 2008. His sobering answer: "Global energy use would double and five new Saudi Arabias would be needed just to meet oil demand. China itself would produce six times as much coal as it does today."[40] And even if China closes the history gap with the United States as a nation, China would not have done nearly as much historical damage to the planet as the United States has on a per capita basis. If we do a historical review from 1751 to 2012, average annual per capita emissions of Americans were about ten times those of Chinese citizens. So whether or not Americans were to become more environmentally aware and energy efficient, the Chinese arguments based on population differentials are not going away anytime soon.[41]

A third argument beyond history and population holds that the developing world should not be asked to make sacrifices to limit climate change. The marginal costs and opportunity costs of sacrifice are much greater in poorer countries, and studies show that the poorest countries, particularly those with long coastlines or low altitudes above sea level, will suffer the most from climate change and catastrophes. Thus, the argument goes that wealthy countries should be willing to pay for anything that the poorer countries contribute to the limiting of greenhouse gas emissions. Although China is now much wealthier than many other countries, it is still a developing country and has positioned itself as a leading representative of the developing world in negotiations over such matters with advanced economies like the United States. But perhaps the only policy proposal that would be more controversial on Capitol Hill than regulations or taxes designed to limit emissions would be foreign aid programs to do so.

Finally, there is the issue of how to calculate emissions given China's position at the end stage of a global production chain. Energy policy experts in the UK estimated that in 2005 a full third of Chinese emissions were caused by export industries.[42] As discussed previously, many of those industries are owned by foreigners, much of the value added is enjoyed by foreigners, and all of their products are consumed by them. So in what sense is it fair to count these as Chinese emissions? It would seem rather that advanced economies are outsourcing not just manufacturing but also environmental responsibility to China.

Despite these impressive hurdles, in 2013–2014 several important Sino-American agreements were reached. Both countries pledged to reduce production and consumption of hydrofluorocarbons (HFCs), which are greenhouse gases, and agreed to reduce emissions and improve fuel-efficiency standards for large vehicles.[43] This progress was possible in large part because the effort on HFCs leverages a preexisting international agreement, the Montreal Protocol on protection of ozone, and the agreement on heavy vehicles only requires executive branch adjustment of existing restrictions. Agreements were also reached to improve research on energy-saving innovations such as "smart grids" and emission-reducing innovations such as carbon sequestration following the burning of coal, gestures that carry few near-term costs and could carry significant long-term benefits. In November 2014, at the Asia-Pacific Economic Cooperation (APEC) summit in Beijing, Presidents Obama and Xi Jinping were able to reach an agreement that, if faithfully implemented by the two sides over time, could prove to be a major breakthrough on the issue. The United States pledged to cut overall emissions from a 2005 baseline by between 26 to 28 percent by 2025, while China pledged to cap the growth in emissions around 2030 and to produce at least 20 percent of electricity from noncarbon sources by that year. Not only might the agreement create a foundation for further limits by the two largest emitters but it might also catalyze others to make meaningful commitments during the Paris climate change conference in 2015. In fact, the Europeans already kicked this ball in a positive direction in October 2014 by committing to reduce 1990-level emissions by 40 percent by 2030.

There are reasons to be both optimistic and skeptical about the importance of the U.S.–China agreement in November 2014, but it is hard to dismiss its significance. Anyone who had discussed this issue with Chinese counterparts will appreciate why it was so difficult to gain an explicit Chinese commitment to peak emissions, even if the date for that peak is a disappointing sixteen years in the future. Because energy use affects the overall economy, anything that limits options for energy use will be highly controversial, particularly in a system like China's in which records on job creation affect officials' career promotion. Environmental standards have been introduced in recent years into the promotion files of cadres alongside other measures of performance. There is evidence that Beijing now understands that environmental issues like water and air pollution are potential threats to regime legitimacy and stability. Sounding as much like an American politician as a Chinese one, in 2014 Premier Li Keqiang encouragingly declared a "war on pollution." China had already begun experimenting in seven key cities with a domestic cap and trade system that, if expanded, could serve to limit overall emissions. Even here, however, the common wisdom among experts on Chinese energy and environment is that cap and trade was preferred over a simpler carbon tax in part because well-connected planning bureaucrats will have more room to get rich off corrupt manipulation of the system under the former than the latter.[44]

On the positive side, it should be noted that the new leadership under Xi Jinping and Li Keqiang so far seems committed to both fighting corruption and cleaning up the local environment, in part by reducing the rate of coal consumption, an approach that should also limit to some degree China's massive emission of greenhouse gases.[45] Overall coal consumption in China has reportedly leveled off since the 2000s despite continued economic growth and may even have shrunk slightly in 2013, demonstrating that China might indeed be able to grow economically in the future without burning ever-increasing amounts of coal in the process.[46] And in August 2014 companies in the aforementioned experimental cap and trade zones were fined for exceeding their allotted carbon emissions, suggesting that some level of monitoring and enforcement is indeed taking place, at least in those locations.[47]

But it would constitute a very big change in Chinese Communist Party practices if environmental issues began to trump job creation in cadres' promotion considerations. Moreover, when environmental issues do enter into such calculations, they are much more likely to be local environmental issues that affect Chinese citizens' lives and social stability directly—such as fine-particulate air pollution or water pollution—than they are to be global environmental issues such as greenhouse gas emissions. Fortunately, there is significant overlap between the two types of pollution. Reducing coal burning and using more renewable energy sources, for example, decreases both ground-level fine-particulate pollution and greenhouse gas emissions in the process.

Unfortunately, not all good things go together: limiting some kinds of pollution does not necessarily limit global warming in the process, and some local environmental remedies could actually make the global situation worse. In January 2013 I attended an academic conference in Beijing during the single worst week on record for urban air pollution in China, which is saying a lot: sixteen of the top twenty polluted cities in the world are Chinese.[48] The phenomenon that week has been dubbed "airpocalypse." It took specialized equipment to measure just how bad the air was that week because the intensity of the fine-particle pollutants exceeded the capacity of the normal monitoring equipment. *The Economist* reported that air toxicity in Beijing that month reached levels forty times what the World Health Organization deems safe.[49] In fact, the whole eastern half of the nation seemed shrouded in thick smog. Massive traffic accidents were reported around the country because drivers had trouble seeing oncoming cars even during normal daylight hours. The government was surprisingly open and self-critical in reporting the issues.[50] That experience gave me some hope that perhaps the ground-level air pollution crisis in China would motivate Beijing to address global warming issues at the same time. My hopes were greatly tempered when I returned home and hosted a meeting at Princeton of physical and social scientists wrestling with the issue of China's rise and climate change. One of the scientists, Princeton professor Denise Mauzerall, stunned me when she stated that, all things being equal, the reduction in low-altitude, fine-particulate pollution in China or anywhere else would increase, rather than decrease, global warming. She offered an elegant reason why this was the case: the yellow shroud that one flies through when approaching Chinese airports serves as a reflective parasol for the sun's rays, shooting a good deal of those warming rays back into space. If China tackles ground-level fine-particulate pollution without significantly reducing the overall burning of carbon in the process (think "clean coal"), then the planet might get warmer even faster as that reflective effect will disappear. It occurred to me almost right away and with great sadness that the logical arrows of domestic politics in China point exactly in this direction—Chinese leaders have many incentives to address urban air pollution that sickens its citizens in the near term and few incentives to tackle overall greenhouse gas emissions, which help create jobs.

As discussed at greater length in chapter 8, some methods of reducing urban air pollution, such as increasing the use of renewable energy, also help limit greenhouse gas emissions, while others, such as the production of synthetic natural gas from coal, actually increase those emissions. And the production of such synthetic natural gas is likely to increase very sharply in the next decade, with the increased GHG emissions potentially outstripping all of the gains made by limiting coal burning in and around Chinese cities. This is precisely why China's commitment to peak emissions in the future, as negotiated at the November 2014 APEC summit, is potentially so significant. If faithfully implemented, the cap on overall emissions will greatly reduce the incentives to address future local urban pollution from coal burning by adopting even higher carbon-intensive solutions like synthetic natural gas.

Unfortunately, this agreement and any follow-on agreement in which China might participate will be difficult to verify. This is not just a technical problem but a political one. The scholar and former National

Security Council official Kenneth Lieberthal reports that when Premier Wen Jiabao suggested potential compromise with U.S. demands on verification at the 2009 Copenhagen conference on climate change, his concession apparently sparked a rare instance of public dissension in the Chinese ranks.[51] Moreover, the Chinese state is poorly structured for tasks such as environmental monitoring. The central government often has insufficient reach to the local level to enforce national policy. Perhaps more important, the environmental regulators at every level of government are generally outranked within the single Party state by the powerful cadres that control important polluting industries like energy companies and steel manufacturers. The courts themselves are run by judges who are Party members and would likely provide little real relief to even the most conscientious regulators.[52]

Without significant government reforms, therefore, Chinese regulators are less likely to be successful in limiting the growth of greenhouse gas emissions and may not even be able to collect credible data on the emissions. Powerful actors will have a strong incentive to hide their emissions and even their coal purchases from Chinese regulators. Given the particularly strong historical allergy in China to ceding sovereignty to foreigners and the inbred lack of transparency of a fifth-generation Leninist political system, it seems very unlikely that China would cede monitoring to foreigners. In fact, the Chinese government has complained strenuously about the U.S. Embassy's online publication of the pollution levels in Beijing. China's posture in Lima, Peru, at the first international climate meeting following the November 2014 APEC summit suggests that Beijing will continue to oppose requirements for international verification of individual states' commitments to limit greenhouse gas emissions.[53]

The Global Economy

IN ADDRESSING THE CAUSES of the Great Depression, the scholar Charles Kindleberger focused on the lack of crisis leadership by the world's leading economies, especially the United States, in the late 1920s. He pointed to the need for the leading state or states to be the "lender of last resort" to countries in financial distress and to maintain open markets for distress goods from countries in crisis even though the global downturn makes protectionism tempting. Kindleberger was calling on countries like the United States to think long-term in future crises and to think broadly about the health of the entire system, not just their own short-term national interests.[54] For reasons discussed above, it will be difficult to encourage China to adopt such farsighted measures to provide long-term support for the international economy unless those same measures also directly serve the interests of China's own economic growth in the near term. So, unfortunately, China is unlikely to provide the kind of responsible leadership Kindleberger calls for.

That having been said, China has been more responsible and supportive of the current international system than its detractors have allowed. Fortunately, achieving coordination with China on trade and finance might be more feasible than in other areas. China has already done more than most developing economies to open itself up to international trade and investment and thereby, as scholar Edward Steinfeld puts it, to "play by our rules." Moreover, like other major economies in the G20, China launched a large stimulus package following the outbreak of the financial crisis in 2008. In fact, when one considers its size in relation to GDP, China's stimulus package was much bigger than its American and European counterparts. And China has been the main engine of growth for the world since 2008, something that benefits everyone.

In the United States, many observers use an unhelpful measure when they accuse China of economic irresponsibility: the unprecedented bilateral trade deficit between the United States and China. That deficit usually runs well over $200 billion per year. But economists generally lend little importance to bilateral trade deficits; they are considered the natural result of the distribution of comparative advantage around the world. Countries will naturally have a mix of bilateral deficits and surpluses with various countries. Instead, economists are interested in whether a country has a persistent current account surplus or deficit with the entire world. If there is a large percentage of GDP on either side of the ledger, this could be bad for the long-term health of the economy in question. Stated in its simplest form, countries like the United States with large current account deficits consume too much in comparison to what they produce, and countries like China with persistent current account surpluses are consuming too little in comparison with production. Especially if the economy in question is large enough, its domestic condition can have negative implications for the international system.

Particularly in the mid-2000s, China was running a large and growing current account surplus with the world. For example, its current account surplus in 2006 was $232 billion USD, about 8 percent of GDP.[55] One of several culprits behind this lack of balance was the value of the Chinese currency on the international market. The exchange rate in China is determined by the government. Normally, when a currency floats on the international market alongside others, a large current account surplus would lead to an increase in the value of the currency in that country. This did not seem to be happening because Chinese government officials were taking steps to prevent it, most notably by planting a good part of the surpluses abroad in U.S. Treasury bonds. A major goal of this effort was to keep Chinese exports and domestic industries competitive against foreign competition. A stronger currency makes a nation's exports less competitive internationally and renders imports more competitive at home. So critics like Paul Krugman charged that China, by suppressing the value of the Chinese RMB, was preying on U.S. workers by selling underpriced products into the U.S. market.[56]

The Chinese practice of sterilizing its surpluses was also seen as distorting to international capital markets, holding down not only inflation through underpriced manufactured goods but also borrowing rates for governments, corporations, and individuals alike in the United States, who were then enabled to continue down the path of long-term fiscal and financial irresponsibility without near-term costs. Governments found it cheaper and easier to run larger deficits, and banks and homeowners were more willing to be involved in risky mortgage schemes that fueled the housing bubble.

Analysts and U.S. government officials at the time were right to criticize China for running such large current account surpluses and for failing to allow its currency to revalue. But the reasoning was different than was often found in the public media. The real problem for the United States was not that an undervalued Chinese currency was stealing U.S. jobs through competition from Chinese imports. The products that China was making for the U.S. market were extremely unlikely to be made in the United States again. If revaluation stripped China of its competitive edge, the manufacturers who would benefit would much more likely be in Vietnam, Indonesia, and India than in Ohio and North Carolina. However, by maintaining an artificially undervalued currency, Beijing was making U.S. exports to China artificially expensive for Chinese consumers and limiting the market for U.S. products in China. This effect is easy to demonstrate. China's currency did begin to revalue against the U.S. dollar in 2005 (and eventually revalued a total of 30 percent from 2007 to 2012). U.S. exports to China grew much faster than U.S. imports from China in that same period (exports to China grew 168 percent, while imports from China grew 75 percent).[57]

This was a real and positive effect for U.S. workers. But China's currency value was routinely overblown by critics of China and critics of the U.S.–China relationship. One reason is the transnational production chain discussed previously. Whatever value China's currency is pegged at, that value will affect China's imports and exports. Yes, China is an exporting behemoth, but it is also a major importer of parts and materials for that exporting sector. An undervalued currency might make the final export products cheaper, but it artificially raises the cost of the imported parts that go into those same products. So globalization considerably offsets the final price advantage that China enjoyed from undervaluing its currency.

Various factors have contributed to the mitigation of the current account surplus problem since 2006: international negotiations with the United States and others; the realization in Chinese elite circles that persistent current account surpluses were unhealthy for China itself; rising wages in China that decrease Chinese export competitiveness and increase the market for imports; and China's recognition during the financial crisis that export markets could dry up in a hurry and that it needs to adjust its economy to emphasize domestic consumption as a source of future growth. China's current account surplus had dropped to a reasonable 2.3 percent of GDP in 2012.[58]

The transition in the Chinese economy to emphasize consumption is difficult and growth is also appreciably slowing. It is interesting to note that a commentator like Paul Krugman, who years earlier had painted China's economy as predatory on the U.S. worker, now worries about the slowing of the Chinese economy and the negative impact that this will have on global growth, including in the United States. In July 2013 he wrote, "No doubt many readers are feeling some intellectual whiplash. Just the other day we were afraid of the Chinese. Now, we are afraid for them."[59] Readers like me had always regarded his earlier zero-sum analyses of U.S.–China economic relations as misguided. But his transformation is worth noting. When even Paul Krugman worries about a Chinese slow-down, it shows that Henry Paulson's diplomatic efforts in 2006 with the Strategic Economic Dialogue were actually quite farsighted. There is a clear lesson here: before we worry ourselves about Chinese economic growth, it might be best to consider the implications of Chinese stagnation!

China, the IMF, and the G20

CONSISTENT WITH SECRETARY PAULSON'S general take on U.S.–China economic relations and Deputy Secretary Zoellick's call for China to be a responsible stakeholder, the Bush administration pushed hard to include China as a significant player in international economic institutions. The United States and other leading economies in the Group of 8 (G8) invited China and several other economies into the expanded G20. China was also invited into the Major Economies initiative, which was launched in Washington in 2008. That grouping wrestled with climate change issues, among others. Finally, the United States urged China to contribute more to and take more responsibility in the IMF and World Bank. This push would produce fruit during the Obama administration. At the 2010 meeting of the G20 regarding the ongoing financial crisis, Beijing was promised a future increase in IMF voting rights, the third increase in as many meetings. Once ratified in member states, the deal would move China from sixth to third, just behind the United States and Japan, in the organization's structure of authority.[60] In 2012, along with other BRICS countries, Beijing took steps to bolster IMF emergency funds in the face of the European crisis. But the scope of the measures are not anywhere near the leadership role envisioned by Kindleberger, who, in any case, could not have imagined an authoritarian developing country as the world's largest economy—nor, most likely, that the largest advanced economy, the United States, would be in such heavy debt.

The hopes and realities related to China's role in the financial and fiscal crisis in Greece offers a good illustration of why it will be difficult for a developing country like China to play the role of lender of last resort. In February and August 2012, during the height of the crisis, Premier Wen Jiabao met with German Chancellor Angela Merkel. There was some hope in Europe and elsewhere that China might be willing to use its sizable reserves to bail Greece out and thereby stabilize the EU, which as a corporate whole constitutes China's largest trading partner and a major source of incoming FDI. After the crisis broke, the decline of exports to the continent cost China many thousands of jobs. Wen Jiabao instead reportedly made a less dramatic and much less risky commitment, promising abstractly to continue to purchase euro bonds for China's foreign exchange portfolio and offering some limited funds through the IMF for emergency lending, but only if those loans were fully guaranteed.[61]

Before the reader jumps to conclusions about China's lack of responsibility in the crisis, consider the following. For all of its fiscal and economic problems, on a per capita basis, Greece is much richer than China (China's GDP per capita in 2012 was $9,300 compared to Greece's at $24,900).[62] Moreover, many of Greece's fiscal problems could be pinned on profligate government spending on social welfare (it is fascinating to me that Wen, a Communist, was calling on the Europeans to practice fiscal austerity!). One influential Chinese newspaper reported in November 2011 that "countries like Greece are spendthrift even when they are heavily indebted. It is said that employees of public sectors of Greece have an annual salary of 14 months, which is guaranteed by the constitution. After retirement they could still receive a 14-month pension in a year, and they are entitled to paid annual leave of at least one month. What is more, many people get off work at 2:30 p.m. for seven months of the year. Half of the budget of Greece is used to pay income and welfare for civil servants, and the number of civil servants in Greece is five times that of Britain."[63] How could Premier Wen justify to Chinese citizens an offer to bail out such a system when China's own social safety net is nascent at best?

One Chinese blogger summed up a common Chinese view by saying that Europeans were trying to "use the money earned from the blood and toil of common Chinese (*laobaixing*) to rescue Europe from the debt crisis so as to allow Europeans to continue living in ease and comfort (*yangzunchuyou*)."[64] The popular nationalistic Chinese newspaper *Global Times* ran a news article in November 2012 in which Australian Prime Minister Gillard is quoted as calling on China to "make a contribution" (*zuo gongxian*) to resolving the European debt crisis, saying that China has a "responsibility" (*you zeren*) to work together with other states to promote global economic expansion and to create job opportunities. An online readers' poll regarding the piece garnered 2,327 responses. The poll offered various emoticons from which readers could choose with labels to describe the emotion. By far the most common reaction to the article (1,974 respondents) was that it was "laughable" (*ke xiao*). In second place, at 246 responses, was "infuriating" (*jinu*).[65] Of course, a reader's poll in a nationalist newspaper does not fairly represent public opinion. But it may represent the people most likely to hit the streets first if the government is seen as overly accommodating to outside powers. A more scientific poll of public opinion, the Beijing Area Survey, shows that foreign aid is not popular in China, even though the bulk of it appropriately goes to the developing world (just over half goes to Africa alone). The plurality of those who expressed an opinion wanted to cut foreign aid (42 percent) and outstripped those who wanted to increase it by almost two to one. One can only imagine how much more dramatic the difference would be if the question was asked about financial support for a country like Greece with a significantly higher per capita GNP than China. The only area in which respondents were less approving of expenditure increases than foreign aid was increased salaries for Chinese government officials![66] It is in this domestic environment that Chinese leaders must decide whether to use China's foreign exchange reserves to play the role of responsible stakeholder.

Even China's impressive domestic stimulus package, arguably its greatest contribution to addressing the global financial crisis, has problems from a global perspective. While maintaining that Chinese growth was essential to global recovery, Beijing has used its stimulus money in a way that favors its more traditional and least efficient economic sectors. Moreover, during the crisis Beijing intensified a preexisting drive to create "indigenous innovation" in Chinese industry. That nativist effort runs against globalization and alienates many foreign businesses and investors. As a result, the Americans and Europeans who are normally the biggest lobbyists in their home countries for positive relations with China have complained to their governments that the program discriminates against their firms and aims to transfer their valuable intellectual property to wholly owned Chinese competitors. Also, and perhaps most ironic, the stimulus package might slow long-term growth because the fervor with which it was implemented, particularly at the local level in China, may have created a series of bad loans, unnecessary infrastructure projects, and real estate bubbles.[67]

None of this is to suggest that China is somehow rewriting the rules of the international economy, but rather that Beijing's stimulus is not the progressive, cooperative, and farsighted effort to bolster the global economy that Chinese diplomats sometimes claim. It seems more a bold and significant effort to bolster domestic job creation in China, even if that means alienating foreign businesses and flouting international trade norms in the process. And some of the Chinese efforts to create jobs at home run against other global governance goals, like encouraging the widespread development of more green production technologies. For example, the efforts by China to force global technological innovators in fields like clean energy to transfer technology to Chinese firms as the price of admission to the Chinese market are not so much the creation of a new international trading system as an apparent violation of the existing one. An April 2011 report of the Institute for Policy Innovation criticizes the Indigenous Innovation program's "attempt to make the transfer of key intellectual property and technological know-how part of the price of the access to its market . . . Not only is this very questionable trade policy and possibly inconsistent with China's commitments to the World Trade Organization . . . it poses one of the biggest threats to the development and diffusion of clean technology to China—a country that desperately needs it." The report continues by stating that in international negotiations on climate change, China also adopts a stance typical of developing countries and rejected by the leading advanced economies that there needs to be a patent-free environment for the transfer of green technologies.[68] The problem, of course, is the classic one. If firms do not enjoy enforceable patents for their innovations, they have little incentive to invest in research and development to create those innovations in the first place.

A second form of Chinese free-riding that has hurt the prospects for the development of greener energy is China's alleged heavy subsidies to solar panel manufacturers. China has been accused in both the European Union and the United States of dumping underpriced solar panels in those markets to squeeze out competition. To the degree that this destroys panel producers in those countries, this is obviously bad for the long-run competition and pricing in that industry. When Europe announced planned tariffs of 47 percent on Chinese solar panels, cells, and wafers in mid-2013 in retaliation, China suggested it might retaliate against the European wine industry, with negative repercussions for Italy and France. Even the biggest victim of Chinese dumping within the EU, Germany, was reluctant to level tariffs because of potential retaliation by China against German machine exports. As a result, the two sides were able to settle the dispute several weeks later in terms considered largely favorable to Chinese manufacturers. Keith Bradsher at the *New York Times* reported that "while Brussels might have had a very strong case in terms of the law or economics, it was fatally weak from the beginning at the political level. Those political weaknesses increased as China's leaders . . . lobbied aggressively to divide Europe on the issue."[69] When the United States slapped tariffs of 24 to 36 percent on Chinese solar panel producers in fall 2012, China retaliated by raising tariffs on American producers of raw materials used in panel manufacturing that are sold by the United States to China.[70] If such mutual retaliation were to persist and escalate, this would have a negative impact on the solar industry. The huge effect of China's fast-paced entry into the U.S. market was demonstrated in reverse when U.S. tariffs put in place in 2014 almost instantly impacted the structure of the U.S. market for non-Chinese solar panel producers, reviving the prospects of American and European businesses that seemed on the eve of extinction.[71]

Chinese subsidies and alleged dumping pose another problem that could undermine government efforts to address global warming. Even when solar panels are at their cheapest for the consumer, solar energy is still much less economically efficient than the burning of fossil fuels. But solar energy has what economists call "positive externalities," or benefits to society outside of the direct economic activity involved, in this case cleaner air and the ability to add electricity to the grid on the hottest days when brownouts from air conditioning are common. It may make good policy sense for governments in advanced countries to subsidize the use of solar energy over dirtier forms of energy, as they have in many places. These subsidies have been quite effective in Germany, for example. Generally gray and overcast Germany is now by far the largest producer of solar energy on the planet. But subsidies require political backing, and nothing helps gain political backing in a democracy more than job creation. So when President Obama talks about green technologies, he talks about jobs. To continually get legislatures to support subsidies, it is very useful to have a concentrated lobby of workers and business owners who will directly benefit from the subsidies and lobby hard for them. In the case of Germany, the relevant lobby would be the owners and workers of existing solar panel producers, who had been quite successful until the early part of the 2010s, when Chinese firms began dominating the global market for panels (in 2013 China enjoyed a full 67 percent of the global market share). Several of the leading German manufacturers have been driven out of business by apparently underpriced Chinese panels since 2011 and some 24,000 German jobs were lost in the industry.[72] Politicians in Germany who support green energy will likely lose political clout in their efforts to secure subsidies and the subsidies will likely decrease. By subsidizing its producers to create market share for infant industries and, in the process, violating the spirit, if not the letter, of WTO trade regulations, China is behaving not like a leader in the global economic system, but like a typical developing country. From the dawn of the industrial revolution, such countries have tried to assist their infant industries through tariff protection and subsidies. But China is such a huge developing country and the world economy is now so interconnected that China's behavior has global consequences for other countries' economies and, in this case, for the effort to address global warming.

Investment and Aid in the Developing World

THE UNITED STATES government has tried hard and with little success to develop a robust aid and investment dialogue with China regarding the developing world. The goal was to foster better understanding of China's programs and policies for the purpose of increasing coordination between Chinese efforts and the efforts of the other major donors. We proposed this idea on several occasions during the Bush administration's second term. We approached the Ministry of Commerce, then under Bo Xilai, who later fell spectacularly from the Party's grace as the Party Chief of Chongqing. We knew that the Foreign Ministry was not nearly as influential on these issues as the Ministry of Commerce, the Finance Ministry, and the national oil companies, among others. But we did not get far. Despite abstractly positive and encouraging statements from its top officials about eventually holding a serious dialogue on these topics, the Ministry of Commerce appeared to be dragging its feet to prevent a high-level dialogue from occurring. In our meetings in 2008 they responded positively to our proposals but then cited the distractions of the Olympics, the Sichuan earthquake, and the typhoon in Burma as filling the ministry's bandwidth for the coming months. My impression was that the diplomats in the Foreign Ministry were often more eager to hold such interagency talks than their colleagues at Commerce. I wondered if that were true because, by attending such a dialogue, they themselves could get a better grasp than they currently had on Chinese business activities abroad. Those activities frequently have a major impact on China's foreign relations, but the diplomats often have little understanding of them, let alone influence over them.

The goal of this effort was not to criticize or check Chinese economic activities in the developing world but rather to create the preconditions for better coordination between the efforts of China, the IMF/World

Bank, and the major aid donors. Under the Millenium Challenge initiatives, those donors had begun a constructive and successful program of linking aid to improvements in governance, particularly in sub-Saharan Africa. China's aid, offered without political conditions, could undercut those efforts, as in the case of a conditional $2 billion IMF loan package offered to Angola in 2004. Improvement in economic transparency in that corrupt and war-torn country was one of the key IMF conditions for the loan. China offered an unconditional oil-backed loan package of the same amount. Angola's government, unsurprisingly, chose the latter. But such directly competitive instances are the rare exception, not the rule. And, as Deborah Brautigam lays out in her excellent book on China's economic activity in Africa, *The Dragon's Gift*, even the 2004 Angola case is more complicated than a simple tale of IMF good and Chinese evil.[73] The costs of lack of coordination between China and other donors are real, but they are best viewed as opportunity costs: the lost chance to pool our efforts in maximally efficient ways so that we could get more bang for the assistance buck—in terms of both creating better development projects and encouraging better governance in the process of creating them. More abstractly, successful joint efforts in development projects in lands distant from both China and the United States would be precisely the kind of project on which the two countries could begin to build a stronger appreciation of their common interests and a stronger foundation for overall bilateral trust.

In what was nascent progress along these lines during the Bush administration, U.S. ambassadors in Ethiopia and Angola had exchanges with their Chinese counterparts on agricultural development projects. In Angola they even agreed to some pilot cooperative efforts. But, as discussed above, China did not seem eager to deepen these relationships at the time. In what might demonstrate a breakthrough in Chinese attitudes toward Sino-American development cooperation under President Xi, in 2013 Beijing proposed greater cooperation with the United States on development aid in Africa, including joint financing and construction of a large dam in the Democratic Republic of Congo. These topics were reportedly discussed during the July 2014 Strategic and Economic Dialogue in Beijing. The Obama administration does not seem as eager as its predecessor to pursue such cooperative efforts with Beijing, so it is still unclear if the Chinese outreach will produce positive results or just more distrust.[74]

Peacekeeping and Humanitarian Intervention

BEIJING VIEWS WITH DEEP SUSPICION one of the great projects of the post–Cold War international system: multilateral humanitarian intervention. In the year following the collapse of the Soviet Union, the United States and others sent an intervention force into Somalia to end the massive famine that had been caused by chaotic fighting among warlord groups and the strategic use of access to food by those combatants.

Washington also played a leading role alongside European states in Bosnia and Kosovo during the Clinton administration. And after an initial expressed allergy to "state-building," the George W. Bush administration would embrace interventionist missions with gusto following the 9/11 attacks. In 2005 the United States would strongly support the effort at the United Nations to ratify a new norm—the Responsibility to Protect—which requires states not only to avoid perpetrating international and domestic crimes against humanity but also to prevent them from happening inside their borders even if the state is not the primary perpetrator. President Obama furthered the trend. Early in his first term, the United States harshly criticized Iranian authorities when protestors were shot and candidates persecuted in the lead-up to the 2009 national election. In early 2011, the United States supported the Arab Spring in Tunisia and, after some reluctance to abandon long-term U.S. ally Hosni Mubarak, in Egypt as well. Washington then pressured Libya's leader Muammar Qaddafi to cease and desist from repressive violence against his domestic opponents and ultimately intervened with the Europeans to support local forces to overthrow his regime. When the Arab Spring came to Syria in the form of civil protest and domestic violence, the Obama administration demanded that Bashar Hafez al-Assad's government step down from power and attempted to create international pressure at the UN to sanction that regime.

Beijing does not like this post–Cold War trend one bit. Sanctions and interventions against the will of sovereign states in the developing world run against China's post-1978 domestic and international ideology. China has been the target of international sanctions following the massacre of the Tiananmen protestors on June 4, 1989, and various actors have threatened China with sanctions on other human rights issues. In the years immediately after Tiananmen, Beijing used postcolonial ideological stances to explain to the Chinese people that the Tiananmen sanctions, many of which have subsequently been lifted, were illegal and unwarranted interference in China's internal affairs. When I was a graduate student based at Peking University in 1990, I recall clearly how CCP propagandists claimed that the advocates of sanctions had ulterior motives designed to repress China. They were accused of using "peaceful evolution" (*heping yanbian*) to make China less stable at home and more culturally "Western." Chinese advocates of liberal democracy were branded dupes or even agents of this international conspiracy and were accused of "total Westernization" (*quanmian xifanghua*). In this narrative, the real goal of international pressure was not the promotion of "so-called human rights" but the subjugation of China in a Western-dominated international order. With that recent experience of sanctions, China has been very reluctant to sanction other sovereign states on such grounds, let alone allow UN-backed military intervention for the purpose of furthering humanitarian or security goals.

That having been said, it would be grossly unfair to say that China does not contribute to the stabilization of countries in crisis. After all, China is by far the biggest contributor to UN Peacekeeping Operations (PKO) and stabilization operations in the UN Security Council. With some 2,000 PKO troops deployed to a wide variety of missions at any time, China contributes more than the other four permanent members of the Security Council combined. Until it agreed to deploy "blue helmets" to Mali in 2013, China had never agreed to send combat troops to PKO or stabilization missions.[75] But China still lost fourteen peacekeeping and stabilization personnel in incidents such as Israeli air strikes in Lebanon and the earthquake in Haiti.[76] China even trains large numbers of other countries' peacekeepers in an impressive facility outside of Beijing that I had occasion to visit in 2010.

As we will see in chapters 6 through 8, China tries to take a traditional political approach to these missions, generally sending troops when their deployment is blessed not only by the United Nations but also by the home government in the nation in question. By creating those preconditions and carefully using its power at the UN Security Council to enforce them, China is able to use its PKO role to check all of the important boxes in the PRC's self-generated national identity: a responsible great power (*fu zeren daguo*); a leader of the developing world; and a postcolonial state with a deep respect for sovereignty. Through PKO operations and the resulting rhetoric, as the scholar Courtney J. Richardson writes, "China is able to be part of the international system, while remaining somewhat aloof from Western notions of the so-called 'international community.' China presents itself as a non-Western, non-imperialist developing state that is a permanent member of the Security Council, able to fund missions and deploy high-value 'enabler units' (engineering, logistics and medical teams)."[77]

China's diplomatic posture toward intervention poses a problem for the United States, European nations, Japan, and other like-minded states. Many times, enforcement of the norms that were eventually embodied in the Responsibility to Protect (R2P) requires action without the permission of the central governments in target states, who are often culpable of either negligence toward or direct involvement in humanitarian crimes. So, for example, China's reluctance or outright refusal to support sanctions, let alone an intervention, in Syria poses great challenges for supporters of a robust interpretation of R2P toward the Assad regime in Damascus. Since China, like Russia, can veto any draft resolution of which it disapproves, states wanting to take action must choose either to circumvent the United Nations altogether, as the United States and NATO did initially in Bosnia and Kosovo, or to try to convince the PRC to find workarounds for its normal reservations by supporting or abstaining when draft resolutions are presented. China's record is mixed on UN interventions. For example, China took surprisingly proactive internationalist positions in Darfur in 2006–2007, the Gulf of Aden in 2008, and Libya in 2011, but adopted a more traditional position on several occasions, actively obstructing UN actions in Zimbabwe, Burma, and Syria. It appears that when one of two conditions are met, China will be more likely to support UN action, or at least stand aside and let it happen: if China and other actors can persuade the central authorities in the target states to acquiesce to UN intervention (e.g., Sudan Darfur) or if those authorities can be portrayed as having totally lost control of their own nation (e.g., Somalia in 1992).

ONE CAN VIEW the glass as one-third full or two-thirds empty on U.S. efforts to get China to play the role of responsible stakeholder on global governance issues. For reasons that will be made clear in the next three chapters, the informed reader should see the glass in both ways. By analyzing and understanding the progress made and setbacks suffered by the United States and the international community in encouraging constructive and assertive behavior by China on a range of global issues, we can have a better sense of how best to manage diplomacy with this developing giant.

PART II

SHAPING CHINA'S CHOICES

CHAPTER 6

The Soviet Collapse
and China's Rise, 1991–2000

THE NEXT THREE CHAPTERS will discuss how the United States has managed the challenges of a rising China since the end of the Cold War. The picture is mixed and the results far from satisfying, but I think it is fair to say that there has been more success than failure, more cooperation than conflict, and more coordination than discord. Whether that record can continue is an open question. In the past few years, China has grown more insecure at home and has rubbed up more frequently and more abrasively against neighbors. And at the same time, China has been asked to do more than ever before to contribute to global governance on economic, environmental, and security issues.

The Administration of George H. W. Bush:
Tiananmen and the End of the Cold War

U.S.–CHINA RELATIONS WERE already tense when the Soviet Union collapsed in 1991. The violent crackdown on peaceful pro-democracy protestors at Tiananmen on June 4, 1989, had put China's relations with the United States in a deep chill for the first time since Nixon's visit in 1972. In response to the massacre, the administration of President George H. W. Bush and many like-minded states joined in sanctions against the Chinese government, particularly targeting arms sales and cooperation with the Chinese military. The Chinese Communist Party, shaken deeply by internal divisions and an obvious legitimacy crisis, fell back on a narrative that further worsened U.S.–China relations. The "instability" in Beijing in June 1989 was attributed to Western anti-China forces and the Chinese dupes who had become their fifth column. True patriots, so the story went, would understand that single-party rule under the CCP was the best protector of China's national interest. Those seeking to undermine CCP rule through political reform were portrayed as misguided or, worse still, guided by foreigners.

The 1980s had been the apex of U.S.–China strategic cooperation, as Deng's PRC and the United States under Ronald Reagan aligned themselves, albeit informally, against the USSR. For all the talk of an independent Chinese foreign policy in the Cold War from 1982–1989, China and the United States both actively opposed the Soviet occupation of Afghanistan and cooperated in arming the anti-Soviet forces there; they also cooperated in the intelligence arena to check the expansion of Soviet power. Generic admonitions against hegemony in CCP propaganda could have been targeting both superpowers but, until 1989, were really only targeting the Soviets. One of the best indicators of China's leaning to the U.S. side during the Cold War is that Beijing even accepted and actually encouraged a moderate strengthening of the Japanese military in this period, knowing that the U.S.–Japan alliance was the strongest bulwark against growing Soviet military presence in the Pacific.[1]

In the late 1980s, Mikhail Gorbachev appeared to leaders in the United States, western Europe, and China to depart in several important ways from his predecessors. The United States and NATO allies appreciated his desire to improve relations across the Iron Curtain in Europe, to pursue serious arms control negotiations, and to experiment with serious domestic political reforms in the USSR. Gorbachev also seemed to be responding to Beijing's own concerns about the Soviet Union's activities on China's periphery. In the early 1980s, Deng had articulated for Gorbachev's predecessors three "obstacles" to improved Sino-Soviet relations; by 1989 Gorbachev had removed them all: reducing dozens of Soviet divisions deployed along China's border; withdrawing the Soviet military from Afghanistan; and ceasing Soviet support for Vietnam's invasion of Cambodia. Meeting those preconditions enabled the first Sino-Soviet summit in decades, with Gorbachev traveling to Beijing on China's terms in May 1989. But because he also pushed political reform—*perestroika*—at home and permitted democratization in the Soviet's Eastern European empire, the CCP elites privately considered Gorbachev a madman.

Perhaps most frustrating to Beijing was the catalytic effect that Gorbachev had on the exploding democracy movement in China. When he arrived in Beijing, the streets were already filled with protestors who had begun their campaign following the April 1989 death of deposed General Secretary Hu Yaobang. Hu was widely viewed by students as an advocate for political reform, and his death provided an occasion to compare him favorably to the surviving leadership of the Party. Gorbachev's visit, which should have been a crowning diplomatic achievement for Deng, only energized the prodemocracy movement and gave the protestors a reference point to which they could compare good, proreform Communists (Gorbachev) against bad, conservative ones (the top CCP leaders like Premier Li Peng and Deng himself). Finally, the Gorbachev summit brought the international media to Beijing in droves. The media then became enthralled with the protest movement and was in place to broadcast its violent demise at the hands of PLA armored divisions. Gorbachev's foreign policy reduced the national security threat to China, but his domestic policies created a much larger security problem for Beijing by calling into question the legitimacy of the CCP. Since, for the CCP, security has always started at home, Gorbachev was much more trouble than he was worth.

The Tiananmen protests and the Tiananmen massacre all occurred in the first six months of the administration of George H. W. Bush. Bush entered office with a significant background in the country as President Richard Nixon's first envoy to Beijing after Nixon's and Kissinger's groundbreaking trips to China in 1971–1972. A moderate Republican who had achieved cooperation with Beijing in the past, Bush resisted domestic cries to withdraw the U.S. Embassy and break economic ties with China. Instead he sent his national security advisor for secret meetings with Deng Xiaoping in a way that violated the spirit of congressional resolutions barring such high-level contacts. The trip quickly leaked to the press and created a firestorm back home.

While Bush approved of some sanctions against China, including those against the PLA, he did not want to sever the overall U.S.–China economic and political relationship, which he presciently predicted would be much more important in the future than it had been even in the second half of the Cold War. He consistently vetoed bills that would have canceled China's most favored nation (MFN) status in trade, preventing a feeding frenzy in Congress with representatives from various districts seeking to protect their local industries and workers with new trade obstacles. After the veto, Bush strategically used the prospect of successful congressional override votes to extract human rights concessions from the Chinese. In this way Bush played the good cop to Congress's bad cop, telling the Chinese that he needed their help in preventing a supermajority from forming in Congress against his vetoes. This hardly emptied the political prisons in China, but it did help win the release of a small number of prominent dissidents to America.

U.S.–China relations held steady for the rest of Bush's first and only term. His very able envoy, Ambassador James Lilley, struggled to maintain high-level contacts with the Chinese government while affirming U.S. values. By sheltering Chinese dissident physicist Fang Lizhi for months at the U.S. Embassy in Beijing, Lilley caused great frustration among CCP elites.[2] The war in Iraq in 1990–1991 and the democratic revolutions in Eastern Europe would preoccupy the Bush administration for the remainder of its time in office. And, in December 1991, the Soviet Union dissolved.

The disintegration of the Soviet empire transformed international politics and had profound impacts on Chinese domestic politics and U.S.–China relations. Not only did the end of Communism in the Soviet Union and Eastern Europe exacerbate the Chinese Communists' concern about domestic legitimacy, but it also accelerated globalization because capital and communication technologies flowed into formerly closed economies and societies. As capitalism prevailed over Communism, the end of the twentieth century and the beginning of the twenty-first was an uncomfortable time to sustain Communist Party rule anywhere, especially in a place moving so quickly toward global integration as China.

Two events occurred in the last months of the George H. W. Bush administration that deserve our attention, since the problems they created would be inherited by his successor, Bill Clinton. Just before the 1992 election, President Bush notified Congress of the government's intention to sell 150 F-16 fighter jets to Taiwan. Then, in December 1992, President Bush deployed U.S. troops to Somalia, taking the lead in the first UN-backed humanitarian intervention of the post–Cold War era.

The Sale of F-16s to Taiwan

THE DISAPPEARANCE OF the common Soviet threat simultaneously elevated and demoted China in the United States diplomatic portfolio. As a potential great power, China gained new importance. But without the common Soviet adversary that had underpinned the U.S.–China relationship, China was no longer such a key component of America's international strategy. In other words, China was less likely to be ignored by the United States, but it was now more likely to be targeted, particularly if Beijing were to behave coercively toward its neighbors. From Beijing's perspective, the shared Soviet threat kept the United States from creating difficulties for the PRC in its relations with Taiwan. The Soviet threat had also justified the strengthening of the U.S. alliance system in Asia to Chinese officials, in ways that would be less acceptable to Beijing once that threat disappeared.

It was in this context that the U.S. government announced the sale of 150 F-16 fighter jets to Taiwan in late 1992. The sale was approved for a combination of domestic and strategic reasons. The planes were made in Texas, a major swing state in pre-electoral polling in the 1992 presidential election. Post–Soviet Russia had become an arms bazaar. The U.S. government knew that China had placed a large order for advanced Su-27 fighters in Moscow. More abstractly, some in the administration, including Ambassador Lilley, who had served in Taiwan as well, wanted to establish a precedent. A 1982 U.S.–China communiqué had declared that the United States intended to reduce its arms sales to Taiwan over time in both quantity and quality. Lilley and others felt that the communiqué should not prevent the United States from fulfilling its commitment under the April 1979 Taiwan Relations Act to provide sufficient defensive arms to Taiwan.[3] (That act also called on the president to maintain sufficient U.S. military capabilities to come to Taiwan's aid should the president choose to intervene in a conflict across the Taiwan Strait.) The Chinese leadership had read the 1982 communiqué to mean that the United States was committed to reducing and eventually ending arms sales to Taiwan. That interpretation has solid grounding in the text but ignores wiggle words implying that the reduction in arms sales was contingent on the peaceful resolution of the two sides' policy differences and the expectation that the threat of war would decline along with the arms sales. U.S. officials also leveled lawyerly technical arguments that the F-16s were the most backward fighter made in America at the time and were, therefore, the most appropriate and least provocative replacements for Taiwan's aging fleet of much older F-5 fighters, which the United States no longer produced and which were crashing at a dramatic rate during training drills. In other words, what Beijing understandably saw as a massive upgrade in Taiwan's air force was being portrayed by the United States as somehow consistent with the spirit of the 1982 communiqué.

American administrations from Bush to the present have argued that the 1982 communiqué is only one element in the U.S. "one China" policy that guides Washington's position toward Taiwan and mainland China. The Taiwan Relations Act is another. Beijing argues that domestic law (the Taiwan Relations Act) should never be allowed to trump international agreements (the three U.S.–China communiqués of 1972, 1979, and 1982). With the exception of legally binding, ratified international treaties, a level to which the communiqués do not rise, Americans tend to view the problem the other way around. Domestic law trumps international agreements.

However one interprets or spins this significant upgrade in Taiwan's defense capabilities, the increase in U.S. military support for Taiwan occurred at an inconvenient time for Beijing. In 1992 Taiwan was in the process of democratization that had been launched by Chiang Kai-shek's son, President Chiang Ching-kuo, just before the younger Chiang's death in 1988. The previously banned pro-independence Democratic Progressive Party was legalized and permitted to back candidates for office. Moreover, the traditionally stalwart anti-independence Nationalist Party, dominated by mainland Chinese refugees from the Chinese Civil War in the Chiang dynasty years, had chosen the first native-born Taiwanese president, Lee Teng-hui, as the successor to the younger Chiang. Lee, fluent in Japanese, had actually served briefly in the Japanese imperial army during the Pacific War, when Taiwan was still a Japanese colony. His selection as president called into question whether the Nationalists would remain dedicated to the concept of Taiwan's eventual unification with mainland China.

In addition to bolstering pro-independence sentiment on the island, the democratization process posed challenges for Beijing, since a democratic Taiwan would potentially attract more support from the United States and its regional democratic allies—Japan, Australia, and the newly democratized South Korea. More abstractly, a successful, liberal democracy on "Chinese Taiwan," as mainlanders often describe it, could put the lie to one of the arguments commonly offered for continued CCP authoritarianism on the mainland: multiparty democracy is somehow "Western," and therefore foreign to Chinese culture. If Taiwan were truly Chinese in a way that precluded permanent independence from the Chinese nation, how then could it also be a "Western" liberal democracy? If Taiwan were somehow not truly Chinese, why not allow it to declare independence? By its mere existence, a democratic Taiwan could pose security challenges for the CCP.

Mainland accusations to the contrary, the purpose of U.S. arms sales to Taiwan was not then and is not now to encourage permanent Taiwan independence nor to subvert the regime on mainland China. I can report from my time hosting working level interagency meetings on the topic that arms are sold to Taipei strictly to ensure that Taiwan is secure from a full-scale invasion or a coercive campaign launched by the PRC to force unification with the mainland. Although the United States ended the 1955 U.S.–ROC Defense Treaty with Taipei and severed official diplomatic relations with Taiwan in January 1979 as part of the normalization of U.S.–PRC relations, Washington sustained strong support for its former ally even before Taiwan democratized in the late

1980s. To be sure, Taiwan's democratization bolstered the spirit of the Taiwan Relations Act. What made matters worse from Beijing's perspective was that, with the collapse of the Soviet Union, the PRC lost a common strategic cause with the United States that might serve to restrain Washington in its support for Taiwan. The sale of the F-16s, then, was seen as part and parcel of a broader problem: the possibility that the United States might offer unconditional support to Taiwan, even if the island were to move toward independence.

The post–Cold War environment thus created a major coercive diplomatic challenge for the United States: to demonstrate to the mainland that coercion of Taiwan would be costly and ultimately unsuccessful while simultaneously reassuring Beijing that U.S. defense cooperation with Taiwan and the substantial U.S. military presence in East Asia were not designed to foster permanent Taiwan independence. Such an outcome would be anathema to most Chinese nationalists, but it would be particularly dangerous for the Chinese Communist Party, given the role that defense of national honor plays in the regime's legitimacy.

Somalia and the Rise of Multilateral Interventionism

THE COLLAPSE OF the Cold War created an explosion of multilateral global governance, international humanitarian intervention, and concerns about proliferation of weapons of mass destruction and their delivery systems among weaker states and nonstate actors. As Dr. Joel Wuthnow at the Center for Naval Analysis reports, during the Cold War the two superpowers almost guaranteed deadlock at the United Nations Security Council, which is governed by a single-veto voting system. UN Security Council resolutions were drafted much less frequently at that time, yet the annual average for vetoes was still four times higher before 1990 than after. As domestic political conflicts and regional instability accompanied the collapse of the bipolar Cold War system, occasions for interventions increased. UN watchdog groups like the International Atomic Energy Agency (IAEA) soon gained real traction in monitoring and fighting nuclear proliferation in places like Iraq, Iran, and North Korea. From 1946 to 1989, the UN Security Council passed only eight resolutions invoking Chapter VII, which refers to members' responsibility to "maintain or restore international peace and security." Chapter VII resolutions can enable economic or military action by member states even when target states are not in agreement with the UN. From 1990 to 2011, 511 such resolutions were passed, more than sixty times the Cold War figure, and the number of troops deployed for UN peacekeeping operations more than quintupled in that time frame.[4]

The UN-backed and U.S.-led Somalia intervention in late 1992 was most important for our purposes as a harbinger of the challenges that increasing multilateral humanitarian missions would pose for China and for U.S.–China relations. The PRC assumed China's permanent seat in the United Nations and on the Security Council only in 1971. It kept a relatively low profile in the organization in its first two decades, with two exceptions: Beijing exhibited vigilance toward any state that accorded official status to the government on Taiwan, and it made occasional interventions in the 1970s on behalf of the Non-Aligned Movement or individual third-world states that seemed to be subject to bullying by either superpower or by western European states. The 1980s were a particularly slow period for China at the UN, as the organization was still largely deadlocked between the United States and the Soviet Union on important security issues, and Deng's government wanted to avoid complicating its relations with the United States while it still faced thirty-five to fifty Soviet divisions on its border.[5]

But after the end of the Cold War, the deadlock broke. In the last weeks of 1992, George H. W. Bush was preparing to leave office, having lost the election to Bill Clinton. He had built a reputation for cool-headed, realistic calculations, the kind that helped him broker a peaceful end to the Cold War in Europe and prevented him from driving to Baghdad to overthrow Saddam Hussein after the successful ousting of Iraq from Kuwait in 1991. Many observers were thus surprised that he decided to intervene militarily in Somalia.

In late 1992 the situation in Somalia was dire. Tens of thousands were already dead, with hundreds of thousands more at risk of starvation or hunger-related illness. The world was outraged by the chaos and the systematic use of famine as a weapon by the warring factions there. Humanitarian convoys of the United Nations mission to Somalia (UNOSOM 1) even came under attack in violation of previous ceasefire agreements. The idea of intervention was widely popular at the United Nations, supported by both developed and developing world delegations. Not wanting to stand in the way, Beijing supported UN Security Council Resolution 794 that authorized a UN force (UNITAF) to be led by the United States. But Beijing was clearly nervous about any precedent that the armed intervention in Somalia might create. In his statement explaining the PRC's yes vote, Chinese Ambassador to the UN Li Daoyu labeled Somalia a "unique situation" that, despite China's reservations, still allowed for a Chapter VII armed intervention.[6] Since there was no functioning central government in Somalia to stop the violence and end the famine on its own, and no legitimate government could oppose the UN action, China could vote to affirm without harming its principled stance on respect for sovereignty. From a U.S. perspective, the Chinese vote on Somalia represented progress. As recently as August 1992, China, along with Zimbabwe and India, was one of only three states abstaining from a Chapter VII UN Security Council resolution designed to condemn violations of the ceasefire in the former Yugoslavia and to protect humanitarian convoys heading to Sarajevo in Bosnia and Herzegovina.

China's thought processes on these matters in the early post–Cold War era would be revealed even more clearly three years later when Beijing adopted a similarly negative and skeptical view as the UN Security Council created a rapid reaction force of 12,500 troops to protect UN peacekeepers who might come under fire in Bosnia. China not only abstained, but its ambassador, Qin Huasun, pointedly reminded fellow council members that Beijing held a very restrictive definition of legitimate peacekeeping operations: "A United Nations peacekeeping force, as the name indicates, is for the purpose of keeping peace rather than fighting." Ambassador Qin warned that once a rapid reaction force was deployed, it would "become a party to the conflict."[7] As Wuthnow argues, China was still committed to keeping a low profile at the UN, so it opposed the move only verbally and ultimately abstained on the resolution that created the rapid reaction force.

The Somalia mission inherited in 1993 by President Bush's successor, Bill Clinton, was largely successful in saving tens of thousands if not hundreds of thousands of lives. But it was marred in the end by the death of eighteen U.S. Army Rangers, who were killed on a botched mission hunting one particularly powerful warlord, Mohamed Farrah Aidid. That ferocious battle, in which many more Somalis than Americans were killed, is captured brilliantly in Mark Bowden's best-selling book *Black Hawk Down*. In the United States, for reasons that still befuddle this author, the entire Somali intervention that saved so many lives was labeled a failure because of the deaths of the Rangers. When Rwanda fell into genocidal domestic violence in 1994, the United States and others failed to react because of the legacy of Somalia. President Clinton would apologize for his lack of action after leaving office, and his regret almost certainly steeled his resolve to intervene in Bosnia and Kosovo against humanitarian crimes later in the 1990s. In the end, inaction in Rwanda only fueled the trend of U.S. post–Cold War interventionism that concerns China so greatly.

The Clinton Administration:
From Threats of Sanctions to WTO Accession

GOVERNOR BILL CLINTON'S election campaign had prioritized punishment of Beijing for domestic problems in China over coordination with the PRC on global affairs. Under the banner "It's the economy, stupid," Clinton also criticized President Bush's overall grand strategy as outdated, claiming that it placed too much emphasis on military security in American foreign policy and not enough on job security at home. This approach endangered U.S. relations with Japan, with which the United States had run persistent trade deficits. If military security no longer trumps economics, then pressuring Japan to open up its markets to American products might take precedence over the maintenance of strong alliance relations with Tokyo. After Clinton's successful election campaign and inauguration, it became clear that this rhetoric was not just electoral politics but also his initial strategic vision toward Northeast Asia.

In his entertaining and well-researched book *About Face*, the

journalist James Mann reviews how most U.S. presidents after Richard Nixon reversed themselves once in office by jettisoning tough
campaign rhetoric and adopting a less confrontational China policy.[8]
The Clinton administration would take much longer than others—
almost eighteen months—to make the adjustment. Candidate Clinton, like Candidate Reagan, blasted his predecessor on China policy,
accusing the sitting president of having been too soft on Beijing. In
Reagan's case, the former governor of California promised to restore
diplomatic relations with Taiwan once in office. Not only did he
never carry through with that promise but he agreed to the highly
accommodating August 1982 communiqué that appeared to limit
arms sales to Taiwan at the behest of Beijing.

But Bill Clinton was different. As a candidate, he blasted President
Bush for maintaining high-level contacts with Beijing after the Tianan-
men massacre and for vetoing the congressional cancelation of China's
most favored nation status, which had been Congress's way of protesting
Beijing's human rights abuses. In a debate with the incumbent, he accused
Bush of "coddling" China's authoritarian leaders, whom he labeled for
good alliterative effect "the butchers of Beijing." When he took office in
January 1993, he adopted a confrontational approach toward China on
human rights. Rather than playing good cop to Congress's bad on the
MFN issue, the Clinton administration directly threatened Beijing with
cancelation of the status. Although China's MFN status was renewed in
1993, the president threatened not to do so in 1994 unless substantial
progress was made on human rights. Distancing himself from his predecessor, he stated, "We no longer have an executive branch policy and
a congressional policy. We have an American policy."[9]

More dramatic, perhaps, was the stance taken when Secretary of
State Warren Christopher visited Beijing in March 1994 during the
annual National People's Congress. In a press conference on his plane,
Christopher publicly demanded progress or, he threatened, MFN
would not be renewed in June. Even to a young China scholar like
myself at the time, this in-your-face approach on human rights seemed
at odds with everything I knew about effective diplomacy toward a
country with a postcolonial historical narrative of victimization. Publicly challenging the CCP with threats of sanctions on human rights is

counterproductive. General criticism on human rights grounds is fine, but such criticism should be coupled with calmer, more quiet diplomacy. That diplomacy should focus on how Beijing could help reduce domestic opposition to good bilateral relations in the United States by demonstrating some improvement on human rights, and, most important, it should forward the idea that improved human rights standards would improve, not undercut, long-term stability in Chinese society. I was in Beijing at the time of the Christopher visit, and I recall learning of the secretary's statement in a meeting with a Chinese government scholar and advisor. He asked me in true puzzlement, "What is he doing?" I assumed, wrongly, that my interlocutor must have had bad information.

In meetings back in the United States later that spring, including one lengthy discussion with a senior State Department official, it became clear to me that the administration had realized this was a feckless approach, not only on strategic grounds, but also on human rights grounds. The Chinese government would feel compelled to stand firm under such direct threats for reasons of reputation; further, if the sanctions were actually leveled and U.S.–China economic ties were severely damaged, the resulting downturn would actually harm Chinese human rights conditions. The administration unconditionally renewed China's MFN status in May, to the outrage of human rights activists in the United States.

But the Clinton administration was wise to reverse course. As a State Department official, I used to give talks at chambers of commerce in China. My message to these business leaders was that they were the true U.S. diplomats, the best transmitters of the American message. U.S. companies promote liberal ideals by setting fair labor standards, spreading ideas about life in an American democracy, and providing opportunities to Chinese personnel who might otherwise feel compelled to work in a state-owned enterprise under a Party chief's direct control. To punish conservatives in the Chinese Communist Party by reducing these opportunities for long-term influence seems ill-advised, to say the least. The bottom line is that, however sincere the motivations behind them, U.S. economic sanctions are simply the wrong tool to promote political liberalization in China.

On strategic issues related to coercive diplomacy and the stabiliz-ing role of the U.S. military presence in Northeast Asia, the Clinton administration came into office emphasizing the importance of eco-nomic relations, even with allies like Japan, over security relations. During much of the Cold War, the United States tolerated discrimi-natory Japanese monetary and trade policies for the sake of allowing our ally to strengthen itself as a regional bulwark against Communism. Early in Clinton's first term, some advisors reportedly reversed the traditional U.S. priority list of security relations over economic ones. They complained that an emphasis on security provided Japan too much leverage in trade negotiations.[10] In early 1994 the United States threat-ened (ultimately unsuccessfully) that if Tokyo did not make progress on importing more items like U.S. car parts, the United States would level economic sanctions on Japan.

Chinese strategic thinkers observed the U.S. approach toward Japan and wondered about the durability of the U.S.–Japanese alliance in the absence of a common Soviet threat. The neo-isolationism in the U.S. public, economic difficulties at home, bilateral trade frictions with Japan, and a lack of strategic focus in the new Clinton administration did not go unnoticed by Chinese experts in the early 1990s.[11] Their reaction might seem unusual at first glance. Rather than celebrating the demise of a regional alliance that could target China in the future, they worried that discord in the U.S.–Japan alliance might threaten China's long-term security interests. The logic was as follows: The U.S. pres-ence in Japan had served to contain Japanese military modernization as it allowed Japan to ride free on U.S. conventional forces and the U.S. nuclear umbrella. If the alliance were to break down, Japan's consider-able economic and technical wherewithal could be turned from the civilian realm to the military realm. Domestic political coalitions could change, with relative pacifists declining and more hawkish elements rising to the fore. Japan could scrap or radically reinterpret its postwar Peace Constitution and become a great power with offensive conven-tional capabilities and, perhaps, nuclear weapons.

Not only did China have ongoing maritime disputes with Japan in the East China Sea, but Japan, they feared, might interfere in rela-tions between Taiwan and mainland China. Taiwan had been colonized by Japan for fifty years, and Japan's imperialism there had been much more humane and much less controversial than Japanese imperialism in other Asian countries. Consequently, many political elements in Taiwan, particularly pro-independence forces, feel a strong affinity toward Japan. At the time, prominent among them was the president and head of the KMT, Lee Teng-hui, who is reportedly more fluent in Japanese than Mandarin Chinese. Also, since Chinese analysts tend to ascribe to Japan several more degrees of aggressiveness and perfidy than actually exist, they worried that many Japanese elites would not want to see the unification of Taiwan with the mainland and would work actively to prevent it.

Nonproliferation and Global Issues

LIKE ITS SUCCESSORS, the Clinton administration was concerned about global issues, such as proliferation of missiles and weapons of mass destruction. But in its China policy, those concerns tended to manifest themselves in bilateral discussions about China's own proliferation behavior rather than in entreaties to help limit objectionable actions by third parties. With the exception of the first North Korean nuclear crisis, China was approached primarily as a source of proliferation, not as a partner in stopping it elsewhere.

In Clinton's first term, Washington would pressure China to halt the sale of M-11 ballistic missiles and technologies to Pakistan and WMD-related items to Iran. On the first issue, sanctions were leveled against China in the form of an embargo on telecommunications technology being sold to China or being launched into space on Chinese rockets for third parties. The logic of the targeted sanctions was that the same domestic interests that profited from proliferation of missiles to Pakistan also profited from satellite launches. The second issue, Chinese arms sales to Iran, included the sale of conventional antiship missiles, nuclear technologies, and precursor components for chemical weapons production. Concern over the latter category of sales led to the infamous trailing of the Chinese ship *Yin He* in 1993 by U.S. naval vessels. The search of the ship by Saudi and Chinese officials, instigated by Washington, turned up nothing and produced only embarrassment in the United States and anger in China.

As John Garver reports, China only signed on to the Nonproliferation Treaty (NPT) in 1992 and had long been skeptical about it and about U.S.-led arms control efforts in general. Over time, and in particular in its second term, the Clinton administration would gain traction in persuading China to limit nuclear cooperation with Tehran and to halt the sale of certain conventional weapons to the Iranian military (the biggest threat here was the Silkworm cruise missiles that could target U.S. Navy ships in the Persian Gulf and the Strait of Hormuz from Iranian soil).[12] For our purposes, it is important to note that all of this progress was achieved on a bilateral basis. To my knowledge, China was not being asked to pressure Iran or third parties to halt Tehran's relationships with other countries, such as North Korea, or to pressure Tehran to forgo domestic WMD-related projects.

Consistent with the bilateral spirit of the discussions, Chinese officials repeatedly raised the subject of U.S. arms sales to Taiwan during the talks on Iran.[13] Experienced U.S. officials tend to stay rigidly on message when avoiding horse trading over U.S. relations with Taiwan. I recall overhearing a conversation between a U.S. official and a Chinese official in the breakfast buffet area of a Chinese hotel near the former U.S. Embassy in early 1998. The U.S. official mentioned the U.S. Navy's concern about Chinese-made cruise missiles deployed in Iran near the Persian Gulf and the Strait of Hormuz. The Chinese official rather bluntly countered with concerns about U.S. weapons sales to Taiwan. The U.S. official took note of the reference but returned directly to the Strait of Hormuz. Even in the casual setting of a breakfast buffet, U.S. officials remain circumspect on arms sales to Taiwan. As a rule, they never include U.S. defense cooperation with Taiwan in negotiations over other matters with China, but from the Chinese perspective the linkage seems natural: why should Beijing help the United States with its Iran problems if the United States hurts China by selling arms to Taiwan?

In my experience as an official and as a scholar studying these topics, the idea of such linkage has never disappeared from the Chinese playbook. But as we will see in chapters 7 and 8, the United States now engages China on Iran not simply as a potential source of proliferation to Iran but as a stakeholder with its own equities in the Persian Gulf and Middle East that might be harmed by Iran's nuclear ambitions. China should do more than forgo sales of destabilizing arms, technologies, and materials to Iran, it should pressure Iran to comply with IAEA protocols and inspections as a nonnuclear signatory to the NPT. This U.S. approach evinces a Chinese response that sounds, to my New York ear, like something the consigliere of a protection racket might say. To paraphrase, the Chinese position goes something like this: "We have established good cooperation on proliferation issues related to North Korea and Iran. This benefits both of our countries. I would hate to see that cooperation harmed by further U.S. arms sales to Taiwan, which would hurt the feelings of the Chinese people."

The First North Korean Nuclear Crisis

ONLY ONE YEAR after acceding to the NPT, China would be put to the test by North Korea, its longtime ally. The 1993–1994 crisis began when North Korea was accused of prevaricating about the civilian nature of its activities at the Yongbyon nuclear facility. IAEA inspectors using methods unknown to the North Koreans discovered evidence that the nuclear facility was reprocessing spent fuel rods into fissile material for nuclear weapons. The Clinton administration entertained preemptive strikes, and the United States, South Korea, and like-minded states condemned North Korea. A resolution by the IAEA Board of Governors and a presidential statement at the UN Security Council in spring 1994 were met with belligerent threats by Pyongyang, including a threat to leave the NPT permanently and a warning that Seoul might be turned into a "sea of fire."[14]

Former president Jimmy Carter helped defuse this serious and often underappreciated crisis in June 1994 with an independent visit to Pyongyang. Over the next several months, Pyongyang negotiated a freeze in reprocessing activities in exchange for energy assistance, including the construction of a light water nuclear reactor for the production of electricity. The Agreed Framework, signed in October 1994, effectively ended the first North Korean nuclear crisis, but it left many questions unsettled: What had become of the plutonium that the IAEA knew North Korea had already reprocessed? Would North Korea pursue highly enriched uranium as an alternative fissile material? And would the new leadership under Kim Jong-il honor the process started by his father, who passed away suddenly the month after Carter's visit?

Although PRC–North Korean relations were at the time strained, as the PRC had infuriated Pyongyang by recognizing the Republic of Korea (South Korea) for the first time in 1992, U.S. diplomats were realistic and even pessimistic about what they could expect from China in terms of coordinated pressure. Given its history of opposition to sanctions, its rather reluctant accession to the Nuclear Nonproliferation Treaty just two years earlier, and its traditionally tight relationship with North Korea, China was hardly eager to join the United States and others in publicly condemning Pyongyang. From March to May 1994, China worked hard behind the scenes to water down the diplomatic language of the IAEA Board of Governors and the UN Security Council. Beijing's goal was to prevent discussion of current or future sanctions against North Korea, to which, Beijing feared, Pyongyang might react in a destabilizing or even violent manner. So China ensured the removal of threats of "further Security Council action" if North Korea were to remain intransigent about its obligations as an NPT signatory.[15]

The chief U.S. negotiator, Robert Gallucci, and his team reported in retrospect that they were relieved and even surprised that China did not veto altogether the resolutions targeting North Korea that were passed by the IAEA Board of Governors in March 1994 and the Security Council two months later. Instead, Beijing abstained when the diluted resolutions came to a vote. China apparently promised the Americans privately to abstain so long as the resolution was "limited." Gallucci and his colleagues judged that China played a "nuanced—but ultimately helpful—role." They believed that China privately warned North Korea that Beijing would not offer a blanket defense of its longtime ally by deploying its Security Council veto. Gallucci and his colleagues believe that this message helped bring Pyongyang back from the brink of war and to the negotiating table. During the 1993–1994 North Korea nuclear crisis, China hardly displayed the leadership it would exhibit as the proactive host of the Six Party Talks in the following decade, but at least it did not obstruct nonproliferation efforts as some in Washington had feared it might. China would forgo vetoes for the entire decade, instead verbally criticizing multilateral governance efforts with which it was uncomfortable. But on North Korea, Beijing was clearly signaling that it would have been willing to veto any resolution that included serious material sanctions or even vague language that suggested such sanctions were a future option.[16]

North Korea as Catalyst for U.S. Security Policy

THE IMPACT OF NORTH KOREA on the security of Northeast Asia seems straightforward. Pyongyang is, pure and simple, a source of instability: it is a violent, rogue regime that has threatened South Korea, Japan, and the United States with direct attacks and has pursued nuclear weapons development in violation of its own pledges in the NPT. But in the 1990s North Korea's acerbic behavior changed the regional security environment in ways that Pyongyang surely never intended and that, arguably, benefited the United States.

The North Korea crisis demonstrated to the Clinton administration that it would need to prioritize security issues in its Asia strategy. More specifically, the crisis exposed both the critical importance of the U.S.–Japan alliance and its potentially fatal flaws. The Cold War U.S.–Japan alliance was very unbalanced. The United States committed itself to the defense of Japan, but that commitment was not reciprocal. There was no notion of collective self-defense, as there is in NATO. Until Prime Minister Shinzo Abe's government changed the interpretation of the constitution along these lines on July 1, 2014, Japanese forces were only obliged to assist U.S. forces in the direct defense of Japan, not in fighting in third areas of concern like North Korea. During the 1993–1994 crisis it became evident that U.S. bases in Japan were essential in almost any East Asian military contingency. While Japan is obliged to provide and subsidize U.S. bases in Japan under long-standing defense guidelines, it became clear that Japan might offer little or no material support to U.S. military actions against North Korea (think logistics, intelligence sharing, and so on). In fact, it was at least hypothetically possible, though unlikely, that Japan could even refuse the United States the right to use its bases for the purposes of striking North Korea.

Japan had already come under criticism in the first Gulf War for its late and largely monetary contribution to allied efforts. Knowing that the U.S. public would not tolerate Japan sitting on its hands while Americans fought a war against bad actors in Japan's own neighborhood, officials in Washington realized that, without revisions to Japan's defense guidelines, the alliance might be one crisis away from its destruction. Moreover, the alliance needed to appear robust for the purposes of coercive diplomacy in a post–Cold War world.[17]

Given these concerns, in 1994–1995, the Pentagon launched a major initiative to strengthen the U.S.–Japan alliance under the leadership of then–Assistant Secretary of Defense for Political Affairs Joseph Nye. The Nye Initiative was first outlined publicly in the 1995 East Asia strategy report in which the United States sought to reassure allies and warn potential adversaries that security in Asia was a priority concern for the Clinton administration and that the United States would not withdraw in the absence of a Soviet threat. Washington made a commitment to maintain at least 100,000 U.S. forces in East Asia. Along with its efforts with Tokyo, the administration also strengthened defense ties with Singapore, Australia, and the Philippines. As part of the broader Nye Initiative, by the late 1990s Washington would secure from Tokyo a commitment to provide assistance to U.S. forces operating in the areas surrounding Japan. In addition to base access guarantees, in its 1997 revised Defense Guidelines Japan committed to rear-area support to the United States in logistics and intelligence sharing and noncombat operations, such as mine clearing. And following a North Korean missile test that flew over Japan in 1998, Japan would also commit fully to cooperation with the United States on research and development of theater missile defense systems.[18]

Why raise all of these issues in a book about the rise of China? In essence, North Korea had altered the psychology of the first post–

Cold War administration in the United States. Chinese tensions with the Philippines and Vietnam over disputed islands in the South China Sea in 1994–1995 (see the discussion on Mischief Reef in chapter 1) also stimulated U.S. efforts to improve defense coordination with its regional allies and security partners, but North Korean provocations were the major driver. After 1994, the U.S. again made security policy in East Asia a clear priority, with implications not just for future North Korea scenarios, but for coercive diplomacy with the PRC.

All things being equal, the strengthening of the U.S.–Japan alliance in the second half of the 1990s might have been viewed as a positive change in Beijing. After all, in the early 1990s Chinese analysts were worried about the potential breakup of the alliance and the unleashing of latent Japanese military potential. But in the complex world of international policies, all things are very rarely equal. Once the United States started to talk about upgrading and strengthening the U.S.–Japan alliance and the countries' economic disputes over car parts fizzled out, Chinese analysts almost instantly began worrying about an opposite path to future Japanese military and diplomatic assertiveness. They now envisioned Japan as an increasingly active junior partner in the alliance, encouraged by the United States to push the boundaries of post–World War II prohibitions on Japanese military assertiveness. As one leading Japan expert in a Chinese government think tank put it in 1998, while Chinese security analysts had generally viewed the U.S.–Japan alliance as a "bottle cap," containing Japan's military development, after the Nye Initiative, they started to worry that it was becoming more of an eggshell, incubating Japan's military assertiveness until Japan burst out of its shell as a strong and independent actor.[19] This is not to say that China suddenly would have preferred the alliance to break down in the short term, but rather that the focus of Chinese concerns had shifted from alliance breakdown to alliance bolstering, with Japan playing a larger military role. What accelerated this transformation in Chinese analysis was, in large part, the Taiwan Straits crisis of 1995–1996. That diplomatic crisis would shift the U.S. security focus in the region from North Korea to China and would negatively color Beijing's perceptions of the U.S.–Japan alliance.

The Taiwan Straits Crisis

THE MAJOR CHALLENGE in U.S. policy toward relations across the Taiwan Strait is to achieve two somewhat contradictory goals at once: on the one hand, Washington needs to maintain a strong enough regional military presence and support for Taiwan's defense to discourage the mainland from coercing or invading the island; on the other hand, the United States needs to reassure Beijing that the purpose of its arms sales and military presence is not to support the permanent legal separation of Taiwan from the Chinese nation (often shorthanded as "Taiwan independence").

Deterrence requires credible threats of punishment and credible assurances that the target's interests will not be harmed as long as it forgoes aggressive behavior. In coercive diplomacy, it is often tricky to balance these two requirements. That challenge is at the heart of what political scientists call "the security dilemma." Actions taken for defensive reasons by one state can seem threatening to another and lead to a reaction that itself is deemed aggressive by the first state, leading to a spiral of tensions. Normally, the deployment of weapons and the adoption of military doctrines useful only for defensive operations sidestep the security dilemma.[20] But in the cross-Strait context, hardy defenses in Taiwan still cause anxiety on the mainland because what mainland leaders fear most is a declaration of permanent Taiwanese independence, not an invasion of the mainland by Taiwan. Thus Taiwan's defense and a strengthened U.S. posture in the region could be seen as protecting pro-independence initiatives and declarations by Taiwan's leaders.

In the first half of 1995, the United States was arguably deficient in both central components of coercive diplomacy. The administration appeared weak in its resolve in the eyes of many Chinese analysts. After all, the United States had withdrawn quickly from Somalia after the death of the Army Rangers, avoided intervention in Rwanda, backed down after ultimatums to China on human rights and most favored nation linkage, and yielded to Japan on trade disputes over car parts. At the same time, the administration appeared to be supporting Japan and Taiwan in ways that might harm China's security. Changes in the U.S.-

Japan alliance in the mid-1990s were accompanied by what appeared to be an upgrading of Washington's relations with an increasingly assertive President Lee Teng-hui on Taiwan.

President Lee had received a PhD at Cornell University in the United States. When he applied for a visa as a sitting president to visit his alma mater for an alumni event in June 1995, Beijing predictably objected. After all, the United States lacked diplomatic relations with Taipei, had recognized Beijing as the sole legitimate government of China since 1979, and had not permitted a sitting leader of Taiwan since then to visit the United States for any purpose but a travel transit on the way to some third location. In what was an arguably botched policy process in both form and content, the Clinton administration first communicated at a very high level (via Secretary of State Christopher) that it did not plan to issue a visa to Lee because it would be inconsistent with the bedrock agreements of the U.S.–China normalization process in the 1970s. But just a few days later, following the passage of a nonbinding but nearly unanimous "sense of the Congress" resolution in favor of Lee's visit, the Clinton administration reversed course and issued the visa.

As fortune would have it, I was an assistant professor at Cornell University at the time. I thought it only natural that my university would invite an esteemed alumnus to speak at an alumni event. Lee was the president of a young democracy and was planning to further the democratization process by holding the first direct elections for president in March 1996. But on strategic grounds, I wondered if it was wise for the U.S. government to issue a visa to a sitting president of the Republic of China, particularly after it had reassured Beijing that it would not. As did almost every China specialist in the U.S. government at the time, I thought the answer should have been no. His visit could spark some sort of crisis in the U.S.–China relationship or even a conflict in the Taiwan Strait. Lee could visit after he left office, I thought.

On a more personal and less important note, I was planning a research visit to China in the weeks just after the alumni gathering and did not relish handing out Cornell name cards to my counterparts in Beijing after the Lee visit and speech. But it was only when I attended his speech with my colleagues at Cornell and heard Lee's message that I realized how uncomfortable the trip was going to be. Not only did Lee break his assurances to Washington that he would avoid politics during his visit but he gave a speech that to mainland Chinese ears sounded like a call for Taiwan to assert its political independence. Especially important was his reference to his nation as the "Republic of China on Taiwan" (as opposed to simply the Republic of China, which constitutionally has a claim to the mainland as well) and his call to "demand the impossible" in terms of breaking out of "Taiwan's diplomatic isolation."[21] I later learned that my interlocutors in Beijing had carefully studied the content of Lee's speech and were none too pleased with his message.

On my way home from the trip to Beijing in July, I read a Chinese newspaper over the shoulder of the airline passenger in front of me. It reported that the PRC had announced plans to test-fire ballistic missiles off of Taiwan. This would be the first of several exercises. In July and August 1995 there were missile exercises; in November and December there were surface and air military exercises; and in March 1996 Beijing began a new round of missile exercises and a buildup of forces across from Taiwan. The crisis reached its apex that same month, when Taiwan held its first direct presidential elections (Lee Teng-hui would be a runaway victor). In the weeks before the election, China ignored U.S. warnings, built up 100,000 forces in the Nanjing Military District across from Taiwan, and fired more missiles near the island. Significantly, unlike in July 1995, in March 1996 the missiles were fired with some accuracy to landing zones relatively near Taiwan's major northern and southern ports of Keelung and Kaohsiung, implying the potential for a future missile blockade, which would devastate Taiwan's trade-dependent economy.[22]

The Clinton administration had spent a good part of the second half of 1995 trying to reassure Beijing that granting a visa to President Lee did not represent a change in the traditional U.S. policy. At the same time, the administration warned Beijing against escalation of cross-Strait tensions in the lead-up to the 1996 presidential elections on Taiwan. But the United States had not yet demonstrated resolve: a credible commitment to counter future Chinese bullying with U.S. military force. In March 1996, President Clinton, wisely in my opinion, decided that Beijing had gone too far and the United States needed to send a deterrent message by deploying two aircraft carrier battle groups off of Taiwan. There is no evidence that Beijing had planned broader military activities beyond the exercises it executed, and it is highly doubtful that it had the military capacity at the time to do anything beyond terrorize Taiwan. So it would be an exaggeration to say that the Clinton administration somehow backed China down or prevailed in the crisis. But it is fair to say that the United States sent a strong signal that it cared deeply about Taiwan's security and Beijing should not assume that the United States would stay neutral in any future conflict across the Strait.

Just a few weeks after the crisis ended, on April 17, 1996, President Clinton and Japanese Prime Minister Hashimoto issued a joint communiqué that called for revitalization of the U.S.–Japan alliance to better guarantee the security of the Asia-Pacific region. This communiqué was the precursor to Japan's revised Defense Guidelines and the commitment to joint development of theater missile defenses that would be formally announced in 1997 and 1998, respectively. These cooperative efforts by Tokyo and Washington meant that it would be more difficult for China to separate Japan from the United States in a future dispute over Taiwan.

While all of these U.S. actions could have frustrated Beijing, leading to increasing enmity toward the United States and its neighbors, in general they had the opposite effect. Fear of U.S. encirclement fostered Chinese reassurance of its neighbors. Beijing embraced a decade-long campaign of multilateral confidence-building in the region. China had previously viewed multilateralism with skepticism, but in 1996–1997 China embraced multilateral diplomacy in East Asia and Central Asia, as described in chapters 1 and 3. In the period following the launching of the Nye Initiative and the crisis in the Taiwan Straits, China created the institutional foundations for the Shanghai Cooperation Organisation and inaugurated the New Security Concept (*Xin Anquan Guan*), adopting a much less belligerent posture toward the ASEAN states.[23] The first meeting of the ASEAN Plus Three (China, Japan, and South Korea) was held in 1997. In addition, China played a reassuring role during the Asian financial crisis that was sparked by financial meltdowns in 1997 in Indonesia and Thailand. China eschewed competitive devaluation of the Chinese yuan to protect its export markets when other regional currencies were devaluing and even offered some financial assistance directly and through the IMF for the hardest-hit economies.

Many international, bureaucratic, and psychological factors undoubtedly contributed to China's change from multilateral skeptic to multilateral champion in the second half of the 1990s.[24] But there is ample evidence to suggest that one of the major catalysts in this evolution was the strengthening U.S. security relationships in the region. Chinese scholar Xia Liping argues that the New Security Concept of 1996 and multilateral confidence-building in Central and Southeast Asia came in response to what Chinese elites saw as "cold war thinking" and "power politics" (a thinly veiled reference to U.S. behavior in the Taiwan Strait and the strengthening of bilateral U.S. alliances).[25] Tsinghua professor Yan Xuetong states that Chinese multilateral initiatives in 1996–1997 were viewed as desirable as a hedge against U.S. regional hegemony.[26] The influential government scholar Zhang Yunling, often credited for being the government advisor who masterminded China's reassurance strategy toward ASEAN, similarly portrays China's constructive approach as a way to counter the China threat theory in Washington and to prevent encirclement of China by U.S. alliances.[27] In a major 2003 opus on China's relations in the Asia-Pacific region edited by Zhang, the Chinese authors called regional multilateral cooperation "an important means by which to prevent the United States from penetrating the Southeast Asian region."[28] In 2006 Zhang and his coauthor, Fudan University scholar Tang Shiping, wrote, "China has pursued a strategy of maintaining amicable relationships with its neighbors and stabilizing its periphery [*mulin youhao, wending zhoubian*] to hedge against the bad times in Sino–U.S. relations. . . . [If] China adopts a moderate approach, most regional countries would be reluctant to adopt a policy of hard containment, and thus China will likely enjoy a benign regional security environment. To this end, China has made strenuous efforts to improve its relationships with its neighboring countries, sometimes by making significant concessions against strong domestic opposition."[29]

Since, as was argued in chapter 3, it is generally in Washington's interest for China to reassure and accommodate its neighbors during its rise, the Clinton administration's demonstration of commitment to East Asian security and resolve in the face of China's bullying of Taiwan and other neighbors can be given some credit for what was a very constructive period in China's regional diplomacy. As we will see in chapter 8, that general trend in Chinese diplomacy would last until the financial crisis of 2008.

There is an important lesson that can be drawn from this period. Contrary to the common assumption that U.S. toughness in East Asia only breeds Chinese intransigence and spirals of tension in the region, the second half of the 1990s demonstrates that a robust U.S. security presence and commitment to East Asia, in the proper diplomatic context, can incentivize China to behave more moderately toward its neighbors. So what is that proper diplomatic context? Having demonstrated resolve, in the years that followed the 1996 crisis the Clinton administration sought to reassure Beijing that the United States did not support Taiwan independence and that the issuance of a visa to Lee Teng-hui and the deployment of the carriers did not represent a change in long-standing U.S. policy.[30] In a visit to Shanghai in 1998, President Clinton publicly and famously reassured the Chinese leadership and public that Washington did not support the following scenarios: Taiwan independence; "two Chinas" or "one China, one Taiwan"; or Taiwan's membership in international organizations for which statehood is a requirement. This statement would, thereafter, commonly be referred to as the "three no's." The Clinton administration would also quickly distance itself from President Lee's assertion to a German journalist in July 1999 that the cross-Strait political situation could best be described as "special state-to-state relations" (dubbed on the mainland the "two-state theory"). After publication of Lee's statement, Washington almost immediately sent high-level envoys to both sides of the Taiwan Strait to clarify U.S. policy.[31]

But Beijing was not entirely reassured. Lingering Chinese concerns about U.S.–Taiwan policy festered in the late 1990s. New sources of friction included a new round of arms sales notifications. U.S.–China tensions were amplified greatly during the Kosovo War in spring 1999. In that war NATO intervened against what was viewed in Beijing as a legitimate Serbian operation against regional separatism. Significantly, it was also the occasion for the U.S. Air Force to accidentally bomb the

PRC Embassy in Belgrade as part of the operations against Milosevic's government. There were multiple casualties, including three deaths, among the Chinese personnel working that night in the embassy. One of Clinton's top China advisors, National Security Council director Robert Suettinger, and leading scholar David M. Lampton both looked back on the period 1999–2000 as a negative turning point in the bilateral relationship.[32]

The Kosovo War

MUCH ATTENTION understandably has been paid to the dramatic and tragic episode of a U.S. bomber destroying the Chinese Embassy in Belgrade. But for China's security analysts, the entire Kosovo operation was suspect from the beginning. International intervention in Yugoslavia over Kosovo set a dangerous precedent for China, as it showed a new willingness on the part of the United States and its allies to carve up ethnically and geographically diverse sovereign countries. Chinese security analysis portrayed the entire Kosovo operation as a realpolitik gambit to increase U.S. and NATO influence in Eastern Europe and to encourage destabilizing separatist movements like the Kosovo Liberation Army at the expense of "non-Western" powers such as Russia and China.[33] Chinese analysts viewed professed humanitarian concerns as a mere pretext for intervention (and the ethnic cleansing of Kosovar Albanians was not reported domestically in China). The NATO Kosovo operation directly pitted the new global governance philosophy of the U.S. and its allies against China's vision of noninterference and its opposition to ethnic or territorial separatism.

China did not take the lead at the UN in opposing action on Kosovo. Russia was so adamantly opposed that the Clinton administration quickly abandoned any attempt to ask the United Nations Security Council to approve military action against Milosevic's Serbian government in Belgrade. But there can be little doubt from Beijing's words and actions and from private conversations that I had in China that Beijing viewed the entire operation as both illegal and dangerous. Beijing did not, of course, want to be dragged into a direct confrontation with NATO, especially in a region so far from China itself. But neither could it remain entirely aloof from the conflict. Like China, Yugoslavia was a nominally socialist country, with restive minority regions (in China, think of Xinjiang and Tibet). So Beijing backed the Serbs and criticized the United States in both the media and in diplomacy. It has been rumored that Beijing also tried to help the Serbian war effort itself, albeit behind the scenes, in areas such as intelligence and communications. Some reports even suggest that Belgrade reciprocated. When a U.S. stealth F-117 fighter bomber was shot down over Yugoslavia in March, Belgrade reportedly allowed Chinese agents to buy key components for study for China's own air defense and stealth aircraft development.[34] According to a well-placed government interlocutor in Beijing in January 2000, there was indeed behind-the-scenes Chinese and Serbian cooperation during the war, although he did not detail what form it took. That interlocutor said that knowledge of that cooperation is one important reason why, to this day, many in Chinese security circles refuse to view the bombing of the Chinese Embassy as accidental. Instead they see it as a punitive strike against China for its support of an enemy of the United States and NATO, noting that the precision-guided bombs struck the military attaché section of the embassy building.

From a domestic perspective, the attack on the Chinese Embassy was a difficult challenge for the Beijing leadership. As former Deputy Assistant Secretary of State Susan Shirk chronicles in her fascinating book *China: Fragile Superpower*, the top leadership was already on heightened alert about domestic stability. Just a few weeks earlier, the Falun Gong had upset the CCP by holding a surprise protest of thousands of adherents directly outside Zhongnanhai, the CCP leadership compound. After the bombing, the Chinese press accused the United States of intentionally targeting the embassy, and one official Chinese newspaper even compared the attack to Nazi atrocities during World War II. The Clinton administration immediately offered formal apologies, but these were largely ignored. With the breaking news and the official government spin, a domestic firestorm was unleashed in China, and the Chinese government, doubly rattled by the bombing and the Falun Gong protest, sought to channel popular anger at the Americans and away from the Chinese government by busing protestors to the site of the U.S. Embassy, which they pelted with rocks for days.[35] In Chengdu, Chinese protestors scaled the walls to the U.S. consular compound and burned the consul's residence.

From a strategic perspective, the Chinese government viewed humanitarian interventions like Kosovo as risky precedents that might encourage separatist movements and enable future great power interventions in civil wars. The danger of this outcome strikes close to home for Beijing. In the months immediately following the Kosovo War, Taiwanese president Lee presented his two-state theory. In this context and in the context of the upcoming Taiwan presidential election of March 2000, in which a pro-independence candidate, Chen Shui-bian, was running for office, Chinese president Jiang Zemin reportedly called for a significant modernization drive in the PLA with a special emphasis on the development of new coercive options for Taiwan scenarios.[36] It was rumored in scholarly and journalistic circles in China at the time that Jiang had grown impatient with the mainland's lack of progress in cross-Strait relations, despite the growing economic interdependence across the Strait, and that he had, therefore, created a timetable within which Taiwan must be coerced into accepting again the broad concept of "one China" and engaging in serious talks on the terms for unification.[37] Beijing's Taiwan white paper of early 2000 seemed at least consistent with these rumors, if not fully confirmatory of them. The white paper, which Chinese premier Zhu Rongji said was explicitly a response to Lee's state-to-state theory, added a new condition that could lead to the use of force by the PRC: Taiwan's "indefinite" (*wu xianqi*) refusal to engage in negotiations on reunification.[38]

A Tale of Two Institutions: Kyoto and WTO Negotiations

THE KOSOVO WAR provided dramatic signals of how difficult it would be to get China to coordinate its diplomatic policy with the United States and like-minded nations. The two other major global governance challenges of the Clinton years—climate change and international trade liberalization—frame the indispensable role that China must play in most global governance issues. When negotiations were made on the Kyoto Protocol, signatories accepted that China was a developing country but ignored its giant footprint. They did so at their peril. All developing countries were given a free pass at Kyoto, including emerging economies like China, India, and Brazil. In fact, Kyoto not only imposed no costs on China, it even provided China some money-making opportunities as signatories could buy out pollution rights by rewarding carbon-reduction efforts in developing countries. But China was no ordinary developing country. It was already a large emitter of greenhouse gases in the 1990s and, as we know from chapters 1 and 4, it was moving headlong in the direction of becoming the world's largest emitter of those gases. The absence of any commitment to reduce Chinese emissions helped doom the treaty domestically in the United States, itself the world's largest emitter at the time. The treaty had no chance of being ratified by the Senate. Free-riding by the United States, in turn, made other signatories much less rigid in their own adherence to it. Very few, if any, major signatories of the Kyoto Protocol have fulfilled their commitments. The treaty, in the end, did little good except to show how the world cannot approach global problems without including a nation as large and influential as China.

WTO negotiations provide the other bookend. In this case, the negotiating parties correctly viewed China as a country that was simply too big to get the special treatment granted to other developing countries and, as a result, the negotiating process produced much more successful results. The "new Democrats" of the Clinton administration were new in the sense that they were strong promoters of free trade (think NAFTA). They very much wanted the General Agreements on Tariffs and Trade (the GATT) to graduate to a World Trade Organization with formal dispute mechanisms, and they worked hard and successfully to bring this about. Meaningful trade deals are always domestically controversial even in the wealthiest countries, but free trade is particularly controversial in poorer and less competitive economies. The GATT had normally allowed much greater protections and much tighter market access for developing countries under the theory that free trade was potentially destabilizing in those countries. Moreover, permitting a higher degree of protection allows governments there to foster infant industries until they become competitive in the international marketplace. This is not unreasonable. Other than the first mover in industrialization, Great Britain, no currently advanced economy has industrialized without early protections for infant industries.

With its large number of people in abject poverty and its low per capita GNP, China had the right economic profile to qualify for developing country exceptions and had long lobbied for those exceptions. But unlike other developing countries, by the late 1990s China had already become a trading giant under the reform program and was on a path to become the world's largest trader of material goods. Charlene Barshefsky, the lead U.S. negotiator with China for the GATT and then the WTO negotiations, labeled China "an 'export powerhouse' whose overseas sales will grow on average by 40 percent each year over the next five years." China, she reasoned, cannot be "accepted as a developing country."[39] In essence, U.S. and European negotiators knew that China was too big to get the normal exceptions because wealthier countries would complain about Chinese predatory trade and would themselves start to default on their own commitments, gutting the WTO. So the United States and others pushed China to accept more market access in areas like agriculture and lower tariffs on manufactured goods than other developing countries in the WTO. The negotiations took many years, but they culminated in an agreement in late 1999 to prepare China for accession to the treaty. In 2000, Washington would grant China "permanent normal trade relation status," the much improved name for what used to be most favored nation status. In 2001 China would join the WTO as a full member. As discussed above, this sparked the rise of foreign direct investment into China and resulted in China's deep integration into regional and global transnational production.

There were major bumps along the way. Premier Zhu Rongji took huge domestic risks in offering such unprecedented trade concessions. It is beyond the scope of this book to list all of the protections eschewed by China that are normally afforded developing countries that accede to the GATT, but they include stricter limits on Chinese industrial and agricultural subsidies than imposed on other developing countries, relatively lax restrictions on the countervailing actions that states can take against China for dumping products below market prices, a requirement for Chinese commitment to national treatment not only vis-à-vis goods but also foreign individuals and enterprises, and special product-specific safeguards against Chinese exports.[40]

Despite these concessions, when Premier Zhu visited the United States in April 1999, President Clinton ignored the consensus among his China advisors that he should accept the generous Chinese offer. The president listened instead to his domestic advisors. He refused to reach an agreement with Zhu, who was reported to be visibly upset when the president gave him the news. Zhu returned home to intense nationalist criticism for having been stiffed by the Americans, who, at the time, were bombing Belgrade in the Kosovo War. As Susan Shirk reports, however, an agreement was ultimately reached later in the year because Zhu Rongji wanted to use the WTO as a bludgeon against entrenched domestic economic interests in China. Those interests, including large state-owned enterprises, were dragging their feet on accepting and implementing his preferred economic reform measures. The WTO supplied Zhu what the Japanese call *gaiatsu,* or "outside pressure," which enabled Zhu to tell domestic conservatives that China's international obligations required him to push through further liberalization measures in the domestic economy.[41] Fortunately for the Clinton administration and the rest of the world, Zhu's near-term economic strategies at home facilitated Beijing's acceptance of China's global economic responsibilities. A parallel process might exist today in the connection between Chinese leaders' need to reduce local air pollution and their willingness to make international commitments to limit greenhouse gas emissions.

THE CLINTON YEARS provided important early lessons for the implications of a rising China in a post–Cold War world. First, China could block directly or hamper significantly efforts at global governance if it either opposed or refused to contribute actively to those efforts. Second, China cannot be treated as a normal developing country because of its sheer size. And third, if China is perceived as free-riding, this can severely impact the willingness of other great powers to contribute to global governance.

Another important lesson is that successful coercive diplomacy with an increasingly powerful China is possible, but such success requires constant management of two rather contradictory imperatives: the need to maintain a reputation for resolve and physical strength while at the same time making clear that the purpose of the U.S. presence and alliance system in the region is not to contain China's economic growth or political influence on the international stage, nor to encourage the territorial breakup of China along the lines of the former Yugoslavia, nor to side unconditionally with China's opponents in maritime sovereignty disputes.

The Clinton years also showed how global governance efforts in North Korea and the former Yugoslavia interacted in important ways with more traditional security issues associated with coercive diplomacy: North Korea mattered for the U.S. alliance system, and changes in that system mattered for China's maritime disputes. Kosovo mattered for China's attitudes about the U.S.–Taiwan relationship and overall view of Washington's goals in the post–Cold War world; and domestic political sensitivities and fragilities in China affected Beijing's calculations about both global governance issues and coercive diplomacy with the United States.

While I have raised several tacit and explicit criticisms of the Clinton administration's policies above, I believe that the president showed a high degree of flexibility and intelligence in reversing course when he deemed such a reversal necessary. In the process, his administration accomplished a great deal in the region. The Nye Initiative created a foundation for a sustained U.S. security presence in East Asia after the Cold War and encouraged a long period of constructive Chinese diplomacy toward its neighbors. Even though the Taiwan crisis was arguably created in large part by clumsy U.S. diplomacy, the administration handled the crisis well by artfully blending credible threats and credible assurances about the limited purpose of those threats. In economic policy, the road was bumpy but, once completed, the WTO initiatives integrated China deeply into the regional and global economies in ways that accord with the common economic and security interests of the United States, its Asian allies, and China itself. There was no blueprint in the Oval Office for how the post–Cold War world would be managed. And, after a very rocky start, the Clinton administration did an admirable job of navigating turbulent and unchartered seas, particularly during its last five years in office.

But despite these achievements, U.S.–China relations were extremely tense when the Clinton administration left office. The fresh wounds of Kosovo had shaken the progress made in the mid-1990s. But more important, in March 2000 the pro-independence candidate, Chen Shui-bian, surprised many on the island and around the world by winning a three-way race for Taiwan's presidency, horrifying Beijing. This was the backdrop inherited by George W. Bush when he assumed office in January 2001.

CHAPTER 7

The Post–9/11 World, 2001–2008

W HEN THE GEORGE W. BUSH administration took office in
January 2001, it inherited the bilateral U.S.–PRC tension from
the Clinton era. The legacies of the Kosovo War and the early 2000
election of a pro-independence president, Chen Shui-bian, in Taiwan
complicated the bilateral relationship. Moreover, the Bush campaign
had labeled China a "strategic competitor" and implied Clinton and
Gore had been too soft toward Beijing. Just as Clinton had done eight
years before, the Bush administration entered office emphasizing confrontation, not partnership with China.

A Very Rocky Ride in 2001

ONE MONTH BEFORE the 2000 presidential elections, future Deputy Secretary of State Richard Armitage issued a report on behalf of a
bipartisan group calling for a strengthened U.S.–Japan alliance and a
more assertive Japanese role within that alliance. The so-called Armitage Report urged Japan to shed some of the historical and legal constraints on collective self-defense and on Japan's ability to project power
abroad. Japan should become an ally more akin to Great Britain, the
authors believed. The new Bush team also wanted to improve Taiwan's

defensive capabilities and streamline arms sales decisions. Chinese analysts predictably distrusted the new administration's defense orientation.

Less than three months into the Bush presidency, the U.S.–China relationship fell into crisis. On April 1, 2001, a Chinese fighter jet clipped a U.S. EP-3 surveillance aircraft in international airspace near China's coast. The Chinese pilot, who was killed in the collision, apparently miscalculated distances while buzzing the lumbering U.S. propeller plane as part of a common intercept. The severely damaged U.S. plane made a miraculous emergency landing on China's Hainan Island with no loss of life. The brave and physically powerful Navy pilot, a former Nebraska high school football linebacker, controlled the plane by applying his considerable leg strength to foot pedals unaided by hydraulics, guiding the plane to the Chinese tarmac and saving the lives of his approximately two dozen crewmembers. He also saved U.S.–China relations from the the specter of American deaths caused by the aggressive act of a Chinese pilot over international waters. While things could have been worse, they also could have been much better. Beijing handled the diplomacy of the crisis in a ham-fisted manner, initially blaming the United States for the collision and then holding the crew for ten days and the plane, packed with U.S. surveillance technology, for much longer. This approach ensured an extended period of distrust, especially between the military establishments of the two countries.[1]

The air crew was released following the procurement of a carefully worded nonapology by U.S. officials about recent occurrences that they "regretted." This allowed Chinese leaders to tell their public and Party brethren that the United States had apologized while allowing the Bush administration to tell its public and its allies the opposite. As long as neither side explicitly corrected the other, all would be fine. Such mutual nondenial is often the stuff of diplomatic compromise.

In the same month, the Bush administration created new tensions with Beijing by announcing its offer to Taiwan of a very large arms sale package (worth over $12 billion USD). President Bush also stated in a television interview that the United States would "do whatever it takes" to help Taiwan defend itself.[2] U.S.-PRC relations regressed to their worst level since the May 1999 U.S. bombing of the PRC's Belgrade Embassy.

September 11, 2001: Common Ground Rediscovered

U.S.-CHINA RELATIONS BEGAN to thaw with Secretary Colin Powell's trip to China in late July 2001. That nascent process of reconciliation would accelerate after the September 11 attacks on New York City and Washington. The terrorist atrocity committed on the world's financial center underscored to leaders in both capitals that, despite the two countries' significant differences, the United States and China have many common interests. Beijing was hardly a leading player in the Global War on Terror that followed the attacks, but the PRC did not stand in the way of U.S.-led effort in its western backyard of South and Central Asia. Instead, Beijing took subtle but constructive positions to help the United States just after the attacks—offering, for example, a small but symbolically important aid program to Pakistan. China thereby buttressed President Pervez Musharraf's domestically controversial decision to cooperate with the U.S. military effort to take down the Taliban regime in Afghanistan, a regime that the Pakistani security and intelligence agencies had been instrumental in creating.[3] Just after the attacks on the United States, Beijing dispatched an experienced high-level official to Pakistan to deliver Beijing's message regarding the need for Pakistani cooperation with the Americans (that diplomat, Wang Yi, would become Foreign Minister in 2013). Pakistan is the closest thing China has to a true and reliable ally and the reverse is also true, so Beijing's words carry real weight in Islamabad.

Coercive Diplomacy: U.S. Alliances and Relations Across the Taiwan Strait

WHILE RELATIONS IMPROVED after 9/11, distrust remained. Beijing still worried that the Bush administration would offer unconditional support to the independence-leaning government in Taiwan. When President Bush, in a speech at Tsinghua University during a February 2002 trip to China, mentioned the Taiwan Relations Act but not the three joint communiqués negotiated with Beijing as the basis of

U.S. policy toward Taiwan, Chinese elites took note. Such an omission might simply have been a mistake. But many in Beijing see nefarious plots in Washington's every utterance. For them it would be hard to accept the notion that Bush's truncated version of the American "one China" policy was simply a gaffe. Perhaps more controversial was the invitation of Taiwan Defense Minister Tang Yao-ming to Florida for a mid-March 2002 defense industry meeting attended by Deputy Secretary of Defense Paul Wolfowitz and Assistant Secretary of State for East Asia James Kelly, among other top officials. Beijing branded this a violation of the 1979 U.S.–PRC normalization agreement (the second joint communiqué).[4]

Other regional developments affected Chinese perceptions. The September 11, 2001, attacks and the wars that followed would provide Japan with military opportunities to support U.S. forces far from the island nation, including noncombat roles in Iraq and in the Indian Ocean near Afghanistan. Under Prime Minister Junichiro Koizumi, Japan also expressed frank concerns about China's regional defense buildup. Newspaper articles in China singled out the United States and Japan for opportunistically exploiting September 11 to bolster their military presence around China. The underlying themes of many Chinese articles in 2002 were that Tokyo had planned to break out of the constraints of its peacetime constitution and the United States had planned to increase its military presence in Central and Southeast Asia even before September 11. The terrorist attacks on New York City and Washington simply provided a pretext for Japan and the United States to implement those plans, the authors argued. One major focus of this criticism was Japan's decision to send Maritime Self Defense Force ships to the Indian Ocean in logistical support of the U.S.-led effort there.[5]

Increased Japanese military activities would have caused concerns in China under any Japanese leadership. But conservative and nationalist trends in Japanese politics seemed to be confirming some elements of the overblown conspiracy theories in China about Japan's long-term strategic intentions. Perhaps most galling to China were yearly visits by Prime Minister Koizumi to the Yasukuni Shrine, a Shinto memorial paying homage to Japan's historical war dead, including fourteen Class-A war criminals from World War II. A museum next to the shrine offers a cartoonish history in which Japan was driven into war by a scheming United States. According to the museum, Roosevelt allegedly provoked the otherwise avoidable war to kick-start the U.S. economy and create jobs as a way out of the Great Depression. Japan, the story goes, was only trying to assist its brethren in mainland Asia in warding off threats from Europeans and Americans, a version of history that is deeply offensive to the many victims of Japanese aggression in the region, not just in China. Koizumi's trips to the shrine soured Japan's relations with China (and with South Korea) and precluded high-level summits and bilateral confidence-building measures between Beijing and Tokyo.

The bilateral Sino-Japanese relationship would be further strained by unruly anti-Japanese nationalism in Chinese society. In August 2004 soccer riots broke out in the wake of the Japanese victory over China in the Asian Cup Soccer Final in Beijing. I attended the match with friends after scalping tickets from a Beijing street merchant who, with a signature sleeveless T-shirt rolled up at the belly, looked somewhat more authentic and less likely than his competitors to sell us some of the many counterfeit ones circulating at the time. Our instincts having been proven correct, we entered the stadium to the sight of official signage above the field hailing regional harmony and peace. But the massive Chinese crowd soon struck up loud and truly obscene chants about the Japanese team, revealing another emotion altogether. The government had ordered security personnel positioned around the stadium. They wore full battle gear in stifling August humidity, making it clear that the government lacked confidence that the propaganda message it had created for the games had taken root in the Chinese crowd. They were right to be worried. When Japan won on a controversial goal and vandalism started outside the stadium after the game, security forces were already in place to limit the scope of the disturbance. Unfortunately for China-Japan relations, this was hardly an isolated event. When Japan pursued membership in the UN Security Council in early 2005, millions of Chinese signed an online anti-Japanese petition against the proposal, street protests filled with invective, and vandalism followed in Shanghai and other Chinese cities.[6]

Taiwan Reassurance

THE STRENGTHENING OF the U.S. military alliance system in Asia under George W. Bush and the demonstration of U.S. resolve to use force on the battlefield helped bolster U.S. deterrence of any PRC military aggression against Taiwan or its other neighbors. But, as discussed in chapter 1, resolve, or the "credibility of threat," is only one part of successful coercive diplomacy. Measures that bolster the credibility of threat can unintentionally undercut coercive diplomacy if they seem provocative and are not accompanied by assurances that the key interests of the target will not be harmed if the target forgoes the use of force. In a period in which Taiwan's leadership was making fairly frequent verbal assertions of Taiwan's independent sovereignty and promoting a series of policy measures to weaken historical links between itself and the mainland, Beijing could have concluded that a demonstration of force was necessary to avoid further erosion of its long-term position in cross-Strait relations, regardless of the degree of U.S. resolve to resist such a move. In his first few years in office, President Chen made several statements that touched upon Taiwan's sovereignty. And, along the same lines, he pushed policy agendas such as public referendums on aspects of cross-Strait relations that suggested he might seek populist means to break out of Taiwan's constitutional constraints on permanent separation from mainland China.

Chen's initiatives and statements often caught the Bush administration by surprise and seemed to violate Chen's private promises to Washington to avoid provoking Beijing in his first term. Strangely, however, Chen's potentially destabilizing antics proved an asset for Washington in its dealings with Beijing. After all, if Washington (and Tokyo) were looking for a chance to wrest Taiwan away from the mainland forever, as many Chinese nationalists had long suspected and U.S. leaders had long denied, President Chen provided a clear opportunity to do so. But the Bush administration eschewed such an opportunity at every turn and, at times, actively opposed Chen's actions. This built a basic foundation of assurance in U.S.–China relations that bolstered U.S.

coercive diplomacy significantly and established trust that was useful in other areas.

In April 2002 then–Vice President Hu Jintao would make an important trip to Washington as he prepared to ascend to the CCP's top spot later in the year. By all accounts, his meetings with his counterpart, Vice President Dick Cheney, went well, and the U.S. government was able to convey the message that it still supported Washington's traditional "one China" policy.

The Bush administration's message would be underscored dramatically in August 2002 during Deputy Secretary of State Armitage's trip to Beijing. Three weeks earlier, Chen Shui-bian had made a speech that asserted Taiwan's sovereignty. On August 3, Chen described relations across the Taiwan Strait as "one country on each side" (*yi bian yi guo*) and suggested that he would pursue a popular referendum to determine Taiwan's status. Chen's formulation went considerably further than Lee Teng-hui's characterization of relations across the Taiwan Strait as "special state-to-state relations" (*teshu de guo yu guo guanxi*). Because the Chinese term *guo* can be translated as either "state" or "nation/country," Lee's formulation could be interpreted as two governments negotiating on an equal basis inside one nation. But Chen's speech referred to China and Taiwan separately, suggesting that he viewed Taiwan as an independent country. If there were any remaining doubt, his government offered the official English translation of the speech with the word *guo* given as "country," not "state."[7] For our purposes, it is also notable that Chen's speech was made in a teleconference with Taiwan compatriots in Japan, a fact that linked Japan to Taiwan independence and, by association, Japan's treaty ally, the United States.

During his August 2002 Beijing visit, Deputy Secretary Armitage distanced himself from Chen's statements. When answering questions to the press about the speech, Armitage replied simply and firmly that the United States "does not support Taiwan independence." Also of importance, during his trip Armitage treated China as a partner in the War on Terror by publicly designating the East Turkestan Islamic Movement (ETIM) an international terrorist organization with links to Al Qaeda. ETIM is a radical organization that seeks independence for the PRC's Xinjiang region. The designation suggested that the United States was not exploiting China's ethnic and geographic splits.[8]

At the Crawford Summit in October 2002, President Bush would have another chance to explain to President Jiang that his administration was not seeking to change the historical U.S. "one China" policy. Then, in the lead-up to the 2004 Taiwan presidential elections, President Bush made the clearest statement yet that Washington actively opposed Chen's unilateral moves in the direction of Taiwan independence. On the campaign trail in Taiwan in late 2003, President Chen had suggested that he would pursue "defensive referenda" on aspects of Taiwan's relationship with the mainland during the presidential election of March 2004. He also suggested the need for constitutional reform and made various verbal assertions of Taiwan's sovereign independence from mainland China. With the visiting PRC premier Wen Jiabao at his side in Washington in December 2003, President Bush asserted that he opposed actions by either side of the Taiwan Strait to unilaterally change the status quo, then criticized President Chen's recent actions and statements. Bush's statement was extremely well received in Beijing.[9]

President Chen won a second term in a much-disputed electoral process that included an apparent eleventh-hour assassination attempt on him and his vice president, Annette Lu. The result dismayed Beijing. The reelected President Chen would return to divisive rhetoric as he campaigned for his party's candidates in the legislative elections in December 2004. China's leadership responded by having the National People's Congress draft and eventually pass an antisecession law, which outlined conditions under which the mainland might use "nonpeaceful" means against Taiwan.[10]

Contributing to China's concerns about regional security in this period were trends in Japanese politics and in U.S.–Japan alliance relations. In Japan, Prime Minister Koizumi continued his yearly visits to the Yasukuni Shrine, aggravating nationalist sentiments in both China and South Korea. And the United States and Japan continued to strengthen the U.S.–Japan alliance pursuant to the 2000 Armitage Report. In February 2005, the leading diplomats and defense officials from both Japan and the United States issued their "2+2" report, which declared a mutual interest in peaceful and stable relations across the Taiwan Strait.[11] From an American perspective, it is only natural that Japan would be concerned about cross-Strait stability and that U.S. bases in Japan would be essential to military intervention if the president were to decide to launch such an effort. But in China any suggestion that Japan might be directly involved in a cross-Strait conflict is politically very sensitive given the bitter history of Japanese imperialism and Taiwan's central role at the beginning (1895) and end (1945) of that saga.

In a revealing 2005 article, an influential Shanghai-based scholar, Wu Xinbo, outlined China's concerns and hopes for the U.S.–Japan alliance. Rather than present the usual diatribe, the article notes that the U.S.–Japan alliance had in the past prevented a more assertive and independent Japanese security policy. Wu saw three key issues of concern: nationalist political trends in Japan under Koizumi; the perception in some quarters in Japan of China's rise as a threat; and Japan's apparent growing attention to and interest in Taiwan, as evidenced by the February 2005 2+2 statement. Wu claimed, however, that these negative reactions had been tempered in the past and could be tempered in the future by proactive diplomacy in Washington and Tokyo to distance those capitals from Chen Shui-bian's gambits on Taiwan and to encourage trilateral dialogue between the United States, Japan, and China.[12]

From 2005 to 2007 the United States and Japan would take actions consistent with the prescriptions in Wu's article. The Bush administration adopted policies that clearly ran counter to any containment strategy, and Washington engaged Beijing in high-level security dialogues at which Beijing was invited to take a larger role on the international stage. This approach took on doctrinal stature through Deputy Secretary Robert Zoellick's speech at the National Committee on U.S.–China Relations gala on September 21, 2005. Zoellick invited China to become a "responsible stakeholder" on the international stage and outlined the philosophy behind the U.S.–PRC Senior Dialogue on Security and Political Affairs (hereafter referred to as the "Strategic Dialogue," the name preferred by China and eventually adopted by the Obama administration). Cooperation and collaboration among China, the United States, and two U.S. allies, Japan and the ROK, during the

Six Party Talks on Korean denuclearization would continue and intensify, especially following the North Korean nuclear test of late 2006.
Beyond North Korea, Washington would continue to engage in productive bilateral discussions with Beijing about how the United States
and the PRC could better coordinate the two countries' responses to
challenges around the world.[13] The same spirit of U.S.–PRC cooperation and the same rejection of a zero-sum mentality in bilateral relations
underpinned the late 2006 initiative to create the Strategic Economic
Dialogue, headed by Treasury Secretary Henry Paulson, on improving
economic conditions within and between the two nations.[14]

Perhaps the most important instances of confidence-building among
the United States, Japan, and the PRC were Washington's and Tokyo's
policies toward relations across the Taiwan Strait in the lead-up to the
March 2008 Taiwan presidential election. President Chen's Democratic
Progressive Party created a popular referendum to apply to the United
Nations under the name Taiwan, rather than the Republic of China,
the constitutional name of the government in Taipei. The referendum,
which was held in conjunction with the presidential election, was partly
a campaign strategy for the DPP. Passage of the referendum could not
change Taiwan's status on the international stage and it certainly would
not have led to Taiwan's admission to the United Nations. But the referendum's passage would have given Chen and his party a quasilegal
foundation from which to launch further pro-independence policies.
Beijing elites were particularly concerned that Chen might push for an
extraconstitutional declaration of independence since he would have
two months in office between the election and the inauguration of his
successor, even if his party were to lose the election, to implement such
a radical strategy.

After repeated efforts at private diplomacy failed to dissuade Chen
and the DPP from pursuing the referendum, the Bush administration
opposed it publicly. This campaign was carried out in a series of high-
level statements in late summer 2007 by Deputy Secretary of State John
Negroponte, Deputy National Security Advisor James Jeffrey, and the
National Security Council Senior Director for East Asian Affairs Den-
nis Wilder.[15] In December, Secretary Condoleezza Rice again rejected
the referendum as "provocative" in a press briefing.[16]

As part of this process, in my capacity as Deputy Assistant Secretary of State for East Asian and Pacific Affairs, I gave a lengthy speech on September 11, 2007, at a high-level U.S.–Taiwan defense conference. My gifted deputy Clifford Hart, the director of the Taiwan Coordination Office at State, contributed greatly to the drafting of the speech. We then had it cleared around Washington in what was a surprisingly smooth and speedy interagency process. The speech was not free of controversy because it criticized a fellow democracy for holding a specific referendum. But after a long series of statements and actions by President Chen that ran against U.S. policy interests, a broad consensus had formed in the Bush administration that something needed to be done to distance the United States from Chen in the eyes of the Taiwan public. In the speech, entitled "A Strong and Moderate Taiwan," I emphasized that while Taiwan's security required a strong military, it also required Taipei to avoid unnecessary, frivolous, and dangerous provocations of nationalism in the PRC. I stated:

> As long as Taiwan maintains a credible defensive capability, the chief threats to its welfare are political actions by Taipei itself that could trigger Beijing's use of force. The United States has repeatedly made clear that the use of force would be unacceptable, and we have repeatedly called on Beijing . . . to reduce its armed threat to Taiwan. But as much as we oppose Beijing's threat to use force, we also take it seriously, and Taipei cannot afford to do otherwise. . . . Responsible leadership in Taipei has to anticipate potential Chinese red lines and reactions and avoid unnecessary and unproductive provocations. . . . The United States has neither the power nor the right to tell the Taiwan people what they can and cannot do. As friends, however, we feel it is our obligation to warn that the content of this particular referendum is ill conceived and potentially quite harmful. Bad public policy initiatives are made no better for being wrapped in the flag of "democracy." . . . We anticipate that Taiwan's perceptive, intelligent citizens will see through the rhetoric and make a sound judgment that the referendum does not serve their interests because it will be fundamentally harmful to Taiwan's external relations.[17]

The speech was widely covered and analyzed in Taiwan's public media. The intended audience had been reached.

It is important to note that in late 2007 major U.S. allies in the region and around the world, many of them democracies, adopted policies toward the referendum consistent with Washington's. Even the European Union, a diverse organization whose decisions are based on consensus, came out in opposition to the referendum. Perhaps most important was Japan's position. During a late December 2007 summit in Beijing, Japanese Prime Minister Yasuo Fukuda would reject the referendum and any other unilateral attempt to change the status quo in cross-Strait relations. Although Fukuda was a bit more reserved than U.S. officials, stating that he did not support the referendum rather than that he opposed it, he clearly implied that he saw the referendum in a very negative light. Taipei newspapers, including the pro-DPP *Taipei Times*, were quick to note Fukuda's negative stance and dismissed the subtle difference in wording.[18]

The consistency of U.S. and Japanese support for the "one China" policy paid dividends. In fact, several weeks after conservative president Ma Ying-jeou's electoral victory in Taipei, President Hu made the first trip to Japan by a Chinese leader in more than ten years. In the days leading up to the trip, an influential Chinese scholar at the CCP Central Party School, Gong Li, pointed out that relations between the two sides were much improved thanks to Japan's rejection of Taiwan's UN referendum and Prime Minister Fukuda's trip to China.[19]

A similar story could be told about U.S. arms sales to Taiwan. Having notified Congress that it planned to sell $3 billion USD in weapons in fall 2007, the Bush administration notified Congress again in fall 2008 that it intended to sell an additional $6.5 billion in arms to Taiwan. As always, this sparked great criticism in Beijing and led to a counterproductive cancelation of military-to-military dialogue between China and the United States until early 2009, after President Obama's inauguration. But despite the large size of the packages, Beijing's response was rather limited and did not derail in any fundamental way relations across the Pacific. Nor did the notification of the weapons sales spoil the improving relations across the Taiwan Strait following the election of KMT president Ma Ying-jeou in March 2008. Ma opposed Chen's pro-independence antics and sought improved relations with the mainland. After his inauguration, the mainland and Taiwan quickly concluded economic agreements and established direct commercial flights across the Taiwan Strait.[20]

The concerted international criticism of the referendum apparently did real damage both to its popularity in Taiwan (an intended consequence of U.S. public diplomacy) and to the popularity of politicians who remained associated with it in the March 2008 elections (an unintended consequence). The coordinated effort also drove home to Beijing a key point: U.S. insistence that Beijing should never coerce Taiwan is not a secret code for U.S. support of Taiwan independence. At every turn, Washington mixed deterrent threats against the mainland's military forces with assurances about the limited purpose of the U.S. security relationship with Taiwan. In a very challenging time in cross-Strait relations, it seems that the Bush administration found a way to bolster regional security.

Seeking China's Cooperation on Global Issues

EVEN WITH THE SUCCESS in Taiwan policy, President Bush had a grander vision than simply preventing unnecessary conflicts. He wanted to shape the choices the leadership in Beijing made about how to use China's increasing influence. Rather than trying to roll back or contain the growth of Chinese power, the United States encouraged Beijing to rely on diplomatic and economic interactions rather than coercion and to use its resulting influence to improve the prospects for security and economic prosperity in Asia and beyond. This endeavour has had mixed results but was on a hopeful trajectory in the three years leading up to the financial crisis of 2008.

For decades, the United States has maintained several dozen formal dialogues with the Chinese. But the Bush administration launched two very important new and overarching diplomatic dialogues that promoted its strategy. Deputy Secretary Robert Zoellick and his Chinese counterpart State Councillor Dai Bingguo created the Strategic Dialogue. Zoellick's successor, John Negroponte, would take the reins of this relatively low-key but quite important dialogue in 2007. As previously discussed, in December 2006 Bush's Treasury Secretary Henry Paulson and his counterpart Vice Premier Wu Yi would more famously launch the Strategic Economic Dialogue, a semiannual meeting on bilateral and global economic affairs.

In the last few years of the Bush administration, I had the privilege of playing a supporting role in both of these major initiatives. It was clear to me that three broad themes contributed to the success of these talks. The first was the focus on channeling rather than containing Chinese rise. By inviting China to play a larger role on the international stage, albeit for a constructive purpose, the Bush administration countered hawkish arguments in China, which hold that the United States and its allies quietly harbor hostile intent and want to keep China from enjoying more regional and global influence.

The second successful theme was the Bush administration's refusal to treat the pursuit of Chinese and U.S. influence in various regions of the world as a zero-sum game. This was wise. In general, increased Chinese activity in developing regions is welcome, and the United States should encourage greater, not less, aid and investment there. Problems do not arise because of some imagined competitive struggle to secure influence and resources but because Chinese policies lack transparency and are not coordinated with major donors and international institutions such as the International Monetary Fund and the World Bank. As a result, Chinese projects can have the potential to undercut global efforts, by offering unconditional loans to governments prone to corruption, for example, when conditionality can be used to improve governance. Development aid has both economic and security implications. Unfortunately, during the Bush administration the United States pursued to no avail the establishment of an assistance dialogue between the U.S. Agency for International Development and those Chinese actors engaged in foreign aid and investment.

The third theme was an expansion of dialogues to address problems in regions around the world. One of the signal changes in the U.S.–China relationship since 2005 has been a move beyond the traditional bilateral issues to ways China and the United States might better coordinate approaches to problems in Africa, Central and South Asia, Latin

America, the Middle East, and Northeast Asia. As part of the Senior (Strategic) Dialogue, China and the United States began a series of regular subdialogues led by U.S. regional assistant secretaries of state and their Chinese counterparts in the Ministry of Foreign Affairs. Ten years earlier, people in these positions in the two countries likely would not have known each others' names, let alone been involved in extensive discussions about how best to foster stability and growth in various parts of the world. The Chinese bring to these dialogues their own robust diplomatic experiences, which often differ from those of their American counterparts in important ways.

Dialogue with China during the latter half of the Bush administration carried several benefits. At a minimum, the two sides made their concerns and strategies toward various problems more clear. Personal relationships among officials were built and sometimes called upon in tense times. But, at the end of the day, the test of success or failure is in the policy adjustments that flow from the dialogues. In this sense, while China remained far from achieving the aspirational status of responsible stakeholder imagined in Zoellick's 2005 speech, its policies underwent significant and constructive changes on certain international security and humanitarian issues that would be hard to explain in the absence of the dialogues.

Economics

IN THE EARLY YEARS of the U.S.–China Strategic Economic Dialogue, a major theme was the undervalued Chinese currency and large Chinese current account surpluses (more exports than imports) to which that undervaluation was contributing. These imbalances created distortions not just in China's economic relations with the United States but potentially in the global economy. By the middle of the 2000s, China was running a very large current account surplus not only with the United States but with the world (nearly 8 percent of GDP). To keep Chinese exports highly competitive on international markets, Chinese officials artificially undervalued China's currency and did not let it float on international markets. The resulting combination of artificially inexpensive Chinese exports and artificially overpriced imports from other countries fueled China's surplus. Arguably, those most affected by China's undervalued currency were not the United States and the wealthiest economies but exporting nations competing with the Chinese. Regardless of any upward price adjustment in Chinese exports that would come with revaluation of the RMB, low-wage industries exporting from China to the United States were unlikely to move back to the United States or to any other advanced economies. But other developing and newly developed countries like Brazil, Indonesia, and South Korea stood to have their exports become more competitive if China's currency were to revalue.

China's RMB revalued roughly 21 percent against the dollar from 2005 to 2008, in part, I believe, because of Secretary Paulson's dialogue. The United States did benefit, albeit not because outsourced jobs returned to America. The big beneficiaries were U.S. exporters. Before this revaluation, the China market had become increasingly important to U.S. exporters. In the five years following China's accession to the WTO in 2001, exports to China grew five times faster than U.S. exports to the rest of the world. Chinese revaluation accelerated that process. In 2006 U.S. exports to China grew nearly twice as fast as U.S. imports from China. Growth in exports continued to outstrip growth in imports by healthy margins in 2007 and 2008 as well. At the end of the Bush administration, China was already the United States' third largest export market.

There are many reasons for this success, and only some of them are directly related to U.S. diplomacy. But a higher valuation of the RMB helped make U.S. products exported to China more affordable to Chinese consumers. In the Strategic Economic Dialogue, the United States also secured contracts for the sale of $8 billion in nuclear power technology to China, for increased air routes between the two countries, and for active cooperation in China between the U.S. Food and Drug Administration and Chinese counterparts. This last accomplishment was perhaps the most surprising. China had been suffering from safety scandals in its exports, from toys to dog food to dumplings. Since inspecting every container from China is an impossibly gargantuan task at stateside ports, the best way to improve product safety is to bring improved inspection capabilities to the factory floors. A smaller cadre of skilled inspectors and scientists can do more good on this score than a large army of customs officials. But it was not easy to convince China to allow foreign inspectors on the ground.

Despite these concrete accomplishments, in my opinion the biggest value of the dialogue was not in such deliverables but in the cooperative spirit exhibited in the discussions. While differences about implementation and interpretation were rife, there was a basic agreement that free trade and flows of investment were good for both economies and for global economic stability. There was a surprising degree of consensus that China needed to improve intellectual property rights protections if it were to develop homegrown innovation; and, in order to address the persistent current account surpluses and the potentially fickle nature of export markets, China needed to base its future growth more on domestic consumption and less on exports and investment. Similarly, there was agreement across the Pacific that the United States needed to adjust its macroeconomy over time to reduce large and persistent current account deficits (importing more than we export) and government debt. There was recognition that the imbalances in both economies had an impact not simply on the bilateral economic relationship but also on global development.

Perhaps most important to me as someone working primarily on security issues was that there was almost no sense in the Strategic Economic Dialogue that either side viewed the other's economic prosperity as a threat or the other's economic woes as a strategic advantage. To the contrary, each country's officials were able to convey their long-term concerns about the other's economy in ways that underscored the danger to both economies and to the global economy if either the United States or China were to suffer a major downturn. The spirit of the discussions was captured well in a truly excellent speech by Chairman of the Federal Reserve Ben Bernanke at China's Academy of Social Sciences in late 2006. Bernanke wisely and fairly raised fundamental macroeconomic problems in both the Chinese and the American economies (including U.S. fiscal debt and financial imbalances) in ways that were visibly appreciated by his Chinese audience, who are more accustomed to U.S. hectoring than self-criticism. Bernanke's willingness to discuss

American problems made his suggestions for Chinese macroeconomic adjustments a much less bitter pill to swallow.

There were also clear differences between the two countries. The United States remained frustrated by widespread intellectual property rights violations and by the lack of openness in various parts of the Chinese economy, especially in finance. Before the financial crisis, U.S. leaders vigorously argued that the ability of American firms to buy majority shares of Chinese financial companies would bring "best practices" to China. While that argument would lose a lot of luster in the second half of 2008, aspects of those earlier arguments about the need for financial liberalization seem to have taken root. In 2013 China launched an experimental special free trade zone in Shanghai. Foreign firms would have more access to investment in financial firms there than they do in the rest of China. The zone would also adopt what Washington has long promoted for all of China, a so-called negative list for foreign investment. Traditionally, in China, foreign investment has been allowed only in explicitly approved sectors (a "positive list"), even though those sectors were quite numerous by the standards of most developing countries. The United States, however, prefers a negative-list approach in which all foreign investments from a treaty country would be permitted and given the same legal standing as domestic investment unless otherwise explicitly restricted by law. In addition to adopting the negative-list approach in the Shanghai zone itself, China recently began negotiating with the United States on a bilateral investment treaty for the entire nation on a negative-list basis, a negotiating approach that was preferred by the Bush administration but rejected by our Chinese counterparts at the time.[21]

For their part, the Chinese complained to Secretary Paulson and his entourage about restrictions on U.S. high-tech exports to China on security grounds. The so-called "China list" bans the export of some thirty-odd technologies to China because they have implications for China's national security establishment. Some Chinese officials claim, falsely, that lifting these export controls would significantly reduce the bilateral trade deficit (in fact, lifting all of the export restrictions would likely reduce the trade deficit by a very small percentage). But a broader Chinese argument on this score is shared by major U.S. corporations and did resonate with American officials. Export controls complicate the operations of U.S. manufacturers like Boeing who assemble parts in China as part of a transnational production chain. The China list for prohibited exports was reviewed under the Bush administration and continues to be reconsidered today with an eye to maintaining a healthy balance between economic opportunities for U.S. firms and U.S. national security.

Another Chinese complaint was about the openness of the United States to Chinese capital. In the past several years, Chinese companies had begun seeking significant investment opportunities in the United States. However, there was concern in Beijing that Washington would block such investments for security reasons through the intentionally opaque deliberations of the executive-branch Committee on Financial Investment in the United States (CFIUS). Many Chinese interlocutors falsely blame this process for Chinese state oil firm CNOOC's failed attempt to purchase U.S. oil firm UNOCAL in 2005. This was not the case. Resistance to the deal came primarily from Congress, not the executive branch. In any case, the Chinese expressed in the Strategic Economic Dialogue and other dialogues that the blocking of this deal had eroded Chinese trust in the U.S. market. Since the interagency CFIUS process is run out of Treasury, the dialogue led by Secretary Paulson provided a good opportunity to set the record straight and to clarify that CFIUS does not particularly target Chinese investments. CFIUS instead prohibits any foreign investment, including by allies like France and the United Kingdom, in sectors of the U.S. economy that would have potentially negative national security implications.

Nonproliferation

North Korea

DESPITE BEIJING'S SEVERE CONCERNS about destabilizing North Korea through international pressure, China has played a relatively assertive leadership role in the international effort to halt and reverse Pyongyang's nuclear weapons program. China's proactive role began in 2003 when it pressured North Korea first into three-way negotiations with Beijing and Washington and, eventually, into the Six Party Talks framework that included Japan, South Korea, and Russia as well. China continued to host and nurture the Six Party Talks through the rest of President Bush's two terms in office. But one can find only limited solace in such progress in terms of China's willingness to accept an assertive leadership role in other aspects of global governance.

Several historical, geographic, political, and military conditions made North Korea in the 2000s a special case for China. Even though relations have been strained during multiple periods after Beijing and Pyongyang signed the 1961 defense pact, North Korea is China's only formal ally, and it is an alliance that is forged in considerable blood from the 1950–1953 Korean War. Geography matters as well. Any conflict on the peninsula would be a disaster for neighboring China, particularly if it involved strikes on nuclear facilities. While preparing for war in Iraq in early 2003, the Bush administration appeared quite belligerent. North Korea had been listed alongside Iran and Iraq as a member of the "Axis of Evil" in President Bush's January 2002 State of the Union Address. Beijing could not ignore the possibility of conflict on the peninsula if a diplomatic solution was not found. In late 2002 a high-level U.S. government entourage visited Pyongyang and presented evidence that North Korea was pursuing highly enriched uranium (HEU) production in violation of its various agreements on nuclear nonproliferation. The U.S. officials claim that their North Korean counterparts admitted to pursuing HEU to supplement plutonium production at the Yongbyon nuclear plant. The North Koreans later denied that they made such an admission and publicly bristled at U.S. accusations. Pyongyang promptly withdrew from the Nonproliferation Treaty and in early 2003 again began reprocessing spent fuel rods at the Yongbyon nuclear facility, an activity that had been frozen there by the aforementioned 1994 Agreed Framework.

Not just Beijing but also Tokyo and Seoul were concerned that if diplomacy failed in this new Korean nuclear crisis, the U.S. might launch air strikes against the recently reactivated Yongbyon nuclear facilities.[22] Envoys flowed into Beijing to urge China to convince Pyongyang to come to the table and, according to public reports, Beijing did just that. Beijing reportedly cut off oil flow to the dependent ally temporarily in winter, citing technical difficulties, and suggested that the 1961 defense commitment to North Korea was conditional on Pyongyang's behavior. Beijing also reportedly offered to serve as an honest broker in North Korean talks with the Americans.[23]

The ordinarily cautious and plodding Beijing acted fairly quickly by Chinese standards. And China likely would have been active diplomatically even earlier were it not for the Party leadership transition that was underway in 2002–2003. At the March 2003 National People's Congress, Hu Jintao would be named president and his foreign policy team would change. The months leading up to this meeting were an awkward time for proactive diplomacy on an important security issue. Once the leadership transition was completed in March, the circumstances above kicked China into full gear and three-party talks (among the DPRK, U.S., and PRC) began in Beijing in April.

Neither the Americans nor the Chinese saw the three-party format as ideal. By August 2003 China and the United States were able to persuade the North Koreans to participate in talks that included Japan, South Korea, and Russia as well. The United States insisted that the talks be about denuclearization of the peninsula, reminding all parties that, after the Cold War, it did not have any nuclear weapons deployed in South Korea. The North always claimed that it had the right to pursue peaceful nuclear energy and, dating back to the 1990s negotiations, even had the gall to state that the Yongbyon facility was part of such a peaceful program. On this pretense, Pyongyang always demanded compensation in the form of energy (heavy fuel oil and a light water nuclear reactor) for any cooperation on its nuclear program. The other members of the Six Party Talks knew that this was farcical because the Yongbyon nuclear facility was detached from the North Korean electrical grid. The only electricity generated by the plant might have been to provide lighting for the plant itself. But there were humanitarian reasons to provide heavy fuel oil to North Korea in any case. Still, truly significant amounts of oil could not be provided at any given time simply because the decrepit North Korean infrastructure lacked the capacity to store large quantities. This meant that the decision to provide the oil was not necessarily a long-term or irreversible one that North Korea could pocket and then continue with nuclear weapons development thereafter without paying costs.

I had the privilege of participating in the U.S. entourage for two rounds of the Six Party Talks. These were arguably the worst (December 2006) and the best (February 2007) rounds of the talks, so I was able to experience a wide range of diplomacy in a short period of time. Negotiating with the North Koreans was often infuriating for the American diplomats and I was often grateful that my role was to advise my boss, Ambassador Christopher Hill, on China's role in the talks, not on how to negotiate with Pyongyang. There was a large cast of characters in the talks, which took place in Beijing's quiet and serene Diaoyutai State Guesthouse compound. China and the United States were represented by two very experienced and distinguished diplomats. In their own way, they both seemed well suited for the task. Chris Hill was Richard Holbrooke's deputy during the Clinton administration and had dealt with bad actors before. He had managed to pound out the details of the Dayton Peace Accords that ended the Bosnia War with Serbia's Slobodan Milosevic, a mobster of the first order. Hill was also accustomed to the cacophony of criticism diplomats face back home anytime they actually negotiate with such bad actors (meaning whenever they offer the other side either assurances or benefits in return for pledges of cooperation). China's lead negotiator was Wu Dawei, a tough, perceptive, and smart diplomat who lacked many of the cosmopolitan niceties of his younger, English-speaking colleagues. A chain-smoking former Red Guard, Wu had the air of someone who had been in his share of street fights. He seemed the perfect interlocutor with a North Korean regime that was, at its core, much more of a crime syndicate than a legitimate nation-state. The fact that Pyongyang's entourage included one sharply dressed and smooth-talking consigliere only heightened my image of the North Korean regime as a mob. I had worked in the construction industry in New York City in the 1980s and had seen such characters before.

On September 19, 2005, the Six Party Talks produced a joint statement that committed all parties, including North Korea, to denuclearization of the peninsula. The statement remains useful to this day as a reminder that the Six Party Talks should be and are about Korean denuclearization, not regional security or regional denuclearization. Anything different could provide Pyongyang the dangerous opportunity to be accepted as a legitimate nuclear state. Implementation fell into disrepair almost immediately, however, because the North quickly interpreted it in a disingenuous fashion. For example, Pyongyang claimed that light water reactors must be sent to North Korea prior to denuclearization, when it was clear to all other parties that such procurement would only follow verifiable North Korean denuclearization. The United States also created complexity in the negotiating process. Four days before the September statement, the United States Treasury Department prevented a Macau bank, Banco Delta Asia, from doing transactions in U.S. dollars, a heavy blow to any bank in a globalized world. Treasury had charged the bank with laundering criminal money from North Korea. To quarantine the effect on the Macau banking industry, the Macau authorities froze the bank's North Korean assets, worth $25 million. This is not a lot of money in the world of international relations, international security, or weapons proliferation. But this was the mouse that roared: Treasury's designation of BDA as a problem institution spooked banks around the world, dissuading them from handling North Korean funds under the wise theory that the large majority of North Korea's international financing had some link to illegal activities. The North Korean leaders could no longer access the cash that financed their luxurious lifestyle and, equally important, allowed them to bribe a sufficiently large sector of their population in order to stay in power.

Treasury launched the Banco Delta Asia (BDA) initiative in conjunction with an innovative financial analyst at State, David Asher. It was a brilliant way to hurt the North Korean regime. Victor Cha, a Georgetown professor and my U.S. government colleague from the National Security Council, recalls in his comprehensive book on North Korea, *The Impossible State,* that a drunken member of the North Korean entourage admitted to him that they were hurting from the measures.[24] The problem with BDA was that it was a brute-force measure designed to hurt North Korea's leadership, not a finely tuned tool of diplomacy. As a law enforcement measure, the designation was hard to rescind— Treasury stood to lose credibility around the world if it did so without cause. Moreover, international banks cannot function without being able to perform transactions in dollars. Treasury's designation of BDA was therefore the nuclear option. Even after the designation was lifted, it was difficult to find an international bank willing to accept the $25 million North Korean transfer from BDA. Bankers preferred to stay below Treasury's radar. They also knew that other banks might shy away from dealing with them rather than be associated with a bank that could be accused of laundering criminal North Korean funds. From a negotiating standpoint, the Treasury designation had limited utility because it had only two modes: on or off. The best negotiating tools are less like an on-off switch and more like a dial that can be used to increase or decrease pressure. As long as the Treasury designation held, North Korea's leaders were in a world of hurt. Once lifted, they could effectively access their money and move to avoid a repeat of this episode.

To put it mildly, Beijing did not like the listing of BDA by Treasury. The timing of the listing, just days before the joint statement, seemed to many like an effort by neoconservatives in Washington to undercut any agreement, thereby neutering the Six Party Talks. A second problem for Beijing was that Macau was its territory, and there was concern that the travails of this one small bank might spread to the finances of the rest of the territory, which is a major gambling hub. Related to this second problem was the potential exposure of mainland Chinese banks to designation for their direct or indirect dealings with North Korean funds. More broadly, the Chinese saw this measure as a sweeping sanction designed to destabilize the regime in North Korea, not simply to provide negotiating leverage related to the nuclear issue. In Bush's first term, his primary goal seemed to be regime change in North Korea, as evidenced by his 2002 "axis of evil" speech. In his second term, he seemed more willing to live, however uncomfortably, with a denuclearized North Korean regime, much to Beijing's relief. But the listing of BDA seemed more consistent with a regime change approach because it affected the bulk of North Korea's international economic activities, on which the regime depended.

North Korea's own behavior in late 2006 helped turn China's focus away from U.S. sanctions and back to the real problem, North Korea's headlong defiance of the international community. North Korea petulantly tested a long-range missile on July 4, 2006. Ruining the holidays of U.S. officials seems to be a page in their rogue state playbook. With little warning to their Chinese allies, and despite China's resistance, North Korea tested a nuclear device for the first time in early October 2006. China's official reaction was particularly harsh, describing North Korean behavior as "brazen" (*hanran*), a term that had been used in the past to describe enemy behavior, such as the U.S. bombing of North Vietnam and Laos during the Vietnam War.

Meanwhile in Washington, one of the more important and surprising aspects of the North Korean negotiations process was taking shape. The United States was preparing a six-point package to offer to North Korea and the other Six Party nations if North Korea were to move verifiably and consistently in the direction of denuclearization. I cannot go into all the details here, but the offer was so generous in the diplomatic, economic, and security realms that any reasonable North Korean leadership not blinded by the desire to acquire a nuclear arsenal would have accepted it. This was not just my opinion or the opinion of other officials in Washington; it was the opinion of the diplomats of all of the other countries involved in the Six Party Talks. I recall being surprised myself by the Bush administration's flexibility when I was first shown a draft of the proposed package in a small meeting on the seventh floor of the State Department. As a China specialist, I noted that the package would appeal to Beijing's leadership, who wanted both denuclearization and long-term stability on the peninsula. For Beijing, regime survival in Pyongyang was a paramount goal. In late 2006 the United States appeared willing to coexist with the North Korean regime as long as it did not have a nuclear weapons program. And denuclearization appeared to be the route for North Korea to break out of its dangerous diplomatic and economic isolation and create a more sustainable economy.

In November 2006 I traveled to Beijing with two senior officials, Undersecretaries of State Nicholas Burns and Robert Joseph, to present the U.S. proposed framework to the Chinese government and to diplomats from the other Six Party nations. Besides the meetings with the Chinese foreign policy leaders, the meeting with the Russian diplomats seemed most important. To this day, Moscow shares the Chinese worry that the United States wants regime change in North Korea and other pariah capitals. The Chinese and Russian interlocutors seemed to me visibly impressed with the moderate content and comprehensive nature of the U.S. vision for North Korea's postnuclear future.

The makeup of the small U.S. entourage was also important. There was a lot of suspicion in the region and in the United States that the Bush administration was internally divided and that any agreement reached would be quickly undercut by opponents to the negotiations. Based in part on the record of U.S. diplomacy in Bush's first term, observers believed that there were still sharp lines between the policy preferences of career diplomats like Chris Hill and political appointees brought in from outside the government, who were considered more ideologically rigid and less willing to compromise. So it was important, in my opinion, that the envisioned framework for a nonnuclear North Korean future was presented in Beijing by Ambassador Burns, the highest-ranking career officer in the State Department, and Ambassador Joseph, the Undersecretary of State in charge of nonproliferation policy, a conservative political appointee widely viewed as being among the officials most skeptical of any accommodation toward Pyongyang. Moreover, Burns had traveled to Beijing to conduct the third round of the Senior (Strategic) Dialogue with China, which was designed by Robert Zoellick and Dai Bingguo to improve U.S.–PRC coordination on matters of global security, including North Korean proliferation. So in form, medium, and timing, the U.S. diplomacy was effective: the Bush administration's message made it clear that Pyongyang, not Washington, was impeding progress; the composition of the entourage demonstrated that the United States government was speaking with a single voice on the issue; and the timing of the message incentivized Beijing to pressure North Korea to return to its commitments in the September 2005 joint statement.

If the flexibility of the United States had not been enough to convince Beijing that its ally, not the United States, was the problem, the behavior of the North Koreans in December 2006 would have removed any doubts. The U.S. diplomats came to the talks that month having circulated their proposal to the other members. The North Korean diplomats, on the other hand, came to Beijing loaded for bear. Even by the high standards of North Korean obstreperousness, their performance was exceptionally rude, aggressive, and undiplomatic. In plenary sessions, not only did the leader of the entourage, Vice Foreign Minister Kim Kye-gwan, bluster about the need for strong nuclear shields to respond to U.S. aggression, he criticized each of the other five national participants of the Six Party Talks for their unfair and aggressive treatment of Pyongyang.

Chris Hill had long since become bored with listening to Kim rail against the United States in hyperbolic terms. In one plenary session that December, he conspicuously opened a newspaper and began to read to demonstrate his indifference to the North Korean tirade of the day. But as Kim worked his way around the room delivering his barrage of invective, he finally settled on the host, China, for a round of critical comments. Hill, who had consistently praised China's efforts at the Six Party Talks, conspicuously closed his newspaper, stating audibly, "Now, *this* is interesting." As if the July Fourth missile tests weren't enough, the stonewalling North Koreans then requested that the December talks be extended through Christmas. Thankfully, Chris Hill refused and we were back on the tarmac in Washington by the evening of December 23.

The diplomatic theatrics of that December were mostly for show, but they were a symbol of something important. In the second half of 2006, North Korea had alienated the rest of the Six Party participants to such a degree that the talks had become a five on one proposition. China signed on to two UN Security Council resolutions sanctioning North Korea after its July missile test and October nuclear test. More important still, as Victor Cha reports, China applied significant bilateral economic and diplomatic pressure on North Korea in late 2006 and early 2007 through its own Party and military channels.[25] Beijing clearly wanted to compel North Korea to negotiate denuclearization in good faith in the Six Party Talks process, a process on the brink of total breakdown in December. As hosts, Beijing stood to lose considerable prestige if the talks failed.

By February 2007, Beijing had gotten Pyongyang's attention. In sharp contrast to their attitude in December, North Korea returned to the talks that month ready to negotiate. The result was the Action for Action plan, in which the United States agreed to provide benefits such as heavy fuel oil in return for a North Korean commitment to disable the Yongbyon nuclear facilities and move toward denuclearization after a full disclosure of North Korean nuclear programs to date. The February 2007 agreement and the negotiations that flowed from it for the next several months was the apex of progress in the talks. It led to the freezing of the Yongbyon facility, the on-site destruction by U.S. government engineers and technicians of key components of the Yongbyon facility's plutonium production capabilities, and the eventual leveling of the plant's cooling tower in June 2008.[26]

This was the only concrete progress that the Six Party Talks produced. The talks would stall again in late 2008 over North Korea's willful misinterpretations of their commitments to the verification processes, including full disclosure of Pyongyang's nuclear weapons–related activity. The talks have not been restored since December 2008 and have been frozen since President Obama took office in 2009. The progress achieved in late 2006 and early 2007 was real but, in the end, temporary and unsatisfactory. In subsequent years North Korea would continue to conduct nuclear tests and test-fire long-range missiles. Moreover, in 2010 it would reveal to a visiting U.S. scientist, Siegfried Hecker, that it actually had a well-developed uranium-enrichment program for the production of fissile material, something the Bush administration had claimed going back to 2002, a claim that administration critics, like Hecker himself, had previously and publicly called into question. In 2013, while the world's attention was on the Obama administration's standoff with Syria, the North Korean regime restarted operations at the Yongbyon nuclear facility (a process that must have required many months of preparation, given the damage done to those facilities by the earlier disablement efforts).

Despite the limited nature of the progress achieved, the negotiation process from late 2006 to early 2007 reveals something important about the conditions under which U.S.–China coordination is possible. When regime change is taken off the table by the United States, and when the behavior of the rogue regime in question, not Washington's policies, is seen as the primary problem, Beijing is much more likely to break with its tradition of passivity and resistance to sanctions. Beijing rarely wants to stand alone in support of a pariah, and its willingness to risk its international reputation as the sole supporter of such a regime is limited. As long as those conditions hold and the United States does not appear to be soliciting China's active support for the overthrow of regimes Washington deems evil, then there are opportunities to foster Chinese cooperation.

Iran

THE RECORD OF U.S.–China cooperation on restraining Iran's nuclear programs during the Bush years was much less encouraging. China signed on to three UN Security Council resolutions from 2006 to 2008 but first worked to water them down. Beijing wanted to limit the effect on the Iranian economy and, especially, on the business relationships between China's state-owned energy companies and the Iranian leadership. China participated actively in the P5+1 process, which involves the five permanent members of the UN Security Council— China, Russia, France, the United Kingdom, and the United States—and Germany. China even hosted a meeting in 2008 in Shanghai. Yet there was a distinct lack of urgency to China's approach, and the international effort to increase pressure on Iran generally was slow and unimpressive. Perhaps more important, as the international community gradually increased pressure on the regime, China's state-owned energy giants continued to pursue new, multibillion-dollar energy contracts with Tehran. This sent a very bad signal that helped undercut the international efforts in which China itself was participating.[27] As a result, even though the Iranian nuclear issue was a high priority for the Bush administration, the international community only applied limited economic pressure on Tehran for its refusal to allow the UN Security Council and the International Atomic Energy Agency to verify that its enriched uranium facilities were for peaceful purposes, a claim that had been widely rejected by the United States, the Europeans, Japan, and many regional actors.

China justified its foot-dragging on Iran in several different ways. It claimed that peaceful negotiation, not pressure, was the best way to manage the Iranian nuclear problem. To professional diplomats, this mantra was a source of great frustration. The entire concept of using serious economic pressure was to enable a meaningful diplomatic, as opposed to military, solution to the problematic Iranian nuclear programs. That pressure and negotiation might be exclusive categories seems naïve at best and disingenuous at worst. Other factors contributed to China's lack of urgency. Chinese analysts had previously underestimated North Korea's ability to develop nuclear weapons, but readily obvious North Korean tests demonstrated that Pyongyang was further along than the Chinese condescended to allow. But the Iranian situation was still not fully clear, and Beijing urged states not to jump to conclusions about Iranian activities. Chinese diplomats sometimes asserted that the lack of clarity on Iran's nuclear programs should stay the hand of the United States, NATO, and especially Israel, which had long called Iran's development of a nuclear weapon a red line. Finally, the diverse economic, strategic, and political cultural reasons offered in chapter 5, and the general distance of Tehran as opposed to Pyongyang made the issue less salient and less pressing to Chinese elites.

In the closing months of the Bush administration, many U.S. experts and officials working on nonproliferation saw the North Korean nuclear test of 2006 as an object lesson that it is much more efficient to counter nuclear proliferation before a country develops fissile material and tests nuclear explosives than after. While Chinese diplomats would likely agree, convincing them to join a pressure campaign on Iran led by the United States and its European allies was another matter altogether.

Humanitarian Disasters and Regional Stability

Sudan Darfur

AFTER THE GENOCIDE in Rwanda, Sudan Darfur constitutes the most infamous example of targeted mass killing in the past twenty years. The killings were perpetrated against as many as two hundred thousand victims, mostly black Africans, by armed Arab militias encouraged and materially supported by the government in Khartoum. For familiar reasons, Beijing initially became a leading champion of Sudan's sovereignty and a defender of the government. The Chinese had made significant energy investments in Sudan. Beijing resisted calls from liberal democracies for regime change, decried regional splittism in multiethnic post-colonial nations, and treated with suspicion the goals and arguments of the global human rights movement, which had championed the cause of Darfur's victims. From the beginning of the atrocities in 2003 until the summer of 2006, Beijing's policy in response to the genocide in Darfur was simple and firm: shield the regime in Khartoum against pressure from the international community, especially at the UN Security Council.

Beijing's policy began to change for the better in the latter half of 2006. As a participant, I could already sense a change in China's tone on Sudan Darfur in discussions in the Strategic Dialogue in Beijing in November 2006. Later that year, China backed a three-phase plan for peacekeeping drafted by Kofi Annan. By early 2007, Beijing was pushing Khartoum to allow implementation of phase two, in which the UN promised to build infrastructure for the eventual deployment of large-scale peacekeeping forces in phase three. President Bush's Special Envoy to Sudan, Ambassador Andrew Natsios, made an important trip to Beijing in early January to bolster what was already positive motion in China's attitudes on Sudan Darfur. In the following month, PRC president Hu Jintao would visit Sudan as part of an African tour. According to a knowledgeable Chinese scholar with whom I discussed the issue, Hu took a long car ride with Sudanese strongman Omar al-Bashir to Chinese-invested oil fields in the southern part of the country. During that ride, Hu made it clear that it would be in Sudan's best interest and in the interest of China-Sudan relations for Bashir to cooperate actively with the United Nations to promote peace in Darfur. Intensive meetings between State Department officials working on Africa policy and their Chinese counterparts were held in early March 2007. In mid-March the PRC Foreign Ministry spokesperson was calling publicly for a UN peacekeeping force to supplement the African Union forces already in Darfur. In early April, the leader of the Chinese delegation for that dialogue, Assistant Foreign Minister Zhai Jun, would visit Sudan, tour the Darfur region, and similarly urge the acceptance of UN peacekeepers. China signed UN Security Council Resolution 1769 on Sudan/Darfur at the end of July, which authorized a joint UN–African Union peacekeeping mission in Darfur for the first time.[28] Earlier, in May, Beijing had announced privately that it would commit three hundred engineering troops to Darfur in support of phase two. The group of more than three hundred Chinese engineers, now in place, constituted the first non-African peacekeeping contingent in Darfur.

Khartoum would eventually allow non-African UN peacekeepers to enter Darfur after previously insisting that only African peacekeepers could operate in the vast region. China had come a long way. In the twelve-month period from July 2006 to July 2007, China's turnaround on Darfur was not quite 180 degrees, but it was quite dramatic nonetheless. Various factors contributed to the change, including Beijing's desire to avoid excessive negative publicity for the upcoming 2008 Beijing Olympics. But the media coverage of China's turnaround was often cartoonish and rarely referred to the diplomatic efforts of the Bush administration (or similar efforts by other like-minded countries concerned about the atrocities in Darfur). For example, Helene Cooper of the *New York Times* reported on April 13, 2007, that Hollywood celebrity activists deserved the credit for the positive turn in Chinese diplomacy. In particular she cited a letter from Steven Spielberg to President Hu in early April. That letter was written as Spielberg's response to a campaign launched by Mia Farrow in March to label the 2008 Games the Genocide Olympics. Farrow had criticized Spielberg for his ongoing work as artistic advisor to China for the Beijing Olympics. Cooper's article suggested that the April trip of Assistant Foreign Minister Zhai to Sudan had been caused by the Spielberg letter, writing, "[After Hu received the Spielberg letter] China soon dispatched Mr. Zhai to Darfur, a turnaround that served as a classic study of how a pressure campaign, aimed to strike Beijing in a vulnerable spot at a vulnerable time, could accomplish what years of diplomacy could not."[29]

State Department officials have long inured themselves to inaccurate and simplistic news reporting, but as I was not a professional diplomat I confess that Cooper's article struck a raw nerve. Cooper missed the important evolution of China's policies toward Darfur, which predated the launch of Farrow's movement. As scholars such as Hong Kong University's Courtney Richardson have argued, many important events had occurred in the months before the Genocide Olympics campaign.[30] Effect cannot precede cause. U.S. diplomacy had been far more effective than Cooper allowed. On March 9, 2007, weeks before Farrow launched her campaign and Spielberg sent his letter, Assistant Secretary of State Jendayi Frazer met with Assistant Foreign Minister Zhai. I participated in those meetings. Not only did the Chinese appear fully open to the idea of an expanded UN role, but during the discussions they even entertained in a cordial fashion Frazer's suggestion that China consider sending noncombat troops as part of a future UN contingent. Four days after the meeting, China's Foreign Ministry spokesperson, Qin Gang, stated publicly that "China hopes the Sudanese government will reach a consensus with the United Nations (UN) and the African Union (AU) as soon as possible on deploying peace-keeping forces in Darfur."[31]

Activists and journalists often focus exclusively on the importance of shaming and sanctioning targeted regimes in producing changed behavior. These approaches have an important place in diplomacy and can contribute to positive outcomes. But context is also critically important. Pragmatic diplomats know that to mobilize skeptical potential third-party partners like China in a multilateral effort to create peace in an area such as Darfur, one must also reassure those potential partners, not just threaten or shame them. The prospective partners need to know that if the goals sought are actually achieved, their important interests in the region will be protected and the partners will receive credit, not further criticism. Without such a foundation of assurance, built over months of diplomacy, I doubt that public relations threats to the Beijing Olympics would have created positive change in Beijing's policies on Darfur. Since many thousands of lives were arguably saved by the UN intervention, this is hardly an academic distinction.

China played a powerful role for peace both by convincing Khartoum to accept a hybrid UN–African Union peacekeeping force and by contributing noncombat Chinese personnel to the non-African contingent. Khartoum never trusted the Americans and Europeans, but China, as a long-term supporter and partner of Khartoum, lent a degree of legitimacy, political gravitas, and safety to the UN mission.

No country likes to be shamed, including China, especially right before the Olympics. But shame was only part of the story. Diplomatic assurances that Beijing's interests would not be harmed if they backed the UN peace process were equally important. In the regional subdialogue and in meetings between Andrew Natsios and his Chinese counterpart Ambassador Liu Guijin, U.S. diplomats consistently pointed out that Washington envisioned Khartoum as a key player in any UN-backed peace. This position reduced the Chinese fears that the UN intervention might become a pretext for regime change (think Bosnia) or regional breakup of Sudan (think Kosovo). Moreover, the U.S. negotiators were able to tie the violence in Darfur to instability in neighboring Chad, which was destabilized by the flow of refugees, many of them armed. By so doing, they credibly portrayed Darfur as an international security issue, removing another Chinese objection to the involvement of the UN Security Council in what might otherwise be seen as a purely domestic humanitarian crisis. Finally, they conveyed that the United States had no designs on Chinese oil claims in the country, only wishing that China would use the leverage that those investments provided to encourage the regime to stem the tide of killing.

Successful diplomacy is generally more about managing problems, not solving them outright. The situation in Darfur is still grim today. But by most reports, it is not nearly as violent as it was in the period 2003–2007. The international peacekeepers were not physically powerful enough or numerous enough to suppress violence by force in such a vast region, but they played an important symbolic role that helped quell the intense fighting of previous years and contributed to subsequent peace deals signed in 2010 between the regime in Khartoum, the regime-backed Janjaweed militia, and rebel groups fighting the regime. This outcome did not happen simply because of the Olympics or because of the potential shame that China would suffer at the hands of mobilized human rights activists. Crediting those factors alone would lead us to miss important lessons about diplomacy with China on global governance issues.

Zimbabwe and Burma

THE CHINESE VETOES of draft UN Security Council resolutions regarding humanitarian disasters in Burma and Zimbabwe (January 14, 2007, and July 18, 2008, respectively) provide a sad and stark contrast to the experience with Sudan Darfur. But that contrast is also useful, especially since both episodes preceded the Olympics. In both instances, the United States and other sponsors of the draft resolutions failed to make a convincing case that these were more than domestic conflicts. China thus opposed referring the cases to the UN Security Council on principle. Moreover, the United States failed to send consistent signals to Beijing that its goal was simply to reduce violence and not to rally international support for regime change.

For example, in the case of Burma, the resolution was doomed by its wording and by mixed signals out of Washington. In essence, Washington and other backers of the resolution were attempting to use the UN Security Council to shame the Burmese junta and, by association, its international economic partners, for Burma's often brutal form of domestic rule. Significantly, the draft resolution called only for condemnation, not sanctions. There were few if any compelling international security reasons for UN Security Council involvement, nor did the proponents of the resolution offer assurances that Chinese interests would be protected in potential follow-on resolutions.

Given the PRC's own record on human rights and domestic repression, Beijing had domestic reasons to oppose international condemnation of Burma. Moreover, Beijing argued successfully that the UN Human Rights Commission, not the UN Security Council, was the appropriate venue for considering humanitarian conditions in Burma (both Russia and South Africa voted no alongside China on the UN Security Council). Influential Americans had contributed to this outcome by simplistically suggesting that the solution to Burma's problems was for the military junta to immediately "step down." But the many Chinese experts on Burma and the much smaller number from the United States knew that the military had effectively ruled Burma since the overthrow of democracy in the early 1990s. No matter how much one reviled the junta, it was the only feasible governing force. Overnight removal of its authority would produce more chaos in a country that was already suffering from violent regional and ethnic conflict. Not only did the PRC have many profitable economic relationships with the existing regime, Beijing did not want to see a chaotic and violent situation on its porous southern border. They imagined a scenario like

Iraq after the United States dismantled the Ba'ath party and fired the military following the U.S. invasion. Off-the-cuff comments about overnight regime change in Burma were, therefore, a poor diplomatic approach with respect to Chinese support.

Gulf of Aden

IN THE LAST MONTHS of the Bush administration, China demonstrated increased willingness to share burdens and coordinate its activities with the international community. Beijing's December 2008 decision to deploy PLA Navy forces to the Gulf of Aden to join an international flotilla combating piracy was important in several respects. China first signed on to a UN Security Council resolution allowing international navies to pursue pirates within the twelve-nautical-mile limit of Somalia's territorial waters. This showed a softening, though not a total rejection, of the principle of noninterference in the internal affairs of states. Security Council members like China and Russia, who were nervous about the new UN "responsibility to protect" doctrine, included in the resolution reference to the approval of central authorities in Somalia for the UN naval engagements. Of course, that country is more characterized by anarchy and warlordism than anything else, so it would be difficult to know if and for how long the international flotilla enjoyed political support in Mogadishu. But the language made it clear that no one should expect China to drop its reservations about Chapter VII UN operations without the consent of the target state.

A second reason that the Gulf of Aden operation is notable is that China agreed to take military action so far from home. Politically, it demonstrated a commitment to global governance and stability that rivaled the deployment to Sudan Darfur. Unlike the December 2004 Indonesian tsunami or Cyclone Nargis in Burma in May 2008, East African piracy was happening very far from China's neighborhood. Of course, as a global trading state of the first order, it would make good sense for China to step up and contribute to multilateral antipiracy missions anywhere in the world. But good sense is often not enough to convince Beijing to pay costs and take risks for the sake of global governance. Hunting pirates might seem a small price to pay, but the Gulf of Aden operation was not risk-free for China. Perhaps most of all, the PLA Navy risked embarrassment. It had never before been asked to sustain operations so far from China's shore, and the logistics and communications challenges were considerable.

The Environment

THE GEORGE W. BUSH administration had a reputation for being indifferent to environmental issues like climate change. China's own reputation on this score during the Bush years was at best mixed. But after years of apparent indifference, Bush embraced the issue of climate change in 2006, perhaps under the influence of his new Secretary of the Treasury, Henry Paulson, a lifelong environmentalist. In December 2006 the United States engaged all of the major net importers of fossil fuels in Asia in a forum on energy security and the environment. Significantly, Beijing hosted that initial meeting of the Five-Country Energy Ministerial. The meeting, which I attended as a representative from the State Department, promoted market-based approaches to energy pricing, sought to reduce government subsidies of energy that served to increase carbon consumption, encouraged the creation of more robust petroleum reserves (but cautioned against using them for purposes other than remedying massive supply shocks), and discussed experimental approaches such as carbon sequestration as a means to reduce greenhouse gas emissions.

The Bush administration also founded the Major Economies Meeting on Energy Security and Climate Change. Launched as a concept in May 2007, the first meeting took place in September of that year. This new forum was designed to avoid two problems of the past. Bush's correct view was that the Kyoto Protocol was doomed from the beginning because it totally excluded two major, rising emitters—China and India—from any responsibility. A second problem was the overwhelming number of countries involved in previous discussions regarding climate change. Since a small number of large economies produce the vast majority of greenhouse gases, it seemed that if one could get some consensus among that smaller group of countries, real progress could be made on limiting climate change, even if a global consensus on required measures was unattainable. Seventeen countries, including India and China, were invited to send representatives to the meetings in 2007 and 2008.

The Obama campaign would criticize the Bush administration for its failure to address climate change in its eight years in office. It is hard to counter that criticism when one looks at the totality of the 2000s. But if mimicry is flattery, then the Obama administration must have seen some merit in the Bush administration's approach in 2007–2008. With some fanfare, the Obama administration launched the Major Economies Forum on Energy Security and Climate Change in May 2009. Despite the single word change in the title, and the politically driven amnesia that usually accompanies the rollout of anything new in Washington, the forum is simply a follow-on to the Bush administration's "Meeting" of the same name.

While bringing greater intensity to the issue than its predecessor, the Obama administration wisely embraced the Bush administration's criticism of Kyoto and Bush's effort to focus on increasing coordination in the policies of the major polluters, including the two developing giants China and India. While the need to motivate China to do more to mitigate greenhouse gas emissions now seems obvious, getting a developing country with enormous domestic concerns to actually contribute to this global effort is quite difficult. And for reasons cited above, without Chinese buy-in developed countries, especially the United States, are likely to find easy excuses to sustain their own lethargy on this important issue.

CHAPTER 8

China's Offensive Diplomacy Since the Financial Crisis, 2009–2014

FEW COUNTRIES WERE MORE deeply affected by the financial crisis than China. This statement might appear jarring to news watchers in the United States. Wasn't China the one major economy that weathered the crisis intact? Didn't the rest of the world rely on that Chinese growth as a life preserver in a stormy sea? The answer to both questions is yes, but the great recession remade Chinese popular and elite psychology. As a result, China became much more confident abroad at a time in which its government became much more nervous at home—a potentially combustible combination.

According to my Chinese interlocutors, large segments of the Chinese public and elites feel that China's global power has risen quickly since the financial collapse of 2008. Many Chinese apparently now believe that their history of international humiliation, long propagated by Chinese educational institutions, media outlets, and Internet sites, might finally be put behind them. The American "hegemon" had taken a mighty blow when Wall Street collapsed. China, by comparison, seemed stable and strong, quickly adopting a massive domestic stimulus package that steadied the economy. The traditional hectoring from the Americans and Europeans about the superiority of their economic and political systems seemed particularly inappropriate now. And U.S. allies in East Asia had to be worried about American resolve, particularly when one considered the costly and unpopular wars in Iraq and

Afghanistan. A powerful China, many believed, no longer had to tolerate routine slights to its national pride from neighbors. Nor did it need to be as passive when the United States sold arms to Taiwan, criticized China's lack of domestic freedoms, or supported dissidents or critics such as Liu Xiaobo or the Dalai Lama.

On the other hand, the Chinese regime was more afraid of domestic instability than at any time since the period around the 1989 Tiananmen uprisings. Internationally, the financial crisis undercut export markets and sources of capital the Chinese required to maintain growth and produce jobs. To make matters worse, a wave of antigovernment protest was spreading from Wall Street to Tahrir Square in Cairo. Despite the Chinese censors' efforts to block news of the Arab Spring and the Jasmine Revolution, it was impossible to keep the wobbling of long-term authoritarian regimes entirely from the public. Even before the financial crisis, public protests in China were on the rise, albeit mostly about local issues. The CCP wanted to prevent them from morphing into national protests against the regime.

Domestically, China adopted by far the largest stimulus package as a percentage of GDP of all the major economies in the world (as much as 14 percent, according to some expert estimates).[1] Unfortunately, by injecting money into flawed state institutions, these emergency efforts served to exacerbate existing problems that were fueling growing popular discontent. China has a startling imbalance of wealth, especially for a country where a red flag flies above a portrait of Chairman Mao in the national square. By marketizing an economy with a large state footprint, Beijing created massive corruption among Party elites and a deep cynicism in the Chinese population about the ethical virtues of their leadership. The stimulus package that Beijing injected into the Chinese economy unfortunately did more than sustain growth, it accelerated the maldistribution of capital to state-owned banks and state-owned firms, and in the process encouraged further corruption and overinvestment by local officials in real estate and infrastructure projects. To make matters worse, a shadow banking system formed in which local financial trusts loaned additional funds at higher than allowed interest rates so that their customers could finance their often already inflated debt.

President Xi Jinping's very public efforts to initiate economic market reforms and crack down on state-sector corruption in late 2013 seemed designed to address all of these problems at once. The Party is considering new market-based approaches to the financial sector to reduce the huge footprint of state-owned banks and state-owned enterprises. There has also been an effort to limit the influence of the aforementioned shadow banks. The Party is also considering allowing farmers to use their land rights as collateral for business loans or to sell the land rights. This could allow them to create nonfarming businesses in rural areas or to ease the process by which they seek formal urban residency with social safety nets attached, instead of living in the cities as floating labor with no free access to public schools and other social services.[2] The Party's goal is to create sustainable economic growth driven by domestic consumption and innovation and an economy less reliant on overseas markets and on profligate bank lending and investment at home by state banks.

If successfully enacted, many powerful interest groups within China stand to lose influence from the reforms and consequentially wealth. It is probably not coincidental then that the reform package has been accompanied by a very tough anticorruption campaign. Top officials, including Politburo Member Bo Xilai, many associates of former Politburo Standing Committee Member Zhou Yongkang, and top PLA general Xu Caihou have all been sacked, stripped of their Party membership, and subjected to criminal prosecution in a manner clearly designed to send a chilling message to corrupt officials throughout the system.

Xi has a confident and outgoing personality, especially in comparison to his stiffer and more bureaucratic predecessor, Hu Jintao. But personality and ambition may not be enough. At this point, no one can be certain of the answer to two critically important questions: Given the large number of influential people who stand to be harmed by deep reforms, will Xi and his deputies be able to effectively implement reform at the central government level and then get local officials to comply? And will the reforms, if effectively implemented, work as planned or will they create economic stagnation, social unrest, or both?

What does all this have to do with China's rise and its foreign relations? The reader will recall that alongside economic performance, a main pillar of CCP legitimacy is its much-trumpeted legacy as defender of Chinese national honor against slights and incursions by foreigners, particularly the reviled Japanese and the U.S. "hegemon." For this reason, Beijing's unfortunate combination of external confidence and internal anxiety renders China more assertive internationally on occasion and more acerbic on others. Chinese assertiveness is only one way for it to destabilize the region. China's destructive reactions to the actions of others can also create enormous problems and in many ways are even more likely and harder to counter. The world is a rough place, and China is moving into it in unprecedented ways. As Chinese power grows, it will be exposed to an increasing number of challenges. Domestic politics problems make China more likely to adopt tough and often counterproductive responses to those challenges.

The Obama Administration: Balancing U.S. Presence and Reassurance

THE OBAMA ASIA TEAM in 2009 was a formidable and experienced one. The Senior Director for Asian Affairs at the National Security Council, Jeff Bader, was a seasoned China hand with significant previous government experience at the State Department and the White House. His deputy for China, Evan Medeiros, who would eventually succeed Bader in the second term, was a young, well-respected academic who worked on Chinese security policy at the RAND Corporation. The new Assistant Secretary of State for East Asian and Pacific Affairs, Kurt Campbell, had been working on Asian security issues for decades and was particularly well known in the capitals of U.S. security partners for his work as Deputy Assistant Secretary of Defense in the Clinton administration. His background at the Pentagon implementing the Nye Initiative had earned Campbell, a former academic, a nickname in Beijing: Dr. Containment.

The new Deputy Secretary of State, Jim Steinberg, inherited the Asia security portfolio from his Bush administration predecessors, Robert Zoellick and John Negroponte. None of these three experienced diplomats would be considered Asia specialists in academic circles, but

Steinberg, like Zoellick and Negroponte, had significant experience working on Asia policy. Steinberg had served as Deputy National Security Advisor in the Clinton administration. At Treasury, Secretary Timothy Geithner had deep roots in Asia. His father is the estimable Asia specialist Peter Geithner. Timothy Geithner learned Mandarin Chinese and studied in China before entering the world of banking. As captain of the economic dialogue with China, he seemed a worthy successor to Henry Paulson, who had conceived of and launched the Strategic Economic Dialogue in 2006. President Obama's intriguing choice for ambassador to China, Jon Huntsman, added real gravitas to his China team. Huntsman, a Republican, left his position as a very popular and successful governor of Utah to become the U.S. envoy to China. He learned Chinese as a young man and, as a former Deputy U.S. Trade Representative and U.S. Ambassador to Singapore, has truly impressive Asia credentials.

One of the many burdens the new Obama administration inherited in early 2009 was a China bearing a mix of cockiness and insecurity that would negatively influence its policies in 2009–2010. Chinese policy improved only somewhat in late 2010 when Beijing began recognizing some of the costs of its acerbic diplomacy. But the years 2011–2014 were hardly smooth ones for Chinese diplomacy, and the Obama administration continued to struggle with dissuading Beijing from bullying its neighbors and encouraging the PRC to play a stabilizing regional role and a more proactively constructive global one.

In terms of coercive diplomacy, the new administration was, like its predecessor, clearly trying to balance credible resolve with assurance. But after the financial crisis struck in 2008, and as the war efforts in Iraq and Afghanistan continued to founder, American power inspired less awe. Meanwhile, because of their domestic problems, Chinese elites were even harder to reassure. No one envied the Obama administration's inheritance.

The only positive note for the Obama administration was the fact that relations across the Taiwan Strait were at their most stable since the early 1990s. Not only had President Chen's 2008 UN referendum failed but the KMT government that succeeded him under Ma Ying-jeou actively pursued improved relations with the mainland. The two sides of the Strait were able to shelve their political disputes and reach multiple economic agreements. Moreover, the Bush administration had announced the intention to sell a large package of arms to Taiwan in its final months of office, relieving the new administration of addressing that thorny issue during its first months.

Still, the challenge for the Obama administration on security policy toward China was a formidable one: how could the United States avoid repeating the pattern in which the first period of a new presidency was fraught with Sino-American tension? The Obama administration attempted this balancing act by upgrading the U.S. diplomatic presence in the region and, at the same time, reaching out to China in the spirit of reassurance. While the administration's instincts were correct, the efforts of its first two years were rhetorically counterproductive.

Bolstering U.S. Presence: The Pivot to Asia

EARLY IN HER TERM in office, at a July 2009 regional gathering, Secretary of State Hillary Clinton declared, "The United States is back" in Asia, after an alleged absence during the grinding wars in Iraq and Afghanistan.[3] The Obama strategy, eventually captured by the term the "Asia pivot," responded to a critical narrative regarding the Bush administration's alleged failings promoted by key Democratic Party Asia experts. For example, in late 2005 Kurt Campbell stated:

> The martial campaigns in the Middle East have had the additional consequence of diverting the United States away from the rapidly changing strategic landscape of Asia precisely at a time when China is making enormous strides in military modernization, commercial conquests, diplomatic inroads, and application of soft power. Rarely in history has a rising power made such prominent gains in the international system largely as a consequence of the actions and inattentiveness of the dominant power. Indeed, Washington has been mostly unaware of China's gains within the past few years, many of which have come at the expense of the United States.[4]

Campbell's influence on the administration's thinking was evident when journalist Fareed Zakaria interviewed President Obama in the Oval Office in January 2012. While denying that he was adopting a containment strategy toward China, the president said:

> The United States has pivoted to focus on the fastest-growing region of the world . . . an area of the world that we had neglected over the last decade because of our intense focus on Iraq, Afghanistan, and the Middle East.[5]

To portray the United States as engaging more effectively with a rising China for influence in Asia had great domestic political appeal. In addition to fitting well with the earlier criticism of the Bush administration, the "pivot" allowed Democrats to portray themselves as strong on national security, particularly as they were planning to withdraw combat troops from Iraq and, eventually, Afghanistan.

Of course, all of this rhetoric hardly matched reality. The United States had never left Asia and the suggestion that we had left and had suddenly returned would do diplomatic harm. Almost all of the major military aspects of U.S. policy now associated with the pivot were in motion before the surge in Iraq in 2006, so the notion that the withdrawal from Iraq under Obama enabled the new approach to Asia is particularly inaccurate. The long process of strengthening U.S. military forces in the region had begun several years before the pivot was announced (e.g., additional submarines and other naval assets in Guam, F-22s to Japan on a rotational basis, littoral combat ships deployed to Singapore, and an increasing U.S. Marine presence in Darwin, Australia). It is typical for decisions about changes in defense posture to take several years to implement. These were no exception.

In economics, the pivot was particularly hard to detect. The Obama administration launched no new economic concepts in its two terms in office. The Korea–U.S. (KORUS) Free Trade Agreement had been negotiated during the Bush administration and had been held up by the Democrats in Congress. The Trans-Pacific Partnership (TPP), actively fostered by the Obama administration in 2013–2014, was originally an initiative launched by Singapore, Chile, New Zealand, and Brunei, four members of the Asia-Pacific Economic Cooperation (APEC) forum, during the second term of the Bush administration. The initiative was designed to address the stalemate in the Doha Round of the WTO. It was fully supported by the Bush administration, who saw it as a way of proliferating "gold standard" free trade deals, such as the U.S.–Singapore Free Trade Agreement, as opposed to the more shallow trade agreements then being signed between China and regional actors. In 2008 the Bush administration agreed to join the TPP negotiations, which expanded to include new participants, most notably Vietnam, another reforming Communist state. The hope was that by including high standards on intellectual property rights, financial services, and agriculture in a new free trade agreement, China would eventually be encouraged to compete by creating deeper free trade agreements of its own and, perhaps, eventually join the Trans-Pacific Partnership itself. The Obama administration laudably pushed for a TPP, particularly in its second term, but it would be a broad rewriting of history to claim that the concept of the partnership itself or the U.S. agreement to negotiate in it was somehow part of the administration's pivot to Asia.

But the pivot was not all empty rhetoric. On the diplomatic front, the Obama administration indeed made significant and positive changes to U.S. regional policy. In particular, the administration would engage in more robust regional diplomacy than its predecessor, especially in Southeast Asia. In 2009 the United States signed the ASEAN Treaty of Amity and Cooperation and thereafter joined the East Asia Summit. The Bush administration had refused to do so in part because Burma is a member of ASEAN and the treaty's first principle is noninterference in the internal affairs of other signatories. High-level American officials would also visit Asia frequently, while U.S. secretaries of state would attend the ASEAN Regional Forum each year under President Obama. Secretary Rice had famously missed two such meetings during the second term of George W. Bush, sending the deputy secretary in her stead. In a postcolonial region, the symbolism of top representation at meetings remains very important.

More important, the Obama administration successfully made these meetings more concrete and meaningful than they had ever been in the past. Previously dismissed as "talk shops" without serious agendas,

Secretary Clinton at the ASEAN Regional Forum in July 2010 and President Obama at the East Asia Summit in November 2011 pushed these organizations to address pressing security issues and to try to fulfill their missions as confidence-building organizations that could reduce tensions over sovereignty disputes (and, thereby, to prevent China's bullying of its smaller neighbors in resolving those disputes).

Perhaps most dramatically, the administration would engage both the junta and the opposition in Burma at a higher official level than the previous administration. These diplomatic contacts positioned Washington to seize the opportunities afforded by the reform-minded leadership under the new authoritarian ruler, Thein Sein. The result was the release of many opposition figures, including Nobel laureate and democracy activist Aung San Suu-kyi, and the dispatch of Asia hand Derek Mitchell as the first ambassador to Burma since the military coup there in 1988.

The problem was not these innovative and proactive policies, but their rhetorical packaging. The administration's public diplomacy created unnecessary problems with both China and its neighbors. There are many deficiencies in terms like "return to Asia" and "pivot." Most obviously, the notion that Washington would be turning its attention (and guns!) on East Asia after leaving Iraq and Afghanistan feeds well into hawkish Chinese narratives about U.S. containment. In a conference that I attended in early 2013, even highly informed Chinese intelligence analysts lumped a series of Bush-era policies with the Obama administration's efforts in "the pivot" and claimed all were designed to exclude and encircle China. I pointed out to my Chinese counterparts, with limited success, that the KORUS free trade agreement was negotiated under the Bush administration and opposed by Senators Obama and Clinton and many other Democrats at the time. Another Bush-era concept, the Trans-Pacific Partnership, was not even created in Washington and was never portrayed by the U.S. government as an aggressive response to China. The U.S. goal in relation to Beijing was not to exclude China from the TPP but to use new agreements like it to catalyze China to compete by further opening its own domestic markets and providing protection for intellectual property rights for the first time.

In addition to negatively impacting Chinese domestic debates, the concept of a pivot also worries others in the region who would rather not choose between a rising China and an American counter-force. Muscular U.S. bluster about regional strength and presence can be counterproductive when states in the region are trying to hedge their bets between China and the United States.

A deeper strategic problem for U.S. diplomacy raised by the pivot is that it makes the United States appear unsteady and unable to handle two problems at once. Friendly governments elsewhere, in Europe and especially in the Middle East, would not welcome a U.S. pivot *away* from their own region. There, many reportedly have worried about the local implications of the announced strategy.[6] In this author's opinion, it would have been better to say that the United States has long had a robust presence in Asia, and with the region's increasing importance the United States is adjusting its diplomatic, military, and economic presence there. This does not fit onto a bumper sticker and does not produce great product differentiation from previous administrations, but it would preclude a lot of the problems associated with the pivot.

Administration officials themselves would recognize problems with the pivot language. Sometime in 2012, the "Asia pivot" would be jettisoned in Washington for the more subtle "Asia rebalance." The latter is a milder and more accurate description of evolving priorities and long-term efforts across administrations to bolster U.S. influence in Asia. But, unfortunately for U.S. diplomacy, "the pivot" proved indelible. In China, the original translation of "the pivot" remains popular to this day: *chongfan yazhou,* or "turn back to Asia." Journalists throughout the region routinely opine about the concrete meaning of "the pivot" in a period of domestic political deadlock in the United States. When tensions flared in the Middle East over Syria, Egypt, and Iran or when President Obama missed an East Asia Summit because of a government shutdown in October 2013, many East Asian observers wondered whether the United States might pivot away again.[7]

Initial Efforts at Strategic Reassurance

DESPITE THE MUSCULAR LANGUAGE about returning to Asia, in its first year in office the Obama team seemed equally determined to avoid unnecessarily provoking Chinese sensibilities on national security issues. Top administration officials understandably wanted to avoid the bilateral tensions witnessed in the early months of the Bush administration over strategic competition, the EP-3 incident, and Taiwan. But the rhetoric and symbolic acts taken to pursue reassurance in the second half of 2009 turned out to be similarly overcooked and counterproductive. As with the pivot, the rhetorical mistakes were later corrected, but by then damage was done.

To start on the right track, President Obama made a point of visiting China in his first year in office. But in the lead-up to the visit, some of his advisors seemed eager, perhaps overly eager, to build trust. For example, Deputy Secretary of State James Steinberg made a speech about China policy at the Center for a New American Security on September 24, 2009. This first major speech by a senior Obama administration official on Asia strategy emphasized the need for "strategic reassurance" in U.S.–China relations. Assurance is established in sustained dialogues and in well-managed diplomacy when problems arise, such as the Bush administration's public and private opposition to Taiwan's provocative UN referendum. But Steinberg's speech seemed to call for efforts to reassure China outside the context of any specific problem or crisis. Citing the political science literature on security dilemmas and tragic spirals of tension caused by power transformations, Steinberg said:

> Now part of this reassurance comes from sustained dialogue. . . .
> But if our efforts are truly to be successful, they must go beyond
> words to actions that reassure. We must each take specific steps to
> address and allay each other's concerns.[8]

This constituted something new. Steinberg was volunteering that the United States also needed to proactively offer China "specific steps" to allay Beijing's security concerns about the United States. I instantly imagined Chinese officials, saying: "Okay, here is an opening list: eliminate arms sales to Taiwan; reduce or eliminate surveillance and reconnaissance operations near the Chinese coast; pressure U.S. allies to back off their claims to islands disputed with China." With that thought in mind, I wondered if and how the speech had been cleared in the interagency process before he gave it. Rumors circulated afterward that it had not.[9]

Similar problems occurred before and during President Obama's trip to China in mid-November. The president had decided not to accept a visit from the Dalai Lama just before heading to China. Anyone who has worked on China policy would understand the inclination to avoid such timing. Presidential visits with the Dalai Lama are a routine part of U.S. policy across administrations. They always cause bilateral tensions, whether or not they occur just before a major event like a presidential trip to Beijing. The practical problem with such a visit just before a China trip is that the relationship with the Dalai Lama would necessarily become a major point of discussion during the president's meetings, stealing time and energy from other issues. So the president decided to pass on the Dalai Lama's invitation for a visit in fall 2009 with every intention of meeting him in the future. But in the context of the strategic reassurance speech, forgoing the visit could be seen by Chinese observers as a specific step. The president was going to China with a clean slate. He had not yet notified Congress about arms sales to Taiwan, and he had declined a visit from the Dalai Lama. Unfortunately, this clean slate, half a product of timing and half of thoughtful strategic diplomacy, would be misread in counterproductive ways by many Chinese observers.

In the lead-up to the president's visit to China, the Chinese side was eager to have Presidents Hu and Obama make a joint statement about the nature of U.S.–China relations. Unfortunately, in my opinion, the U.S. team agreed. The result was a laundry list of unobjectionable statements about common interest, common goals, and aspirations for cooperation on specific issues from avian influenza to a U.S.–China gas and oil forum. At more than 4,000 words, it reads very much like the product of two countries' separate interagency processes. But one specific section of the document immediately caught my eye. Seemingly in the spirit of Steinberg's strategic reassurance speech, in a section entitled "Building and Deepening Strategic Trust," the two sides agreed to respect each other's "core interests." The text reads:

The two countries reiterated that the fundamental principle of respect for each other's sovereignty and territorial integrity is at the core of the three U.S.–China joint communiqués which guide U.S.–China relations. Neither side supports any attempts by any force to undermine this principle. The two sides agreed that respecting each other's core interests is extremely important to ensure steady progress in U.S.–China relations.[10]

This section directly followed a paragraph on "the Taiwan issue," an infelicitous phrase preferred by the CCP to describe problems in relations across the Taiwan Strait.

It is difficult for Americans to pin down U.S. core national interests. What would they be—life, liberty, and the pursuit of happiness? The task is not so hard for specialists on the PRC. State Councillor Dai Bingguo, China's top foreign policy official at the time, wrote a lengthy essay in late 2010 summing up the PRC's core interests in three categories (*fanchou*): the continued monopoly on power of the Chinese Communist Party regime; territorial integrity and sovereignty; and an environment conducive to continued economic development.[11] For U.S. diplomacy, the problem is clear: the United States only agrees with the third of these three principles. While the United States does not take measures to cause political instability in China or overthrow the regime there, Washington has actively promoted peaceful political liberalization and a move away from one-party rule. And while there is nothing wrong in principle with the United States respecting China's sovereignty and territorial integrity, the United States does not agree on the critically important details of Beijing's sovereignty claims to Taiwan, the Senkaku/Diaoyu Islands, or the islands and waters of the South China Sea. Over the coming months, administration officials would apparently come to realize that the inclusion of "core interests" in a joint statement was a mistake. The Chinese government used the phrase with sharply increased frequency after 2009.[12] But, to my knowledge, it has not been repeated by senior U.S. government officials.

The problems with the Obama administration's overeager reassurance campaign would become evident in early 2010 when China reacted harshly to the normal U.S. policies that particularly offended Beijing.

According to my Chinese interlocutors, many in China had come to the conclusion that the Obama administration was different from its predecessors in its basic approach to China. Either because the administration realized that the United States was weaker than before the financial crisis or because the Obama team had a different philosophical approach to the bilateral relations, it appeared to many Chinese as more accommodating and sensitive to Chinese concerns than its predecessors. My better-connected contacts said that this view was not shared among officials at the top of the foreign policy establishment, but it was commonly held by both the general public and many in the Party who were not as experienced in foreign affairs. So in early 2010 when the Obama administration behaved like its predecessors—selling arms to Taiwan, criticizing Beijing for infringing on freedom of the press, and arranging for the president to meet with the Dalai Lama—there was real disappointment and a harsher than normal reaction in Beijing. Threats of retaliation were leveled against U.S. firms that were selling arms to Taiwan. Prominent commentators, including military officers, suggested in state-run media that China should dump U.S. Treasury bills to punish the United States in its time of economic turmoil. At a minimum, they said, China should reduce cooperation in policy arenas important to the United States, like North Korea and Iran. In their view, the Obama administration clearly violated China's "core interests." It is only logical, according to many Chinese observers, that Beijing should in turn refuse to assist the United States in pursuing what Beijing believes to be U.S. core national interests, such as preventing nuclear proliferation or helping stabilize the U.S. economy.

The top leadership in China wisely eschewed policies that would harm both the United States and China, such as manipulating the purchase or sale of Treasury bills. But the pressure on the leadership from nationalist voices inside and outside the Party was intense. This domestic insecurity helps explain China's ideological and acerbic reactions to several challenges on China's periphery in 2010 that were not of Beijing's making. The result was arguably the worst year for Chinese diplomacy in the reform era. Beijing responded clumsily to North Korean belligerence toward Seoul, sovereignty disputes in the South China Sea, and Japan's arrest of a Chinese fisherman near the disputed Senkaku/

Diaoyu Islands. In the process, Beijing undercut the achievements of the previous twelve years of constructive reassurance toward its neighbors, from Japan to Vietnam to India. By the end of the year, Beijing had upset its bilateral relations with almost all of its neighbors. The only countries Beijing hadn't offended were Russia and a couple of Southeast Asian nations.

The most dramatic change since the financial crisis was China's North Korea policy. Rather than pressuring Pyongyang after its nuclear and missile tests in spring 2009, Beijing seems to have doubled down on its economic and political ties with Kim Jong-il. Knowledgeable observers believe that trade and investment relations between China and North Korea deepened from 2008 to 2011. There was also frequent high-level public diplomacy between Chinese and North Korean leaders, including two visits by Kim to China in 2010. In October, Zhou Yongkang, a member of the Chinese Communist Party's Politburo Standing Committee, stood with top members of the Kim regime during the anniversary celebration of the Korean Workers' Party. This attention was most welcome in Pyongyang during the regime's sensitive transition period, in which Kim had been grooming his youngest son, Kim Jong-un, to take power.

Driven by the fear of a precipitous collapse of a neighboring Communist regime following the elder Kim's stroke in 2008 and the reduction of Chinese influence on the Korean Peninsula, Beijing fell back on long-held conservative foreign policy principles supporting North Korea. In particular, it stood by the Kim regime during the course of several crises sparked by Pyongyang in 2010. In May, an international commission determined that a North Korean submarine had indeed sunk the South Korean naval ship *Cheonan* in March; for its part, China refused to review the evidence and protected North Korea from facing direct criticism in the UN Security Council. In so doing, Chinese leaders alienated many in the international community, especially South Korea, Japan, and the United States. Beijing similarly protected North Korea from international condemnation after Pyongyang revealed in fall 2010 that it had secretly developed a uranium-enrichment facility. And after North Korea shelled a South Korean island in November, Beijing once again adopted an agnostic pose, simply calling for calm and warning all sides against any further escalation. The only specific warning it could muster was its ultimately unsuccessful effort to dissuade U.S. warships involved in joint U.S.–South Korean naval exercises from entering the Yellow Sea, which overlaps with China's exclusive economic zone. The Chinese actions and inactions deeply offended the South Korean government and public, which quite correctly felt victimized by North Korea's aggressive acts.

China also adopted abrasive policies in the maritime domain in the years just after the financial crisis broke. In 2009, Chinese ships harassed the unarmed U.S. Navy ship *Impeccable* in international waters off the Chinese coast. Chinese diplomats also overreacted to U.S. Secretary of State Hillary Clinton's diplomacy regarding the management of sovereignty disputes in the South China Sea at the ASEAN Regional Forum in Vietnam in July 2010. China is the only nation in the region that claims all the disputed islands in the sea. Its expansive claims are also ambiguous, relying on maps that predate the People's Republic of China and sometimes on vague terms such as "historic waters" or "relevant waters," which carry no validity in international law. At the meeting, Clinton wisely and assertively called for the peaceful settlement of differences, freedom of navigation, a legal basis for all claims rooted in customary international law, and multilateral confidence-building measures. Even though Clinton did not specifically name China and her comments did not change the United States' traditional neutrality on maritime sovereignty disputes, the U.S. initiative was unwelcome in Beijing. The Chinese foreign minister's harsh and bullying reaction at the conference—warning "small countries" in the region against collaborating with outside powers in dealing with the disputes—created tension between China and the relevant ASEAN states and between China and Japan, which, like the United States, has no territorial claims in the South China Sea but is concerned about maintaining freedom of navigation and regional security.

In September 2010 Beijing reacted harshly to Japan's arrest of a Chinese fishing boat captain and his crew near the disputed Senkaku Islands, following an incident in which the Chinese boat apparently rammed a Japanese Coast Guard vessel on purpose. Japan threatened to prosecute the captain under domestic law rather than just deport him to China. The negative Chinese reaction to Japan's jailing of the fishing boat captain was predictable, but the Chinese government was especially bellicose in its response: Beijing restricted rare-earth shipments to Japan, on which Japanese electronic manufacturers are highly dependent; further, the Chinese Foreign Ministry demanded an official apology and reparations even after the Japanese had already acceded to Chinese demands to release the ship's captain and crew. This may have impressed domestic audiences in China, but it deeply alienated the Japanese public, which, according to all polling data, developed very negative views of China. What is most striking, perhaps, is that all of this trouble occurred while the Democratic Party of Japan—traditionally considered very accommodating to China—was Japan's ruling party. The timing of the tense state of Chinese-Japanese relations thus speaks volumes about the opportunity costs of China's diplomatic truculence.

According to my sources in China, domestic factors helped produce these deleterious effects on Chinese foreign policy. For domestic and bureaucratic reasons, Beijing elites felt the need to react stridently to all perceived slights to national pride and sovereignty. When, for example, various Asian states sided with Clinton at the ASEAN meeting in Hanoi, Chinese Foreign Ministry officials felt compelled to respond in caustic terms that alienated several of China's southern neighbors. Similarly, no one believes that China truly supports North Korea's military provocations or development of nuclear weapons. But Beijing's concerns about maintaining domestic stability in North Korea, peace on the Korean Peninsula, and social stability in China have prevented Chinese officials from criticizing North Korea publicly or allowing the UN Security Council to do so. What is more, these interests also apparently prevented Chinese officials from refuting conspiracy theories in the Chinese media and on the Internet that the United States and South Korea plotted to provoke tensions on the Korean Peninsula to justify military exercises near China's borders. On the contrary, the Foreign Ministry only fed the fire in July and November 2010 by warning the United States not to place warships in waters near China without Beijing's permission. This move may have won some favor with the Chinese military and the Chinese public, but the diplomatic costs of being seen to pardon or even defend Pyongyang's actions were high in Seoul,

Tokyo, and Washington. As many Chinese analysts will privately state, and some brave ones have publicly argued, a truly assertive great power would not allow a small pariah state to hijack its foreign policy in such a fashion. Beijing was acting as much out of fear at home as it was cockiness abroad.

In my opinion, the Obama administration responded constructively and strategically to the deteriorating conditions in East Asia. After being rebuffed by China for cooperation on North Korea and the South China Sea, Washington decided to actively address the issues without China. Beijing elites and other regional players noticed that Obama and his principal advisors—Secretary of State Clinton, Secretary of Defense Robert Gates, and National Security Advisor Thomas Donilon—traveled often to the region, including in November 2010 when Obama and Clinton went on separate multination tours of Asia. More concretely, the U.S.–South Korean military exercises in the Yellow Sea following the November attack by North Korea and the trilateral meeting of Japanese, Korean, and U.S. security officials in Washington demonstrated that the United States and its partners have diplomatic and security options even without China's active cooperation. Beijing does not like such initiatives. The notion that North Korean belligerence might be able to break the logjam in Japanese and South Korean relations particularly grabbed the attention of observers in Beijing, as I noted during my sabbatical research trips to China in 2010–2011. It seems from public reports that China finally restrained North Korea toward the end of 2010. Pyongyang had threatened Seoul with military action if South Korea carried through with a December 2010 military exercise. The exercise was completed without such retaliation. In part because of a firm response by the United States and its allies, Beijing shifted by year's end from enabling North Korean aggression through inaction and obstruction to a more constructive and proactive stance.

A similar though somewhat less dramatic story can be told about the South China Sea, where in 2013 the efforts by some ASEAN members, the United States, and Japan seem to have pushed China into accepting in principle multilateral discussions of a code of conduct to help prevent escalation of the territorial disputes. As was the case with the Nye Initiative during the Clinton administration, a robust set of U.S. policies in

Asia toward allies and nonallied partners helped lead to more constructive Chinese diplomacy. But China is now both stronger internationally and less secure at home than it was in the mid-1990s, so its shift in late 2010 seemed more tactical and issue-specific, while the change to more reassuring diplomacy in the 1990s was more sweeping, leading to over ten years of creative and constructive diplomacy toward the region.

It is analytically useful to ask what explains the acerbic turn in Beijing's foreign policy in 2010. The answer is sobering because most of the factors, unfortunately, are still in place. Many in China believe China is significantly stronger and the United States weaker after the financial crisis. Domestic voices calling for a more muscular Chinese foreign policy have created a heated political environment. Popular nationalism, the growth in the number of media outlets through which Chinese citizens can express their views, and the increasing sensitivity of the government to public opinion have provided space for criticism of Beijing's U.S. policy. Such critiques have notably come from active-duty military officers and scholars at state-run think tanks and universities. Gone are the days when Chinese elites could ignore these hawkish voices. For example, in 2010, during the period leading up to the transition of power from Hu Jintao to Xi Jinping in 2012, Chinese officials had to foster their reputations as protectors of national pride and domestic stability. Some prominent Party members did not survive, including Politburo member and Chongqing Party Chief Bo Xilai. Such an environment does not lend itself to accommodation to foreign pressure or being too solicitous of Washington.

In the area of coercive diplomacy, the United States and its allies would continue to face challenges in the maritime realm. In spring 2012 the dispute between China and the Philippines over Scarborough Shoal (Huangyan Dao in Chinese) would come to a head. The Chinese maritime security agencies had been increasing their presence incrementally in the South China Sea for the past several years, and according to Filipino authorities, Chinese fishermen continued to hunt giant clams—an endangered species—in disputed waters. In April 2012 the Filipino Navy arrested some Chinese fishermen allegedly engaged in such activities. Chinese maritime surveillance ships responded by sealing the mouth to the Shoal's lagoon and preventing entrance to all Filipino ships. While Manila looked for backing from the United States, Washington called for dialogue and de-escalation, as the United States does not recognize any disputant's sovereignty over the Shoal. While it would appear that Manila had taken the first step in this dispute, China's hyperactive response seemed both escalatory and patterned. In other words, it often appears that Beijing is waiting for provocations by others to legitimize Chinese actions that will consolidate control over the islands that China has claimed for decades but not administered in the past. This strategy seemed most transparent when, in July 2012, Beijing announced the formation of a new government administration, Sansha City, a part of Hainan Province. The "city" government has jurisdiction over expansive Chinese claims in the South China Sea to the largely uninhabited Spratly Islands (Nansha in Chinese), Paracel Islands (Xisha), and Macclesfield Bank (Zhongsha).

The Senkaku/Diaoyu Islands have remained a regional hot spot in the past three years and, much more than Scarborough Shoal, a potential source of escalation to U.S.–China conflict. Japan has claimed and administered the islands since their 1971 transfer to Japanese jurisdiction by Washington as part of the post–World War II reversion of Okinawa to Japan. As discussed in chapter 4, unlike any other maritime disputes in the region, the United States does side with one claimant in this one. While the United States takes no position on the sovereignty of the islands, it does recognize Japanese administrative control. As such, Washington has declared that the U.S.–Japan Defense Treaty applies to the islands. For its part, China has been trying unsuccessfully to get Japan to recognize that a dispute exists over the islands and to negotiate with Tokyo on that basis. China's claim to the islands harkens back to the World War II Cairo and Potsdam declarations, in which China was promised the return of all booty captured by imperial Japan dating back to the 1895 Treaty of Shimonoseki. That treaty ended the Sino-Japanese War, perhaps the most degrading chapter in China's century of humiliation. Tokyo has refused, arguing that Japan seized the unpopulated islands as *terra nullius* (unclaimed territory) in the late nineteenth century, not as war booty.

China has been trying to challenge and erode Japanese sole administrative control of the islands for the past several years, increasing not only fishing activity near the islands but patrols by maritime security forces and, on occasion, the Chinese Air Force. Two years after the Japanese arrest of the Chinese fishing boat captain, tensions again came to a head in September 2012 when Prime Minister Noda of Japan decided that the central government should purchase the islands, previously owned privately by a Japanese family. Noda's logic was compelling and his effort was meant as a way to limit, not exacerbate, tensions with China. Noda faced a problem that was not sufficiently appreciated by Chinese observers. The hypernationalist leader of the Tokyo municipal government, Governor Ishihara, had been raising private funds through right-wing organizations to purchase the uninhabited islands from the family. There is little doubt that this group would have taken provocative actions on the islands that would incite Chinese nationalism. As the funds poured into Ishihara's coffers, Noda decided to preempt by having the central government purchase the islands first.

Unfortunately for Japan, for the United States, and, arguably, for China itself, the "nationalization" of the islands by the Japanese government was seen in China as a provocative change in the status quo. Beijing claims that when Japan normalized relations with the PRC in 1972 and when it signed a Treaty of Cooperation with China in 1978, Tokyo had agreed to shelve the dispute over the islands, thereby recognizing that a dispute existed and promising not to stoke the embers. In this Chinese interpretation, by "nationalizing" (*guoyouhua*) the islands and now refusing to recognize any dispute, Tokyo was the provocateur, brazenly changing the status quo. Violent protests against Japan broke out all over China. Some Chinese driving Japanese cars were injured by angry mobs. Sino-Japanese diplomatic relations fell into a deep chill and Chinese naval and air activities around the islands increased. The Chinese-Japanese economic relationship in both trade and investment has never fully recovered.

For what should be obvious reasons, the United States has a huge stake in preventing escalating tensions between Japan and China. At the same time, the United States greatly values both the alliance with Japan and, more abstractly, Washington's reputation as an ally. This creates a real dilemma for U.S. policy makers: how to deter China from provoking Japan while dissuading Japan from taking provocative actions of its own. In November 2013, China unexpectedly declared an air defense identification zone (ADIZ) over the East China Sea, to include the air space over and around disputed islands. To make matters worse, on December 26, 2013, Prime Minister Abe became the first sitting Japanese prime minister since Koizumi to visit the controversial Yasukuni Shrine.

The creation of an ADIZ itself is not so much the issue. The concept is a U.S. invention from the early Cold War. Many nations have subsequently declared them. Under the original conception, an ADIZ is designed to give coastal nations warning of aircraft approaching with the intent to enter the nation's territorial airspace, which by tradition extends twelve nautical miles out to sea. Such aircraft, such as civilian jetliners, should alert the country when approaching the nation's airspace. The Chinese ADIZ announcement was considered particularly provocative for several reasons. The rollout occurred without prior warning and in an already tense time with Japan. The Chinese ADIZ overlaps not only Japan's ADIZ but also South Korea's. The initial announcement claimed that all aircraft traveling in the zone, not just those intending to enter Chinese airspace, needed to notify Chinese authorities. In other words, a plane traveling from Japan to Australia, with a route well outside Chinese airspace in the East China Sea, would be expected to notify Chinese authorities in the same way a plane would have to do were it traveling from Japan to Guangzhou. There is no international law governing air defense identification zones, all of which are unilaterally declared, but this expansive interpretation went beyond the spirit of the norm created by the United States. The broader Chinese interpretation seemed to have implications for U.S. and Japanese military flights over international waters near China. The 2001 EP-3 incident recounted in chapter 7 demonstrates that China has an unusually expansive definition of the two-hundred-nautical-mile exclusive economic zone (EEZ) afforded by the UN Convention on the Law of the Sea. (China requires permission for all non-Chinese military activities in and above its EEZ.) Moreover, the Ministry of National Defense ominously claimed the right not only to monitor the ADIZ but to take "emergency defensive measures" against aircraft not complying with the Chinese demands. Finally, and perhaps most important, the Chinese ADIZ overlaps the preexisting Japanese

ADIZ that extends over the Senkaku Islands. To my knowledge, this is the only overlapping ADIZ in the world in which a sovereignty dispute exists within the overlapping sector.[13] Even if, in the end, China interprets the ADIZ narrowly, Japanese and American planes heading toward the Senkaku Islands without notification could be treated as heading toward Chinese airspace. On a political level, even the possibility of such a scenario could be used to erode the notion that Japan has uncontested administrative control of the islands, which has implications for the U.S. argument for why the U.S.–Japan alliance extends to the islands.

The government of Japan responded to the ADIZ announcement by renouncing it, demanding it be rescinded, and ordering its civilian air carriers, which are dependent on Tokyo, to refuse to abide by it. The United States was also highly critical but more than a little unclear in its response, sometimes calling for a reversal of the Chinese decision, other times claiming that the United States would not recognize the Chinese ADIZ, and other times simply requesting that the ADIZ be implemented carefully. But two strong statements were made, one diplomatic and the other physical. Diplomatically, the United States reminded China and Japan that it recognized Japan's administrative control over the islands and that the islands therefore fall under Article V of the U.S.–Japan Defense Treaty. In addition, soon after the ADIZ announcement, two unarmed American B-52s flew a publicly announced exercise off the Senkaku Islands, driving home the point that the United States would not be deterred from military operations in international waters or international airspace near China.

But public reports also suggest that the United States was sending restraining messages to Japan and Korea, particularly when Vice President Joe Biden visited Tokyo, Beijing, and Seoul in December 2013. Japanese leaders, who believe China is trying to bully them, worry greatly about anything that looks like U.S. even-handedness on the Senkaku issue, and many in Japan do not understand why Washington does not just recognize the islands as sovereign Japanese territory. But Washington, unfortunately, has reason to worry not just about China, but also Japan. The conservative Prime Minister Shinzo Abe, who took office in December 2012, has promised to strengthen the Japanese military and to try to reinterpret and eventually change the Japanese peace constitution that under previous interpretations precluded Japanese commitment to collective self-defense with allies and under UN mandates (Japan's lack of responsibility to come to the military aid of allies or the United Nations in anything but the defense of Japan itself is what has made the U.S.–Japan alliance so lopsided). Those same restrictions also prevent Japan from developing robust offensive strike capabilities, even conventional ones. Abe has used the disputed islands as a mobilizing cause for his reform effort, and on July 1, 2014, his government announced that the current Japanese constitution will be interpreted by Abe's cabinet as allowing for collective self-defense.

The United States generally supports a more active military role for Japan. The worry would be if Abe tried to stir up trouble unnecessarily over historical issues as part of this self-strengthening effort. Abe's visit to the Yasukuni Shrine in December 2013 was likely no more than a nationalist display. But the United States was strongly opposed to the visit, and in an unprecedented move, the U.S. Embassy in Tokyo criticized Abe publicly for the visit.

In late March 2014, the Chinese Coast Guard provoked negative reactions in the Philippines by harassing and attempting to block a Filipino ship bringing supplies and fresh troops to a Filipino Navy ship that had been grounded on the disputed Second Thomas Shoal in 1999 and occupied by Filipino Marines ever since. The U.S. military reportedly monitored the standoff with its new P-8 surveillance plane, sending a signal that the United States opposed Chinese bullying of the Philippines even if it did not take any position on Manila's sovereignty claim on Second Thomas Shoal. In May 2014 Beijing further provoked tensions with Vietnam by sending a large oil rig to disputed waters near the Paracel Islands. This action sparked anti-China riots in Vietnam and prompted a tough diplomatic response from U.S. officials, including Secretary of Defense Chuck Hagel in a speech at the annual Shangri-La Dialogue in Singapore.

So what explains all this tension in China's diplomacy? Despite the image of a more powerful China seeking to drive events under the rubric of a new grand strategy, Beijing—with a few important exceptions—has been reacting, however abrasively, to unwelcome and unforeseen events that have often been initiated by others. On the other hand, there seems to be a pattern in which, when provoked, China reacts harshly and provocatively, seizing the opportunity to make advances in sovereignty disputes. Those advances sometimes take physical form such as control of Scarborough Shoal; sometimes they take political form, as we saw in the creation of the East China Sea ADIZ; and sometimes both. In the past few years, Chinese Coast Guard and military ships and planes have increased their activity near disputed islands and shoals.

This reactive assertiveness has been supplemented by the type of proactive assertiveness we saw in the creation of Sansha City or in the dispatch of the oil rig off the Paracel Islands. The word on the street in China is that Xi Jinping is more assertive at home and abroad than his predecessor. But the differences, if any, are a question of degree. China is still reacting in certain circumstances, as it did to the resupply of the Filipino ship on Second Thomas Shoal. Moreover, the distinction between reactive assertiveness and proactive assertiveness may not carry great meaning for those engaging China. The reactive assertiveness of 2010 posed the same kind of challenges for the United States, U.S. regional allies and security partners, and other neighbors of China as does the proactive variety. And, as discussed above, the growth of Chinese power and presence offshore, the normal activities of countries like Vietnam, which are also growing in economic and military wherewithal, and the existence of a number of maritime disputes will create plenty of opportunities for China to be assertive and destabilizing in its behavior, regardless of whether it is the first to instigate tensions in any given situation or not. Moreover, as Chinese power grows in relation to its neighbors and the United States, regional actors have incentives to challenge China in disputed areas now, rather than waiting until later when China's ability to back its expansive claims has grown even stronger.

Global Governance and Humanitarian Intervention

THE ARAB SPRING created great turmoil for China's foreign policy toward the Middle East and North Africa. On the one hand, the fall of the regime in Egypt seemed to undercut U.S. power in the region. On the other, popular uprisings against secular dictatorships by Islamic forces was not in China's domestic interest. Since national security in China really means state security, censors tried their best to suppress images of authoritarians being overthrown by organized, angry publics. The Islamist character of the movements was also notable because of China's ongoing difficulties in maintaining stability in Xinjiang province, where China's minority Muslims live in large numbers.[14]

The instability caused by the Jasmine Revolutions or Arab Spring also carried international implications for Beijing. China is a leading importer of African and Middle Eastern energy, and Arab nations in the Middle East and North Africa were traditionally among China's most stalwart allies in efforts to preserve the principle of noninterference in countries' internal affairs. But the Arab Spring and Sunni concerns about Iran's newfound influence after the U.S. invasion of Iraq rendered certain Arab nations, especially Saudi Arabia and Qatar, more interventionist in their foreign policies. This change became manifest in places like Libya and Syria, where erstwhile partners challenged Chinese traditional approaches. However anti-American the populations of Arab states remained, they were pushing ideas regarding political reform and regime change that sounded more like Hillary Clinton or Paul Wolfowitz than Zhou Enlai or Yang Jiechi. If Beijing openly criticized Arab governments for their domestic governance, China's leaders potentially exposed themselves to similar criticisms at home. But if Beijing actively opposed foreign interference, it stood to alienate multiple governments in the Arab League and the African Union.[15]

China faced this dilemma most acutely during the crisis in Libya in early 2011. When the Arab Spring reached that country and Colonel Qaddafi turned his military against the city of Benghazi, the international community condemned his government. Over the course of decades, Qaddafi had alienated many different kinds of governments. Even Russia, traditionally opposed to humanitarian intervention by the international community, seemed ready to throw Qaddafi under the bus. China had significant energy investments in the country and tens of thousands of citizens working there. The UN Security Council voted on and passed two resolutions on Libya. The first, UNSCR 1970, was passed unanimously on February 26, 2011. It referred Qaddafi's government to the International Criminal Court (ICC) for investigation of crimes against humanity.[16] UN Security Council Resolution 1973 passed on March 17, 2011, with five abstentions, including China. It created a no-fly zone to protect the civilian population, particularly in Benghazi, against attack.[17]

The first resolution was more remarkable than the second. When I first read in the morning paper that the resolution had passed unanimously, I dropped my coffee. China rarely surprises me in this way, but for Beijing to vote yes on a resolution that refers a fellow authoritarian regime to the ICC was far beyond my expectation. I was aware that the Obama administration and European diplomats had prepared favorable conditions for passage by getting the Arab League and the African Union to support condemnation of Qaddafi. But I still expected a Chinese abstention, along with a critical comment about the resolution. Instead, China voted yes, and its ambassador offered a short and very vague comment, stating that "China was very much concerned about the situation in Libya. The greatest urgency was to cease the violence, to end the bloodshed and civilian casualties, and to resolve the crisis through peaceful means, such as dialogue. The safety and interest of the foreign nationals in Libya must be assured. Taking into account the special circumstances in Libya, the Chinese delegation had voted in favour of the resolution."[18]

The reference to "special circumstances" suggests that Beijing did not want this vote to be seen as a precedent. I later discovered that the vote was considered controversial within the Chinese government. A few Chinese officials whom I met later in 2011 were actually unaware that China had voted yes, rather than abstaining. One military officer complained about the vote and said that PLA officers had roundly criticized the decision in meetings with their Foreign Ministry colleagues.

China joined Russia in abstaining on the second resolution, the one to use force in Libya. The content of Ambassador Li Baodong's statement regarding China's abstention helps us understand the "special circumstances" under which Beijing had voted for the ICC resolution. On the occasion of the use of force resolution, according to the official UN news release, Ambassador Li argued in much more traditional fashion that "the United Nations Charter must be respected and the current crisis must be ended through peaceful means. China was always against the use of force when those means were not exhausted. His delegation had asked specific questions that failed to be answered and, therefore, it had serious difficulty with the resolution. It had not blocked the passage of the resolution, however, because it attached great importance to the requests of the Arab League and the African Union."[19] China's desire to avoid alienating the Arab League and the African Union helps explain why China did not veto this resolution and, I believe, why China had taken the truly extraordinary step of referring Libya to the ICC three weeks earlier.

Any lessons from these events and any progress achieved in getting China to soften the principle of nonintervention were seemingly lost when the Europeans and the United States interpreted UNSCR 1973 very broadly and launched military strikes to help bring down Qaddafi's regime and to facilitate his summary execution by the rebels. Mildly put, this was a huge stretch of the UN's mandate and could easily be portrayed as a violation of international law. Qaddafi was executed by the rebels far from Benghazi, and when he was killed, his forces no longer posed a major threat to the civilian population. China's criticisms of the UN operation predictably began as soon as the first military missions were flown out of NATO bases and continued throughout the war.

The lessons of Libya would have strong consequences for how China and Russia addressed UN action during the Syrian Civil War. After Libya, China more predictably opposed any UN condemnation of Assad's regime, much less any sanctions. China joined Russia in vetoing three draft resolutions in 2012 to condemn and sanction Assad's regime, in August 2013 blocked consideration of a use-of-force resolution, and in May 2014 vetoed a draft resolution to refer the Syrian Civil War to the International Criminal Court.[20] While Putin's Russia took the lead in opposing U.S. and European efforts at the UN, China was steadfast in its support of the Russian position, despite the fact that countries like Saudi Arabia, with whom China has had close ties, strongly supported the rebels and wanted the UN to actively oppose Assad as well. China also found diplomatic comfort in the region because Iran was strongly supportive of Assad and strongly opposed to the UN draft resolutions. China would join Russia in supporting UN efforts to remove chemical weapons in Syria. But unlike the earlier resolutions, Assad's government didn't oppose the move; it had decided to give up its chemical weapons. Moreover, any international effort to remove the weapons would, by necessity, involve Assad's government as a partner, bolstering his regime's stability and international legitimacy in the process. So while the earlier resolutions could be seen to encourage regime change under new norms of "responsibility to protect," the chemical weapons agreements were fully consistent with traditional international norms of sovereignty.

Sadly, the experience of Libya and Syria may have moved Beijing into a more cautious and rigid posture on humanitarian intervention than it had adopted in the last years of the Bush administration. Unlike the Bush administration's policies toward Sudan and toward piracy in the Gulf of Aden, the Obama administration's position early in the crises in Libya and Syria called for regime change. After the UN mandate in Libya was expanded to include the use of NATO airpower to support local rebels seeking regime change, there was no chance of securing Chinese or Russian support for UN pressure on Assad in Syria. Although the outcome at the UN was probably already sealed by the Libya example, it certainly did not help that the Obama administration stated at the beginning of U.S. involvement in Syria that a minimum acceptable outcome of any peace negotiation was that the Assad regime step down from power.[21] In other words, prior to the chemical weapons deal with the Assad regime, which nearly guaranteed its protection from international military pressure, U.S. coercive diplomacy toward Assad's government was all threat and no assurance: an obvious recipe for failure. Since, after Iraq, the United States no longer had the will to remove an Arab regime by force, the Obama administration's position guaranteed Assad the strong backing of international opponents to internationally engineered regime change, and China is still certainly in that category.

Despite the clear setbacks in Libya and Syria, China's position on peacekeeping and on peacemaking continues to evolve. In summer 2013 Beijing agreed for the first time to send combat troops as part of its peacekeeping mission to Mali.[22] Such a decision may have been made so that China could gain experience at armed rescue of the increasing number of Chinese citizens working in dangerous locations abroad.

For example, more than thirty thousand Chinese citizens had required evacuation from Libya.[23] And China has pressing security considerations for its energy operations in war-torn South Sudan. China was very active both in observing the elections in South Sudan that produced the nation's independence in 2011 and in attempting to broker a peace deal there when civil war broke out in late 2013. Of course, Beijing has enormous material stakes in peace in South Sudan because Chinese energy companies are the biggest foreign investors in the considerable energy resources of that new nation. Still, these types of incentives that flow from the growth of China's global economic footprint might eventually help socialize China into understanding the costs of instability in any part of the world and into supporting the international community's efforts to stabilize such areas.

Nonproliferation

North Korea

AS NORTH KOREA continued to develop its nuclear weapons and missile capabilities during the Obama years, China offered a mixed response. The uncertainties created by the financial crisis combined with the uncertainty following the reported stroke of Kim Jong-il in summer 2008 rendered Beijing even more protective of North Korea than it had been in the previous three years. Even though the Six Party Talks had broken down in 2008 over the issue of verification, domestic stability in North Korea dominated Beijing's strategy. Beijing applied no pressure on the North; in fact, 2009 and 2010 were banner years for China's economic relations with their long-term ally. The Obama administration aptly accused China of "enabling" North Korea's misdeeds. The outwardly warm relations between Beijing and Kim Jong-il's government were underscored by Kim Jong-il's three visits to China in 2010–2011 and many trips by multiple high-level Chinese entourages to Pyongyang.[24]

There were only two hiccups in the PRC–DPRK relationship in the last three years before Kim Jong-il's death in December 2011. The first was Beijing's accession to a new UN Security Council sanctions resolution in June 2009 (UNSCR 1874) following North Korea's second nuclear test. That resolution for the first time called for a full arms embargo on North Korea. But this resolution apparently had only limited implications for the overall economic relationship between Pyongyang and Beijing, and there is reason to doubt that military-related sanctions had been strictly enforced by Beijing in any case. For example, what appeared to be a Chinese-made truck for a mobile missile launcher was trotted out for a North Korean military parade in April 2012. Even if this truck had been sold before UNSCR 1874 was passed in June 2009, its direct relevance to North Korea's nuclear and missile programs would have placed it on the prohibited list for UN sanctions going back to 2006. If public reports and the discussions of my interlocutors in Beijing are accurate, the second hiccup in Beijing's relations with Pyongyang would have come in late 2010 when China apparently restrained North Korea from carrying through with its threatened military retaliation against planned South Korean military exercises.

Aside from these exceptions, Beijing's official policies generally provided succor to Pyongyang through Kim Jong-il's death in 2011. Chinese elites often blamed North Korea's poor diplomatic and security environment for Pyongyang's unwillingness to respect its previous commitments in the Six Party Talks. The Obama administration, having decided that the Bush administration had been too eager to pursue talks in its final months in office, adopted a relatively aloof posture toward the resumption of negotiations. The response in Beijing was to argue that North Korea stood on the cusp of adopting Deng Xiaoping–style reforms, if only it could receive enough security assurances to permit them. If sincere, these Chinese impressions about the prospect for reforms must have come from meetings with Kim Jong-il and his son and chosen successor, Kim Jong-un. The Chinese interpretation held that the United States and South Korea's conservative leadership under President Lee Myung-bak were obstructing a process that might bring North Korea out of the cold and eventually foster denuclearization.

Despite Beijing's persistent protectiveness, some Chinese elites were losing patience with North Korea. I was told in 2010–2011 that there was a lively debate on China's North Korea policy underway inside and outside Chinese foreign policy circles. A growing number of influential Chinese seemed to be coming to the conclusion that the special relationship with politically backward and outwardly obnoxious North Korea was creating a bad diplomatic reputation for China. Moreover, by threatening its neighbors, North Korea was deepening cooperation between the United States and its regional allies in ways that did not serve China's long-term national security interest. A couple of bold academics braved the slings and arrows of Chinese nationalists and called for a fundamental rethink of China's approach to the peninsula.[25] At an international conference that I attended in 2010, one Chinese professor called China's foreign policy toward North Korea that of an "adolescent" great power. He argued that a more mature approach would require eschewing support for North Korea and, instead, cooperating with American, Japanese, and South Korean officials to address a common security concern.

The death of Kim Jong-il in December 2011 could only have exacerbated Beijing's concerns about the stability of its neighbor. The transition to a young, inexperienced, and untested successor, Kim Jong-un, seemed fraught with uncertainty. In this context the Obama administration did something that received more criticism than it deserved. It reached out to North Korea diplomatically to try to achieve some interim deal that could facilitate a return to the Six Party Talks. This effort resulted in the February 29, 2012, "Leap Day Agreement," in which the United States agreed to restore humanitarian food aid to the North if the North halted progress on its nuclear and missile programs. Pyongyang launched a failed missile test weeks later, willfully scuttling the deal.

Were the people on point in the U.S. diplomatic effort—Ambassador Glyn Davies and his deputy, Ambassador Clifford Hart—so naïve as to think this effort would likely halt the North Korean programs? Having worked closely with both of these hard-headed and experienced diplomats, I can say that the answer is almost certainly no. But, as with the late 2006 package offer to North Korea made by the Bush administration, I believe that their approach was a wise one. By showing Beijing that the United States remained ready to negotiate in good faith after a hiatus of more than three years, the full onus of responsibility for failure rested squarely on the new North Korean leadership. Chinese experts and officials might otherwise blame the United States or its South Korean ally for the DPRK's obstreperous behavior. That North Korea alone had caused tensions was particularly important to drive home to the Chinese after the United States and NATO had helped bring down Qaddafi. After all, Qaddafi had voluntarily given up his nuclear program and then was subjected to regime change and execution. It was all too easy for Chinese elites to blame American aggression rather than their own passivity for the lack of progress on denuclearization in Iran and North Korea. This desire to shift the burden from China to the United States became very clear in the interviews I had with academics and officials in China in 2011. At the end of the day, only China can put meaningful economic and political pressure on North Korea. Since it seems so reluctant to do so, particularly in a period of transition, the only way to spur meaningful international action is to underscore North Korean culpability. The Leap Day Agreement helped create such clarity.

In December 2012, Pyongyang would conduct a more provocative missile test, successfully launching a satellite into space. Like the Soviet Sputnik launch in 1957, this test portends North Korea's future ability to deliver a nuclear warhead on an intercontinental ballistic missile. In February 2013, North Korea conducted its third nuclear test, to the frustration not only of the United States and its allies but of China and Russia. Pyongyang also announced that the pursuit of an advanced nuclear weapons arsenal was a national goal.

At the time, the Chinese Communist party was undergoing its ten-year political transition. Xi Jinping had been chosen general secretary in fall 2012 and would be named president in Spring 2013. Beijing did not need these provocations in any year, let alone during a transition. The UN Security Council passed new resolutions after the missile and nuclear tests, UNSCR 2087 and 2094, the latter being the most significant as it targeted North Korean banking networks involved in proliferation activities. Since North Korean banks abroad are only rarely involved in economically productive activities, a broad interpretation of this resolution—which also included banks involved in evading existing UN sanctions—followed by strict enforcement could put a tight squeeze on North Korean criminal finance, the life's blood of the regime.

In June 2013 Presidents Obama and Xi held an unusual "shirt-sleeves" summit at the Annenberg Estate in Sunnylands, California. The two presidents agreed that their countries should seek a "new type of great power relationship" to avoid the tensions and conflict normally associated with rising powers. Cooperation on North Korea and Iran figured prominently in the U.S. side's vision of how two competing great powers can build trust by addressing mutual problems. Deeply influenced by the logic of Robert Zoellick's 2005 "responsible stakeholder" speech, the Obama administration was trying to leverage Xi's desire to reinforce the U.S.–China relationship by urging greater Chinese cooperation on global governance. As the former State Department official and scholar Alan Romberg summed up in a report following the summit, while China was still unwilling to assist the United States and others in destabilizing the North Korean regime, it seemed willing to place a higher priority than in the recent past on pressuring Pyongyang to prevent proliferation of weapons or nuclear materials from North Korea to other countries and, perhaps, to roll back the North Korean nuclear program.[26] Romberg's analysis seemed confirmed in September 2013 when China's Ministry of Commerce produced a lengthy list of items that were not to be sold to North Korea by Chinese entities. The real bite on North Korea will be determined by actual implementation, not by the itemizing of a sanctions list, but the publication of the list itself was a significant political act and a slap in the face of China's long-term ally.

Chinese experts have insisted to me in private conversations that President Xi is less tolerant of Pyongyang's destabilizing behavior than Hu Jintao was. In addition to the sanctions list, they point to the downgrading of the "special" relationship between Beijing and Pyongyang, which normally was managed by the CCP's International Liaison Department, to a more normal bilateral relationship, managed primarily by the Foreign Ministry. In addition, President Xi visited Seoul for a summit with President Park Geun-hye but has not yet met Kim Jong-un since taking office. In an important gesture, Xi joined Park in expressing concern about the North Korean nuclear program and calling for denuclearization of the peninsula. These recent events may not be followed by serious Chinese pressure on North Korea, as Washington would like, but they are certainly progress over what President Obama called the "willful blindness" of Xi's predecessor, Hu Jintao, to North Korean provocations in 2010.[27]

It is unclear how the debates in China about the costs of PRC–DPRK friendship to China's diplomatic portfolio will eventually turn out. But a recent article by a high-ranking retired PLA officer provides some hope. General Wang Hongguang, former Deputy Commander of the critically important Nanjing Military District (opposite Taiwan), wrote in response to a *Global Times* editorial emphasizing that maintenance of North Korean stability is in China's interest: "I agree with this, and at the same time I also think that North Korea's abandonment of nuclear weapons is more in line with China's interests because [such abandonment] . . . is a precondition for stability." General Wang expressed concern about the stimulative effect of North Korean activities on U.S. alliances in the region and on their missile defense programs, cited the danger of fallout and seismic repercussions on China from North Korean nuclear tests, and worried about the catastrophic impact on China of a U.S. first strike on North Korean facilities in a future shooting war. He concluded that "China is the main country threatened by North Korea's possession of nuclear weapons." He criticized China for having "only played the role of bringing the United States and North Korea together" for talks and labeled this posture "quite awkward." He called on China instead to employ "all resources to strongly urge North Korea to abandon nuclear weapons."[28] General Wang's article was music to the ears of former and current U.S. diplomats working on this problem.

Following Kim Jong-un's reported execution of his previously powerful uncle in December 2013, Peking University professor Niu Jun published a scathing commentary in Hong Kong. Niu excoriated the brutal and bloody North Korean regime, which he called "very inappropriate" to East Asia's contemporary geostrategic environment, and predicted it could not survive very long. Niu also challenged China's traditional policy of protecting North Korea as a strategic buffer, which he says "lacks appropriate foundation and would have been discontinued long ago if not for the ideological factor." He claims that the Chinese public regards as a joke (*xiaohua*) positive official news stories about

North Korea. On strategic grounds, Niu blasts arguments of Chinese hard-liners who equate in a simpleminded fashion their leadership's call for "taking action" on the international stage (*you suo zuowei*) with support for actions designed to "oppose the West." Professor Niu opines that popular pressure for a change in China's North Korea policy might eventually override the "ideological factors" that have maintained the traditional policy of protecting the North.[29] The United States, and most of the rest of the world, can only hope that Professor Niu is right.

Iran

AS OUTLINED IN CHAPTER 5, the Chinese position on Iran is complex. The Obama administration and some like-minded European states have managed to adopt more significant multilateral and unilateral sanctions on Iran's energy and financial sector than ever before. The effect on Iran's economy has been significant, particularly in the financial sector. There is little doubt that the increasing pressure helped bring Tehran to the negotiating table to discuss its nuclear programs under the newly elected President Hassan Rouhani. An interim deal to limit uranium-enrichment activities in exchange for some relief from sanctions was reached in Geneva in November 2013 and extended in November 2014. It is too soon to tell whether the deal that was struck will last and if it will provide a firm foundation for further progress in nuclear negotiation.

What has China's role been in this process? China clearly welcomed a deal that would help stabilize the Iranian economy and, as a member of the P5+1 process, China was involved in sealing the interim agreement. But did China contribute to the international pressure that helped bring about Iranian accommodation and, if so, what does that mean for future Chinese cooperation on global nonproliferation? This is much harder to judge. China did sign on to relevant UN Security Council resolutions, including UNSCR 1929 in June 2010, but only after watering them down to protect China's own economic interests and to reduce the damage to Iran's overall economy. Most of the real international pressure on Iran has come from domestic laws and regulations enacted by the United

States and other leading economies that raise disincentives for third parties to invest in the Iranian energy sector or to work with Iranian banks
that are believed to be financing Tehran's extensive nuclear and missile
programs. Based in both its material interests and its traditional view on
sovereignty, China sees such unilateral measures, outside the UN and
the P5+1 process, as illegitimate. But Chinese firms, including energy
firms and banks, want to have access to U.S. and European markets, so
they will often comply with the prohibitions of the unilateral laws. In
a series of six-month waiver extensions, the U.S. State Department has
been able to exempt China from U.S. domestic sanctions legislation on
Iran by citing "significant" reductions in crude oil purchases by China.
From China's own statistics, it imported 20 percent less crude oil from
Iran in 2012 than in 2011, and the reduced rates continued into 2013,
earning China another six-month waiver in December of that year. But
questions remain. For example, was the reduction really the result of
a conscious decision by Beijing to support nonproliferation or was it
simply the result of grudging measures taken by Chinese companies to
avoid unilateral sanctions? One sign that there has not been a fundamental change in China's political attitudes toward these questions is
that Chinese importation of fuel oil, which is not covered by the U.S.
laws, reportedly increased from $1 million per year in 2012 to $495
million in the first seven months of 2013. As the congressionally funded
U.S.–China Economic and Security Review Commission concluded
from this data in its 2013 report, this dramatic use of a loophole in the
law suggests that China's relative compliance on crude oil did not indicate that Beijing agrees with the U.S. legislation.[30] And we should also
ask how long the effective reduction in Chinese purchases will last in
any case, particularly when the apparent thaw in relations between Tehran and Washington and its allies might further delegitimize in Chinese
eyes the unilateral measures by the United States and the Europeans. As
soon as an interim deal was struck, there were public reports that a Chinese firm was pursuing a new deal for significant future crude oil purchases.[31] And the latest available data suggest that Chinese oil purchases
from Iran indeed increased by 48 percent in the first half of 2014 over
the same period in 2013, reducing pressure on Iran to reach a permanent
deal on its nuclear programs. [32]

The Environment

THERE IS NO ISSUE that touches on the themes of this book more clearly than the global struggle to address climate change. Serious Chinese greenhouse gas emission reduction efforts could negatively affect China's domestic economic development and, therefore, one pillar of the legitimacy of the CCP regime.[33] Moreover, while China is now by far the largest emitter, responsible for 25 percent of global CO_2 emissions, developed countries are understandably blamed for having created the bulk of the problem, and the easy escape valve of accusing the great powers of past misdeeds fits well with postcolonial nationalism.[34] To appear to sacrifice China's own economic growth prospects without massive sacrifices in the United States and Europe would open China's leaders to the accusation that they are not defending China's honor, the other great pillar of CCP domestic legitimacy. Until the APEC summit in November 2014 in Beijing, the United States seemed unwilling to break this logjam by making significant new commitments of its own. Without Chinese sacrifices that accompanied such U.S. commitments, any proposal to cut greenhouse gas emissions by the Obama administration would be particularly domestically controversial in the United States. The two countries were caught in a trap of sorts. They might have loosened the grip of that trap significantly at the APEC meeting through deft diplomacy by both leaderships.

The Obama administration expanded its promise of numerical cuts at Copenhagen by committing the United States to cut by 2025 at least 26 percent of the greenhouse gases emitted in 2005. It was probably no coincidence that the commitment was not rolled out until the midterm elections were complete. On the one hand, President Obama had little to lose in his last two years in office after the Republicans gave the Democrats a drubbing earlier that November, seizing a majority in both houses of Congress. On the other, one has to wonder whether that new Congress will allow the executive branch to implement the regulations necessary to bring about the promised cuts. The new Senate majority leader, Mitch McConnell, from the coal state of Kentucky, attacked the deal immediately, complaining that the United States would need to make economic sacrifices from now until 2025 to cut emissions, while China had only promised to cap emissions around 2030, after sixteen more years of growth. To complicate the administration's policy further, Senator James Inhofe of Oklahoma, perhaps the most vocal climate change denier in Washington, is slated to become the chair of the Senate Committee on Environment and Public Works. These powerful actors might be able to limit the regulatory power of the Environmental Protection Agency so that it is unable to implement the president's preferred plan of action.[35]

The Chinese government's promise of peak emissions around 2030 was disappointing not only to these senators but also to optimistic environmentalists on both sides of the Pacific who had hoped for a cap in 2025, or even earlier. Five more years of growth in Chinese emissions is quite consequential, especially when that added growth compounds into the future at the higher peak. Analysts differ on how much of an actual policy sacrifice Beijing offered in the negotiations with the Americans, since ongoing changes in the Chinese economy toward more service industries and the existing trajectory in the renewable energy sector might render the promises less impressive. But in my opinion, the senators and other domestic critics of the deal are not correct when they say that the Obama administration failed to achieve anything significant. China became the first major emitter in the developing world to commit to an overall cap on carbon emissions and even offered a 20 percent target for the use of noncarbon sources of electricity (wind, solar, hydroelectric, and nuclear). This is an enormous change in basic psychology from the Chinese position at Copenhagen just five years earlier, outlined below. The difference has implications for many issues—from limiting the use of certain carbon-intensive solutions to reduce urban pollution to convincing other significant emitters to make commitments to quantitative limits themselves. Compliance by and verification in China will be difficult to establish, and the likelihood of Chinese backsliding or shirking will, of course, only be increased if U.S. domestic politics prevent implementation of President Obama's commitments, which come due before the Chinese ones. But we should not dismiss the importance of the deal that was struck. And it could, after all, be the first of several future deals with more significant implications for the long-term health of the planet. To understand why, it is useful to track the many problems American and Chinese negotiators faced in earlier years.

The December 2009 summit in Copenhagen exhibited the problems that needed to be overcome in 2014. China came into the conference portraying itself as an increasingly powerful leader of the developing world. Beijing's entourage worked hard to organize the BASIC countries (Brazil, South Africa, India, and China) around a position that made maximum demands on the developed countries for both dramatic commitments to reduced overall emissions and significant transfers to the developing world to help pay for the damage caused by climate change and for the costs of any remediation efforts.[36] Meanwhile, the same states rejected any quantitative restrictions on emissions from the emerging markets and the developing world more generally.[37] China itself did make a somewhat meaningful gesture of pledging unilaterally to reduce the carbon intensity in its economy by 40 to 45 percent by 2020. Carbon intensity refers to the amount of carbon emitted for each yuan or dollar of China's gross domestic product; even if it falls, overall emissions can grow if the economy continues to grow as well.[38] What Beijing assiduously avoided was a commitment to quantitative limits on overall future emissions that could negatively impact economic growth rates. Moreover, China remained resolutely opposed to allowing international verification organizations to monitor its compliance with any deal.[39] Finally, Chinese negotiators knew that as China's economy developed toward services and away from the production of the cheapest and dirtiest manufactured goods, carbon intensity would drop to a large degree without great effort by the state, even if overall emissions continued to grow at rates that would harm the global environment.

Jeffrey Bader, President Obama's right-hand advisor on Asia policy at the National Security Council, produced a balanced and fascinating memoir soon after returning to private life. His description of the Chinese diplomatic behavior at the Copenhagen conference is both informative and incisive. He points out that Beijing's entourage, led by Premier Wen Jiabao, arrived in Copenhagen on a mission to prevent any significant costs to China and to place blame on the United States and Europe for the failure to reach a meaningful accord. While the soft-spoken and outwardly humble Wen was his normal diplomatic self, some lower-ranking members of the Chinese entourage expressed anger and frustration in front of President Obama in a way that might have served their interests back home but was both bad protocol and bad diplomacy.

President Obama was successful in one aspect of his negotiating strategy at Copenhagen. By intensively engaging the Chinese and the other major developing states' representatives, he was able to ensure that China would bear some blame for a total failure. China thus signed on to the conference's final accord, a weak document with a small fund for transfers from developed countries to the developing world (not to include China), no new binding commitments on either quantitative outputs or carbon intensity, and no protocol for monitoring or verification.[40] As Bader put it, "The Chinese would have wrecked the conference [altogether] if left to their own devices. Thanks to Obama's cajoling, they, and Wen in particular, realized at the last minute that China would bear the lion's share of the blame if the conference collapsed."[41] In fact, despite Wen's efforts, the Europeans still blamed China for preventing a more meaningful agreement. Bader's description of China's frustration with this diplomatic result is very telling. He writes, "The Chinese seemed bewildered by these [European] assessments, suggesting the dimensions of the time lag between the growing reality of China's economic strength today and its own still limited perception of its responsibilities."[42] While China sees itself as a developing country, others see it as a giant.

There were follow-on conferences in Cancun, Durban, Doha, and Warsaw. None of these produced results that would seriously limit future emissions. Moreover, while some progress was made on the issue of verification of current and future agreements, those protocols are limited to those receiving transfer payments from the developed countries, meaning that China will not be subject to international verification.

China's disastrous domestic environmental conditions, including rampant pollution of the air, water, and soil, could limit its long-term economic growth. Environmental problems have already been a major source of protest from angry farmers and urban dwellers whose families are adversely affected.[43] For largely domestic reasons, in recent years the Chinese government has invested heavily in green technologies, renewable energy, and pollution reduction. It has also created a domestic carbon-trading scheme designed to reduce overall air pollution.[44] *The Economist* wrote that the aforementioned January 2013 "airpocalypse" across urban China

> injected a new urgency into local debate about the environment—and produced a green-policy frenzy a few months later. In three weeks from the middle of June, the government unveiled a series of reforms to restrict air pollution. It started the country's first carbon market, made prosecuting environmental crimes easier and made local officials more accountable for air-quality problems in their areas. It also said China—meaning companies as well as government—would spend $275 billion over the next five years cleaning up the air. Even by Chinese standards that is serious money, equivalent to Hong Kong's GDP or twice the size of the annual defence budget.[45]

Beijing has used pressure on highly polluting state-owned firms to use energy more efficiently. China has reportedly reduced its carbon intensity by 20 percent over the last five years and its growth in CO_2 emissions to half the rate of economic growth.[46]

As discussed in chapter 5, since Copenhagen, China has adopted measures unilaterally or in negotiations with the United States and others to try to limit growth in coal burning, to make more fuel-efficient and less polluting vehicles, and to seek global reductions of hydrofluorocarbon production and consumption under the Montreal Protocol framework. Skeptics might point out that China has mainly plucked low-hanging fruit, relying on more efficient use of fossil fuels, something that has direct economic benefits in any case, and coasting on the natural turn of a quickly developing economy to cleaner service industries for growth. The results require little or no sacrifice and say little about China's willingness or ability to pay significant costs in the future. But we must also recognize that China has worked hard to limit the use of coal and has invested massively in noncarbon energy sources. As the *New York Times* reports, in the past decade China has built the world's largest wind-power complex. And if developments unfold according to plan, China will triple its already massive hydropower output and will increase nuclear power six times by 2020. China is also increasing the use of natural gas in its fossil-fuel mix, as the burning of natural gas is much less polluting than the burning of coal or petroleum.[47]

Unfortunately, not all good things go together. One problem is that the reduction of smog and low-altitude particulates and the reduction of carbon emissions do not always go entirely hand in hand. One basic reason, as stated in chapter 5, is that those particulates provide a parasol that reflects the sun's rays into space. Lessening of that parasol effect would cut somewhat into the considerable global benefits of burning less coal in and around Chinese cities. There is another, even more concerning reason that the goal of reducing urban air pollution does not necessarily dovetail with the goal of reducing greenhouse gas emissions. Some efforts to reduce airborne particulates could themselves actually increase China's carbon footprint. For example, if China turns a large portion of its massive coal reserves into synthetic natural gas (SNG) for burning in urban electrical plants, smog might be significantly reduced in those cities. And Chinese leaders have reasons to pursue this course. The domestic health and political problems created by urban smog, much more than remediation of global warming, are driving Beijing's overall energy policy reforms. The problem, according to experts, is that when one considers the carbon emissions involved in creating, shipping, and burning synthetic natural gas made from coal, carbon emissions increase anywhere from 30 to 80 percent over simply burning the coal![48] As of 2013 Beijing had reportedly approved nine SNG plants, and by one estimate thirty more have been proposed.[49] In 2014 Greenpeace reported that twenty-one plants had already been approved and as many as fifty plants had been proposed, outstripping China's already ambitious government plan.[50] Once the large sunk costs for building the plants are paid, it will be economically and politically harder to stop using them, despite the terrible global implications.[51] In a very depressing article, Greenpeace research predicts that the growth in CO_2 emissions from increasing Chinese SNG will likely outstrip in only one year the entire U.S. commitment to reduce emissions from now until 2020 and will nearly match the EU's own commitment on that score. More to the point, perhaps, the research suggests that the new emissions from SNG will far outstrip the global benefits of China's rather active campaign to limit coal burning in many provinces.[52] That coal control campaign is, predictably, aimed more at reducing ground-level fine particulate pollution than it is targeted at reducing greenhouse gas emissions, but the two effects overlap significantly in the case of limiting coal burning, so there were potential large-scale global benefits as well. Unfortunately, the opposite is true for replacing coal burning with SNG consumption, and China apparently plans to consume massive amounts of SNG in coming decades.

Of course, unlike SNG, Chinese development of renewable energy such as wind power or solar energy generally has benefits for both the local environment and the global environment. And Beijing committed to invest nearly $300 billion in renewable energy in its current five-year plan (2011–2015), a truly impressive amount.[53] While creating energy from renewable sources is more expensive than burning coal or oil, less reliable and predictable than those carbon-based methods (wind varies, and the sun only shines half the day), or both, there are some straightforward economic incentives for Beijing to invest in these technologies. China's economy is highly globalized, and the prospect of a fertile global marketplace for cleaner energy and green technologies encourages China and others to get in on the ground floor by investing in these sectors now. The problem is not China competing globally in these emerging markets. That is a good thing. The potential problem is how China might choose to compete in those markets. Past experience does not paint a bright picture. If heavily subsidized Chinese firms are allowed or encouraged to dump their goods in third markets to create market share or simply to reduce excess capacity from overinvestment, China could undercut the healthy development of green industries elsewhere and, in the process, reduce the power of domestic lobbies in other countries for government subsidies for environmentally responsible energy production. We have already seen this pattern in Chinese solar panel exports, as discussed in chapter 5.

Similarly, if Chinese firms steal the intellectual property of foreign green technology firms as they produce new technologies, this theft could seriously harm incentives for innovation around the world in areas like wind turbine production. China's track record to date on such matters is not a good one. It is difficult to see China creating the culture and institutional capacity to enforce global intellectual property rights norms anytime soon.

The November 2014 agreement between the United States and China could help address some but not all of these problems. The Chinese made a commitment to cap overall emissions. Even if the peak of emissions will come much later and reach much higher than environmentalists in China and abroad had hoped, any notional peak, if enforced, undercuts the logic of using particularly carbon-intensive solutions like SNG to reduce low-altitude fine-particulate pollution in the cities. China's top leaders have real incentives to confront powerful polluting interest groups at home in order to tackle urban pollution, a potentially destabilizing political problem in China. And even as we recognize the potentially negative aspects for climate change of some solutions to urban pollution—like SNG or the reduction of the cooling parasol effect of fine-particulate pollution—we also must recognize that, in general, the goals of reducing urban pollution and of limiting climate change for the most part dovetail. So the 2014 agreement, with its notional future cap on emissions, might actually be a win–win outcome for both American climate change negotiators and Chinese leaders looking to address dire environmental conditions at home. Any agreement by Chinese leaders with international actors to seek a peak in emissions around 2030 might be used as leverage at home to deepen reform of government regulatory bureaucracies so that they can better enforce central government policy mandates on both fine-particulate pollutants in the cities and carbon emissions. The reader will recall how China's accession to the WTO reportedly assisted Premier Zhu Rongji in pushing through desired domestic reforms of the state sector. Without better enforcement and verification in China, other countries might accuse Beijing of backsliding on its commitments and lose domestic backing for their own commitments accordingly. And even after the 2014 APEC summit, China still seems adamantly opposed to international verification requirements for any deals it strikes.

It is easy to point fingers at China for intellectual property rights rip-offs, dumping, refusal to accept quantitative emissions targets, and rejecting international verification, but China has strong reasons to point the finger back toward the United States and the Europeans, who have produced such a high percentage of the accumulated carbon in the global atmosphere. China has valid ethical reasons to make demands of developed countries that those countries, especially the United States, will find difficult to meet, especially if China does not significantly limit its own emissions. This tragic Sino-American dynamic is one of the many reasons that the United States itself has been irresponsible on climate change. In essence, Beijing and Washington have enabled each other to do less than is needed to address this increasingly serious global problem.

The China Challenge

TWO ASPECTS OF CHINA'S RISE pose problems for the United States. The first is a traditional security challenge: How do we negotiate the rise of an increasingly powerful actor in a region of great global importance? This challenge is real. A Sino-American conflict is not inevitable or even likely, but I consider such a conflict possible, and that is worrisome enough. Avoiding this conflict will require a strong U.S. presence in Asia combined with deft diplomacy to assure China that the United States seeks neither to halt China's rise on the global stage nor to foment domestic instability within China itself.

The second problem is arguably more difficult to solve: How do we persuade a large but still developing country with a nationalist chip on its shoulder to contribute to the international system? Because that system is now so tightly integrated after decades of globalization, a major perturbation anywhere can affect us all. And since China is so large, it can disrupt global governance efforts either by consciously obstructing them or simply by refusing to participate in solving a wide range of problems—from proliferation of nuclear weapons, to civil conflict and humanitarian disasters, to international financial instability, to climate change.

So how should the United States confront these challenges? The United States is not now and never has been powerful enough to dictate to China what it should or should not do. But especially in coordination with its allies, security partners, and others, the United States does have the power to shape the choices of a rising China so as to encourage Beijing to adopt policies that are positive for regional and global stability and to forgo policies that could destabilize East Asia and undercut the global order.

A sophisticated and constructive strategy toward China combines two elements not normally associated with each other: a very strong U.S. military presence in East Asia with a consistent diplomatic posture that invites China to participate in regional and global governance. Without a reassuring diplomatic mission, many inside and outside China might see the strong U.S. military presence as containment—the dawn of a new cold war. With a strong presence in place, Washington should suggest peaceful channels through which the United States and China can cooperate regionally and globally and thereby reduce bilateral tensions while still allowing for increasing Chinese power and prestige. Without the strong presence, however, many in China might view U.S. entreaties for cooperation and confidence-building as signs of U.S. weakness, and Beijing might be more tempted to settle its differences through coercion. The combined effect of a military and a diplomatic presence should be to show China that such a campaign of coercion would not only fail but also further the outcome that Chinese strategists fear most: the encirclement of China by countries aligned with a mobilized and adversarial United States.

For U.S. leaders, the regional security challenges and the global governance challenges created by China's rise are linked. Success in one area could breed success in the other. Serious failure in one, however, could also spoil the prospects of success in the other. One of the best ways to foster Sino-American mutual trust is to find areas for cooperation outside of East Asia, where mutual suspicions between Washington and Beijing should be lower than they are over sensitive territorial issues like Taiwan or the Senkaku Islands. If global governance issues are handled deftly, China may become more assertive internationally and more constructive at the same time. If China does improve its performance on global governance and the response from the United States is positive, strategic mistrust of a rising China in Washington and in East Asian capitals should decline, and at the same time, Chinese citizens hoping for a more prominent role in world affairs should be satisfied. Getting China's foreign policy to improve—to be assertive without being aggressive—may be the greatest challenge facing the next few generations of U.S. diplomats.

Combining U.S. Strength and Diplomatic Moderation

IN PART BECAUSE they see Sino-American conflict as nearly inevitable, prominent pessimists, such as John Mearsheimer, prescribe a U.S.-led containment effort against a rising China.[1] As discussed in chapter 3, the periods from which pessimists tend to draw their theoretical lessons, the nineteenth and twentieth centuries, were very different from the twenty-first century; now a thick web of economic interdependence in the form of transnational production links us all. Regional and global institutions also help ameliorate tensions. In the meantime, all the great powers in the world either have nuclear weapons or are allied with a nuclear power. Great powers have no incentive and no credible threat to invade and occupy each other as they had in the past.

Even if we were to accept Mearsheimer's outdated logic about a zero-sum Sino-American power competition, an active attempt by Washington to harm the Chinese economy and isolate China diplomatically whenever possible, as the United States did to the Soviet Union in the Cold War era, would be extremely ill advised. A straightforward containment effort toward China today would almost certainly fail because the United States would be extremely hard-pressed to enlist any other country in such an effort, and an attempt to do so would likely cause irreparable damage to the U.S. alliance system in the region and around the world. In a net assessment of the two nations' relative power, the United States has many advantages, but there is no area where that advantage is greater than the U.S. network of alliances and security partnerships in Asia and beyond. Throwing that advantage away under the banner of enhancing American power would be as ironic as it were tragic.

Unfortunately, zero-sum views of U.S.–China relations are most popular in China itself. Raised on a volatile blend of Marxism-Leninism and postcolonial nationalism, many Chinese elites see the world as a brutal struggle for material power in which stronger powers will want to oppress a weaker China. As a Chinese academic once told me, John Mearsheimer is seen by many Chinese as the one honest American strategist, willing to admit that the United States has deep-seated national interests in delaying and halting China's rise. Many Chinese nationalists treat with suspicion American advice about how to improve China's foreign policy and reform its domestic governance. They view the "responsible stakeholder" concept as an unfair burden on China and see the problems the concept is designed to address as being more American, or "Western," than they are Chinese. They also view U.S. advice that Beijing reduce censorship and repression, improve the rule of law, and provide legitimate venues for peaceful social discontent as a Trojan horse. Borrowing from official government propaganda about the dangers of democratization and the loosening of the CCP's grip on power, they argue that the United States is trying to weaken China by westernizing and splitting it.

The irony, of course, is that many U.S. officials sincerely agree with Premier Wen Jiabao's outgoing comments: political reform must accompany economic reform if China is to continue to modernize and grow in a stable fashion. And contrary to a realpolitik, zero-sum view, the United States wishes China well. The United States views democracy as a foundation of national strength and stability, and the notion that it spreads democracy to weaken countries rather than to strengthen them is one of the more bizarre manifestations of Chinese postcolonial nationalism.

To demonstrate the common interests between the two nations, it is useful to imagine the dangers to the United States if China were to fall into domestic political and social disarray. The resulting nation would not only lose its ability to fight proliferation, it could itself become a major source of it. Likewise, China would have neither the capacity nor the incentive to cooperate with other powers to address financial crises, regional instability, environmental degradation, and the spread of potentially epidemic diseases like avian influenza or Ebola. A China with severe domestic problems might be much more neuralgic and internationally conflict-prone. Unless the domestic paralysis was near total, such a China would still likely have enough material power to pose grave risks to the United States, but at the same time Chinese politicians might have stronger incentives to react to real or perceived slights on the international stage in hypernationalist ways to preserve and enhance their power at home. This would be true even if such a China did not have the slightest pretense of becoming a peer competitor of the United States.

Although the United States should not feed Chinese fears about U.S. hostility, Chinese anxiety about a U.S. containment effort could carry some benefits for the United States: the potential for future encirclement may encourage Chinese strategists to be more accommodating. Under conditions in which Chinese analysts believe in the possibility of containment, even the most pessimistic realpolitik thinkers might join their more optimistic colleagues in prescribing moderate policies. Chinese strategists sometimes recognize that more coercive Chinese policies toward neighbors increase both the willingness and the ability of Washington to encircle and constrain China. Just as many American experts understand that any attempt by the United States to contain China's rise now would likely weaken the United States, many Chinese observers think bullying by Beijing will create a tighter and more expansive set of U.S.-led security relationships in the region.

A fine example of this phenomenon is provided by Professor Yan Xuetong of Tsinghua University, a highly intelligent and prolific Chinese commentator who, like Mearsheimer, tends to view U.S.–China relations as a zero-sum struggle. But rather than calling for a more hostile Chinese stance, Yan actually recommends that Beijing behave in an accommodating and reassuring fashion toward its neighbors so as to reduce the ability of the United States to encircle and strangle China and to prevent regional spirals of tension, thus allowing China to play its full role in global governance. Ironically, he calls for those policies precisely because he sees an intense struggle for relative power between a rising China and a declining United States. In a provocative *New York Times* editorial entitled "How China Can Defeat America," Yan writes, "China's quest to enhance its world leadership status and America's effort to maintain its present position is a zero-sum game. It is the battle for people's hearts and minds that will determine who eventually prevails. And, as China's ancient philosophers predicted, the country that displays more humane authority will win."[2]

When Yan's op-ed was first published, a very moderate Chinese colleague asked me what I thought. My reaction was mixed. There are indeed competitive elements in U.S.–China relations, but I fully reject Yan's argument that they create an overall relationship that is a zero-sum game. Nevertheless, I welcome Yan's prescriptions. By cooperating with its neighbors and contributing to global governance, China will indeed be increasing its power and prestige, but in ways that serve rather than challenge U.S. national interests. After all, the real security question posed by China's rise in Asia is not how to keep China down but how to maintain regional stability and guarantee the security and interests of China's neighbors.

Shaping China's Choices in the Military Security Sphere

EVEN THOUGH U.S.–CHINA RELATIONS are not a zero-sum game, a complex web of geography, political psychology, domestic politics, and shifting distributions of material power will force both countries to make constant adjustments in the years ahead. One does not need to envision replays of the two world wars or the Cold War to recognize the security challenge presented by China's rise. The trick for U.S. leaders is how to maintain a strong military, economic, and diplomatic presence in East Asia without triggering a defensive and destabilizing reaction in Beijing. The United States must encourage China to compete in mutually beneficial areas such as constructive bilateral and multilateral diplomacy. It must advocate for deepening economic integration and discourage China from bullying its way to great power status. Providing China's neighbors the opportunity to cooperate with the United States in security, economic, and diplomatic affairs without jealously begrudging their positive economic and diplomatic relations with China should preserve U.S. advantages in the region and push China toward healthier forms of competition with the United States.

The post–Cold War history of East Asia offers several confirming examples of the policy analysis outlined herein. During the early years of the Clinton administration, we saw a poor combination of a weakening U.S. presence and an assertive diplomatic policy against Beijing.

The strain on the U.S.–Japan alliance over economic differences, the administration's direct threat to sanction China economically to promote domestic political reform, and the clumsy handling of Taiwan president Lee Teng-hui's application for a visa in 1995 helped promote a crisis in the region and great tension in U.S.–China relations. In a nutshell, the United States seemed both weak and threatening to China, the opposite of the ideal strategy. But the administration's resolute military response to the 1995–1996 Taiwan Strait crisis and the concurrent effort to strengthen U.S. alliances in the region embodied in the Nye Initiative went a long way toward convincing Beijing that the U.S. presence would remain strong in the post–Cold War era. At the same time, the Clinton administration reassured China through words and actions that the purpose of the strengthened U.S. presence was not to promote eventual Taiwan independence from the Chinese nation, Beijing's biggest security concern during the presidency of Lee Teng-hui.

China's response to this balanced set of policies was to emphasize multilateral diplomacy and economic integration with its neighbors. Consistent with this "peaceful rise" strategy, Beijing consciously shelved sovereignty disputes in the East and South China Seas, thereby minimizing tensions with ASEAN and with Japan. Moderates in China were able to convince their more strident colleagues that this approach was best by pointing to the failure of Chinese coercion and the competitive costs of the opposite strategy. That reassuring Chinese foreign policy continued well into the next decade. It arguably served the interests of everyone in the region, as well as the United States, and was a signal achievement of the Asia policy of the Clinton administration's second term.

The Bush administration came into office correctly perceiving the need for a strong U.S. military, economic, and diplomatic presence in the region. The new administration sought to bolster that presence with firm commitments to allies and security partners, together with new free-trade initiatives in Asia with willing partners like Singapore and South Korea. But the Bush team had also tried to distance itself from the Clinton administration on the campaign trail and, in the process, adopted an immoderate diplomatic stance toward Beijing, labeling China a "strategic competitor" rather than a potential "strategic partner" (the label assigned by the Clinton administration as a future aspiration, rather than a present descriptor). Top Bush advisors also called for Japan to be more like the UK and to break out of its pattern of self-restraint in military affairs that had been in place since the end of World War II. They similarly promised increased U.S. support for Taiwan's defense. Especially following the EP-3 crisis in early 2001 and the announcement of a very large arms sales package for Taiwan, many in Beijing perceived the new president as unconditionally supportive of Taiwan. Taiwan's president at the time, Chen Shui-bian, was, if anything, more dedicated to pursuing Taiwan independence than his predecessor, so Beijing's perception only served to intensify its mistrust of the new administration, which ratcheted up tensions unnecessarily in East Asia.

What was missing in the early Bush administration policies was reassurance to China about the purpose of the U.S. regional presence and revitalized alliances. Some very unwelcome events provided an opportunity for the Bush administration to correct this problem. The terrorist attacks on 9/11 reminded thoughtful observers in both capitals of the common interests between Beijing and Washington. They also provided a new reason for the United States to strengthen its security cooperation with key regional partners such as Japan and Singapore and to increase the U.S. presence to China's west in Central Asia. Normally, such a series of actions would destabilize U.S.–China relations by increasing China's fears about U.S. encirclement. In fact, those increased fears were still very much present in Chinese strategic circles through the beginning of 2002. But Bush administration officials, including Vice President Cheney, made concerted efforts to reassure Beijing that U.S. policy toward China had not changed—that the talk about rethinking China policy was just campaign rhetoric.

Even more reassuring was the way Washington openly distanced itself from Chen Shui-bian's pro-independence activities in Taiwan from 2002 to 2008. This served to reduce the currency of Chinese conspiracy theories about U.S. intentions. Moreover, it built a foundation for trust that not only stabilized the East Asia region but also, I believe, helped create momentum for cooperation on global governance issues like North Korea, Sudan Darfur, and piracy off of Somalia from 2006 to 2008.

The Obama administration came into office at a time of reduced tensions in cross-Strait relations. Chen Shui-bian's controversial March

2008 referendum on seeking membership in the UN under the name
Taiwan had failed to receive the required number of votes. Also, the
KMT's Ma Ying-jeou, who was more moderate in his posture toward
the mainland, was elected on the same day. Cross-Strait détente is generally welcomed in Washington. Ironically, however, the lack of tensions
in relations across the Taiwan Strait deprived the Obama administration
of the opportunities afforded to the Clinton and Bush administrations
to reassure the PRC about U.S. strategic intentions without appearing
overly weak or compromising in the process.

Key aspects of the Obama administration's approach to Asia were
laudable and consistent with the balanced strategy suggested above,
especially the effort to improve diplomatic and economic relations with
Burma and upgrade U.S. diplomatic participation in regional organizations, such as the ASEAN Regional Forum and the East Asia Summit.
The problem for the first-term Obama administration was its rhetoric about China policy and about Asia strategy more generally. Rather
than establish a strong and moderate posture toward a rising China,
those rhetorical gaffes pulled in opposite directions. The effort to seek
strategic reassurance of China outside of any specific context (e.g., a
prior move by Taipei toward permanent independence for Taiwan) and
the agreement in the 2009 U.S.–China Joint Statement to respect the
PRC's "core interests" unintentionally sent a signal to Chinese observers that the new administration was going to be more accommodating
toward China than any since the end of the Cold War. Many in China
believed that either because the administration had a different strategic orientation than its predecessors or because the financial crisis had
weakened America, they were witnessing a significant change in U.S.
posture. This belief came crashing down in early 2010 when China
realized that U.S. policy toward Taiwan arms sales, human rights, and
the Dalai Lama had in fact not changed despite those rhetorical assurances. Beijing reacted harshly, and distrust of the United States was
greatly intensified in Chinese strategic circles.

That Chinese distrust of the Obama administration was fed and
intensified by the administration's other rhetorical flourish: the description of its Asia strategy as a "return" to the region, a "pivot" toward the
region, and a "rebalance" of U.S. priorities away from the Middle East

and Central Asia and toward East Asia. This unnecessary and largely inaccurate narrative made almost everything positive that the administration did in the security and diplomatic fields in the region—and those positive steps are important and considerable—initially seem to many Chinese analysts and observers to be part of a new encirclement strategy. The U.S. "black hand" was seen behind all efforts by Japan and Southeast Asian states, such as the Philippines and Vietnam, to assert their claims in sovereignty disputes in the East China Sea and the South China Sea. And even the least threatening and least novel aspects of Obama administration policies often appeared both new and potentially threatening in Chinese eyes—for instance, the ratification of the free trade agreement with Korea that was negotiated by the Bush administration and the Obama team's pursuit of the Trans-Pacific Partnership in trade with an array of regional actors, which was also hatched in the region itself during the Bush years.

Moving forward, the United States needs to maintain a strong military, diplomatic, and economic presence in Asia and to provide potential victims of Chinese bullying with an alternative security partner in the United States. The United States should insist that sovereignty disputes are handled peacefully and should encourage and facilitate multilateral confidence-building in disputed areas, but should assiduously avoid taking sides in those disputes or getting directly involved in their settlement. U.S. government officials have sometimes used fuzzy rhetoric that clouds the important distinctions between managing disputes and resolving them. It is one thing for Washington to call for multilateral confidence-building to keep existing disputes from escalating in a region that is important to the United States; it is quite another for a nonclaimant, like Washington, to prescribe multilateral methods to settle the disputes themselves. U.S. prescriptions for multilateral negotiations over sovereignty disputes would appear not only meddlesome but feckless as the existing multilateral organizations in the region seem ill suited for that task. Those organizations, such as ASEAN, include claimants and nonclaimants alike and, more generally, lack the necessary internal cohesion to take on such a challenge. But despite some lack of rhetorical clarity by government representatives on certain occasions, the Obama administration's policies toward the East China Sea and South China Sea disputes have been generally consistent with long-held U.S. positions on those disputes and were assertively and constructively stated in regional security forums. Secretary Clinton's statement at the July 2010 ASEAN Regional Forum set a new standard for clarity, strength, and balance in U.S. policy toward the South China Sea disputes, and President Obama successfully turned the East Asia Summit in 2011 from a talk shop into a forum that wrestled for the first time with the pressing security concerns in the region.

In line with this approach, President Obama signed a base access agreement with the Philippines during his 2014 tour of four Asian nations. The Philippines' own postcolonial nationalism contributed to the removal of U.S. bases there in the 1990s. Chinese bullying of the militarily weak ally over the past few years made an American presence more welcome, and the base access agreement demonstrated to China the costs of its coercive behavior. It will be helpful for Beijing to recognize that its more assertive and coercive actions toward its neighbors will likely only deepen U.S. defense relationships in the region. For example, Obama was wise to publicly reassure Tokyo that no amount of Chinese assertiveness will make Washington reconsider either Japan's sole administrative control of the Senkaku Islands or the alliance's applicability to them.

Unfortunately, however, the exaggerated rhetoric that the administration chose to describe its overall regional strategy seemingly confirmed nationalist Chinese narratives about U.S. efforts to encircle and contain China and likely contributed to Beijing's decision in the past few years to pursue its maritime claims against regional rivals more assertively. Especially in the context of tensions over recent mutual accusations of cyber-spying and online intellectual property theft, the administration's strategic rhetoric rendered the overall tone of U.S.–China relations unnecessarily harsh. Even in the era of the budget sequester, the United States still carries a big stick, but it has not been speaking softly.

Finding Common Interests and Avoiding Red Lines

THE UNITED STATES must elicit Chinese support for global governance, but doing so requires a degree of subtlety, sophistication, and empathy that is often absent from America's own foreign policy and is harder still to sustain across a coalition. The United States and like-minded states need to focus on the considerable common interests we have with China on everything from finance and trade, to nonproliferation, to stability in various regions of the world, to global environmental protection. But those multilateral efforts need to eschew preconditions and stated objectives that trigger Beijing's allergies toward international intervention to overthrow regimes. In eliciting Chinese support for multilateral efforts, the international community needs to focus more on solving specific behavioral problems by problematic states—such as nuclear activities prohibited by preexisting commitments to the Nuclear Nonproliferation Treaty or wanton killing of targeted civilian populations—and focus less on regime change. This last part is particularly important. When the United States and its allies seek to overthrow regimes, Chinese elites see a dangerous precedent, and they also perceive the effort as an attempt to deprive China of some legitimate economic or diplomatic benefit in that region, rather than as an attempt to restore regional stability.

The first Bush administration and the Clinton administration endeavored to keep China from actively supporting bad behavior (such as selling nuclear materials or missile technologies to Iran) and to get China to stand aside during multilateral security initiatives, such as UN authorization of the first Gulf War or UN sanctions on North Korea in the lead-up to the Agreed Framework. But in the twenty-first century, this is no longer enough. Even Chinese passivity and the maintenance of normal economic relations with global pariahs provides enough sustenance to those bad actors to undercut global efforts to pressure them. The international efforts to pressure North Korea and Iran over their nuclear programs are prime examples of this problem.

Although the Obama administration's choice of rhetoric was different, Robert Zoellick's "responsible stakeholder" initiative during the second term of the George W. Bush administration is still at the heart of U.S. China policy. The Obama administration embraced Beijing's preferred phrase: "new type of great power relations" (*xin xing daguo guanxi*). I think it unwise to seek common labels with Beijing, as China tends to interpret them radically differently and to use those self-serving interpretations against the United States and its allies diplomatically when predictable differences arise. But the spirit of Obama's approach is very much in line with that of his predecessor: the best way to avoid the tragic spirals of tension that accompanied power transitions of the past is to build bilateral trust through cooperation on common projects, many of which are multilateral in nature. So, for example, from 2002 to 2008, the United States not only built trust by distancing itself from Taiwan independence but by fostering varying levels of cooperation with China in multilateral initiatives like the Six Party Talks on Korean denuclearization, the UN peacekeeping effort in Sudan Darfur, and the antipiracy efforts off the Gulf of Aden.

It is worthwhile to reflect on how these improvements in cooperation came about. In the case of North Korea, China brought maximum pressure to bear after the first nuclear test in 2006, which Beijing viewed as an affront by its Cold War ally. But an underappreciated part of that story was the U.S. effort to reassure China that the international pressure on North Korea was intended not to overthrow the government there or deprive China of its own economic and diplomatic interests in the country, but simply to stop the nuclear program. The diplomatic package presented by the Bush administration in fall 2006 appeared to offer a way for the North Korean regime to break out of its diplomatic isolation and to improve its economy if it would only give up its nuclear programs. This was a far cry from President Bush's "axis of evil" speech, delivered prior to the invasion of Iraq, suggesting that the only solution to the North Korean problem was the elimination of its leadership. (This may in the end prove true, but it is not good diplomacy to say so, especially if other key actors disagree.) Similarly, on Sudan policy, U.S. diplomats, including this author, were careful to disabuse skeptical Chinese elites of the notion that the purpose of a UN-sponsored Darfur mission would be regional secession for Darfur. Moreover, Washington needed to convince those Chinese elites that we did not begrudge China its oil investments in Sudan and that U.S. and European efforts to pressure the regime in Khartoum were not secret designs to undermine China's energy interests.

This was not an easy sell, as the Chinese looked back to the Kosovo War in 1999. China had opposed the NATO operation against Yugoslavia, and Chinese citizens bitterly recall that the United States devastated their embassy in one of many air strikes on Belgrade. At a deeper and more political level, Chinese elites understood that the "simple" humanitarian mission to oppose ethnic cleansing could easily eventually morph into internationally armed support for Kosovo independence from Yugoslavia. They were right, in the end. Kosovo independence was formally cemented in early 2008. In Darfur, U.S. diplomats needed to convince the Chinese that carving up Sudan was not the goal of the United States or its European allies. In that effort, it was helpful to have the African Union's support for the U.S. and EU approach. The participation and backing of an organization of developing states with traditionally anti-interventionist, postcolonial attitudes and diverse regional and ethnic tensions of their own lent credence to the American and European assertion that their goal was not to overthrow the state in Khartoum or to break up the country along territorial lines. Without those assurances, the social opprobrium related to the impending Olympics in 2008 likely would not have been enough for Beijing to change its policy on Sudan. With those assurances, Beijing chose to pressure the Sudanese leadership to accept a hybrid UN–African Union force and contributed hundreds of engineers.

In securing China's participation in the Gulf of Aden operation, it was relatively easy for the United States and others to convince a large trading state like China of our common interests in combating piracy. There was wariness in Beijing, however, that the operation might lead to greater U.S. and allied penetration of the Horn of Africa. The fact that the United States was involved in a large and diverse international coalition of navies almost certainly reduced Chinese resistance. The UN resolution that allowed for hot pursuit of pirates into Somali territorial waters also included an important concession for Beijing; the resolution stated that the Somali "central authorities" had agreed in advance to such intrusions into Somali territory.

The Bush years also carry important negative lessons for U.S. diplomacy toward China and the region. The inclusion of North Korea and Iran alongside Iraq in the "axis of evil" speech, and the invasion of Iraq itself in early 2003, arguably stimulated Beijing to agree to a multilateral approach to the North Korean nuclear issue out of fear that Pyongyang would be next on the target list for military attack. But the Bush administration's suggestion in its first term that only regime change could solve the problems gave Beijing elites a psychologically soothing excuse for the lack of progress in nuclear talks, once those talks had started. The problem, they argued, was not that there was insufficient pressure on North Korea from China and the rest of the international community. The real problem was that there was insufficient reassurance from the United States that the governments in countries like North Korea and Iran, governments labeled as pariahs by Washington, would not be subverted through economic pressure or overthrown by foreign invasion if they were to curtail their nuclear activities.

A similar dynamic led China to veto UN Security Council resolutions condemning the Burmese junta and Zimbabwe's brutal regime for domestic human rights violations. Not only did Beijing argue that the Security Council was the wrong venue for human rights concerns, China's diplomats worried that verbal condemnation could be the precursor to stronger international measures designed to destabilize the target governments. Particularly in the case of ethnically divided Burma, which lies on China's southern border, rhetoric employed by U.S. officials about the need for the junta simply to "step down" raised the specter for Chinese officials of a power vacuum followed by a bloody civil war on China's periphery. And even though Americans were frustrated with the Burmese junta and China's refusal to pressure that government, the Chinese had logical and understandable concerns about the dangers that would be created by overnight regime change in Burma.

The Obama years also provide fairly stark lessons of what works and what does not work in gaining assertive Chinese support for global governance efforts. When constructive efforts clearly fit into China's own near-term domestic agenda and require little foreign interference in China or in other countries, it is relatively easy to secure China's support. So when the G20 countries were designing coordinated stimulus packages in response to the financial crisis, no one offered a bigger domestic package as a percentage of GNP than China. But this did not necessarily signal a new era in China's global consciousness and willingness to make sacrifices for global order. Beijing had strong domestic reasons to keep the engine of growth humming; and while government stimulus packages are not always efficient, Beijing's stimulus package was an easy sell at home because it kept people working at a time when export markets had been hit hard. To be fair, the benefits of China's stimulus still spread far beyond China. China was almost the sole engine of global growth in the darkest moments of the financial crisis. But Europeans and others had much less success petitioning Beijing to use its massive foreign exchange reserves to help bail out countries in crisis, such as Greece. Fortunately, in the end the Greek crisis did not pull down the European financial system, but if it had, China would have been hurt badly by the shrinking of one of its largest markets. Still, it was very difficult indeed to convince a poorer developing country with a social safety net in its nascent stages of development to bail out a much richer country that had gone bankrupt in large part because it had woven an overly lavish social safety net for its citizenry.

On climate change until 2014, only limited progress had been made in gaining China's collaboration. Where China has behaved most impressively is conservation, long-term investments in renewable energy sources, and the replacement of coal with natural gas, wind, solar, and nuclear energy whenever possible. These remedies address China's own local environmental concerns in reducing low-atmosphere air pollution and also jibe well with China's own short-term and long-term economic interests in getting in on the ground floor of global green energy markets. One policy lesson is that, as with China's WTO accession, international negotiators should attempt to find positive links between their own requests of China and the Chinese leadership's desire to tackle environmental and economic problems at home. In the case of the WTO, the demands for a relatively open Chinese trade and investment sector compared to other developing countries dovetailed with the top leaders' desire to reform the politically powerful state-owned sectors of the Chinese economy. In the case of climate change negotiations, the push for a cap on China's overall emissions dovetails with the Chinese leaders' desire to take on powerful, inefficient, and often corrupt sectors of the state in the energy, transportation, and national resource sectors to limit domestic pollution that has reached epidemic proportions and threatens social stability. Moreover, pursuit of green energy helps create a foundation for long-term economic growth that is

rooted more in innovation and less in dirty forms of energy consumption. But not all good things go together; boding ill for a serious Chinese contribution to the reduction of greenhouse gases are the following
sobering trends: China's alleged dumping of solar panels in Europe and
the United States; systematic intellectual property rights theft, which
could impact areas like wind-power production; the creation of new
carbon-intensive processes like producing synthetic natural gas from
coal to reduce urban pollution; persistent administrative problems in
effectively monitoring and regulating emissions; and continued rejection of international monitoring and verification of any commitments
Beijing might make.

On the diplomatic front, as we saw at the failed Copenhagen meetings in late 2009, China labeled itself a developing country and tried
to rally other large developing countries to blame the developed countries for climate change and thereby lessen the burdens on themselves
for reduced emissions. The fact that the United States had such a poor
record of making any economic sacrifices to reduce global greenhouse
gas emissions only energized the BASIC (Brazil, South Africa, India,
and China) countries' obstructionism. In its second term, the Obama
administration finally turned its attention seriously to the issue, placing
the equivalent of a carbon tax on coal plants through regulatory measures under the Clean Air Act in 2013. Some of the critics of this move
were insincere in saying that such unilateral administrative actions will
do no good—many of them, after all, do not even accept that global
warming is occurring. Critics of unilateral U.S. policies to limit emissions have a point, however, when they say that it would have been
much more effective if the prospect of such a U.S. reduction could
be used to leverage binding international agreements with the Chinese and others. But, although the agreement reached in Beijing in
November 2014 is not legally binding, in a sense the United States did
indeed leverage its own specific commitments to cuts by 2025 to gain
Chinese acquiescence to the aforementioned cap in 2030. Given the
domestic controversies in China regarding any sacrifices that might
affect growth or might injure China's national pride, the U.S. commitments likely helped Chinese leaders accept the potentially controversial commitment to peak emissions. The commitment itself should,

all things being equal, help empower those leaders to create policies and institutional mechanisms that will limit local and global pollution in the future.

But all things are rarely equal. It is too soon to tell if the Obama administration's Climate Action Plan will withstand legislative challenges in the United States, let alone improve the conditions for international negotiations on climate change, but the atmosphere going into the Paris climate summit in 2015 seems much better than in 2009 before Copenhagen. And it can fairly be said that nothing the United States had done previously had held out much prospect of gaining compromise from other countries on this issue; many other countries would have to doubt that a supermajority in Congress in the United States would, in any case, ratify a binding treaty calling for international reductions in greenhouse gas emissions negotiated by a U.S. president. So President Obama would have limited leverage and credibility abroad in negotiating binding joint reductions of greenhouse reductions. This is all the more true with a Republican-controlled Senate. The use of executive-branch regulatory authorities and the pursuit of parallel unilateral commitments from others, as the Obama administration pursued in Beijing, seem to me to have been the best approach in an imperfect world.

Since new technologies and innovations will likely provide the most effective way to address climate change, it will be important to see if the United States can make any progress with China on issues such as intellectual property rights violations and dumping so that technology sharing and even cross-border development of environmental technologies might become more feasible. The most important technologies in the Chinese context will be ones that reduce not only greenhouse gas emissions but, at the same time, the ground-level pollution that plagues Chinese cities and poses a risk for regime stability. Chinese elites have clearer political incentives to absorb and utilize such technologies than they do to adopt measures that limit greenhouse gas emissions alone. Sadly, China provides both the greatest laboratory in the world for technologies that might reduce carbon emissions and, at the same time, one of the world's most dangerous environments for foreign businesses, scientists, and engineers to unveil their technological innovations.

On nonproliferation and humanitarian intervention, the Obama administration inherited many of the problems of its predecessor. China did not want to see either Iran or North Korea develop nuclear weapons programs, but neither did it want to allow, let alone participate in, sweeping sanctions that could destabilize those countries. Such a process is wrong in principle from the PRC's perspective. Moreover, foreign pressure aimed at regime destabilization could harm substantial Chinese economic and political interests there.

The only way to really sanction Iran successfully is to target the energy sector and the financial sector that supports it. Chinese officials, however, do not want to harm relations with a traditional diplomatic partner in a geostrategically important part of the world. Moreover, to target the energy sector in Iran would undermine China's own interests and could destabilize Iran in ways that bring back bad memories in Beijing of President Bush's "axis of evil" speech.

China has agreed to various UN Security Council resolutions sanctioning specific entities and individuals in Iran, but it has worked consistently to water down those resolutions to prevent harm to Chinese business dealings and to avoid harm to the Iranian public (Chinese shorthand for preventing domestic instability). In 2011–2013 China curtailed some of its investment and energy activities in Iran, most likely because Chinese state-owned enterprises feared they might get clipped by domestic sanctions levied by European countries and by the U.S. Congress. It seems that such Chinese self-restraint began breaking down as soon as an interim deal was struck between Iran and the P5+1 countries in November 2013. We know that Chinese oil imports from Iran increased sharply in the first half of 2014. Since the interim agreement was extended for several months in November 2014, and executive branch leaders in both the United States and Europe have an incentive to prevent new legislative sanctions while the talks continue, we should expect Chinese companies to take more courage to invest in Iran as well. In a strange and disheartening sense, an extended interim agreement with Iran is an ideal outcome for China, the only net importer of energy involved in the negotiations willing to significantly ramp up economic cooperation with Iran while Tehran maintains a significant HEU enrichment capability. China thereby enjoys a near-monopoly position in the Iranian economy. And China's economy is so large that it can keep Tehran afloat even if stricter sanctions are maintained by the other negotiating partners.

In North Korea, China's general penchant to prioritize stability above denuclearization was only intensified when Kim Jong-il suffered a stroke in 2008 and Pyongyang prepared to pass the torch to his untested young son. The Obama administration's more patient approach to North Korea, eschewing Six Party Talks until Pyongyang accepted its earlier obligations, fit Beijing's strategy well in 2009 and early 2010. The diplomatic lull gave Beijing the space to deepen its economic relations with North Korea without paying an excessively high diplomatic cost, even after North Korea tested a nuclear device in 2009. But North Korean belligerence against the South in March (the sinking of the *Cheonan*) and October (the Yeonpyeong Island shelling) revived the diplomatic costs for China of its protective stance toward its dysfunctional ally.

The Obama administration's deft diplomatic reaction to the crisis in Korea in 2010—increasing security cooperation with both Seoul and Tokyo and encouraging them to increase bilateral coordination with each other—carries important lessons on how to use a strong presence to shape China's choices in a positive manner. The administration had wisely approached China first for help in pressuring Pyongyang, but received no such support. Washington subsequently used its alliance system to respond instead, and did so in ways that worried Beijing. From all public reports, Beijing then decided that Pyongyang's belligerence was becoming too costly to tolerate. Not only was Pyongyang's aggression risking war, it was also stimulating the United States and its allies to tighten their coordination on China's periphery. As a result, Beijing reportedly discouraged further conventional provocations by Pyongyang in late 2010 in a way that arguably served the interests of everyone in the region. Unfortunately, it was very difficult, if not impossible, for the Obama administration to build on this lesson and to elicit significant Chinese pressure on Pyongyang on the nuclear issue. And uncertainties about domestic politics in North Korea, with the reported execution of some top generals and Kim Jong-un's own uncle, seem to have rendered Beijing even more cautious about pressuring its obstreperous neighbor in strong and persistent ways.

The international humanitarian intervention in Libya and its aftermath provides one of the most important lessons for the effort to shape the choices of a rising China. Much to the surprise of many China experts, including this one, the United States and the Europeans gained Beijing's support on the UN Security Council for referring Qaddafi's government to the International Criminal Court for investigation of humanitarian abuses. That referral to the ICC, arguably, marks the pinnacle of U.S. efforts to encourage China to soften its stance on noninterference. China eventually abstained on the subsequent UN Security Council resolution calling on the use of force to protect the population of Benghazi. The fact that Beijing almost immediately expressed reservations about NATO air operations in Libya shows that preventing a Chinese veto likely required skillful diplomacy.

How did the Obama administration and the European allies achieve these positive results? Before approaching China for its diplomatic support in New York, the Americans and the Europeans wisely ensured that they had support from the regional groupings in Africa and the Middle East. With the African Union and Arab League in support of pressure and international intervention against Qaddafi, it was difficult to argue in China or anywhere else that this was a typical case of great power imperialism in the developing world. Less philosophically, if China were to obstruct UN action under those conditions, Beijing stood to alienate a vast swathe of developing countries. So the Obama administration benefited from a strong hand when approaching Beijing diplomatically about Libya. The Obama administration also benefited from Russia's own disillusionment with Qaddafi, which guaranteed that Beijing would be alone on any veto to the use of force. The Americans also pushed for a very moderate wording of the UN Security Council resolution—focusing on the safety of the people of Benghazi rather than on regime change.

Unfortunately, the positive side of the ledger in the lead-up to the Libya intervention was negatively balanced after NATO airpower was mobilized. From Beijing's perspective, the scope of the NATO military operation very quickly exceeded the UN mandate (and the Russians concurred with the Chinese analysis). What was ostensibly an effort to protect the citizenry of Benghazi quickly became a mission to destabilize and destroy the Qaddafi regime. For principled reasons, Beijing does not like internationally sponsored regime change. For practical reasons, Beijing worries with some justification that the United States and its allies are much better at breaking regimes than they are at replacing them with stable governments. China had considerable investments in the energy sector in Libya and needed to extract tens of thousands of its citizens from the fighting and chaos. All of these concerns came to a head in Libya as NATO became the de facto air force for Qaddafi's vengeful opposition.

Since China generally does not trust the United States and its allies in these matters, my impression in 2011 was that there was more frustration in Beijing about NATO actions than there was surprise. The predictable result was early, strong, and persistent opposition to any UN Security Council resolutions targeting the Assad regime in Syria. Chinese and Russian opposition at the UN left the Obama administration in the ironic and unenviable position of threatening military strikes on an Arab state without UN Security Council backing (the parallels to the Bush administration's threats against Saddam Hussein's regime in 2002–2003 were all too clear). Making matters worse, before demanding peace talks to end the civil conflict in that country, the administration declared that the only acceptable outcome of successful political talks would be the removal of Assad from power. Chinese analysts astutely pointed out that by providing zero assurances for Damascus, Assad and his supporters would have absolutely no reason to negotiate with the opposition or international mediators in good faith. In other words, the United States lost an opportunity to address the regime's odious behavior—the mass slaughter of innocents—by focusing on its loss of legitimacy and the need for it to abdicate power.

The international diplomatic cost of using NATO air power in Libya had profound effects. Not only did it complicate efforts to get UN backing for humanitarian intervention elsewhere, the NATO mission also made it more difficult to persuade China to collaborate with Washington on nuclear nonproliferation in other parts of the world. Several years earlier, Qaddafi had chosen to give up his nuclear weapons program in a verifiable manner. His reward? Opponents supported by NATO airpower shot him dead in the street. Since 2011, I have heard the narrative of the overthrow and execution of Qaddafi several times during discussions with Chinese interlocutors about Iran and North Korea. Elites in

China understand that North Korea is more a headache than an ally, and they will often admit that Iran has been provocative in pursuing a nuclear program and supporting rebel and terrorist groups abroad. But none of that necessarily means that Beijing is willing to pay the costs of forgoing economic relations with those countries, or to run the risk that a tougher UN sanctions regime might lead to instability in those countries. Given this situation, Beijing elites can ease their psychological dissonance on the issues by convincing themselves and trying to convince their foreign diplomatic partners that China's relatively passive and accommodating approach to these countries is not the main stumbling block to progress on denuclearization: rather, they argue, the unwillingness of the United States to reassure those regimes about their safety in a postnuclear scenario disincentivizes them to cooperate with multilateral efforts.

To succeed in pursuing global governance goals with some degree of Chinese support, the United States will need to avoid, whenever possible, beginning the process by demanding regime change in the target country. Even if regime change is secretly the U.S. hope—understandable in places with particularly bad governance—invoking that goal publicly reduces the breadth and power of the coalition that might pressure a regime. This is true whether the proscribed behavior is the development of nuclear weapons programs, killing of ethnic minorities, or imprisonment or torture of members of opposition movements. Jumping from a policy that targets proscribed behavior to one that targets the government's ability to stay in power provides the target government with little incentive to cooperate on the specific matter at hand, and little prospect of gaining Chinese support for the effort. And given China's size on the international stage, China's refusal to join in various sanctions in favor of maintaining normal relations with the country in question would provide enough sustenance to the targeted regime to both continue with the proscribed behavior and to stay in power. So even if we really want the government to go, the best strategy might be to focus on the regime's behavior and work on inducing China to join in sanctions.

In addition to unnecessarily alienating Beijing by means of excessive and unrealistic demands, the United States should listen to Chinese concerns about the potential that poorly designed humanitarian interventions can create greater instability in areas like Syria, Burma, Sudan, or Libya. If central authorities disintegrate with little left to replace them, chaos and violence will often ensue. Just because Beijing's own political interests are served by rejecting international pressure on authoritarian regimes does not mean that Chinese elites are wrong to question the wisdom of creating chaos in the name of humanitarianism. Moreover, precisely because Beijing maintains normal relations with so many of these countries and Chinese state-owned enterprises invest there, Chinese officials often have more political experience on the ground in such places than Americans (and more reasons to be concerned about instability and increased violence there). This is one of several reasons why it is helpful for the United States to partner first with regional multilateral groupings before approaching the Chinese. Those groupings have the biggest stake in long-term stability and the most local knowledge, and given their own histories of bullying by the great powers, their participation lends great credence to the sincerity and viability of the goals laid out by leaders of more distant developed countries. The prospect in Beijing of improving China's relations with those actors in the developing world through cooperation, and the fear of alienating them by Chinese stonewalling at the UN, can greatly increase the likelihood of active and constructive Chinese participation in such multilateral efforts, as we saw when Beijing referred Qaddafi's regime to the ICC.

All of these considerations should be woven into a strategy that accepts and even encourages China's rise to greater power and prominence in international politics but shapes China's choices so that it is more likely to forgo bullying behavior that destabilizes East Asia and more likely to accept burdens as a responsible stakeholder in global governance. The history since the end of the Cold War suggests that achieving these objectives is both difficult and possible. Success requires an unusual mix of strength and toughness on the one hand and a willingness to reassure and listen to the Chinese on the other. The United States government is highly experienced and well structured for coercive diplomacy of great powers, but it is inexperienced and much less well structured to induce a developing country to contribute assertively to solving global problems. As China's power continues to rise in an unusually complex environment in Asia, the United States will need to hone its existing skills at coercive diplomacy and alliance management. And as China's global footprint grows, the United States will need to develop new diplomatic skills of empathy and persuasion to encourage Beijing to contribute its fair share to efforts to stop nuclear proliferation, maintain financial stability, halt humanitarian disasters and restore regional order, and limit climate change.

APPENDIX

APPENDIX 1.1. PRC CONVENTIONAL MISSILE THREAT (BY TARGET)

Key NE Asia Targets in Range	Missile Threat	Maximum Range
Taiwan; northern half of South Korea; Paracel Islands	DF-11 SRBM; DF-15 SRBM	600 km
U.S. bases in Japan and South Korea; Philippines; Singapore; Spratly Islands	DF-21 ASBM; DF-21 MRBM; CJ-10 LACM; FB-7 with ASCM; B-6 with ASCM	1500+ km
Guam, Straits of Malacca	DF-3, B-6 with LACM	3300 km
Source: *Military and Security Developments Involving the People's Republic of China 2012* (Office of the Secretary of Defense, May 2012), 42.		

APPENDIX 1.2. PRC MISSILE THREAT (BY SIZE OF ARSENAL)

Missile Category	Quantity	Launchers	Estimated Range
Intercontinental Ballistic Missile (ICBM)	50–75	50–75	5400–13,000+ km
Intermediate-range Ballistic Missile (IRBM)	5–20	5–20	3000+ km
Medium-range Ballistic Missile (MRBM)	75–100	75–100	1750+ km
Short-range Ballistic Missile (SRBM)	1000–1200	200–250	300–600 km
Ground-launched Cruise Missile (GLCM)	200–500	40–55	1500+ km
Source: *Military and Security Developments Involving the People's Republic of China 2011* (Office of the Secretary of Defense, 2011), 78.			

APPENDIX 1.3. SUBMARINES BY PURPOSE
(CUMULATIVE TOTAL NUMBERS)
1995–2010

	1995	2000	2005	2010
Ballistic Missile Submarines	1	1	2	3 (2009)
Nuclear-powered Attack Submarines (SSNs)	5	5	6	6
Diesel Attack Submarines (SSs)	77	60	~51–52	54

Source: Ronald O'Rourke, *China Naval Modernization: Implications for U.S. Navy Capabilities—Background and Issues for Congress*, CRS Report for Congress, March 23, 2012, 33–34.

APPENDIX 1.4. SUBMARINES BY MODEL
(NEW COMMISSIONS ONLY)
1995–2010

	1995–1999	2000–2004	2005–2009	2010	Cumulative total 1995–2010
Ballistic Missile Submarines					
Jin (Type 094)	--	--	1	1	3
Nuclear-powered Attack Submarines (SSNs)					
Shang (Type 093)	--	--	2	--	2
Diesel Attack Submarines (SSs)					
Ming (Type 035) *(Note: not considered "modern" by DOD)*	6	3	--	--	9
Kilo (Russian-built)	4	1	7	--	12
Song (Type 039)	1	7	5	--	13
Yuan (Type 031) *(Note: may have AIP)*	--	--	3	1	4

Source: *Jane's Fighting Ships 2011–2012*, and previous editions. Cited in Ronald O'Rourke, *China Naval Modernization: Implications for U.S. Navy Capabilities—Background and Issues for Congress*, CRS Report for Congress, March 23, 2012, 16.

APPENDIX 1.5. FOURTH-GENERATION FIGHTER AIRCRAFT

Aircraft Type	Role	Quantity	Approximate Date Range of Major Procurement
Russian-built			
Su-27	Air superiority	76	1990s
Su-30 MKK2	Fighter-bomber	76	2000s
Indigenously built			
J-10 (based off F-16)	Multirole fighter	60–80	2000s
J-11B (based off Su-27)	Air superiority	95–116	2000s
J-15 (based off J-11B)	Carrier-capable	--	Under development

Sources: The numbers here come from "Air Forces," Sino-Defense.com, http://www.sino defence.com/airforce/default.asp, accessed July 23, 2012. Oriana Mastro and Mark Stokes, *Air Power Trends in Northeast Asia: Implications for Japan and the U.S.–Japan Alliance*, Project 2049 Institute, n.d., 7–9, cite Russian estimates that China's fourth-generation fighters number 350–500, somewhat more than listed here. On the J-15, see Daniel Kostecka, "Problems and Prospects for China's Ship-Based Aviation Program," *China Brief* 12, no. 1 (January 6, 2012).

APPENDIX 1.6. OTHER CAPABILITIES OF INTEREST: ADVANCED AIR DEFENSE

Surface-to-Air Missiles (SAM)
Russian-built: SA-10B (S-300PMU); SA-20 PMU1/PMU2 (S-300PMU1&2)
Indigenous: HD-6D, HQ-7, HQ-9, HQ-12, HQ-16
Fourth-generation Fighters
Su-27/Su-30; J-10/J-11; JH-7
Bombers
B-6G bombers
Shipboard Area-Air-Defense (AAD)
?

Sources: *Military and Security Developments Involving the People's Republic of China 2011* (Office of the Secretary of Defense, 2011), 4, 32; Chapter Six: "Asia," *The Military Balance* 112, no. 1 (2012), 238.

APPENDIX 1.7. OTHER CAPABILITIES OF INTEREST: CRUISE MISSILES

Land-Attack Cruise Missiles (LACM)
YJ-63, YJ-64, KD-88, DH-10, YJ-100
Antiship Cruise Missiles
Nearly a dozen variants, including SS-N-22 and SS-N-27B (Russian)
Relevant Platforms for Sea and Air-launched Cruise Missiles
Conventional- and nuclear-powered attack submarines: Kilo, Song, Yuan, and Shang classes
Surface combatants: Luzhou, Luyang I/II, Sovremenny II
Maritime strike aircraft: JB-7/7A; B-6G; Su-30MKK
Source: *Military and Security Developments Involving the People's Republic of China 2011* (Office of the Secretary of Defense, 2011), 29–30.

APPENDIX 1.8. MOBILE NUCLEAR FORCES

Launcher and Missile	Initial Deployment	Range	Warhead	Number of Warheads (as of January 2012)
Land-based				
Road-mobile, solid-fueled, three-stage DF-31 (CSS-10 Mod 1) ICBMs	2006	>7200 km	1 x 200–300 kt	10–20
Road-mobile, solid-fueled, three-stage DF-31A (CSS-10 Mod 2) ICBMs	2007	>11,200 km	1 x 200–300 kt	10–20
Road-mobile ICBM capable of carrying MIRV	? – under development	?		0
Aircraft		From location of aircraft		
H-6–delivered gravity bomb	1965	3100 km	1 x bomb	~20

SLBMs		From location of submarine		
Solid-fueled, two-stage JL-1 (CSS-N-3)	1986	>1770 km	1 x 200–300 kt	12
Solid-fueled, three-stage JL-2 (CSS-NX-14)	2014 (estimated)	>7,400 km	1 x 200–300 kt	36
Source: Shannon N. Kile, Phillip Schell, and Hans M. Kristensen, "Chinese Nuclear Forces," in *SIPRI Yearbook 2012* (New York: Oxford University Press, 2012), 327–31; *Military and Security Developments Involving the People's Republic of China 2011* (Office of the Secretary of Defense, 2011), 3; *Military and Security Developments Involving the People's Republic of China 2012* (Office of the Secretary of Defense, 2012), 7, 23.				

APPENDIX 3.1. TOP TEN OECD AID DONORS TO SUB-SAHARAN AFRICA

	2008
United States	7.202
France	3.37
Germany	2.703
United Kingdom	2.594
Japan	1.571
Netherlands	1.516
Canada	1.347
Spain	1.114
Norway	1.028
Sweden	1.026

Figures represent billion USD.
Source: *Geographical Distribution of Financial Flows to Developing Countries 2013: Disbursements, Commitments, Country Indicators*, OECD Publishing, February 6, 2013, 22–67, doi: 10.1787/fin_flows_dev-2013-en-fr.

NOTES

INTRODUCTION

1. If we exclude the value of services, China surpassed the United States to become the leading trading state in the world in 2012. See http://www .bloomberg.com/news/2013-02-09/china-passes-u-s-to-become-the-world-s-biggest-trading-nation.html.

2. Dai Bingguo, *"Jianchi Zou Heping Fazhan Daolu"* [Adhere to the Path of Peaceful Development], Zhongyang Zhengfu Menhu Wangzhan, The Central People's Government of the People's Republic of China Web site, December 6, 2010, http://www.gov.cn/ldhd/2010-12/06/content_1760381.htm. For an English translation, see USC U.S.–China Institute, http://china.usc.edu/ShowArticle.aspx?articleID=2325&AspxA utoDetectCookieSupport=1.

CHAPTER 1. CHINA'S RISE: WHY IT IS REAL

1. World Bank, http://data.worldbank.org/indicator/NY.GNP.PCAP.CD.

2. GDP per capita (PPP) in 2012. CIA World Factbook, https://www.cia .gov/library/publications/the-world-factbook/geos/us.html.

3. Harry Harding, *China's Second Revolution: Reform After Mao* (Washington, DC: Brookings Institution, 1987).

4. "China Eclipses U.S. as Biggest Trading Nation," Bloomberg News, February 10, 2013, www.bloomberg.com/news/2013-02-09/china-passes-u-s-to-become-the-world-s-biggest-trading-nation.html.

5. In 2012, China's total trade with the United States was $536 billion USD. U.S. trade with Canada was $617 billion. See United States Cen-

sus Web site at www.census.gov/foreign-trade/statistics/highlights/top/top1212yr.html.

6. For World Bank data on Chinese exports and imports, respectively, as a percentage of GDP in 2007 and 2011, see http://data.worldbank.org/indicator/NE.EXP.GNFS.ZS/countries; and http://search.worldbank.org/data?qterm=Imports%20of%20goods%20and%20services&language=EN.

7. Estimates of foreign direct investment (FDI) from respectable sources vary widely based on accounting methodology, but there is a consensus that China surpassed the United States to become the top target of FDI in 2012. Reuters reports that FDI increased 5.5 percent in 2013 to $117 billion USD, meaning that it was just over $110 billion in 2012. "China 2013 Foreign Investment Flows Hit Record High," Reuters, January 14, 2014, http://www.reuters.com/article/2014/01/16/us-china-economy-fdi-idUSBREA0F0EI20140116. *Forbes* magazine placed China at number one in the first half of 2012 with $59 billion USD in that six-month period compared to $57 billion USD for the United States. See "China Leads in Foreign Direct Investment," *Forbes,* November 5, 2012, http://www.forbes.com/sites/jackperkowski/2012/11/05/china-leads-in-foreign-direct-investment/. Using a different methodology, the OECD concludes that in 2012, China's inbound FDI was a much higher $253 billion USD and almost 50 percent higher than the comparable figure for the United States, which was in second place at $175 billion. See *FDI in Figures,* OECD Investment Division, http://www.oecd.org/daf/inv/FDI%20in%20figures.pdf.

8. See Indian Department of Commerce at http://commerce.nic.in/pressrelease/pressrelease_detail.asp?id=402; and http://indiatoday.intoday.in/story/india-china-trade-hits-all-time-high-of-usd-73.9-billion-in-2011/1/171137.html.

9. See OECD Factbook 2011–2012: *Economic, Environmental and Social Statistics,* http://www.oecd-ilibrary.org/sites/factbook-2011-en/04/01/05/index.html?itemId=/content/chapter/factbook-2011-37-en.

10. For an authoritative overview, see Deborah Brautigam, *The Dragon's Gift: The Real Story of China in Africa* (Oxford: Oxford University Press, 2009).

11. International Monetary Fund, Direction of Trade Statistics database, www.imfstatistics.org.

12. See Peter Wonacott, "In Africa, U.S. Watches China's Rise," *Wall Street Journal,* September 2, 2011, http://online.wsj.com/article/SB10001424053111903392904576510271838147248.html; and "The Chinese in Africa: Trying to Pull Together," *The Economist,* April 20, 2011, http://www.economist.com/node/18586448.

13. International Monetary Fund, Direction of Trade Statistics database, www.imfstatistics.org. Accessed via Global Insight database.

14. This data is based on Katherine Koleski, *Backgrounder: China in Latin America* (U.S–China Economic and Security Review Commission, May 27, 2011), http://origin.www.uscc.gov/sites/default/files/Research/Back grounder_China_in_Latin_America.pdf. Another official Chinese report places foreign direct investment to Latin America at 15 percent of overall Chinese FDI for 2010, but after subtracting the "investment" in the tax havens of the Caymans and Virgin Islands, the figure drops to only 1.3 percent of China's global FDI. *Statistical Bulletin of China's Outward Foreign Direct Investment* (China Ministry of Commerce, 2011), pp. 82–84, http://images.mofcom.gov.cn/hzs/accessory/201109/1316069658609 .pdf.

15. Dawn C. Murphy, testimony at hearing "China and the Middle East," June 6, 2013, U.S.–China Economic and Security Review Commission, http://www.uscc.gov/sites/default/files/MURPHY_testimony.pdf; and David Shambaugh and Dawn Murphy, "U.S.–China Interactions in the Middle East, Africa, Europe, and Latin America," in *Tangled Titans: The New Context of U.S.–China Relations*, ed. David Shambaugh (Lanham, MD: Rowan and Littlefield, 2013). See also Geoffrey Kemp, *The East Moves West: India, China, and Asia's Growing Presence in the Middle East* (Washington, DC: Brookings Institution Press, 2010); and Ben Simpfendorfer, *The New Silk Road: How a Rising Arab World Is Turning Away from the West and Rediscovering China* (Basingstoke, UK: Palgrave Macmillan, 2009).

16. Thomas J. Christensen, "Chinese Realpolitik: Reading Beijing's World-View," *Foreign Affairs* 75, no. 5 (September–October 1996).

17. Thomas J. Christensen, *Worse Than a Monolith: Alliance Politics and Problems of Coercive Diplomacy in Asia* (Princeton, NJ: Princeton University Press, 2011).

18. For a discussion of CAFTA, see http://www.asean-cn.org/category_279/ index.aspx.

19. See pages 90 and 247–49 for a review of these criticisms.

20. For the official declaration of the summit, see http://www.focac.org/eng/ ltda/dscbzjhy/DOC32009/t606841.htm.

21. See the forum Web site at http://english.mofcom.gov.cn/article/zt_china portuguese/.

22. See the forum Web site at www.cascf.org.

23. See the forum Web site at http://cncforumenglish.mofcom.gov.cn/.

24. For an excellent review, see Joel Wuthnow, *Chinese Diplomacy and the UN Security Council: Beyond the Veto* (London: Routledge, 2013).

25. For Secretary Gates's own account, see Robert M. Gates, *Duty: Memoirs of a Secretary at War* (New York: Alfred A. Knopf, 2014), 527–28.

26. Andrew S. Erickson and Austin M. Strange, *No Substitute for Experience: Chinese Antipiracy Operations in the Gulf of Aden*, vol. 10, *China Maritime Studies* (Newport, RI: U.S. Naval War College, 2013), http://www.usnwc.edu/Research---Gaming/China-Maritime-Studies-Institute/Publications.aspx.

CHAPTER 2. THIS TIME SHOULD BE DIFFERENT: CHINA'S RISE IN A GLOBALIZED WORLD

1. Richard K. Betts and Thomas J. Christensen, "China: Getting the Questions Right," *The National Interest,* Winter 2000–2001.

2. Aaron L. Friedberg, *A Contest for Supremacy: China, America, and the Struggle for Mastery in Asia* (New York: Norton, 2011).

3. John J. Mearsheimer, "China's Unpeaceful Rise," *Current History,* April 2006.

4. Carl Kaysen, "Is War Obsolete?" *International Security* 14, no. 4 (Spring 1990), 42–64; and John Mueller, *Retreat from Doomsday: The Obsolescence of Major Power War* (New York: Basic Books, 1989).

5. Peter Liberman, *Does Conquest Pay? The Exploitation of Occupied Industrial Societies* (Princeton, NJ: Princeton University Press, 1998).

6. Helen V. Milner, *Resisting Protectionism: Global Industries and the Politics of International Trade* (Princeton, NJ: Princeton University Press, 1988).

7. Stephen G. Brooks, *Producing Security: Multinational Corporations, Globalization, and the Changing Calculus of Conflict* (Princeton, NJ: Princeton University Press, 2007), 46.

8. Brooks, *Producing Security,* 19.

9. Robert Koopman, Zhi Wang, and Shang-jin Wei, "How Much of Chinese Exports Is Really Made in China? Assessing Foreign and Domestic Value-Added in Gross Exports," Office of Economics working paper no. 208-03-B, U.S. International Trade Commission, March 2008, p. 3, http://www.usitc.gov/publications/332/ec200803b_revised.pdf.

10. Edward S. Steinfeld, *Playing Our Game: Why China's Rise Doesn't Threaten the West* (New York: Oxford University Press, 2010), 17.

11. Steinfeld, *Playing Our Game,* 85.

12. Ibid., 86.

13. Aaron L. Friedberg, "Ripe for Rivalry: Prospects for Peace in a Multipolar East Asia," *International Security* 18, no. 3 (Winter 1993–1994), 5–33.

14. Takashi Inoguchi, "Arguing the Regional Community Building in Northeast Asia," paper presented at the Beijing Forum, November 16–18,

2005. A 2007 World Bank Study claimed that in that year, 49 percent of East Asian nations' exports were intraregional and 53 percent of their imports were intraregional. See also Mona Haddad, "Trade Integration in East Asia: The Role of China and Production Networks," World Bank Policy Research working paper 4160, March 2007, http://www-wds .worldbank.org/external/default/WDSContentServer/IW3P/IB/2007/0 3/06/000016406_20070306101249/Rendered/PDF/wps4160.pdf.

15. Koopman, Wang, and Wei, "How Much of Chinese Exports Is Really Made in China?," 1.

16. Steinfeld, *Playing Our Game*, 85.

17. EIU World Investment Service (online), October 12, 2012, Economist Intelligence Unit, https://eiu.bvdep.com.

18. Evan A. Feigenbaum and Robert A. Manning, "A Tale of Two Asias," *Foreign Policy*, October 31, 2012, www.foreignpolicy.com/ articles/2012/10/30/a_tale_of_two_asias.

19. IMF trade data from International Monetary Fund, Direction of Trade Statistics database, 2013, www.imfstatistics.org. For World Bank data on Chinese exports and imports, respectively, as a percentage of GDP in 2011, see http://data.worldbank.org/indicator/NE.EXP.GNFS.ZS/coun tries; and http://search.worldbank.org/data?qterm=Imports%20of%20 goods%20and%20services&language=EN.

20. EIU World Investment Service (online), Economist Intelligence Unit, https://eiu.bvdep.com.

21. Ibid.

22. H. Fung, J. Yau, and G. Zhang, "Reported Trade Figure Discrepancy, Regulatory Arbitrage, and Round-Tripping: Evidence from the China–Hong Kong Trade Data," *Journal of International Business Studies* 42, no. 1 (2011), 152–76, doi:http://dx.doi.org/10.1057/jibs.2010.35.

23. Thomas J. Christensen and Jack Snyder, "Chain Gangs and Passed Bucks: Predicting Alliance Patterns in Multipolarity," *International Organization* 44 (Spring 1990), 137–68.

24. Michael Barnhart, *Japan Prepares for Total War: The Search for Economic Security, 1919–1941* (Ithaca, NY: Cornell University Press, 1987).

25. Ja Ian Chong and Todd H. Hall, "The Lessons of 1914 for East Asia Today: Missing the Trees for the Forest," *International Security* 39, no. 1 (Summer 2014), 7–43.

26. G. John Ikenberry, *Liberal Leviathan: The Origins, Crisis, and Transformation of the American World Order* (Princeton, NJ: Princeton University Press, 2011), chapter 8.

27. Charles Kupchan, *No One's World: The West, the Rising Rest, and the Coming Global Turn* (New York: Oxford University Press, 2012).

28. Martin Jacques, *When China Rules the World: The End of the Western World and the Birth of a New Global Order* (New York: Penguin Books, 2009), 16.

29. Robert Kagan, *The Return of History and the End of Dreams* (New York: Alfred A. Knopf, 2008); Robert J. Lieber, *Power and Willpower in the American Future: Why the United States Is Not Destined to Decline* (New York: Cambridge University Press, 2012); and Aaron L. Friedberg, *A Contest for Supremacy: China, America, and the Struggle for Mastery in Asia* (New York: W. W. Norton, 2011).

30. For a typical reference to westernizing and separatist conspiracies against China on an official Chinese Communist Party Web site, see *"Wo Dang Weihu Xinjiang Wending Fandui Minzu Fenliede Zhanlüe Sikao Ji Qi Lishixing Gongxian"* [Our Party's Strategic Thought and Its Historical Contributions in Supporting Xinjiang's Stability and Opposing Ethnic Separatism], *Renmin Wang*, February 20, 2013, http://dangshi.people.com.cn/n/2013/0220/c85037-20541376.html.

31. Pan Wei, "Western System versus Chinese System," China Policy Institute, University of Nottingham, briefing paper no. 61, July 2010, p. 2.

32. For Wang Jisi's clever parsing of the differences between globalization and westernization, see *"Quanqiuhua Shi Bushi Xifanghua?"* [Is Globalization (the Same as) Westernization?], Aisixiang.com, August 4, 2003.

33. Raj M. Desai and James Raymond Vreeland, "What the New Bank of BRICS Is All About," The Monkey Cage, *Washington Post*, July 17, 2014, http://www.washingtonpost.com/blogs/monkey-cage/wp/2014/07/17/what-the-new-bank-of-brics-is-all-about/; Shannon Van Sant, "BRICS Bank Viewed as IMF Competitor," Voice of America, August 12, 2014, http://www.voanews.com/content/brics-launches-new-development-bank/2410633.html; "China's $50 Billion Asia Bank Snubs Japan, India," Bloomberg News, May 12, 2014, http://www.bloomberg.com/news/2014-05-11/china-s-50-billion-asia-bank-snubs-japan-india-in-power-push.html; Jamil Anderlini, "China Expands Plans for World Bank Rival," *Financial Times,* June 24, 2014, http://www.ft.com/intl/cms/s/0/b1012282-fba4-11e3-aa19-00144feab7de.html#axzz3BRDsFWi8\.

34. See Marcia Don Harpaz, "China and the WTO: New Kid in the Developing Bloc?," research paper no. 2-07, International Law Forum, Hebrew University of Jerusalem (February 2007), 74–76, for a useful chart outlining the relatively strict standards applied to China compared to other developing countries.

35. EIU World Investment Service (online), Economist Intelligence Unit, https://eiu.bvdep.com.

CHAPTER 3. WHY CHINESE POWER WILL NOT SURPASS
U.S. POWER ANYTIME SOON

1. Martin Jacques, *When China Rules the World: The End of the Western World and the Birth of a New Global Order* (New York: Penguin Books, 2009).
2. Arvind Subramanian, "The Inevitable Superpower: Why China's Dominance Is a Sure Thing," *Foreign Affairs* 90, no. 5 (September–October 2011), 66.
3. Joshua Kurlantzick, "How China Is Changing Global Diplomacy: Cultural Revolution," *New Republic,* June 27, 2005, 16.
4. David Shambaugh, *China Goes Global: The Partial Power* (Oxford: Oxford University Press, 2013).
5. For the views of U.S. respondents to a Gallup poll about global economic leadership, see http://www.statista.com/statistics/218198/opinion -of-worlds-leading-economic-power. See also Pew Research Center, "U.S. Favorability Ratings Remain Positive, China Seen Overtaking U.S. as Global Superpower," July 13, 2011, http://www.pewglobal .org/2011/07/13/china-seen-overtaking-us-as-global-superpower/.
6. Jacques, *When China Rules the World;* Subramanian, "The Inevitable Superpower"; and Christopher Layne, "The Global Power Shift from West to East," *National Interest,* May–June 2012, http://nationalinterest .org/article/the-global-power-shift-west-east-6796?page=1.
7. Sheena Chestnut and Alastair Iain Johnston, "Is China Rising?," in *Global Giant: Is China Changing the Rules of the Game?,* eds. Eva Paus, Penelope B. Prime, and Jon Western (New York: Palgrave Macmillan, 2009), chapter 12; Joseph Nye, *The Future of Power* (New York: Perseus, 2011), especially chapter 6; Michael Beckley, "China's Century? Why America's Edge Will Endure," *International Security* 36, no. 3 (Winter 2011–2012), 41–78; and Robert Lieber, *Power and Willpower in the American Future: Why the United States Is Not Destined to Decline* (New York: Cambridge University Press, 2012).
8. CIA World Factbook, https://www.cia.gov/library/publications/the-world-factbook/geos/ch.html; and https://www.cia.gov/library/publications/the-world-factbook/geos/us.html.
9. "OECD Economic Surveys: China," March 2013, http://www.oecd.org/ eco/surveys/Overview%20China%202013-Eng%20modified.pdf. Similar predictions were made by the IMF in 2011, http://www.guardian .co.uk/commentisfree/cifamerica/2011/apr/27/china-imf-economy-2016.
10. GDP per capita (PPP) in 2012, CIA World Factbook, https://www.cia .gov/library/publications/the-world-factbook/geos/ch.html; and https:// www.cia.gov/library/publications/the-world-factbook/geos/us.html.
11. Agustino Fontevecchia, "China Gambles That a Credit Crunch Can Rein

in Shadow Banking," *Forbes,* June 24, 2013, http://www.forbes.com/sites/afontevecchia/2013/06/24/china-is-right-to-use-liquidity-crunch-to-target-shadow-banking-but-leverage-raises-risks/. For the negative fallout in the region, see Bettina Wassener, "Asian Markets Falter After Central Bank Statement," *New York Times,* June 24, 2013, http://www.nytimes.com/2013/06/25/business/global/chinese-central-bank-says-liquidity-at-reasonable-level.html.

12. Jonathan Kirshner, *Currency and Coercion: The Political Economy of International Monetary Power* (Princeton, NJ: Princeton University Press, 1995), 64–82.

13. Robert D. Atkinson, testimony at hearing "The Impact of International Technology Transfer on American Research and Development," December 5, 2012, U.S. House of Representatives, House Science Committee, Subcommittee on Investigation and Oversight, p. 6, http://science.house.gov/sites/republicans.science.house.gov/files/documents/HHRG-112-SY21-WState-RAtkinson-20121205.pdf; see also Spike Nowak, "On the Fast Track: Technology Transfer in China," *China Briefing,* September 3, 2012, http://www.china-briefing.com/news/2012/09/03/on-the-fast-track-technology-transfer-in-china.html.

14. James McGregor, *No Ancient Wisdom, No Followers: The Challenges of Chinese Authoritarian Capitalism* (Westport, CT: Prospecta Press, 2012), 31–54; see also Adam Segal, "China's Innovation Wall: Beijing's Push for Foreign Technology," *Foreign Affairs,* September 28, 2010.

15. Quoted in McGregor, *No Ancient Wisdom,* 34.

16. Robert J. Lieber, *Power and Willpower in the American Future: Why the United States Is Not Destined to Decline* (New York: Cambridge University Press, 2012), 41.

17. Lieber, *Power and Willpower,* 49.

18. For data on U.S. and Chinese global patents in green technology, see Chris Israel, "Survey of the Global Policy Landscape for Green Technology and Intellectual Property," Institute for Policy Innovation, policy report 193, April 2011, http://www.ipi.org/docLib/20120106_Green_Tech.pdf. In 2012 the United States held more than half the global patents in nanotechnologies, while China held fewer than 5 percent. See the Reuters news report at http://www.reuters.com/article/2013/02/14/us-patents-nanotechnology-idUSBRE91D0YL20130214, February 14, 2013.

19. For Chinese deficits in branding, see Bruce Dickson, "Revising Reform: China's New Leaders and the Challenges of Governance," *China: An International Journal* 10, no. 2 (August 2012), 34–51.

20. Beckley, "China's Century?," 61.

21. See William Overholt, "Reassessing China: Awaiting Xi Jinping," *Washington Quarterly* 35, no. 2 (2012), 121–137.

22. International Monetary Fund, Direction of Trade Statistics database, 2013, www.imfstatistics.org. Accessed via Global Insight database.

23. Ibid.

24. U.S. Energy Information Administration, "China Poised to Become World's Largest Net Oil Importer Later This Year," August 9, 2013, http://www.eia.gov/todayinenergy/detail.cfm?id=12471.

25. International Monetary Fund, Direction of Trade Statistics database, 2013, www.imfstatistics.org. Accessed via Global Insight database.

26. Ibid.

27. U.S. Trade with Sub-Saharan Africa, January–December 2012, United States Department of Commerce, International Trade Commission (Washington, DC, 2013), http://trade.gov/agoa/agoa_main_004064.pdf.

28. Deborah Brautigam, *The Dragon's Gift: The Real Story of China in Africa* (Oxford: Oxford University Press, 2009), 162–188.

29. Naohiro Kitano and Yukinori Harada, "Estimating China's Foreign Aid, 2001–2013," JICA Research Institute, JICA-RI working paper no. 78, June 2014, p. 17, http://jica-ri.jica.go.jp/publication/workingpaper/estimating_chinas_foreign_aid_2001-2013.html.

30. This data is culled from the Japan International Cooperation Agency (JICA), China's most recent foreign aid white paper, and USAID figures. The JICA report estimates China's total global bilateral foreign aid for 2013 at approximately $6 billion USD. The Chinese 2014 foreign aid white paper states that China's percentage of global foreign aid allocated to Africa is approximately 50 percent per year. USAID data shows that 25 percent of U.S. aid is allocated to Africa, which equals approximately $7.75 billion USD for 2012. See Kitano and Harada, "Estimating China's Foreign Aid, 2001–2013"; "China's Foreign Aid," white paper, July 2014, Information Office of the State Council, People's Republic of China, http://news.xinhuanet.com/english/china/2014-07/10/c_133474011.htm; USAID, "Foreign Assistance Fast Facts FY 2012," https://eads.usaid.gov/gbk/data/fast_facts.cfm#region.

31. See the UN Conference on Trade and Development (UNCTAD) report, http://unctad.org/en/publicationslibrary/webdiaeia2013d6_en.pdf, p. 7.

32. See Amy Copley, Fenohasina Maret-Rakotondrazaka, and Amadou Sy, "The U.S.–Africa Leaders Summit: A Focus on Foreign Direct Investment," Brookings Institution, July 11, 2014, http://www.brookings.edu/blogs/africa-in-focus/posts/2014/07/11-foreign-direct-investment-us-africa-leaders-summit.

33. Thomas J. Christensen, testimony at hearing "China in Africa: Implications for U.S. Policy," June 4, 2008, U.S. Senate, Committee on Foreign Relations, Subcommittee on African Affairs, Senate Hearing 110-649, U.S. Government Printing Office, http://www.gpo.gov/fdsys/pkg/CHRG-110shrg45811/html/CHRG-110shrg45811.htm.

34. Shoaib-ur-Rehman Siddiqui, "Venezuela Says China's Oil Exports up to 600,000 bpd," *Business Recorder,* July 7, 2012, http://www.brecorder.com/markets/energy/america/66303-venezuela-says-china-oil-exports-up-to-600000-bpd-.html, and "Venezuela Analysis Brief," U.S. Energy Information Administration, http://www.eia.gov/countries/country-data.cfm?fips=VE.

35. "Venezuela: Chavez Buys Enemy U.S.'s Fuel While Lauding Iran," *Petroleum World,* July 11, 2012, http://www.petroleumworld.com/story t12071102.htm.

36. "Zambian Miners Kill Chinese Manager During Pay Protests," *Mmegi* Online, August 7, 2012, http://www.mmegi.bw/index.php?sid=11&aid=292&dir=2012/August/Tuesday7. See also coverage in the *Guardian* and on BBC, http://www.theguardian.com/world/2012/aug/05/zambian-miners-kill-chinese-supervisor; and http://www.bbc.co.uk/news/world-africa-19135435.

37. International Monetary Fund, Direction of Trade Statistics database, 2013, www.imfstatistics.org. Accessed via Global Insight database.

38. For China numbers, see *Statistical Bulletin of China's Outward Foreign Direct Investment,* China Ministry of Commerce, 2011, pp. 82–84, http://images.mofcom.gov.cn/hzs/accessory/201109/1316069658609.pdf. For U.S. investment numbers, see OECD Statistics, http://stats.oecd.org/Index.aspx?DatasetCode=FDI_FLOW_PARTNER.

39. Katherine Koleski, *Backgrounder: China in Latin America,* U.S.–China Economic and Security Review Commission, 2011, 9, http://origin.www.uscc.gov/sites/default/files/Research/Backgrounder_China_in_Latin_America.pdf, citing *2009 Statistical Bulletin of China's Outward Foreign Direct Investment,* China Ministry of Commerce. See also Thomas Lum, Hannah Fischer, Julissa Gomez-Granger, and Anne Leland, "China's Foreign Aid Activities in Africa, Latin America, and Southeast Asia," Congressional Research Service, February 25, 2009, 13, http://china.usc.edu/App_Images//crs-china-aid-latin-america-africa-se-asia-090225.pdf.

40. *2011 Statistical Bulletin of China's Outward Foreign Direct Investment,* China Ministry of Commerce, 82–84, http:/images.mofcom.gov.cn/hzs/accessory/201109/1316069658609.pdf.

41. See OECD Statistics, http://stats.oecd.org/Index.aspx?DatasetCode=FDI_FLOW_PARTNER.

42. Chestnut and Johnston, "Is China Rising?," chapter 12.

43. Jacques, *When China Rules the World*, 7.

44. Lieber, *Power and Willpower*.

45. Military and Security Developments Involving the People's Republic of China 2011, Office of the Secretary of Defense, 43, www.defense.gov/pubs/pdfs/2011_CMPR_Final.pdf.

46. U.S. Office of Naval Intelligence, "The People's Liberation Army Navy: A Modern Navy with Chinese Characteristics," August 2009, p. 22, http://fas.org/irp/agency/oni/pla-navy.pdf.

47. John Pomfret, "Military Strength Is Eluding China," *Washington Post*, December 25, 2010.

48. Kevin Bacon, "Pentagon: 'Too Early' to Call China's J-20 a Stealth Fighter," *Stripes Central*, January 26, 2011.

49. Tai-ming Cheung, quoted in Kathrin Hille, "China: Doing It All Yourself Has Its Drawbacks," *Financial Times*, July 7, 2012, http://www.ft.com/intl/cms/s/0/200c0ae8-b485-11e1-bb2e-00144feabdc0.html#axzzlzwAOLvm9.

50. See Tai-ming Cheung, "What the J-20 Says About China's Defense Sector," China Real Time Report, January 13, 2011; see also Phillip C. Saunders and Joshua K. Wiseman, *Buy, Build, or Steal: China's Quest for Advanced Military Aviation Technologies* (Washington, DC: National Defense University Press, 2011).

51. Zachary Fryer Biggs, "U.S. Military Goes on Cyber Offensive," *Defense News*, March 24, 2012, http://www.defensenews.com/article/20120324/DEFREG02/303240001/U-S-Military-Goes-Cyber-Offensive.

52. "U.S. Cyber Offense 'Best in the World': NSA's Gen. Keith Alexander," *Washington Times*, August 26, 2013, http://www.washingtontimes.com/news/2013/aug/26/us-cyberwar-offense-best-world-nsas-gen-keith-alex/.

53. Michael O'Hanlon, cited in Lieber, *Power and Willpower*, 133.

54. G. John Ikenberry, *Liberal Leviathan: The Origins, Crisis, and Transformation of the American World Order* (Princeton, NJ: Princeton University Press, 2011), 239.

55. Randall Schriver, "The China Challenge," paper presented to the Center for Strategic and International Studies working group "With One Hand Tied: Dealing with China During a Period of Preoccupation," June 13, 2005, 6–7; Aaron Friedberg, "The Struggle for Mastery in Asia," *Commentary* 110, no. 4 (November 2000), 17–26; and Richard Baum, Kurt N. Campbell, James A. Kelly, and Robert S. Ross, "Whither U.S.–China Relations?" roundtable discussion, *NBR Analysis* 16, no. 4 (December 2005), 25.

56. Kurlantzick, "How China Is Changing Global Diplomacy," 16.
57. Charles Krauthammer, "China's Moment," *Washington Post*, September 23, 2005.
58. For an excellent review of the evolving Asia architecture, see Victor Cha, "Complex Patchworks: U.S. Alliances as Part of Asia's Regional Architecture," *Asia Policy*, no. 11 (January 2011), 27–50.

CHAPTER 4. WHY CHINA STILL POSES STRATEGIC CHALLENGES

1. John Arquilla, *Dubious Battles: Aggression, Defeat, and the International System* (Washington, DC: Taylor & Francis, 1992).
2. For a review of Chinese coercive capabilities, including the DF-21D, see Department of Defense, *Annual Report to Congress on the Military Power of the People's Republic of China*, 2009, 2010, and 2011.
3. Ibid.
4. Lieutenant General Wang Houqing and Major General Zhang Xingye, chief eds., *Zhanyi Xue* [Military Campaign Studies] (Beijing: National Defense University Press, May 2000), military circulation only, 28. The authors, writing in 2000, state, "Our weaponry has improved greatly in comparison to the past, but in comparison to the militaries of the advanced countries [*fada guojia*], there will still be a large gap not only now but long into the future. Therefore we not only must accelerate our development of advanced weapons, thus shrinking the gap to the fullest extent possible, but also [we must] use our current weapons to defeat enemies. . . . [We must] explore the art of the inferior defeating the superior under high-tech conditions." A more recent doctrinal work for China's rocket forces, the Second Artillery, that is classified in the Chinese system but is now available outside China similarly discussed China's modernizing nuclear arsenal and conventional rocket forces as a means to confront enemies with superior conventional and nuclear forces; see Yu Xijun, ed., *Di Er Pao Bing Zhanyi Xue* [The Science of Second Artillery Campaigns] (Beijing: PLA Press, 2004). This fascinating doctrinal volume has become available from Chinese-language booksellers outside the PRC and at libraries at George Washington University, Harvard University, Oxford University, and the U.S. Naval War College.
5. Thomas J. Christensen, "Posing Problems without Catching Up," *International Security* 25, no. 4 (Spring 2001), 5–40.
6. Andrew F. Krepinevich, *Why AirSea Battle?* (Washington, DC: CSBA, 2010), especially p. 24.
7. For a review of China's nuclear modernization, see Senior Colonel Yao

Yunzhu, "China's Perspective on Nuclear Deterrence," *Air and Space Power Journal*, March 2010; Taylor M. Fravel and Evan S. Medeiros, "China's Search for Assured Retaliation: The Evolution of Chinese Nuclear Strategy and Force Structure," *International Security* 35, no. 2 (Fall 2010), 48–87; and Thomas J. Christensen, "The Meaning of the Nuclear Evolution: China's Strategic Modernization and U.S.–China Security Relations," *Journal of Strategic Studies* 35, no. 4 (August 2012), 447–87. For an excellent overview of the dangers of escalation of initially limited conflicts, see Avery Goldstein, "China's Real and Present Danger," *Foreign Affairs*, September/October 2013, http://www.foreignaffairs.com/articles/139651/avery-goldstein/chinas-real-and-present-danger.

8. For the work that originally coined the term "stability-instability paradox," see Glenn Snyder, "The Balance of Power and the Balance of Terror," in *The Balance of Power*, ed. Paul Seabury (San Francisco: Chandler Publishers, 1965), 184–201. For strategists writing in this vein, see Henry Rowen and Albert Wohlstetter, "Varying Responses with Circumstances," in *Beyond Nuclear Deterrence: New Aims, New Arms*, eds. Johan J. Holst and Uwe Nerlich (New York: Crane, Russak, 1977), 225–38; and Colin Gray, "Strategic Stability Reconsidered," *Survival* 109, no. 4 (1980), 135–54. For a complete review of this literature, see Robert Jervis, *The Meaning of the Nuclear Revolution, the Prospect of Armageddon* (Ithaca, NY: Cornell University Press, 1989), chapter 1.

9. See Jervis, *The Meaning of the Nuclear Revolution*, chapter 3; and Thomas Schelling, *Arms and Influence* (New Haven, CT: Yale University Press, 1967), 18–25.

10. Amos Tversky and Daniel Kahneman, "Prospect Theory: An Analysis of Decision under Risk," *Econometrica* 47, no. 2 (March 1979), 263–91. For interesting applications of the theory to international relations, see Rose McDermott, *Risk Taking in International Relations: Prospect Theory in Post-War American Foreign Policy* (Ann Arbor: University of Michigan Press, 1998); Barbara Farnham, ed., *Avoiding Losses/Taking Risks: Prospect Theory and International Conflict* (Ann Arbor: University of Michigan Press, 1994); and James W. Davis, *Threats and Promises: The Pursuit of International Influence* (Baltimore, MD: Johns Hopkins University Press, 2000), 32–35.

11. Jervis, *The Meaning of the Nuclear Revolution*, 168–73.

12. Yu Xijun, ed., *The Science of Second Artillery Campaigns*, 299.

13. For a review of these writings, see Christensen, "The Meaning of the Nuclear Evolution."

14. Yu Xijun, ed., *The Science of Second Artillery Campaigns*, 294.

15. Ibid., 272.

16. For a masterful overview of China's historical handling of its sovereignty

disputes on land and at sea, see Taylor Fravel, *Strong Borders, Secure Nation: Cooperation and Conflict in China's Territorial Disputes* (Princeton, NJ: Princeton University Press, 2008). For analysis of China's most assertive recent reactions to Japanese and Filipino behavior in the South China Sea and East China Sea, see Taylor Fravel, "China's Island Strategy: 'Redefine the Status Quo,'" *The Diplomat,* November 1, 2012, http://thediplomat .com/china-power/chinas-island-strategy-redefine-the-status-quo/.

17. See Kevin O'Brien and Rachel E. Stern, "Introduction: Studying Contention in Contemporary China," in *Popular Protests in China,* ed. Kevin O'Brien (Cambridge, MA: Harvard University Press, 2008), 12.

18. Kathrin Hille, "China: Citizens United," *Financial Times,* July 29, 2013, citing the work of Professor Sun Liping of Tsinghua University.

19. For a good summation of the challenges facing the Xi Jinping government, see Bruce Dickson, "Revising Reform: China's New Leaders and the Challenges of Governance," *China: An International Journal* 10, no. 2 (August 2012), 34–51.

20. For a photo of this protestor, see http://world.time.com/2012/09/17/ china-island-dispute-spurs-anti-japan-protests/#photo/china_protests_ 02/?&_suid=13568909926410943316569297229.

CHAPTER 5. GLOBAL GOVERNANCE: THE BIGGEST CHALLENGE OF ALL

1. Robert B. Zoellick, "Whither China: From Membership to Responsibility?" Remarks to the National Committee of U.S–China Relations, New York City, September 21, 2005, http://2001-2009.state.gov/s/d/former/ zoellick/rem/53682.htm.

2. Susan Shirk, *China: Fragile Superpower* (New York: Oxford University Press, 2007).

3. Pan Wei, "Western System versus Chinese System," China Policy Institute, University of Nottingham, briefing paper no. 61, July 2010, p. 15.

4. Gu Wei, *"Aiguozhuyi yu Fuzeren Waijiao"* [Patriotism and Responsible Diplomacy], *Journal of the Guangzhou Institute of Socialism,* no. 1, 2012, 99–104, oversea.cnki.net.

5. Pan, "Western System versus Chinese System," p. 15.

6. "Comprehensive Report of the Special Advisor to the DCI on Iraq's WMD, with Addendum (Duelfer Report)," Central Intelligence Agency, April 25, 2005, http://www.gpo.gov/fdsys/pkg/GPO-DUELFERRE PORT/content-detail.html.

7. Sheena Greitens, "Illicit Activity and Proliferation: North Korean Smuggling Networks," *International Security* 32, no. 1 (Summer 2007), 80–111;

and Victor Cha, *The Impossible State: North Korea, Past and Future* (New York: Ecco Books, 2012).

8. Jayshree Bajoria and Xu Beina, "The China–North Korea Relationship," *Backgrounders,* Council on Foreign Relations, last updated February 21, 2013, http://www.cfr.org/china/china-north-korea-relationship/p11097; and Bates Gill, "China's North Korea Policy: Assessing Interests and Influence," Special Report 283, United States Institute of Peace, July 2011, http://www.usip.org/sites/default/files/resources/China's_North_Korea _Policy.pdf.

9. For data on Chinese-Iranian trade, see European Commission Web site, http://trade.ec.europa.eu/doclib/docs/2006/september/tradoc_113392.pdf, p. 5. For an overall discussion of Chinese-Iranian economic relations, see Scott Harold and Alizera Nader, *China and Iran: Economic, Political and Military Relations,* RAND, Center for Middle East Public Policy, 2012, http:// www.rand.org/content/dam/rand/pubs/occasional_papers/2012/RAND_ OP351.pdf; and Brandon Fite, "U.S. and Iranian Strategic Competition: The Impact of China and Russia," Center for Strategic and International Studies, March 2011, http://csis.org/files/publication/REPORT_Iran_ Chapter_X_China_and_Russia_Final_Revision2212.pdf.

10. Shannon Tiezzi, "How China Complicates the Iranian Nuclear Talks," *The Diplomat,* November 25, 2014, http://thediplomat.com/ 2014/11/how-china-complicates-the-iranian-nuclear-talks/; and Louis Charbonneau and Parisa Hafezi, "No Easy 'Plan B' for Iran if Nuclear Talks with Major Powers Collapse," Reuters, November 23, 2014, http://www.reuters.com/article/2014/11/23/us-iran-nuclear-contin gency-idUSKCN0J70VX20141123.

11. See Bruce W. Bennett and Jennifer Lind, "The Collapse of North Korea: Military Missions and Requirements," *International Security* 36, no. 2 (Fall 2011), 84–119; and Ferial Ara Saeed and James J. Przystup, "Korea Futures: Challenges to U.S. Diplomacy of North Korea Regime Collapse," *Strategic Perspectives* 7 (September 2011), Center for Strategic Research, Institute for National Strategic Studies, National Defense University Press, http://ndupress.ndu.edu/Portals/68/Documents/stratperspective/inss/ Strategic-Perspectives-7.pdf.

12. According to research by Harvard's Alastair Iain Johnston, three PLA researchers made this argument in 2010 in a book on the Korean peninsula crisis of that year. See Johnston, "China's New Assertiveness?" *International Security* 37, no. 4 (Spring 2013), 7–48.

13. For a revealing review of the many modern, economically advanced locations in China that former North Korean leader Kim Jong-il toured on his multiple visits, see Victor Cha, *The Impossible State,* 151–52.

14. I offer an analysis of this history in Thomas J. Christensen, *Worse Than a Monolith: Alliance Politics and Problems of Coercive Diplomacy in Asia* (Princeton, NJ: Princeton University Press, 2011), chapters 2–3.

15. For an example, a recently published and relatively comprehensive Chinese history of events leading up to China's intervention in Korea, see Xu Yan, *Mao Zedong yu KangMei YuanChao Zhanzheng: Zhengque er Hui-huangYunchou Weiwo* [Mao Zedong and the War to Resist America and Aid Korea (The Korean War): A Correct and Glorious Mapping-out of Strategy)] (Beijing: PLA Publishing House, 2003).

16. Shen Zhihua, *Mao Zedong, Si Dalin, yu Chao Zhan: Zhong Su Zui Gao Jimi Dangan* [Mao Zedong, Stalin, and the Korean War: The Top-Secret Sino-Soviet Archives] (Hong Kong: Cosmos Books, 2008), 208.

17. Christensen, *Worse Than a Monolith,* chapter 2.

18. For the original Chinese language, see *"Xi Jinping: Zai Jinian Zhongguo Renmin Zhiyuanjun Kangmeiyuanchao Chuguo Zuozhan 60 Zhounian Zuotanhui Shangde Jianghua"* [Xi Jinping: Speech at the Conference Commemorating the Sixtieth Anniversary of the Chinese People's Volunteer Army and the War of Resisting America and Assisting Korea], Xinhua, October 5, 2010, http://news.xinhuanet.com/politics/2010-10/25/c_12700037 .htm. For a complete English translation that differs a bit from the author's own, see "Xi Jinping's Speech Marking China's Entry into the Korean War," BBC Monitoring Reports, October 28, 2010, http://www.access mylibrary.com/article-1G1-240787853/text-xi-jinping-speech.html. Accessed on July 22, 2013.

19. Erica S. Downs and Suzanne Maloney, "Getting China to Sanction Iran," *Foreign Affairs* 90, no. 2 (March–April 2011).

20. Dawn C. Murphy, testimony at hearing "China and the Middle East," June 6, 2013, U.S.–China Economic and Security Review Commission, http://www.uscc.gov/sites/default/files/MURPHY_testimony.pdf; and David Shambaugh and Dawn Murphy, "U.S.–China Interactions in the Middle East, Africa, Europe, and Latin America," in *Tangled Titans: The New Context of U.S.–China Relations*, ed. David Shambaugh (Lanham, MD: Rowan and Littlefield, 2013).

21. Erica Downs, "Getting China to Turn on Iran," *The National Interest,* July 19, 2012.

22. Downs and Maloney, "Getting China to Sanction Iran."

23. For statistics on Chinese-Iranian trade, see European Commission Web site, http://trade.ec.europa.eu/doclib/docs/2006/september/tradoc_113392 .pdf, p. 5. For overall discussion of Chinese-Iranian economic relations, see Scott Harold and Alizera Nader, *China and Iran: Economic, Political and Military Relations,* RAND, Center for Middle East Public Policy, 2012,

http://www.rand.org/content/dam/rand/pubs/occasional_papers/2012/RAND_OP351.pdf. For a discussion of the impact of sanctions on Chinese-Iranian economic relations, see Nikolay A. Kozhanov, "U.S. Economic Sanctions Against Iran: Undermined by External Factors," *Middle East Policy* 18, no. 3 (Fall 2011), 144–60, http://search.proquest.com/docview/900126888?accountid=11243; and Erica Downs, testimony at hearing "China and the Middle East," Panel II: China's Energy and Other Economic Interests in the Middle East, June 6, 2013, U.S. China Economic and Security Review Commission, http://www.uscc.gov/sites/default/files/Downs_Testimony.pdf.

24. John W. Garver, *China and Iran: Ancient Partners in a Post-Imperial World* (Seattle: University of Washington Press, 2006).

25. Garver, *China and Iran,* chapter 4.

26. Wang Liping and Xia Shi, *"He Anquan Beijing Xiade Yilang Hewenti yu Zhongguo Waijiao Zhanlüe Xuanze"* [The Iranian Nuclear Issue and China's Foreign Policy Strategic Choices in the Backdrop of Nuclear Security], *Guoji Zhengzhi* [International Politics], June 2010.

27. Downs and Maloney, "Getting China to Sanction Iran."

28. William Chandler, "Breaking the Suicide Pact: U.S.–China Cooperation on Climate Change," Carnegie Corporation, May 2008.

29. Chandler, "Breaking the Suicide Pact," p. 1.

30. Jonathan Kaimin, "China's Reliance on Coal Reduces Life Expectancy by 5.5 Years, Says Study," *The Guardian,* July 8, 2013, http://www.theguardian.com/environment/2013/jul/08/northern-china-air-pollution-life-expectancy/print.

31. Chandler, "Breaking the Suicide Pact," p. 2.

32. Thomas Friedman, "Aren't We Clever?" *New York Times,* September 18, 2010, http://www.nytimes.com/2010/09/19/opinion/19friedman.html?_r=0l; and Thomas Friedman, "The New Sputnik," *New York Times*, September 26, 2009, http://www.nytimes.com/2009/09/27/opinion/27friedman.html?_r=3&em.

33. U.S. Energy Information Agency, Country Reports: China, updated April 22, 2013, http://www.eia.gov/countries/cab.cfm?fips=CH.

34. "The World's Biggest Polluter Is Going Green, but It Needs to Speed Up the Transition," *The Economist,* August 10, 2013. The CDIAC estimates that China's emissions in 2012 were already nearly twice the U.S. emissions, and in the previous three years U.S. emissions had dropped while China's had increased.

35. "Nuclear Power in China," World Nuclear Association, updated December 2014, http://www.world-nuclear.org/info/Country-Profiles/Countries-A-F/China--Nuclear-Power/.

36. Joe McDonald, "China Starts Building Nuclear Power Plant," January 6, 2013, http://www.huffingtonpost.com/huff-wires/20130106/as-china-nuclear-power/?utm_hp_ref=homepage&ir=homepag.

37. Cass Sunstein, "The World Versus the United States and China? The Complex Climate Change Incentives of the Leading Greenhous Gas Emitters," *UCLA Law Review* 61, no. 6 (2008), 1675–1700.

38. Makiko Sato and James Hansen, "Updating the Climate Science: What Path Is the Real World Following?," Figure 27: Current and Cumulative Fossil Fuel Carbon Dioxide Emissions, Dr. James Hansen Web site (online updates to James Hansen, *Storms of My Grandchildren* [New York: Bloomsbury USA, 2009]), http://www.columbia.edu/~mhs119/UpdatedFigures/.

39. Sato and Hansen, "Updating the Climate Science," Figure 24: Cumulative Per Capita Carbon Dioxide Emissions.

40. Chandler, "Breaking the Suicide Pact," p. 2.

41. Sato and Hansen, "Updating the Climate Science," Figure 24: Cumulative Per Capita Carbon Dioxide Emissions.

42. Christopher L. Weber, Glen P. Peters, Dabo Guan, and Klaus Hubacek, "The Contribution of Chinese Exports to Climate Change," *Energy Policy* 36, no. 9 (2008).

43. See "United States and China Agree to Work Together on Phase Down of HFC's," June 13, 2013, Office of the Press Secretary, the White House, http://www.whitehouse.gov/the-press-office/2013/06/08/united-states-and-china-agree-work-together-phase-down-hfcs; and "Media Note: Report of the U.S.–China Climate Change Working Group to the 6th Round of the Strategic and Economic Dialogue," July 15, 2014, Office of the Spokesperson, U.S. Department of State, http://www.state.gov/r/pa/prs/ps/2014/07/229308.htm.

44. For a UN report on the problem of corruption in cap and trade schemes around the world, see "The Importance of Corruption on Climate Change: Threatening Emission Trading Mechanism," UNEP Global, Emissions Alert Service, March 2013, http://www.unep.org/pdf/UNEP-GEAS_MARCH_2013.pdf. For a good overview of the nascent Chinese cap and trade scheme, see Guoyi Han, Mari Olsson, Karl Hallding, and David Lunsford, "China's Carbon Emissions Trading," Stockholm Environmental Institute, 2012, http://www.sei-international.org/mediamanager/documents/Publications/china-cluster/SEI-FORES-2012-China-Carbon-Emissions.pdf.

45. Chris Buckley, "China's Plan to Limit Coal Use Could Spur Consumption for Years," *New York Times,* July 24, 2014, http://www.nytimes.com/2014/07/25/world/asia/chinese-plan-to-reduce-coal-use-could-allow-increases-for-years.html?hpw&action=click&pgtype=Homepage

&version=HpHedThumbWell&module=well-region&region=bottom-well&WT.nav=bottom-well&_r=1.

46. Justin Guay, "Chinese Coal Consumption Just Fell for the First Time This Century," Renew Economy, August 20, 2014, http://renewecon omy.com.au/2014/chinese-coal-consumption-just-fell-for-first-time-this-century-49062; and Lu Hui, "Smoggy Beijing to Ban Coal Use," Xinhua, August 4, 2014, http://news.xinhuanet.com/english/china/2014-08/04/c_133531366.htm.

47. Wang Jing, "Two Guangdong Firms Face Punishments over Failures in Emissions Program," Caixin Online, August 8, 2014, http://english .caixin.com/2014-08-08/100714692.html; and He Huifeng, "Guang-dong Proposes Illegal Polluters Pay Fines Equal to 30pc of Losses," *South China Morning Post,* August 13, 2014, http://www.scmp.com/ article/1572853/30pc-penalty-proposed-serious-polluters-guangdong.

48. "The Most Polluted Place on Earth," CBS News, January 8, 2010, http:// www.cbsnews.com/8301-18563_162-2895653.html.

49. "The World's Biggest Polluter Is Going Green, but It Needs to Speed Up the Transition," *The Economist,* August 10, 2013.

50. For unusually frank Chinese news coverage of the smog crisis, see *"Quan-guo 33 Ge Jiance Chengshi Kongqi Zhiliang Zhishu Chao 300 Womende Kongqi Zenmele?"* [Nationwide 33 Cities Monitoring Air Quality Index Exceed 300, How Is Our Air?]" *Renmin Ribao,* January 13, 2013, http://news.xin huanet.com/politics/2013-01/13/c_114345643.htm; and *"Beijing: Wumai 'Huimaqiang' Kongqi Zhiliang Zaixian Yanzhong Wuran"* [Beijing: Haze "Backstroke" Air Quality Is Again Experiencing Serious Pollution], Xin-hua Net, January 19, 2013, http://news.xinhuanet.com/politics/2013-01/19/c_114426474.htm.

51. Kenneth Lieberthal, "Climate Change and China's Global Responsibili-ties," *Upfront,* Brookings Institution, December 23, 2009.

52. Kenneth Liebethal, *Managing the China Challenge: How to Achieve Corporate Success in the People's Republic* (Washington, DC: Brookings Institution Press, 2011).

53. Edward Wong, "At Climate Meeting, China Balks at Verifying Cuts in Emissions," *New York Times,* December 9, 2014, http://sinosphere.blogs .nytimes.com/2014/12/09/at-climate-meeting-china-balks-at-verify ing-cuts-in-carbon-emissions/?emc=edit_tnt_20141209&nlid=2930400 1&tntemail0=y&_r=0.

54. Charles P. Kindleberger, *The World in Depression, 1929–1939* (Berkeley, CA: University of California Press, 1973).

55. Current account surplus, World Bank, http://data.worldbank.org/indi cator/BN.CAB.XOKA.CD?page=1; and current account surplus as per-

cent of GDP, http://data.worldbank.org/indicator/BN.CAB.XOKA .GD.ZS?page=1.

56. Paul Krugman, "Holding China to Account," *New York Times,* October 2, 2011, http://www.nytimes.com/2011/10/03/opinion/holding-china-to-account.html.

57. See Jamil Anderlini, "China Hints at Halt to Renminbi Rise," *Financial Times,* March 12, 2012, http://www.ft.com/intl/cms/s/0/972b0948-6c33-11e1-b00f-00144feab49a.html#axzz2btkMS0J6; and United States Census Bureau, "Trade in Goods with China," http://www.census.gov/foreign-trade/balance/c5700.html#2012.

58. World Bank, http://data.worldbank.org/indicator/BN.CAB.XOKA.GD.ZS.

59. Paul Krugman, "Hitting China's Wall," *New York Times,* July 18, 2013.

60. For quota and voting percentages after the reforms, see http://www.imf .org/external/np/sec/pr/2011/pdfs/quota_tbl.pdf.

61. Keith Bradsher and Liz Alderman, "China Considers Offering Aid in Europe's Debt Crisis," *New York Times,* February 2, 2012; and Wei Lingling, "As Merkel Visits, China Cautiously Vows Euro-Zone Aid," *Wall Street Journal,* August 30, 2012.

62. CIA World Factbook, for China: https://www.cia.gov/library/publica tions/the-world-factbook/geos/ch.html; and for Greece: https://www .cia.gov/library/publications/the-world-factbook/geos/gr.html.

63. Pan Yuan, "China Rescuing Europe from Expanding Debt Crisis 'Pseudo-Proposition,'" *Zhongguo Qingnian Bao* [China Youth Daily], November 22, 2011. OSC translated text T05:46:54Z, World News Connection.

64. *"Yong Zhongguo Laobaixing de Xue Han Qian. Qu Jiuzhu Ouzhou Zhai Weiji, Rang Ouzhor ren Jixu Yangzunchuyou"* [On the Question of Using the Money Earned with the Blood and Sweat of Ordinary Chinese People to Rescue Europe from the Debt Crisis to Allow European People to Continue to Live in Ease and Comfort], http://blog.sina.com.cn/ a66569199l u2011-10-29 00:52:35. Accessed on August 1, 2013.

65. *"Ao Zongli Jilade Huyu Zhongguo Wei Ou Zhai Weiji 'Zuo Gongxian.'"* [Australian Prime Minister Gillard Calls on China to "Make a Contribution" in the European Debt Crisis], *Global Times,* November 8, 2012, http://world.huanqiu.com/exclusive/2012-11/3258277.html.

66. *"2013 Nian Beijingdiqu Jingji Fazhan Genzong Diaocha 'Shuju bianma yu pinshuo fenbu shouce (Guoji guanzhu bufen)'"* [2013 Beijing Economic Development Tracking Survey "Data Coding and Frequency Distribution Manual (International Issues Section)"], Beijing University Research Center for Contemporary China, November 2013, p. 37. I am grateful to Alastair Iain Johnston, who participated in the survey research, for sharing this data.

67. William Overholt, "Reassessing China: Awaiting Xi Jinping," *Washington Quarterly* 35, no. 2 (2012), 121–137.

68. Chris Israel, "A Survey of the Global Policy Landscape for Green Technology and Intellectual Property," Policy Report 193, Institute for Policy Innovation, April 2011, 17.

69. Keith Bradsher, "Weak Finish from Europe on Chinese Solar Panels," *New York Times,* July 28, 2013.

70. Diane Cardwell, "China's Feud with West on Solar Leads to Tax," *New York Times,* July 19, 2013; and "China, EU Reach Settlement on Solar Panels," Associated Press, July 27, 2013.

71. Diane Cardwell and Keith Bradsher, "Solar Industry Is Rebalanced by U.S. Pressure on China," *New York Times,* July 25, 2014, http://www .nytimes.com/2014/07/26/business/energy-environment/solar-industry-is-rebalanced-by-us-pressure-on-china.html?hp&action=click&pgtype =Homepage&version=HpSumSmallMediaHigh&module=second-column-region&region=top-news&WT.nav=top-news&_r=1.

72. "China, EU Reach Settlement on Solar Panels," Associated Press, July 27, 2013.

73. Deborah Brautigam, *The Dragon's Gift: The Real Story of China in Africa* (Oxford: Oxford University Press, 2009), 273–77.

74. Geoff Dyer, "Beijing Invites U.S. to Link Up over Africa," *Financial Times,* August 5, 2014.

75. Kathrin Hille, "China Commits Combat Troops to Mali," *Financial Times,* June 27, 2013, http://www.ft.com/cms/s/0/e46f3e42-defe-11e2-881f-00144feab7de.html#axzz2btC52zHU.

76. "Secretary-General at China Peacekeeping Centre," press release, UN Department of Public Information, June 19, 2013, http://www.un.org/ News/Press/docs/2013/sgsm15120.doc.htm.

77. Courtney J. Richardson, "A Responsible Power? China and the UN Peacekeeping Regime," *International Peacekeeping* 18, no. 3 (June 2011), 288.

CHAPTER 6. THE SOVIET COLLAPSE AND CHINA'S RISE, 1991–2000

1. Thomas J. Christensen, *Worse Than a Monolith: Alliance Politics and Problems of Coercive Diplomacy in Asia* (Princeton, NJ: Princeton University Press, 2011), chapter 6.

2. James Lilley, *China Hands: Nine Decades of Adventure, Espionage, and Diplomacy in Asia* (New York: Public Affairs, 2004), chapter 20.

3. James Mann, *About Face: A History of America's Curious Relationship with China, From Nixon to Clinton* (New York: Vintage Books, 2000), chapter 14.

4. Joel Wuthnow, *Chinese Diplomacy and the UN Security Council* (New York: Routledge, 2012), 3–4.

5. Ibid., chapter 1.
6. Ibid., 24.
7. Qin Huasun, PRC Ambassador to the United Nations, in Security Council Document S/PV.3542, January 30, 1995, quoted in Wuthnow, *Chinese Diplomacy and the UN Security Council*, 22.
8. Mann, *About Face*.
9. President Clinton, White House announcement on Executive Order 12850, "Conditions for Renewal of Most Favored Nation Status for the People's Republic of China," May 28, 1993, quoted in Robert L. Suettinger, *Beyond Tiananmen: The Politics of U.S.–China Relations, 1989–2000* (Washington, DC: Brookings Institution, 2003), 167.
10. For an insider's look at concerns about how acrimonious economic disputes were harming the alliance, see David L. Asher, "U.S.–Japan Alliance for the Next Century," *Orbis* 41, no. 3 (Summer 1997), 343–75.
11. In particular, three military officers whom I interviewed in 1994 stressed these themes. For fears about Democrats and neo-isolationism, see Cai Zuming, *Meiguo Junshi Zhanlüe Yanjiu* [Studies of American Military Strategy], internally circulated (Beijing: Academy of Military Sciences Press, 1993), 223; Liu Liping, *"Jilie Zhendanzhong de Meiguo Duiwai Zhengce Sichao"* [The Storm over Contending Positions on U.S. Foreign Policy], *Xiandai Guoji Guanxi* [Contemporary International Relations], no. 6 (1992), 15–16; and Li Shusheng, *"Sulian de Jieti yu MeiRi zai Yatai Diqu de Zhengduo"* [The Disintegration of the Soviet Union and U.S.–Japan rivalry in the Asia Pacific], *Shijie Jingji yu Zhengzhi* [World Economy and Politics], no. 7 (July 1992), 56–58. For an article about the emphasis on trade and the lack of strategic focus in Washington, see Lu Zhongwei, *"Yazhou Anquanzhong de ZhongRi Guanxi"* [Sino-Japanese Relations in the Asian Security Environment], *Shijie Jingji yu Zhengzhi* [World Economy and Politics], no. 3 (March 1993), 23–35, 42.
12. John W. Garver, *China and Iran: Ancient Partners in a Post-Imperial World* (Seattle: University of Washington Press, 2006), chapters 6–8.
13. Garver, *China and Iran*, 216.
14. For an excellent insider's account, see Joel S. Wit, Daniel B. Poneman, and Robert C. Gallucci, *Going Critical: The First North Korean Nuclear Crisis* (Washington, DC: Brookings Institution Press, 2004). Also see Victor Cha, *The Impossible State: North Korea, Past and Future* (New York: Ecco Books, 2012).
15. Wuthnow, *Chinese Diplomacy and the UN Security Council*, 28.
16. Wit, Poneman, and Gallucci, *Going Critical*, 198–99.
17. For the importance of the 1994 Korean crisis in Clinton administration officials' calculations, see Kurt M. Campbell, "The Official U.S. View,"

in Michael J. Green and Mike M. Mochizuki, *The U.S.–Japan Security Alliance in the Twenty-first Century* (New York: Council on Foreign Relations Study Group Papers, 1998), 85–87.

18. This history is reviewed in more detail in Thomas J. Christensen, "China, the U.S.–Japan Alliance, and the Security Dilemma in East Asia," *International Security* 23, no. 4 (Spring 1999).

19. Liu Jiangyong, "New Trends in Sino–U.S.–Japan Relations," *Contemporary International Relations* 8, no. 7 (July 1998), 1–13.

20. Robert Jervis, "Cooperation under the Security Dilemma," *World Politics* 30, no. 2 (January 1978), 167–214. Although scholars differ on definitions of what specifically constitutes a destabilizing offense and a stabilizing defense in the current literature, they all focus on states' capacity for fighting across borders and seizing enemy-held territory as the measure of the offense-defense balance. See, for example, Van Evera, "Offense, Defense, and the Causes of War," *International Security* 22, no. 4 (Spring 1998), 5–43; and Charles L. Glaser and Chaim Kaufmann, "What Is the Offense-Defense Balance and Can We Measure It?" *International Security* 22, no. 4 (Spring 1998), 44–82.

21. Author interviews in Beijing, June–July 1995. For the full text of President Lee Teng-hui's speech "Always in My Heart," Cornell University, June 9, 1995, see http://taiwanauj.nat.gov.tw/ct.asp?xItem=13324&CtNode=122.

22. For a good analytic review and recapitulation of the crisis, see Robert S. Ross, "The 1995–96 Taiwan Strait Confrontation: Coercion, Credibility, and the Use of Force," *International Security* (Fall 2000), 87–123.

23. Robert Sutter, *China's Rise in Asia: Promises and Perils* (Lanham, MD: Rowman & Littlefield, 2005), 81.

24. For a rich analysis of China's shifting attitudes toward multilateral institutions in the mid-1990s, see Alastair Iain Johnston and Paul Evans, "China's Engagement with Multilateral Security Organizations," in *Engaging China: The Management of an Emerging Power,* eds. Johnston and Robert S. Ross (New York: Routledge, 1999), pp. 235–272, especially pp. 258–260.

25. Xia Liping, *"Lun Zhongguo Guoji Zhanlüe Zhong de Xin Anquan Guan"* [A Study of the New Security Concept in China's International Strategy], in *Xin Shiji Jiyuqi yu Zhongguo Guoji Zhanlüe* [The Period of Opportunity in the New Century and China's International Strategy], chief eds. Chen Peiyao and Xia Liping (Beijing: Times Publishers, 2004), 58.

26. For Yan Xuetong's views, see "PRC's Wang Jisi: China May Leave G8 in Future; Scholars Support Multilateralism," *Wen Wei Po* (Hong Kong, internet version), in Chinese, Foreign Broadcast Information Service, June 22, 2005, doc. CPP20050622000094, p. 64.

27. Zhang Yunling, *"Zonghe Anquan Guan Ji Dui Wo Guo Anquan de Sikao"*

[The Comprehensive Security Concept and Reflections on Our Nation's Security], *Dangdai Yatai* [Contemporary Asia-Pacific Studies], no. 1 (2000), 1–16.

28. Zhang Yunling, chief ed., *Weilai 10–15 Nian Zhongguo Zai Yatai Diqu Mianlan de Guoji Huanjing* [The Security Environment China Will Face in the Southeast Asia Region in the Next 10–15 Years] (Beijing: Chinese Academy of Social Sciences Press, November 2003), 309.

29. Tang Shiping and Zhang Yunling, "China's Regional Strategy," in *Power Shift: China and Asia's New Dynamics,* ed. David Shambaugh (Berkeley: University of California Press, 2006). The U.S. scholar Michael Glosny cites multiple works by Chinese authors that view improved relations with ASEAN as a means to avoid those states' linking up in an encircling alliance with a revitalized U.S.–Japan alliance. See "Heading toward a Win-Win Future? Recent Developments in China's Policy toward Southeast Asia," *Asian Security* 2, no. 1 (February 2006), 24–57.

30. Suettinger, *Beyond Tiananmen*, 200–63; Nancy Bernkopf Tucker, *Strait Talk: United States–Taiwan Relations and the Crisis with China* (Cambridge, MA: Harvard University Press, 2009), 205–12; Patrick Tyler, *A Great Wall: Six Presidents and China: An Investigative History* (New York: Public Affairs, 2000), 320–22; Mann, *About Face*, 320–30; and Alan D. Romberg, *Rein In at the Brink of the Precipice: American Policy toward Taiwan and U.S.–PRC Relations* (Washington, DC: Henry L. Stimson Center, 2003), 161–62.

31. David M. Lampton, *Same Bed, Different Dreams: Managing U.S.–China Relations, 1989–2000* (Berkeley, CA: University of California Press, 2001), 61; Romberg, *Rein In at the Brink*, 185–89; Suettinger, *Beyond Tiananmen*, 382; and Richard Bush, *Untying the Knot: Making Peace in the Taiwan Strait* (Washington, DC: Brookings Institution, 2005), 218–19. For a transcript of President Lee Teng-hui's July 9, 1999, *Deutsche Welle* interview, see http://www.taiwandc.org/nws-9926.htm.

32. Suettinger, *Beyond Tiananmen*, chapter 9; and Lampton, *Same Bed, Different Dreams*, 55–61.

33. Author interviews with military officers, civilian government experts, and Western nations' military attachés in Beijing, spring 1999 and January 2000. For official analyses that link the Kosovo operation to American and Japanese containment strategies toward China through interference in China's internal affairs, see Gao Qiufu, ed., *Xiao Yan Weigan: Kesuowo Zhanzheng yu Shijie Geju* [The Kosovo War and the World Structure] (Beijing: Xinhua Publishers, July 1999), internally circulated, especially chapter 3.

34. See, for example, Associated Press, "Chinese Stealth Fighter Jet May Use

U.S. Technology," *The Guardian*, January 23, 2011, at http://www.the guardian.com/world/2011/jan/23/china-stealth-fighter-us-technology.

35. Susan L. Shirk, *China: Fragile Superpower* (New York: Oxford University Press, 2007), chapter 8.

36. Suettinger, *Beyond Tiananmen*, 402.

37. For an article based on the timetable rumor circulating in Beijing, see Willy Wo-lap Lam, "Dual Edge to 'Liberation' Timetable," *South China Morning Post*, March 1, 2000. For an analysis of the timeline issues, see Alan Romberg, "Cross-Strait Relations: In Search of Peace," *China Leadership Monitor*, no. 23 (Winter 2008), http://media.hoover.org/documents/CLM23AR.pdf.

38. Taiwan White Paper, February 2000, in *Beijing Review*, March 6, 2000, 16–24. For Premier Zhu's statement about the origins of the white paper, see Romberg, *Rein In at the Brink*, 192.

39. Charlene Barshefsky, quoted in Marcia Don Harpaz, "China and the WTO: New Kid in the Developing Bloc?," research paper no. 2-07, International Law Forum, Hebrew University of Jerusalem (February 2007), 12.

40. Harpaz, "China and the WTO."

41. Shirk, *China: Fragile Superpower*, chapter 8.

CHAPTER 7. THE POST–9/11 WORLD, 2001–2008

1. The best coverage of the EP-3 crisis is by a major player in the events at the U.S. Embassy in Beijing, John Keefe, who was special assistant to Ambassador Joseph Prueher at the time. See his monograph, *Anatomy of the EP-3 Incident, April 2001* (Alexandria, VA: Center for Naval Analyses, 2001).

2. President Bush made this comment in a televised interview with Charlie Gibson of ABC News on April 25, 2001.

3. On October 1, 2001, the official Chinese news agency, Xinhua, reported that Jiang Zemin had spoken with President Musharraf directly by phone and had promised 10 million RMB in aid. For coverage of U.S.–China relations just after 9/11, see Thomas J. Christensen, "China," in *Asian Aftershocks: Strategic Asia 2002–2003,* eds. Richard Ellings and Aaron Friedberg with Michael Wills (Seattle: National Bureau of Asian Research, 2002), 51–94.

4. For official CCP reaction to the visit of ROC Minister of Defense Tang Yao-ming, see "China Summons U.S. Ambassador to Make Representations," Xinhua News Agency, March 16, 2002; and "U.S.–Taiwan Secret Talks on Arms-Sales: Analysis," *People's Daily* Online, March 18, 2002,

FBIS CPP-2002-0118-000088. For press reports of Chinese reactions, see Murray Hiebert and Susan V. Lawrence, "Taiwan: Crossing the Red Lines," *Far Eastern Economic Review*, April 4, 2002; and Willy Wo-lap Lam, "China's Army to Prepare for Military Struggle," CNN.com, March 13, 2002.

5. For Chinese press reactions to U.S. basing in Central Asia, see, for example, Gao Qiufu, "U.S. Wishful Thinking on Its Military Presence in Central Asia and Real Purpose," Beijing *Liaowang*, April 29, 2002, FBIS CPP-2002-0506-000066; He Chong, "The United States Emphasizes the Purposes of the Long-Term Stationing of Troops in Central Asia," Hong Kong *Tongxun she*, January 9, 2002, FBIS CPP-2002-0109-000124; and Shih Chun-yu, "United States Wants Long-Term Military Deployment to Control Central Asia," Hong Kong *Takung Pao*, January 11, 2002, FBIS CPP-2002-0111-000037. For descriptions of U.S.–Japanese activities during the war on terrorism, see "Two MSDF Ships Set Sail for Indian Ocean," *Kyodo News*, February 12, 2002; and "MSDF to Extend Anti-Terror Tour," *Yomiuri shimbun*, May 10, 2002. For Chinese reactions to those deployments, see *"9-11 Cheng Guanjian Zhuanzhe Riben Junshi Xingdong Huoyue Wei Wushinian Zhi Zui"* [September 11 Was the Most Critical Turning Point in 50 Years for the Invigoration of Japanese Military Activity], *Nanfang Dushi Bao*, April 16, 2002; and *"Riben Jin Jun Dongnan Ya Qitu He Zai"* [For What Purpose Is Japan Planning to Enter Southeast Asia Militarily], *Canwang Xinwen Zhoukan*, May 3, 2002. For PRC criticism of U.S. policy toward North Korea, see Yan Guoqun, "Sunshine Policy Is Shining Again," Beijing *Jiefangjun bao*, April 11, 2002, FBIS CPP-2002-0411-000088.

6. Robert Marquand, "Anti-Japan Protests Jar an Uneasy Asia: Demonstrations Spread from Beijing to Several Southern Cities Sunday," *Christian Science Monitor*, April 11, 2005, http://www.csmonitor.com/2005/0411/p01s04-woap.html. For a novel political analysis of the anti–Japanese protests in China, see Jessica Chen Weiss, *Powerful Patriots: Nationalist Protest in China's Foreign Relations* (New York: Oxford University Press, 2014).

7. "Chen Stresses Urgency for Referendum Legislation for Taiwan's Future," Taipei Central News Agency, August 3, 2002; and Taipei Office of the President, "Apparent Text of Chen Shui-bian's Speech on Taiwan's Future, Referendum" (in Chinese), August 3, 2002, FBIS CPP-2002-080-3000098. For the CCP's official reaction, see "Text of Taiwan Affairs Spokesman's Remarks on Chen's Call for Referendum," Xinhua News Agency (in Chinese), August 5, 2002, FBIS CPP-2002-0805-00002.

8. Alan D. Romberg, *Rein In at the Brink of the Precipice: American Policy toward Taiwan and U.S.–PRC Relations* (Washington, DC: Henry L. Stim-

son Center, 2003), 207–208. For the official U.S. position on the Armitage visit, see U.S. Department of State, Transcript of Deputy Secretary of State Richard Armitage Press Conference—Conclusion of China Visit, Beijing, August 26, 2002. For very positive Chinese coverage of the meetings, see Li Xuanliang, *"Zhongguo Daodan Guande Hen Yan"* [China Severely Restricts Missiles], and Song Nianshen, *"Meiguo Shou Ci Rending 'Dongtu' Jiu Shi Kongbuzuzhi"* [For the First Time the United States Maintains That "ETIM" Is a Terrorist Organization], *Huanqiu Shibao* [*Global Times*], August 29, 2002.

9. For the very positive reaction in China to Bush's statement, see John Pomfret, "China Lauds Bush for Comments on Taiwan," *Washington Post,* December 11, 2003.

10. For coverage of the political tensions in the lead-up to the December 2004 legislative elections and the creation of the antisecession law, see Thomas J. Christensen, "Taiwan's Legislative Yuan Elections and Cross-Strait Relations: Reduced Tensions and Remaining Challenges," *China Leadership Monitor,* no. 13 (Winter 2005), http://media.hoover.org/documents/clm13_tc.pdf.

11. For an assessment of the U.S.–Japan joint statement, see Yuki Tatsumi, "U.S.–Japan Security Consultative Committee: An Assessment," *Pacific Forum* 10, http://www.csis.org. For a general treatment of Asia's reaction to Japan's treatment of history, see Hugo Restall, "'Opposing the Sun': Japan Alienates Asia," *Far Eastern Economic Review,* April 2005. Also see Wang Te-chun, "Strengthening of U.S.–Japan Alliance Explicitly Aimed at China," *Ta Kung Pao,* February 20, 2005, FBIS TOO:22:31Z. The article is an interview with influential Chinese Academy of Social Sciences Japan Scholar Jin Xide. Jin calls the then-forthcoming 2+2 statement the second major adjustment to the alliance after the Guidelines Review of the 1990s.

12. Wu Xinbo, "The End of the Silver Lining: A Chinese View of the U.S.–Japan Alliance," *Washington Quarterly* 29, no. 1, 119–30.

13. For an overview of U.S.–China relations in this period, see Thomas J. Christensen, "Shaping the Choices of a Rising China: Some Recent Lessons for the Obama Administration," *Washington Quarterly* 32, no. 3 (July 2009), 89–104.

14. For the text of the speech, see "Whither China: From Membership to Responsibility?," Robert B. Zoellick, Deputy Secretary of State, remarks to the National Committee on U.S.–China Relations, September 21, 2005, New York City, http://www.ncuscr.org/articlesandspeeches/Zoellick.htm.

15. For expert coverage of the U.S.–PRC–Taiwan triangle in this period, see Alan Romberg, "Applying to the U.N. in the Name of Taiwan,"

China Leadership Monitor, no. 22 (Fall 2008), http://media.hoover.org/documents/CLM22AR.pdf.

16. Thom Shanker and Helene Cooper, "Rice Has Sharp Words for Taiwan, as Gates Does for China," *New York Times,* December 22, 2007, http://www.nytimes.com/2007/12/22/world/asia/22diplo.html.

17. "A Strong and Moderate Taiwan," Thomas J. Christensen, Deputy Assistant Secretary of State for East Asian and Pacific Affairs, speech to the U.S.–Taiwan Business Council's Defense Industry Conference, Annapolis, Maryland, September 11, 2007, http://2001-2009.state.gov/p/eap/rls/rm/2007/91979.htm.

18. For Japanese opposition to the referendum expressed by Prime Minister Yasuo Fukuda to Premier Wen Jiabao during the former's December 2007 trip to Beijing, see AFP Beijing, "Tokyo Opposes Taiwan UN Referendum," in *Taipei Times,* December 29, 2007, http://www.taipeitimes.com/News/front/archives/2007/12/29/2003394696.

19. Ma Hao-liang, "China-Japan Relations Will Usher in a Period of Relative Stability," *Ta Kung Pao,* Internet version, May 3, 2008, FBIS T08:50:47Z.

20. For comprehensive coverage of trends in cross–Strait relations in this period, see Alan D. Romberg, "Cross-Strait Relations: Ascend the Heights and Take a Long-Term Perspective," *China Leadership Monitor,* no. 27 (Winter 2008), http://media.hoover.org/documents/CLM27AR.pdf; and Alan D. Romberg, "Cross-Strait Relations: First the Easy, Now the Hard," *China Leadership Monitor,* no. 28 (Spring 2009), http://media.hoover.org/documents/CLM28AR.pdf.

21. "China, U.S. to Start Negative List BIT Negotiations," Xinhua News Agency, July 10, 2014, http://news.xinhuanet.com/english/china/2014-07/10/c_133472362.htm.

22. For an unusually frank article by a PRC scholar pointing to the catalytic role played in diplomacy by increasing U.S. threats of force, beginning in February 2003 and carrying through the early stages of war in Iraq, see Shi Yinhong, "Crisis and Hope—North Korean Nuclear Issue against Backdrop of Iraq War," *Ta Kung Pao,* April 15, 2003, FBIS CPP-2003-0421-000045.

23. Shi Yinhong, "Crisis and Hope"; and John Pomfret, "China Urges North Korean Dialogue," Washington Post Foreign Service, April 4, 2003. On Chinese oil cutoffs, see Howard French, "North Korea's Reaction on Iraq Is Subdued So Far," *New York Times,* April 2, 2003. On sanctions and the rendering of PRC defense commitments to North Korea conditional on Pyongyang's behavior, see Leslie Fung, "China Washes Hands of N. Korea's Antics," *Straits Times,* April 5, 2003.

24. Victor Cha, *The Impossible State: North Korea, Past and Future* (New York: Ecco Books, 2012), 266.

25. Ibid., 268.

26. For the text of the February Six Party Talks agreement, see North Korea—Denuclearization Action Plan, February 13, 2007, http://2001-2009.state.gov/r/pa/prs/ps/2007/february/80479.htm.

27. See UN Security Council Resolution 1737, SC/8928, December 23, 2006, http://www.un.org/News/Press/docs/2006/sc8928.doc.htm; UN Security Council Resolution 1747, SC/8980, March 24, 2007, http://www.un.org/News/Press/docs/2007/sc8980.doc.htm; and UN Security Council Resolution 1803, SC/9268, March 3, 2008, http://un.org/News/Press/docs/2008/sc9268.doc.htm.

28. See UN Security Council Resolution 1769, SC/9089, July 31, 2007, http://www.un.org/News/Press/docs/2007/sc9089.doc.htm.

29. Helene Cooper, "Darfur Collides with Olympics, and China Yields," *New York Times,* April 13, 2007.

30. Courtney J. Richardson, *The Chinese Mirror Has Two Faces? Understanding China's United Nations Peacekeeping Participation*, PhD Dissertation, Tufts University, 2012.

31. Qin Gang, Foreign Ministry Press Briefing, March 13, 2007, http://syd ney.chineseconsulate.org/eng/xwdt/t303512.htm.

CHAPTER 8. CHINA'S OFFENSIVE DIPLOMACY
SINCE THE FINANCIAL CRISIS, 2009–2014

1. Albert Keidel, "China's Stimulus Lesson for America," Carnegie Endowment for International Peace, November 2008, http://carnegieendow ment.org/files/chinas_stimulus_lesson_for_america.pdf; and David Barboza, "China Plans $586 Billion Economic Stimulus," *New York Times,* November 9, 2008, http://www.nytimes.com/2008/11/09/business/world business/09iht-yuan.4.17664544.html?_r=0.

2. Evan Feigenbaum and Damien Ma, "After the Plenum: Why China Must Reshape the State," *Foreign Affairs,* December 16, 2013.

3. "U.S. 'Is Back' in Asia, Secretary of State Hillary Clinton Declares," *Daily News,* July 21, 2009, http://www.nydailynews.com/news/world/u-s-back-asia-secretary-state-hillary-clinton-declares-article-1.429381.

4. Richard Baum, Kurt M. Campbell, James A. Kelly, and Robert S. Ross, "Whither U.S.–China Relations?" roundtable discussion, *NBR Analysis* 16, no. 4 (December 2005), 25.

5. Fareed Zakaria, "Inside Obama's World: The President Talks to TIME

About the Changing Nature of American Power," *Time,* January 19, 2012, http://swampland.time.com/2012/01/19/inside-obamas-world-the-presi dent-talks-to-time-about-the-changing-nature-of-american-power/.

6. Tomas Valasek, "Europe and the 'Asia Pivot,'" *New York Times,* October 25, 2012; Gideon Rachmen, "The U.S. Pivot to Asia—Should Europeans Worry?," Center for European Policy Analysis, April 2, 2012, www.cepa .org; and Vali Nasr, "The U.S. Should Focus on Asia: All of Asia," *The Atlantic,* April 11, 2013.

7. John J. Brandon, "Obama's Asia Pivot on Shaky Ground," Asia Founda- tion, October 2013, www.Asiafoundation.org; Wenwen Wang, "Middle East Unease a Drag on Washington's 'Pivot to Asia,'" *Global Times,* Octo- ber 21, 2013, www.globaltimes.cn; and Michael Auslin, "Obama Pivots from Asia to Syria," *Wall Street Journal Asia,* September 3, 2013.

8. "China's Arrival: The Long March to Global Power," Deputy Secretary of State James B. Steinberg, keynote address, Center for a New American Security, September 24, 2009, http://www.cnas.org/files/multimedia/ documents/Deputy%20Secretary%20James%20Steinberg's%20Septem ber%2024,%202009%20Keynote%20Address%20Transcript.pdf.

9. Josh Rogin, "The End of the Concept of Strategic Reassurance," *The Cable,* November 6, 2009, http://thecable.foreignpolicy.com/posts/2009/11/06/ the_end_of_the_concept_of_strategic_reassurance#sthash.dezp7guz.dpbs.

10. "U.S.–China Joint Statement," November 17, 2009, White House Office of the Press Secretary, http://www.whitehouse.gov/the-press-office/us- china-joint-statement.

11. Dai Bingguo, *"Zhongguo de Hexin Liyu You San Ge Fanchou"* [China's Core Interests Have Three Categories], PRC Ministry of Foreign Affairs, December 7, 2010, http://news.ifeng.com/mainland/detail_2010 _12/07/3379812_1.shtml.

12. For an excellent analysis of the increased frequency of the use of "core interests" in the Party's official mouthpiece, the *People's Daily,* from 2009, see Michael Swaine, "China's Assertive Behavior—Part One: On 'Core Interests,'" *China Leadership Monitor,* no. 34, (2011), http://media.hoover .org/sites/default/files/documents/CLM34MS.pdf.

13. Peter Dutton, testimony at hearing "China's Maritime Disputes in the East and South China Sea," January 14, 2014, House Foreign Affairs Committee, pp. 6–11, http://docs.house.gov/meetings/FA/FA05/201401 14/101643/HHRG-113-FA05-Wstate-DuttonP-20140114.pdf; and Kim- berly Hsu, "Air Defense Identification Zone Intended to Provide China Greater Flexibility to Enforce East China Sea Claims," staff report, U.S.– China Economic and Security Review Commission, January 14, 2014,

http://origin.www.uscc.gov/sites/default/files/Research/China%20 ADIZ%20Staff%20Report.pdf.

14. Dawn C. Murphy, testimony at hearing "China and the Middle East," June 6, 2013, U.S.–China Economic and Security Review Commission, http://www.uscc.gov/Hearings/hearing-china-and-middle-east-web cast, p. 3; Bruce Dickson, "No 'Jasmine' for China," *Current History* 110, no. 737 (September 2011), 211–16; and *2013: Report to Congress,* U.S.–China Economic and Security Review Commission, November 2013, 295–324.

15. *2013: Report to Congress,* U.S.–China Economic and Security Review Commission, November 2013, 295–324.

16. United Nations Security Council Resolution S/RES/1970, adopted on February 26, 2011, http://www.un.org/en/ga/search/view_doc.asp?sym bol=S/RES/1970(2011).

17. United Nations Security Council Resolution S/RES/1973, adopted on March 17, 2011, http://www.un.org/en/ga/search/view_doc.asp?symbol =S/RES/1973(2011).

18. For the official UN news coverage of the resolution, with commentary by Security Council members, visit http://www.un.org/News/Press/ docs/2011/sc10187.doc.htm.

19. For the official UN Security Council news release, visit http://www.un .org/News/Press/docs/2011/sc10200.doc.htm.

20. The three draft resolutions on Syria in 2012 were s/2011/612; s/2012/ 538; and s/2012/77, http://www.un.org/depts/dhl/resguide/scact2012_en .shtml; and http://www.un.org/depts/dhl/resguide/scact2011_en.shtml. For coverage of the May 2014 vote, see "Russia and China Veto UN Move to Refer Syria to ICC," BBC News, May 22, 2014, http://www.bbc.com/ news/world-middle-east-27514256.

21. Chas W. Freeman and Dawn C. Murphy, "China and Syria," *China Forum* (TV talk show), September 22, 2013, U.S.–China Policy Foundation, Washington, DC, http://uscpf.org/v3/china-forum-program-index/.

22. "China Sends Security Forces for Peacekeeping Mission in Mali," Xinhua, December 4, 2013; and "Chinese Troops Bolster UN Peace-keeping Mission in Mali," *South China Morning Post,* January 17, 2014, http://www.scmp.com/news/china/article/1407574/chinese-troops-bolster-un-peacekeeping-mission-mali.

23. "China's Miraculous Evacuation from Libya Widely Applauded," Xinhua special report, Beijing, March 7, 2011. Xinhua provided by World News Connection.

24. Kim Jong-il visited China in May 2010, August 2010, and May 2011. See

Wei Wang, "Kim Jong Il's Seven Visits to China," China.org.cn, December 21, 2011, http://www.china.org.cn/world/2011-12/21/content_2421 1950.htm.

25. Zhu Feng, "China's North Korean Contradictions," Project Syndicate, December 2, 2010, http://www.project-syndicate.org/commentary/china-s-north-korean-contradictions.

26. Alan Romberg, "The Sunnylands Summit: Keeping North Korea in Perspective," *38 North*, June 13, 2013, http://38north.org/2013/06/aromberg061413/.

27. Romberg, "The Sunnylands Summit"; and "China Tightens Sanctions on North Korea," Voice of America, September 24, 2013, http://www.voa news.com/content/china-tightens-nuclear-sanctions-against-north-korea/1756023.html.

28. Wang Hongguang, "North Korea's Abandonment of Nuclear Weapons Is More in China's Interest," *Beijing Huanqiu Wang* (in Chinese), December 16, 2013. Translation provided by Open Source Center in document CHR201321852669388.

29. Niu Jun, "*Gaibian Chao Zhengce Yao 'You Suo Zuowei'*" [Changing North Korea Policy Requires "Taking Action"], *Ming Pao*, December 18, 2003.

30. *2013 Report to Congress*, U.S.–China Economic and Security Review Commission (Washington, DC: U.S. Government Publishing, November 2013), 299–300, 318.

31. Chen Aizhu, "Exclusive: China May Raise Iran Oil Imports with New Contract: Sources," Reuters, December 31, 2013, http://www.reuters.com/article/2013/12/31/us-china-iran-zhenrong-idUSBRE9B U03020131231.

32. Shannon Tiezzi, "How China Complicates the Iranian Nuclear Talks," *The Diplomat*, November 25, 2014, http://thediplomat.com/2014/11/how-china-complicates-the-iranian-nuclear-talks/.

33. Björn Conrad, "China in Copenhagen: Reconciling the 'Beijing Climate Revolution' and the 'Copenhagen Climate Obstinacy,'" *China Quarterly* 219 (June 2012), 435–455.

34. Jan Burck, Franziska Marten, and Christoph Bals, "The Climate Change Performance Index: Results 2014," *Germanwatch*, November 2013, 6, http://germanwatch.org/en/7677.

35. Valerie Volcovici and David Lawder, "Republicans Vow EPA Fight as Obama Touts China Climate Deal," Reuters, November 12, 2014, http://www.reuters.com/article/2014/11/12/us-china-usa-climate change-mcconnell-idUSKCN0IW1TZ20141112.

36. Radoslav S. Dimitrov, "Inside UN Climate Change Negotiations: The

Copenhagen Conference," *Review of Policy Research* 27, no. 6 (2010), 796, 802–805.

37. Axel Michaelowa, "Copenhagen and the Consequences," *Intereconomics,* 2010, DOI: 10.1007/s10272-010-0319-6.

38. Gloria Jean Gong, "What China Wants: China Climate Change Priorities in a Post-Copenhagen World," *Global Change, Peace and Security* 23, no. 2 (2011), 159–75, DOI: 10/1080/14781158.2011.580958.

39. Gong, "What China Wants"; and Conrad, "China in Copenhagen," 451–52.

40. Dimitrov, "Inside UN Climate Change Negotiations"; and Peter Christoff, "Cold Climate in Copenhagen: China and the United States at the COP 15," *Environmental Politics* 19, no. 4, 637–56.

41. Jeffrey Bader, *Obama and China's Rise: An Insider's Account of America's Asia Strategy* (Washington, DC: Brookings Institution, 2012), 67.

42. Bader, *Obama and China's Rise*, 67–68.

43. Conrad, "China in Copenhagen," 435–55.

44. Alex Y. Lo, "Carbon Emissions Trading in China," *Nature Climate Change* 2 (November 2012).

45. "The East Is Grey," *The Economist*, August 10, 2013, http://www .economist.com/news/briefing/21583245-china-worlds-worst-polluter-largest-investor-green-energy-its-rise-will-have.

46. Ibid.

47. Chris P. Nielson and Mun S. Ho, "Clearing the Air in China," *New York Times*, October 25, 2013.

48. Christina Larson, "China Wants to Cut Down Coal—And That's Bad for Global Warming," *Businessweek*, September 30, 2013, http:// mobile.businessweek.com/articles/2013-09-30/chinas-synthetic-natural-gas-plants-could-accelerate-climate-change.

49. Chi-Jen Yang and Robert B. Jackson, "China's Synthetic Natural Gas Revolution," *Nature Climate Change* 3 (October 2013), www.nature.com/ natureclimatechange.

50. Christine Ottery, "China's Planned Coal-to-Gas Plants to Emit Over One Billion Tons of CO_2," Greenpeace International, July 25, 2014, http:// www.greenpeace.org/international/en/news/Blogs/makingwaves/ China-coal-to-gas-plants-to-emit-billion-tons-of-CO2/blog/50013/.

51. Brad Plumer, "China's Plan to Clean Up Air Pollution Could Be a Climate Disaster," *Washington Post,* September 26, 2013, http:// www.washingtonpost.com/blogs/wonkblog/wp/2013/09/26/chinas-efforts-to-clean-up-air-pollution-could-be-a-climate-disaster/.

52. Ottery, "China's Planned Coal-to-Gas Plants."

53. Du Juan, "China to Invest Trillions [RMB] to Cope with Climate Change," *China Daily*, July 30, 2013.

EPILOGUE: THE CHINA CHALLENGE

1. John J. Mearsheimer, *The Tragedy of Great Power Politics* (New York, W. W. Norton, 2001).
2. Yan Xuetong, "How China Can Defeat America," op-ed, *New York Times,* November 20, 2011.

INDEX

Page numbers in *italics* refer to figures and maps.
Page numbers beginning with 319 refer to endnotes.